Word Matters

Irene C. Fountas & Gay Su Pinnell

with a chapter by Mary Ellen Giacobbe

Word Matters

Teaching Phonics and Spelling in the Reading/Writing Classroom

HEINEMANN

Portsmouth, NH

Heinemann
361 Hanover Street
Portsmouth, NH 03801–3912
www.heinemann.com

Offices and agents throughout the world

The authors and publisher wish to thank those who generously gave permission to reprint borrowed material:

Figures 10-3, 10-4, 10-5, 10-6, 10-7, 17-1, 17-2, and 17-3 from *An Observation Survey of Early Literacy Achievement* by Marie M. Clay. Copyright © 1993 by Marie M. Clay. Published by Heinemann, Portsmouth, NH, and Auckland, New Zealand. Reprinted by permission of the author and publisher.

Figures 12-2 and 12-3 from *Guided Reading: Good First Teaching for All Children* by Irene C. Fountas and Gay Su Pinnell. Copyright © 1996 by Irene C. Fountas and Gay Su Pinnell. Published by Heinemann, Portsmouth, NH. Reprinted by permission of the publisher.

Figures 12-5 and 12-6 from *Help America Read: A Handbook for Volunteers* by Gay Su Pinnell and Irene C. Fountas. Copyright © 1997 by Gay Su Pinnell and Irene C. Fountas. Published by Heinemann, Portsmouth, NH. Reprinted by permission of the publisher.

Figure 17-4 from *Reading Miscue Inventory: Alternative Procedures* by Y. M. Goodman, D. J. Watson, and C. L. Burke. Copyright © 1987. Published by Richard Owen Publishers, New York, NY. Reprinted by permission of the publisher.

Running Records by Marie Clay. Used by permission of the author and publisher, Heinemann Education, Auckland, New Zealand.

Library of Congress Cataloging-in-Publication Data
Pinnell, Gay Su
   Word matters : teaching phonics and spelling in the reading/writing classroom / Gay Su Pinnell and Irene C. Fountas with a chapter by Mary Ellen Giacobbe.
      p.   cm.
   Includes bibliographical references (p. 395) and index.
   ISBN 13: 978-0-325-09977-4
   Previously published under ISBN 0-325-00051-4 (alk. paper)
   1. Reading—Phonetic method. 2. English language—Orthography and spelling—Study and teaching. 3. Language arts. I. Fountas, Irene C. II. Giacobbe, Mary Ellen. III. Title.
LB1573.3P55   1998
372.46'5—dc21   98-34167
                         CIP

Editor: Lois Bridges
Production: Melissa L. Inglis
Cover design: Ellery Harvey
Manufacturing: Erin St. Hilaire

Interior photography © Mark Morelli, Cambridge, MA

Printed in the United States of America

4 5 6 7 8 9 10 PAH 24 23 22 21
Digitally Printed PAH October 2021

We dedicate this book to literacy teachers across the country—

our partners in teaching and learning about word matters.

G. S. P.

I. C. F.

Contents

CONTENTS

Acknowledgments

We wrote this book building on the foundation of our own experiences as teachers as well as on our thorough examination of the research. Our learning is continuous; we learn daily from our colleagues and from the teachers with whom we work. We first thank the teachers who have so generously shared their teaching, their classrooms, and their students' learning; they include Kate Bartley, Mark Canner, Marie Crispen, Amy Davis, Kim Del Isolla, Florence Metcalf, Irma Napoleon, Ida Patacca, Pat Prime, Stephanie Ripley, Kate Ruben, Susan Sullivan, Jean Westin, and Melissa Wilson.

We have had the privilege of working alongside expert, supportive colleagues in the early literacy project and Reading Recovery at The Ohio State University and Lesley College. We are deeply grateful for our ongoing learning and collegiality with Diane DeFord, Rose Mary Estice, Mary Fried, Peg Gwyther, Justina Henry, Carol Lyons, Andrea McCarrier, and Joan Wiley at OSU and with Sue Hundley, Diane Powell, and Mary Snow at Lesley College.

We have also been privileged to learn from great teachers in literacy and language education. To Marie Clay, whose work continues to deepen our understanding of how children learn to become literate, to Martha L. King, who over the years has strengthened our appreciation for language and all its fascinating aspects, and to Charlotte S. Huck, who always helps us remember the magic of words and the joy of reading, we extend our continued respect and appreciation. And, special thanks to our colleague Mary Ellen Giacobbe, who generously shared with us and with our readers her expertise and insights in a chapter in this book.

We express our love and appreciation to our families, whose confidence in this work made it possible, especially to our mothers, Catherine Fountas and Elfrieda Pinnell, who have always counseled us with wise words. We are most appreciative to Ron for his loving patience, encouragement and support throughout the whole process.

We express our appreciation to Polly Taylor for her support in preparing the manuscript, to Heather Kroll for her invaluable persistence and assistance with myriad details, and to Jennifer Gleason for her spirited teamwork.

Over the last ten years, our research and development work in classrooms has been supported by philanthropic organizations interested in the improvement of literacy education. We express gratitude to the Charles A. Dana Foundation, the Martha Holden Jennings Foundation, the Noyce Foundation, and the John D. and Catherine T. MacArthur Foundation. We thank Uri Treisman for his vision and Joan Wylie for her attention to the challenges of school improvement and her encouragement for our work.

Finally, the team at Heinemann deserves all of our gratitude for their extraordinary patience and support as we conceptualized and worked on this book. The conversations we had with publisher Mike Gibbons and literacy editor Lois Bridges were invaluable. They are two very committed and professional people who have helped us in our thinking. We also are most grateful to Heinemann's director of production, Renée LeVerrier, for her boundless energy, to Roberta Lew for her meticulous assistance with permissions, and especially to our production editor, Melissa Inglis, who provided invaluable administration of the production of the book. Thanks to Renée Nicholls as well for her masterful copy editing.

We are indebted to our remarkable editor, Lois Bridges, whose advice has been so valuable and whose knowledge, sensitivity, and ability to use words has greatly enhanced our ability to communicate.

Introduction

The key word in the title of our book is *teaching*. We have lived our entire adult lives as teachers of literacy. In our view, language and literacy are the essential societal tools we must ensure that all children will learn and use. Becoming a literate person entails multiple facets. First, we want our students to enjoy their literacy, using it to enhance the quality of their lives. Loving to read as we do, we are motivated to share our love of good books with every child we teach. We also share with children our love of writing. Writing is a way to communicate, to express our thoughts, and to organize and reflect on our lives. We also recognize that writing skill contributes immeasurably to a successful life. We want to help our students use literacy to achieve economic and personal freedom. Highly literate people can learn and develop the skills the future requires; furthermore, a literate society is a thinking society. Its citizens are not easily controlled.

Those are lofty goals, ones we recognize that we share with other educators. As literacy teachers, we must also consider what we do on a daily basis to help our young students acquire effective reading and writing skills. With each additional year of teaching experience we gain, we realize anew just how complex the teaching-learning process really is. Thoughtful teachers might state the issues they face every day in this way:

▌ I want my students to understand what reading and writing are for, so I want them to read books they choose for real purposes. But, don't I sometimes have to choose books for them on their level of skill?

❚ I want to be sure my students enjoy reading. But, isn't there a time when they just need to focus on specific skills?

❚ I want to teach my students to figure out words in the context of reading and to spell words in the context of writing. But, don't I have to teach some phonics and spelling in a focused way?

The answer to these concerns is always "yes," and "no." We must ensure that children develop what are typically referred to as "skills" while, at the same time, they are becoming joyful and analytic users of literacy. In this book, we present and promote a concept we call *word solving*. Our goal is to teach our children to become *word solvers*. This means that as they read they can take words apart to help them in their search for meaning, and that while they write they are able to construct words from such essential elements as letters and letter clusters.

Our friend and teacher Martha King, Professor Emeritus at The Ohio State University, has often spoken of teaching as casting a broad net by involving children in the reading and writing process with all its complexities. The children focus on the meaning—on the interesting story they are reading or writing and on what they are finding out from reading or reporting in writing. Teachers, who have their students' developing skills in mind as they cast the net, make sure that they regularly bring the net to the surface to examine what is being "caught" or learned. They want to engage their students in the experiences that make it possible for them to understand the functions of literacy, to actually *use* what they are learning in meaningful ways. At the same time, teachers want to direct their students' attention to the information and actions that will foster their literacy development.

In this book we have tried to share an organized way of thinking about reading, writing, and word study—three contexts for learning. In each context, children explore words and learn about them in a different way, but in each instance they are learning about the words that comprise our language. We believe that all three components are necessary and, in combination, provide effective literacy instruction for all children.

We know that children who read more are likely to become better readers and that children who write more are likely to learn how to spell better. Therefore it makes sense to design a curriculum that invites children to spend a great deal of time in reading and writing extended text. Our goal is to teach them the tools they need to approach new words that are embedded in texts they want to read or that occur in the texts they want to write. Word learning, in fact, is not so much about learning individual words as about learning how the written language "works."

This book is about how children learn word solving and how teachers teach word solving. Literacy programs today include more writing and more reading of quality literature than ever before in our educational history. Yet we continue to encounter waves of controversy regarding children's literacy success and the role of specific knowledge and skills such as phonological awareness, visual perception, and spelling. Arguments batter the field of literacy education; nevertheless, in our work with teachers, administrators, and teacher educators, we observe more consensus among colleagues than is evident from reading the popular press or even the academic journals. *Most educators agree that*:

❚ Phonological awareness is an important factor in early reading and writing success.

❚ Children need some powerful, explicit, meaningful, and interesting instruction in phonics and other principles of how words are constructed.

❚ Children need numerous opportunities to use phonological information while reading and writing continuous text.

❚ Fluent, simultaneous processing of visual, phonological, syntactic, and semantic cues while reading for meaning is the foundation of all literacy.

There is disagreement, however, on just *how* to ensure that young readers and writers develop competence in using phonics and spelling skills as they read and write. Instructional approaches, teaching interactions, timing, materials, and curriculum designs are all issues over which educators and researchers argue. In this book, we go back to our observations of children's reading and writing behavior as the source of knowledge about how children develop reading and writing competence over time, and we provide a conceptual system for helping each reader and writer become a joyful, fluent user of written language.

In teaching literacy we are working with the nature and structure of our language. Oral and written language are rule-governed systems that represent the body of knowledge children need to understand in order to become effective readers and writers. As teachers, we need an overall map and a clear understanding of that body of knowledge. But the journey into literacy for each child is different, especially in the beginning stages. Children first acquire particular knowledge and then systematize it. Ultimately, *children need*:

❚ Knowledge of an ever-increasing core of words.
❚ Knowledge of patterns that occur in words.
❚ Knowledge of strategies for solving words.

Our educational program must ensure that all children become word solvers. Furthermore, the children must be able to perform these operations fluently, with flexibility, and in a largely unconscious way so they can center their attention on the meaning of what they are reading or writing.

The key is good first teaching, based on the teacher's understanding of the system of written language. Teachers need to understand phonics and spelling in order to assess what children know and then to support development of children's knowledge. A central theme in the book is our responsibility to observe and assess the behavioral evidence that reveals children's knowledge of the symbol system and conventions. We want to facilitate each child's journey but we are, of necessity, working with groups in classrooms, a challenging task. The skillful teaching that ensures individual learning requires close, thoughtful observation as well as systematic ways of planning and organizing instruction for groups. As teachers, we need:

▌ To understand how the written language system works.

▌ To understand the reading and writing processes.

▌ To know how to build knowledge of high-frequency words and how to teach for word patterns and strategies through focused word study lessons.

▌ To create a coherent curriculum in which word study, reading, and writing are connected through children's interests, purposes, and discovery.

▌ To assess and document learning about words and how they work.

▌ To work with others to ensure a high-quality word solving program.

Our approach to teaching phonics and spelling is to teach concepts within classrooms where children constantly use oral and written language for authentic purposes. The plan for teaching in such classrooms does not exclude well-designed, focused experiences that help children attend to and use information from letters, sounds, words, and parts of words. We conceptualize phonics and spelling instruction within a broad framework of literacy learning that is content-rich, includes many different kinds of reading and writing, and includes a range of teaching approaches from highly supportive instruction to encouraging the children's independent actions and practice.

Phonics is an essential part of the reading process, and spelling is a key aspect of the writing process. We will describe how work in each area complements and supports learning in the other. To construct words, for example, the writer must write letter by letter. We know that the writer might know clusters that represent sound sequences and/or meaning chunks, think of them as a group, and write them quickly, all at once; however, ultimately each letter must be recalled and written in sequence by the competent writer. In order to do that, children need to know how to construct letters and put them into the space on the page from left to right, using space to define words. Taking words apart while reading requires the reader to attend to visual aspects of the word—sometimes sounding out the word or part of the word from left to right, sometimes recognizing clusters of letters within a word, sometimes recognizing meaningful parts and/or endings—and to check the analysis with all other information in the text to be sure that it fits with meaning and syntax. We are describing a complex set of interrelated strategies. We wrote our book to help teachers support the learning of these strategies as they engage children both in reading and writing stories and in the direct teaching of skills.

We also make a place in our curriculum for *word study*, which we describe as a process of inquiry. Learning about words can be interesting and enjoyable; as teachers engage in word study activities with children, they will find that the children often discover more about words than planned for in the lesson. And the process of discovery spills over into reading and writing as it "echoes" across a morning's or a week's work with children. Through this process, children can see the value of knowing about letters, sounds, and words.

In our recent book *Guided Reading: Good First Teaching for all Children* (Fountas and Pinnell 1996), we addressed guided reading in a comprehensive way, providing both a theoretical rationale and practical information on quality instruction. We see this book on phonics and spelling as a companion volume in which we focus on aspects of the reading and writing processes that require strong teaching if all children are to become independent, competent readers and writers. A third volume, *Voices on Word Matters* (1999), further expands these concepts through a collection of original articles by outstanding researchers and educators.

We present *Word Matters: Teaching Phonics and Spelling in the Reading/Writing Classroom* in five sections. Section 1 focuses on how children learn about letters and words and presents contexts for learning. In Section 2, we explore oral language as a foundation for literacy learning and provide a summary of what teachers need to understand about language. A major theme of this section is what teachers need to know about phonological and orthographic awareness and the role of those important processes in reading and writing. We emphasize observation and assessment as tools for teachers to expand their own knowledge base as well as to determine student progress. We also look at how children learn about phonics and spelling through the language play that is so important in early childhood.

Section 3 takes us into word study, with descriptions of and guidelines for designing effective ways to help children focus on letters, sounds, words, and how they work. We describe how teachers can set up and implement intentional instruction to bring critical concepts to children's attention. Criteria for selecting and using this kind of instruction are clear within every chapter; you will find that this instruction:

❚ Is interesting and, often, fun.
❚ Makes up a brief part of the language arts curriculum.
❚ Involves children in active learning rather than passive drill.

∎ Is within children's capability yet offers enough challenge to be interesting and productive for learning.

∎ Promotes interest in words and motivates children to engage in their own inquiry about how words work.

∎ Has high payoff in terms of students' using the skills later within reading and writing contexts.

We use word study centers, word walls, and word sorts to construct knowledge about how words work and to provide for multilevel learning in the primary classroom. We describe designs for lessons on words that help children take ownership of their own learning and that promote connections across word study, reading, and writing. In addition, we introduce a word study system to support spelling. Lists of words and other reproducible materials are included in the appendixes so that teachers can readily implement the approach we describe.

In Section 4, we explore word learning and word solving within writing and reading. Interactive writing, a setting for group instruction, is a powerful process for demonstrating how words work; here, children learn many strategies they can use in their own writing. Guest author Mary Ellen Giacobbe helps us think about phonics and spelling as an integral part of the writing workshop. You will find her practical descriptions and useful materials most helpful in implementing this effective approach. We also explore shared and guided reading as contexts within which to help children learn and use important word-solving skills.

Our last section is designed to bring colleagues together to consider how children learn to become word solvers. We explore the developmental shifts over time that we can expect as children learn more about words. It is useful for teachers to work together to conceptualize a word-solving program that spans grade levels and helps all children use their strengths to learn more. Teaching for change is an integral part of this section. We suggest benchmarks for progress that will help school teams assess the impact of their own programs, and we also present work with parents as an important component of helping children become word solvers. Finally, to support collegiality and continuous learning, we have provided Suggestions for Professional Development at the end of every chapter.

We hope that this book initiates a rich dialogue among teachers as they create strong reading/writing curriculums. Our goal is powerful teaching that enables all children to become word solvers in the process of becoming effective readers and writers who enjoy the many rewards of literacy.

1

A Quality Literacy Program: Supporting Young Word Solvers

In this section, we explore what it means to become a word solver and what it means to support children's learning about how words work. We begin with eight principles of literacy learning and go on to describe the high-quality literacy program that is needed for all children to become effective word solvers. The learning involved in becoming a word solver is more specifically described in Chapter 3. Chapters 4 and 5 focus on the resources and tools, especially interactive word walls and charts, that are essential for an effective instructional program. The ideas we introduce in this section are explored in greater depth throughout the book.

8!

Eight Principles of Literacy Learning

Today's classrooms are filled with beautiful, engaging children's books. Our students are reading high-quality literature and creating their own writing that reflects a variety of genres and purposes. Yet, a consistent, agreed-upon vision for literacy education eludes us as we struggle over the role of phonics, spelling, and the conventions of our written language in learning to write. As teachers, we want our students to learn the basic skills that will enable them to become effective readers and writers. At the same time, we must never lose sight of our overarching goal for all children: that they understand and experience the myriad functions of literacy as well as the pure joy inherent in reading and writing.

Drawing upon our observations of children in many learning contexts, we have identified the following eight key principles. We state these in terms of children's needs. In this way, they challenge us as educators to provide a rich and balanced program that offers a full range of learning opportunities for all children.

1. Children need to understand the purposes of literacy so they can fully appreciate and enjoy literacy in their lives.

2. Children need to hear written language so they can learn its structure and take in new information and ideas.

3. Children need to become aware of the sounds of language, to enjoy those sounds, and to use this knowledge as a tool in becoming literate.

4. Children need to have many experiences working with written symbols so they can learn how to look at letters and use this information to read and write.

5. Children need to explore words and learn how words work so they can use this information effectively and efficiently in reading and writing.

6. Children need to learn the conventions of print and how books work so they can use this knowledge as readers and writers.

7. Children need to read and write continuous text so they can use and expand their knowledge about letters, sounds, words, and language.

8. Children need to develop flexibility and fluency to enhance comprehension and enjoyment of reading and writing.

Let's explore each one in turn and consider how each contributes to successful literacy learning.

Children need to understand the purposes of literacy so they can fully appreciate and enjoy literacy in their lives.

From her earliest years, a child sees the many functions of print in her home and neighborhood. Literate people demonstrate reading and writing for real purposes—reading menus, writing shopping lists, looking up sporting events. Indeed, there are thousands of ways that people unconsciously use literacy in daily life. Many children try out literacy for themselves before they've had any formal instruction; they listen to stories, and they pretend to read and write. This functional aspect of literacy is key because we learn the value of any human activity by using it.

Early experiences with print can help children understand the purposes of literacy as they incidentally learn what print is and how it works. At home and in preschools and kindergarten classrooms, for example, we have observed young children:

■ Signing in as they come into the classroom.

■ Finding their materials by looking for their names.

■ Labeling their block constructions.

■ Writing menus in a play restaurant.

■ Hearing stories read aloud several times each day.

■ Exploring books on their own.

■ Working in a group to write lists of things to do or buy, messages or letters (see Figure 1-1), and their own versions of familiar stories such as The Three Bears.

These examples are only a few of the many ways that teachers involve young children in meaningful experiences with print. Throughout the grades, children need many opportunities to engage in meaningful literacy experiences in school that parallel the uses of literacy in people's lives. At the same time, teachers can help children understand why it's a good idea to learn what words are and why learning to read and write matters.

Children need to hear written language so they can learn its structure and take in new information and ideas.

It is obvious that the written and oral versions of any language share a common vocabulary and sentence structure. However, we can also observe some important differences. Most people can tell the difference between an oral and written style of "grammar." Two examples of written language structures are

> "Once upon a time in a small
>   kingdom . . ."
> "Hurry," exclaimed the rabbit, "we'll be
>   late!"

These structures aren't heard in oral language unless someone is reading aloud or telling a story. Many of us have observed a young child pick up a book and, as Clay (1991a) described it, "talk like a book," approximating the language of stories and producing it. Children who know how to "talk like a book" are fortunate because they have had opportunities to hear the books read aloud. As they hear the same story many times, they can "absorb" the stories and make them their own.

These children have internalized the structure or "syntax" of written language, and they are using words they would not usually hear in oral language. They are also expanding their vocabularies and their repertoire of language structures, knowledge that is important in beginning literacy. Children know what to expect from written language and how it is supposed to sound.

Wherever possible, we have used plural pronouns to avoid sexist language. When we use a generic singular pronoun, we have alternated the masculine and feminine by chapter.

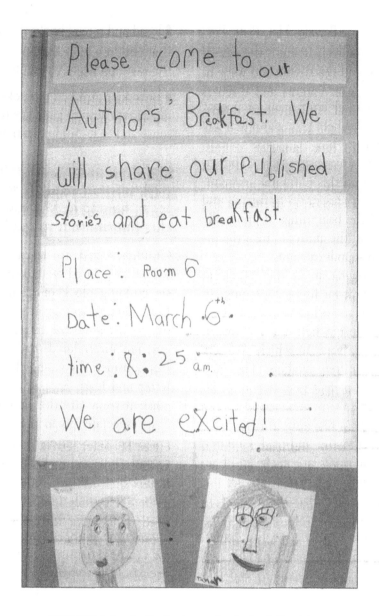

FIGURE 1-1   An Invitation to the Author's Breakfast

They can confirm whether or not what they are reading makes sense and sounds right.

Children need to become aware of the sounds of language, to enjoy those sounds, and to use this knowledge as a tool in becoming literate.

When we listen to people talk, we hear streams of sounds that we put together in ways that make meaning—words and parts of words that follow each other in rule-governed ways. Largely, we are unaware of the sounds of

language; we are focusing on what the words are telling us. For young children at some point in time, it is necessary to notice the sounds of language and consciously attend to them. Five-year-old Madeleine, for example, knows that *Madeleine*, *Margaret* (her baby sister's name), and *Mommy* all sound alike at the beginning. This means that she can notice the sounds in words as they are said orally.

There is a natural human tendency to enjoy the sounds of language. For example, we delight in poetic alliteration, and we enjoy rhythm and rhyme. When young children learn *Pease Porridge Hot, Pease Porridge Cold*, they are likely to enjoy the sounds of the language and the rhyme and want to say it over and over. Parents and teachers can use this natural enjoyment of poetry, song, and rhyme to help young children pay close attention to how language sounds. Books such as *Goodnight Moon* (Brown 1947) capitalize on this natural enjoyment. In young children's responses to rhymes and games, we find the beginnings of phonemic awareness, that is, the ability to hear the individual speech sounds in words.

Why is knowing about the sounds in words so important for literacy learning? In English and in many other languages, there is a close relationship between the sounds we speak and the ways in which they are represented in written symbols. The relationship is not a perfect one; but in an alphabetic written system, it is critical for the users of language to recognize this relationship and use it to write and read. Children who realize that words are made up of sequences of sounds, called *phonemes* by linguists, can more easily relate these sounds to the sequences of letters and to letter groups. As children learn to read and write, understanding the sound-letter relationship is key, and this understanding begins in oral language experiences.

It is particularly important for children who are English learners to experience a wide, rich range of oral language. There are more than 5.3 million school-aged children in the United States whose primary language is other than English. Teachers who work with these English learners know how important it is to engage them in daily conversations. Teachers of English learners:

∎ Repeat and expand phrases and sentences in a natural way so that children hear English structures again and again and begin to use them with some confidence.

∎ Use pictures and concrete objects to make themselves understood.

∎ Read and reread books that are favorites so that children have a chance to internalize the text and begin to join in on refrains.

∎ Introduce children to books with simple, repetitive, natural language that will make sense and that children can easily repeat.

Children need many experiences with written symbols so they can learn how to look at letters and use this information to read and write.

Children need to learn how to attach sounds to printed symbols or letters as a basic building block of reading and writing. Learning how to look at letters and learning how to use letter information are two different, but interrelated, bodies of knowledge. Just consider: the young child must notice a letter and learn enough about it to distinguish it from all other letters. That is not easy, especially given the very small differences between letters such as *h*, *n*, and *u*. Orientation also makes a difference; when letters such as *d* or *b* are turned around or over, even their names change. Children need to look for features like tails, sticks, curves, and tunnels. Knowing what to look for can be a daunting task when faced with the whole alphabet.

What we have overlooked for too long is the fact that before a child can attach a sound to a symbol, she must first be able to see the letter symbol as an individual entity different from other symbols (Clay 1991a, 266). A whole network of knowledge surrounds a single letter: it has a shape, it's connected to a sound, it has a name, it can be connected to other letters in a word, and it can appear in different ways—large, small, in italics, in color, and so forth; yet, remarkably, the letter is always the same in important ways. Children need to be able to recognize letters in isolation, but, even more important, they need to be able to distinguish letters that are surrounded by other letters—embedded in print.

FIGURE 1-2   Children Engaged in Letter Sorting

Children need to explore words and learn how words work so they can use this information effectively and efficiently in reading and writing.

Chances are, a child's first experience with learning to look at print has to do with the child's own name. It is not an accident that Madeleine recognized the /m/ phoneme. She can also find the M&M's and the meat in the grocery advertising page. And, she announced to her mother one day that *Daddy* also has an *m*. Puzzled, her mother explained that there was no *m* in *Daddy*; then Madeleine mentioned that when you call Daddy at the office, you push *mem-1* on the telephone (the memory feature). Children who are connecting print to themselves begin to notice print in the environment. Madeleine is learning what to look for as she notices the *m* again and again. She uses the information in many ways, such as in one of the notes that she wrote at age four (Figure 1-3).

It is obvious that Madeleine used her name as an important resource in learning to read. Most young children build a network of understandings around their names, including:

❚ My name is a word.
❚ A word is a sequence of letters that go together.
❚ The letters in a word progress in a certain direction.
❚ Words have meaning.
❚ Words are written the same way every time. **predictable**
❚ Words are defined by white space on either side.
❚ Words can be short or long (they can have one letter or many).
❚ Other words start like my name or end like my name.
❚ I can say the word and connect sounds to some of the letters in a word.
❚ Words can be put together to make a message.
❚ Words have different meanings when put together with other words.

7

FIGURE 1-3   Madeleine's Note, Age 4

❚ Words have parts that are like other words.
❚ One word can be used to help me recognize another word.

These ideas are increasingly complex in nature, but as children work with words, they gradually learn more, enabling them to systematize their knowledge.

At first, through a broad range of experiences such as shared reading and group writing, children may learn to identify a few words. The first few words a child learns are very important because that child is learning how to learn words. These first words, usually including the child's name, are exemplars. We are reminded of the kindergarten child who announced, "Ever since I learned the word *the*, I just see it everywhere!" Building a body of knowledge of words that occur frequently in language is useful because children learn to recognize them easily in print, write them quickly, and use the information they possess about these words to write or figure out new words.

We have described attention to the sounds and visual features of letters as if they are two separate areas of learning; however, we recognize that these two areas are coordinated and reciprocal processes. Learning in one helps learning in the other. Saying words slowly helps children write the words or parts of words and get better at spelling them. The knowledge of the letter-sound relationship also makes it easier for children to read these words in text. For example, children must learn that words do not always look the way they sound. *Eight* has two sounds and five letters, and sounds like the word *ate*. It will be important for children to engage in activities that help them recognize clusters of letters or patterns that may be connected to sounds.

Children need to learn the conventions of print and how books work so they can use this knowledge as readers and writers.

Some of the important understandings about print involve the purely arbitrary conventions that people have created to make written language accessible. For example, words are written from left to right in a straight line across a page. When the edge of a page is reached, print begins again on the left. This convention requires our eyes to move left to right and sweep back to the left, a movement that occurs automatically for experienced readers. We also attach spoken words to the clusters of letters on a page; this convention helps readers attend to the critical information needed to recognize words. For the young child, it means making a "space and time transformation" (Clay 1991a); that is, spoken words come out in time and written words are arranged in space. Children learn to match one spoken word to one written word, reading left to right; this is both a conceptual and a motor task. Other conventions of print include:

❚ Left page before right page when reading.
❚ Punctuation.
❚ Upper- and lowercase letters.
❚ Paragraphing.
❚ Print layout, such as spacing of words and lines of text.

For some young children, the fact that we look at the print rather than the picture as we read may be completely new information. We can help children develop knowledge of print conventions even before they learn letters or words or letter-sound relationships because a wide range of literacy experiences contributes to the knowledge base. As children write, in groups or on their own, they have to place words across a page. As they read, they must follow a line of print with their eyes. Hundreds of experiences with reading and writing help the young child to build an understanding of these conventions of print.

Children need to read and write continuous text so they can use and expand their knowledge about letters, sounds, words, and language.

Children do not need to know all the letters or sounds, or even very many words, before beginning to read text. They can be involved in meaningful and enjoyable reading and writing from the beginning. As young readers and writers engage with text, the phonological (sound) and orthographic (letter) information and the conventions of print become more available, because as children interact with the text, they use these sources of information. For example, five-year-old Rosa reads a simple caption book called *At the Zoo* (Peters 1995). On the first page, the text says:

I like the giraffe and the giraffe likes me.

The language pattern is repeated on each page, and the illustration helps her to read the word *giraffe*. The text is an easy one for Rosa to read even though she would not be able to read all of the words in isolation. She is using her knowledge of language and of the world to propel her through this text, but she is also learning some important things about reading. Each time she engages in reading the text she attends to more of the print features. For example:

❚ She practices word-by-word matching and the motor movement of reading by using her finger to assist her eyes, pointing to each word as she reads it. This sentence is fairly long for a beginner, so it is important that the child is first able to say the sentence orally, with teacher assistance, before attempting to read it. If the child cannot produce the sentence in oral language, the text will be very difficult to read.

❚ She uses her knowledge of the words *I*, *the*, and *and*, which are all familiar to her through many experiences in reading and writing. These words anchor her reading so that she can check whether her finger is in the right place. One of the things we like about this text is that these familiar words are used many times. Rosa will need to read many texts using high-frequency words to build her strength and instant recognition.

❚ She notices that sometimes the word *like* is used and sometimes the word *likes* is used. That prompts her to notice the endings of words. She is beginning to understand that word endings make a difference in the meaning of a text and how it sounds.

❚ She has the opportunity to figure out the word *me*, which contains a letter-sound combination that she knows, *m*, and a letter, *e*, that she knows by name. She can find the word *me* in the text, and she reads it over and over on page after page. By the time she finishes *At the Zoo*, she has a good acquaintance with the word and soon will be able to use it as an example to connect it to words like *he* and *be*.

❚ She notices that *tiger* has an *r* in it; so does her name. She also notices that *giraffe* has an *r* in the middle.

Rosa does not know all of the letter-sound relationships; she cannot decode all the words. However, she has the opportunity to use what she does know. She is engaged in an enjoyable and meaningful experience while she simultaneously expands her knowledge of letters, sounds, and words. From the very beginning, Rosa is putting together her understandings so that they make sense.

Children need to develop flexibility and fluency to enhance comprehension and enjoyment of reading and writing.

Finally, what does it mean to be a good, independent reader or writer? Two characteristics are predominant: fluency and flexibility. We will discuss each of these characteristics briefly.

Fluency, in our view, involves both rate of reading (speed) and the phrasing that good readers use when they read aloud. When we talk about fluency we are referring to the way readers put words together in phrases, to the expression and intonation they use, and to the speed and ease with which they read. In a study of the oral read-ing fluency of fourth graders, we found a high relationship between words per minute, accuracy, and a qualitative measure of "expression" or phrasing. And, all those measures were highly correlated with the scores on the standardized tests of the National Assessment of Educational Progress 1995. Several systems contribute to fluency in reading:

❚ Fast processing—recognizing words and spelling patterns quickly and automatically while keeping attention on the meaning of a text.

❚ Using language and meaning systems to check on reading and predict while reading.

❚ Fluent processing of visual (letter), phonological (sound), syntactic (language structure), and semantic (meaning) cues, the foundation of all reading.

❚ Continuous checking to be sure that what is read makes sense, sounds right, and matches the print.

All of those aspects help readers maintain fluency. Readers develop the fast processing system, for example, as they encounter various spelling patterns repeatedly in the text. In this way, these patterns become quickly recognizable. Readers develop fluency and phrasing as they read material that makes sense to them. Young children must read material that enables them to retain their knowledge of language while they focus on the details of printed language. When children are able to use their knowledge of language, they can anticipate what the print might say; then they either confirm their prediction with the actual text or figure out the text as they read it. Either way, language knowledge always enables readers to make sense of text and to gain momentum while reading the text.

Fluency is also important to the writer. As writers compose their messages, the ability to write many words easily frees their attention for the act of composition. We would not want writers to laboriously figure out every word; only new words should require slowing down and analyzing the parts. Fluency in early writing is enhanced when:

▌ Children know a large core of words and can produce them quickly, and automatically.

▌ Children understand useful spelling patterns that they can use to make many more words.

▌ Children can associate letters and sounds quickly and easily, and use this information in the process of writing.

▌ Children can compose a message and reproduce it easily because they are not too distracted by laborious processes in writing the words.

Readers and writers also need to be flexible. Clay (1991a) has said that a good reader can change directions at any point in time. Good readers who approach a word they do not know have many ways of solving it. For example, readers can:

▌ Recognize it as a familiar word and check whether it makes sense and sounds right.

▌ Derive the new word by analogy to a word or words they already know (using *my* and *tree* to figure out *try*).

▌ Search for meaning in pictures and text.

▌ Predict based on meaning or syntax and check against visual information.

▌ Think about what would make sense and sound right given some aspect of the word.

▌ Partially sound letters of the word and fit this partial information with meaning and language structure.

▌ Sound out parts of the word and link them to known words or parts of words.

▌ Analyze the word letter by letter, using larger clusters as much as possible (Fountas and Pinnell 1996).

Also, readers must be flexible in their ability to read different kinds of texts. For example, when we read for information, the demands on processing are slightly different than when we read for enjoyment or escape. Young readers need many experiences with different kinds of texts—letters, lists, stories, descriptions, directions, fiction, and informational texts—so they will become flexible readers and will be able to tackle a variety of texts with confidence.

There is a parallel need to write for many purposes and to produce many different kinds of written documents. When children are just beginning as writers, it may be hard for them to create a wide variety of texts because they need very easy material to read, and their first messages may be personal. But as they learn more, variety becomes increasingly important. Group situations, such as interactive writing and shared reading, offer teachers opportunities to demonstrate the construction of different kinds of texts and to encourage children to create their own.

Suggestions for Professional Development

1. The eight principles described in this chapter are expressed as children's needs in the chart in Figure 1-4. For each of the eight, think about and note how you are meeting children's needs with instructional components and/or specific activities in your instructional programs. Then, for each of the eight, identify one goal that you want to achieve in your classroom this year. Discuss reading, writing, and other word-solving activities.

2. Share your results with a colleague and make a plan and timeline to accomplish your goals.

3. Schedule a follow-up meeting with your colleagues to review the changes you have made and what you have learned.

Eight Principles of Literacy Learning		
Children need:	In my classroom, I:	My goal is:
• To understand the purposes of literacy so they can fully appreciate and enjoy literacy in their lives.		
• To hear written language so they can learn its structure and take in new information and ideas.		
• To become aware of the sounds of language, to enjoy those sounds, and to use this knowledge as a tool in becoming literate.		
• To have many experiences working with written symbols so they can learn how to look at letters and use this information to read and write.		
• To explore words and learn how words work so they can use this information effectively and efficiently in reading and writing.		
• To learn the conventions of print and how books work so they can use this knowledge as readers and writers.		
• To read and write continuous text so they can use and expand their knowledge about letters, sounds, words, and language.		
• To develop flexibility and fluency to enhance comprehension and enjoyment of reading and writing.		

FIGURE 1-4   Eight Principles of Literacy Learning

Designing a Quality Literacy Program

Guided by the eight principles of literacy learning, we can now consider a quality literacy program that provides for learning in multidimensional ways. Word learning, in particular, cannot be confined to simple, brief lessons. Children need to see words, use them, think about them, play with them, figure them out in reading, spell them in writing, and hear them in many contexts over and over again. Even as adults we continue to learn new words. Sometimes we learn a new word and then "hear" it several times within the next week or so. This is not a coincidence. Encountering an interesting new word captures our attention and makes us more alert to the various meanings and uses of the word in multiple contexts. Children, too, need similar experiences to truly appreciate and claim words as their own. Our instructional programs must be multifaceted, providing children with many opportunities to learn about the various aspects of literacy.

Becoming a competent word solver is definitely one of the basic first steps that children must take. If children cannot work with words—solving new and unfamiliar words so they can spell them in writing and figure them out in reading—we will not

have achieved the goals of our literacy program. Ultimately, word solving is the essential analytic skill needed for reading and writing. Successful reading and writing depend on the reader/writer's ability to:

- Use visual features of words.
- Use the relationships between sounds and letters and letter clusters.
- Use spelling patterns.
- Coordinate these skills with attention to meaning and the syntax or "grammar" of language.

As Clay (1991a) has said, readers must read with divided attention to solve words without losing meaning or fluency. As well, writers must be able to construct words without losing the message they want to convey.

It is our job as teachers to design a literacy program that will help children become interested in words, become effective and fast at word solving, and be able to use word-solving skills while reading and writing meaningful messages, stories, informational pieces, and other kinds of written language. In this chapter we present twelve characteristics of a quality literacy program that includes word study.

Promoting Interest in Language

An *effective literacy program promotes curiosity about and interest in words and the sounds of language*. As children use language, finding satisfaction and enjoyment, their interest in words grows. Participating in chanting rhymes, singing songs, and saying or hearing poetry delights young children. This natural enjoyment is the foundation for becoming literate.

As children hear stories, poetry, and nursery rhymes read aloud, they simultaneously experience the beauty and rhythm of written language while they observe the print connected to it. In this way, children learn that messages are constant when they are encoded in print, and that these messages can be said over and over, providing enjoyment again and again. Moreover, children are developing an interest in written words, even before they can read them. It is natural for children in a language-rich classroom to find words fascinating: the way they look, the way they sound, the way they mean, and the way they are put together to communicate meaning.

Reading aloud to English learners opens the door to their full participation in the oral language of the classroom. But what about word study? For a child who does not know the language very well, word study can be treacherous. Just imagine what it would be like to try to take apart isolated words, build new words, or make connections between words when you do not know how to pronounce them or even know what they mean. So, this first characteristic, building interest in language, is especially important for English learners. As teachers of English learners, we must:

❚ Be sure that children understand the meaning of phrases, poems, and stories that we are using to build interest in language.

❚ Provide lots of opportunities for children to say the words over and over.

❚ Be tolerant of diverse pronunciations; what matters is that children are using and enjoying the sounds of language.

Building on the Teacher's Expertise

A quality literacy program is built on the teacher's understanding of the reading and writing processes, which includes a thorough knowledge of how letters and words work in the alphabetic system. As teachers, the more we understand about the language system and about the operations involved in reading and writing, the more effective we can be at observing children and teaching them.

Reading and writing are complex processes acquired over time in unique ways by individual children. Effective readers can use all sources of information in print as they read for meaning. They notice errors and work at solving problems so that they are able to learn more each time they read. These skills include the ability to read phrases or words sound by sound or part by part. Effective writers can attend to the message they want to communicate as they construct sequences of words, letter by letter, part by part. Your understanding of what good readers and writers know how to do will guide your decision making about instruction.

It is also important for us as teachers to understand oral and written language. How can we design a curriculum that helps children learn how words work unless we understand the basic elements of the linguistic system? We need to understand how words are related to each other in the way they sound, look, and mean so that we can help children go beyond simplistic, rote knowledge of words to become discoverers of interesting connections between words. A goal of the word study curriculum is to help children develop a deep knowledge of powerful principles that they can apply in flexible ways. We are not interested in the tedious accumulation of lists of words; we aim to help students develop the effective strategies they need to solve *any* word they meet.

What about a teacher who works with English learners? Knowing the necessary language concepts is, indeed, a challenging task because it not only means making explicit and systematizing some of your understandings of the English language, but it also requires acquiring some understanding of the English learner's language if that is possible. We know that when children learn language they acquire a phonological or sound system and an underlying knowledge of the rules of grammar through which they can generate an infinite number of sentences in their language. Knowing some of the words of the English learner's language and how to pronounce them, and knowing some of the basic syntactic structures, will help you discover what the child understands about language. Whenever possible, incorporate into the books and rhymes you read aloud words from other languages. All children enjoy practicing the pronunciation of words in a language not their own, so this diversity will appeal to everyone in the class. In addition, the diversity of language helps children pay attention to the element of sound. All the while, you are sensitizing children to the sounds of language.

Using Assessment for Instruction

In a quality literacy program, teachers use systematic observation and assessment to identify children's understanding and to inform teaching. In order to be effective, you need detailed knowledge of the children in your program so you can adjust tasks and materials to help children make the most of their strengths. Through systematic observation, you can collect behavioral evidence of learning. The running record (Clay 1993a), for example, is a powerful tool for recording the details of reading behavior. This technique provides a "shorthand" way to observe a child's reading of any text and to code the behavior so it can later be analyzed. The running record technique provides an accuracy score so the difficulty of the text for that child can be de-

termined; more important, it provides a way to see how readers are processing the text and using strategies to figure out words they don't know. (For more information about how to take and use running records, see Clay [1993a], Fountas and Pinnell [1996], and Johnston [1997].)

To take a running record, you sit beside the child so that you both can see the book and you can unobtrusively record reading behavior using a coding system. Figure 2-1 shows how the coding might look for one child's reading of a simple text.

In Figure 2-1, Shante is attending to meaning and language structure cues and also checking the first letters of words. She deals competently with the compound word *sidewalk* and takes apart the word *over*. She notices a letter cluster in *streets*. Shante is analyzing words left to right using letter-sound relationships, but she is also using a cluster or part of a word. She is relating a word she knows to a word she is trying to figure out. The text is easy for her; she has only a few problems to solve and she does so while attending to the meaning of this simple book.

Your analysis of these records guides the way you interact with your students, and guides the materials and books you select for reading instruction. Running records help you learn the range of strategies children are applying in reading; that is, how children are using many different sources of information. Running records provide specific information with regard to letter and word learning and how the children are using this information while reading text.

Children's writing samples provide another kind of behavioral evidence. Through examining and analyzing writing samples, you can learn the degree to which the child understands the alphabetic system, including how sequences of letters communicate meaning. Samples collected over time provide evidence of ongoing learning.

If we know something about the language that English learners speak in their homes and we observe them carefully, we

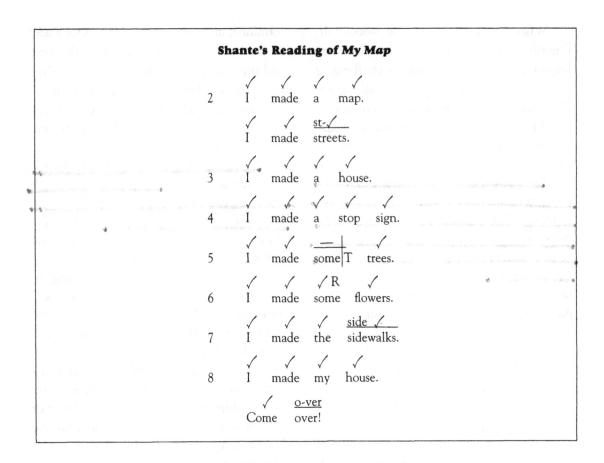

FIGURE 2-1   Shante's Reading of *My Map*

can see that they are probably using what they know about language as a system. They may make errors, for example, that are logical when we consider the way their home language is structured. When observing English learners, it does not help merely to notice "deficits." We need to learn how these learners are approaching all aspects of English, both oral and written, and to note their strengths. Even knowing a few words is a starting point for learning more about words.

Systematic observation of both reading and writing provides important information about the effectiveness of the literacy program and the teaching within it. What children do when they read and write is an indicator of what has been taught. Teachers can reflect on their teaching. What has been emphasized? What has been neglected? Ongoing assessment can guide the school literacy program to broaden its impact and reach all children.

Teaching for Word-Solving Strategies

Teachers emphasize word-solving strategies or the thinking that readers and writers can apply in a generative way; that is, they help children apply techniques to many new words in different settings. When children learn to read and write, they do learn letters and specific words. In this book, we will discuss many ways to help children in this endeavor. But reading and writing are not simply about recognizing letters and acquiring reading and writing vocabularies. The way children use this information while processing text and writing text is what makes the difference in becoming competent, independent readers and writers. When children have developed a system for using print, they can apply the processing systems to the reading and writing of increasingly challenging texts.

Teachers must be particularly sensitive

when English learners are trying to become familiar with print in a language that is not their own. A "bottom line" guideline is that children should not be expected to read something they do not understand. A great deal of oral language must surround all interactions with print. Writing and reading books with simple, natural-sounding patterns and familiar topics will help to build knowledge of both the English words and their visual configuration in print. In this way children can build a base for the more complex word analyses; phonological and orthographic patterns will become more available when the territory is familiar. For all learners, essential knowledge includes an understanding of how letters and words work so that they are not limited to memorizing or learning "sight" words but can write and read an infinite number of words because they have effective tools.

Treating Word Solving as a Process

Teachers value the learners' partially correct attempts as important indicators along the way to correct responding. Active learning is a key to achieving competence in reading and writing. Anyone who has worked with children in remedial reading knows that frequently these students become passive. They stop trying to figure out words or write words and simply wait for someone to tell them. It would be very easy for this to happen to English learners who are performing by rote, without understanding what they are trying to read or write. The partially correct responses of readers provide a window of opportunity for the teacher, who can ask:

■ What do these learners know about the language system—their own and/or English?

■ What parts of word solving do the learners understand and use?

As teachers, we do want children to read and spell most words accurately, but we want children to keep working at words that they

do not yet fully know. Making attempts, receiving affirmation for partial correctness, and receiving feedback to get better are all part of learning. Children's attempts always have a logic. When they try things out, even when they are not fully correct, they are revealing their working hypotheses about reading and writing. The errors a child makes (on the way to self-correction) give teachers a window of observation that will help them know what he is attending to and how he is currently using knowledge. Teachers who understand reading and writing as a complex process that changes over time are sensitive to how each response reflects the child's logic and understanding at a particular point in time. Using this information, teachers are able to note strengths and build on them.

Providing Active, Multilevel Learning Opportunities

Teachers provide daily, active, multilevel word study opportunities. The words *daily*, *active*, and *multilevel* present several challenges for us as teachers. Each child in a classroom deserves daily teaching that engages her interest and enables her to participate with confidence and competence, while giving her opportunities for new learning. The teaching must be daily, which means that time must be set aside for productive learning activities. Also, the time must be well used by appropriate-level activities and good examples that help children develop effective word-learning strategies.

The learning must also be active. When children are actively solving words and using them, they learn more effectively (see Figure 2-2). The understandings become their own because they have engaged with them, not simply heard them.

Finally, the activities must be multilevel, meaning that each child must be able to profit from them at an individual level of understanding. It is obvious that in a class of twenty to thirty students, there will be a wide range of ability and understanding

FIGURE 2-2   Children Engaged in Word Study

about letters, words, and how words work. In a first-grade class, for example, some children may still be learning the alphabet letters and a few high-frequency words, while others may have a large collection of known words that they can use in many different ways. Other children may be learning English and may need meaningful, successful practice of some of the basic aspects of the language.

Multilevel activities are designed so that multiple understandings may be taken from any one activity. Multilevel activities generally are "open-ended," meaning that a variety of different responses are possible and that more advanced learners can go beyond the particular lesson. Children who are advanced in their knowledge of words, for example, will have the opportunity to go beyond the lesson at hand and to explore the principle widely, generating more examples or discovering related principles. For English learners, there may be small-group attention, working with words together and engaging in conversation so that they can more easily see the principle involved. As in

any other planned educational experience, it is necessary to adjust instruction to individual learners.

Teaching for a Shift in Behavior

Teachers provide explicit teaching of principles and strategies that allow each learner to move forward. The success of a literacy program rests on the quality of teaching students receive. Teachers make hundreds of decisions within a school day. Some of the decisions are preplanned; others are made during moment-to-moment interactions that build on knowledge students bring to the situation. Good plans are essential and provide a base for powerful teaching; you can start by being aware of the behaviors that indicate what your students know and can do. By using observation records, you can make better plans, tailoring individual interactions to each child's responses in a way that allows all learners to move forward. The goal is to provide clear, easy-to-understand examples that help students learn the basic principles of word study. Then, students practice and apply these principles, with teacher support, and practice again with supportive interactions that help build the process.

Centering the Teaching on Children

Effective literacy education involves teaching children, not simply following a set program. Program designs and outlines provide structure and support for our teaching, but as teachers we know that our work is not about teaching a program. It is about teaching our individual students how to be good readers and writers of stories, informational pieces, and the extensive range of literacy processes that will be required of them in school and later in life. We see children as individual learners who bring their own life experience and language knowledge to the literacy process. Our role is to design the program they need.

Viewing children as individual learners and working with them in groups may seem at odds; however, no matter what size group we are working with, we always recognize that children are individuals and we do our best to tune in to their individual strengths and knowledge bases. Teaching to individual strengths is what makes the teaching powerful.

The power of teaching is often in the moment-to-moment interactions we have with individuals or groups of children. That is why many different kinds of materials and many different kinds of program designs "work" with most children. The power is in the teaching. The more skilled we can become at observing children and interacting with them, the higher their achievement.

Promoting Self-Monitoring Behaviors

The program promotes self-monitoring or checking on oneself in word solving. Good readers and writers are independent. They know how to use the knowledge they have in flexible ways. They are self-regulated rather than teacher-dependent. Young children can begin to use even the limited set of knowledge

they have in a self-monitoring way. Part of the instruction in a literacy program provides for self-monitoring. With regard to word solving, we want readers and writers to:

❙ Notice when words don't look right, sound right, or make sense.

❙ Know how to search for more information in reading or writing.

❙ Know how to use existing knowledge in strategic ways to get to what they do not know.

❙ Know when to ask the teacher for help.

❙ Know when and how to look for answers in other sources, such as word walls or dictionaries.

Having skills such as these helps students work independently, creating space for the teacher to work with small groups and individuals. These skills are useful because they provide young children with an increasing sense of self-control and self-management. Being able to make decisions and solve one's own problems in writing, reading, or any other class activity is part of learning.

Including a Variety of Interactions

The literacy program includes individual conferences, small-group teaching, and whole-class lessons. Individual conferences provide specific help to the individual reader or writer. This immediate assistance allows the child to move forward in completing tasks, but more important, it provides the feedback that helps to refine the processing systems the child is developing. Small-group teaching is organized based on the strengths and needs of individual children who are similar enough to benefit from effective group instruction. Whole-class lessons concentrate on what everyone in the class needs to know. Short, focused lessons (as in writing workshop or shared reading) are effective.

For efficiency in teaching, we must group children in various ways. For guided reading (discussed in Chapter 3), we suggest small groups of two to eight children who have similar reading behaviors and who read similar levels of text. Writing workshop usually involves the whole group in a minilesson that is followed by independent work and the opportunity to have an individual conference with the teacher. Sometimes, a writing minilesson might involve only a portion of the class, or follow-up sessions might involve small groups of children looking at particular aspects of the writing process. Word study, as we will describe in more detail in later chapters, is likely to involve a range of whole-group, small-group, and independent activities.

When working with both large and small groups of children, we know that we must plan well. We will work hard to organize and structure their learning so we make best use of our time and children know what is expected.

Using Effective Management and Resources for Independent Learning

The program is characterized by using effective management and assuring that classrooms are well supplied with appropriate tools, resources, and references to support independent learning. The word *system* is key to creating and implementing an effective literacy program. There is a structured, systematic process for each kind of instruction provided—for spelling, for guided reading, for writing workshop, and so forth. The system provides for flexible decision making related to the needs of individual learners. Teachers have the larger system in mind but are willing to group and regroup, tailoring instructional moves to where children need to go. Ongoing, systematic assessment is part of the management plan so that teachers have the information they need to make flexible decisions and to guide teaching.

The environment for learning includes the full range of materials that children will need to work independently and to support their learning at appropriate levels. For example, a set of books that are organized by level and labeled can help children to make good choices in their own reading. A well-organized and labeled writing center makes it possible for children to handle supplies efficiently and to work on their own. References and resources provide support for writing so that the teacher is not always the only source of information. A well-supplied and organized classroom has many benefits:

❚ Children have rich input not only from the teacher but from material resources.

❚ Children can work independently in productive literacy activities.

❚ Children benefit from intensive instruction for guided reading, spelling, or writing lessons, as the teacher is freed to work with small groups.

❚ Children learn much about self-management.

These resources and references are carefully selected. Many of the materials are constructed with children so that they are made anew each year. Chapter 4, in which we discuss the word study environment, provides some good examples. Here are some suggestions for considering the quality of resources and references:

❚ Carefully select resources and references, considering the appropriate nature and level of difficulty of each to support students. For example, some commercially produced materials may feature a format that is too difficult or demand conceptual understanding beyond the children's developmental ability.

❚ Create some of the resources and references together with children so they'll feel ownership and develop a full understanding of the nature and use of each.

▌ Use references and resources (such as interactive wall charts) as an ongoing part of word study.

▌ Demonstrate the use of references and resources regularly as a good alternative to "asking the teacher."

▌ Realize that English learners may need more demonstration and practice to use references and resources in the English classroom. You may want to work with them in a small group.

▌ Make it possible for English learners, and indeed, all children, to see their own lives and language reflected in the references and resources of the classrooms (for example, in illustrations and vocabulary).

Educating and Involving Parents

An integral part of a quality literacy program is educating parents in the goals, instructional processes, and assessment practices that document learning. Parents need to have a basic understanding of and realistic expectations about how children learn letters, sounds, and words, and how they learn to use this information in the reading and writing process. Parents need to know what will be taught and what to expect. They need to know what to look for as evidence of their children's learning literacy, including learning individual words and the strategies for figuring out words in reading and writing.

In an effective school literacy program, parents have the opportunity to learn ways to support their children in word learning. Parents can play a critical role in any literacy program by:

▌ Showing interest in children's reading and writing.

▌ Appreciating their first approximated attempts.

▌ Noticing when children are checking on themselves and working at problem solving.

▌ Listening to children reading, beginning with easy books.

▌ Helping children begin to write.

The more parents can focus on what children are trying to say, and the more they notice progress based on both correct and partially correct responses, the more support they will give their children in building the reading and writing process. The school can provide assistance and guidance to parents to help them interact effectively with their young children as they begin to write and read.

Assuring Quality at All Levels

Implementing a quality word study curriculum is not possible unless there is also a quality literacy program in the classroom. The best word study curriculum will be useless without parallel opportunities for children to engage in reading and writing for a variety of purposes. It is difficult, also, to implement a high-quality literacy program in a classroom without collaboration among colleagues. For example, if materials to support reading, writing, and word study are analyzed by grade-level teams and across grade levels, more strategic purchasing and organizing is possible.

Schedules, too, are subject to school-wide operations. Teachers need blocks of uninterrupted time to implement an effective word study curriculum in a quality literacy program. The classroom day is crowded. As you read this book you may find yourself saying, "How can I find the time to use these good ideas for word study without removing time for reading and writing?" The truth is that we must have both authentic reading and writing and focused exploration of letters, sounds, and words.

One of the first steps toward a quality program is simply identifying the time and finding ways to use it well. Colleagues, including teachers and administrators, can help each other analyze classroom schedules and also make adjustments in the school schedule to support more learning time. If we are serious about creating literate children who exemplify the portrait of competence sketched at the beginning of this chapter, then we must have the experiences necessary to support their learning. There is no other time in the child's life when we can so efficiently achieve this goal; it must be now.

Suggestions for Professional Development

1. Discuss with colleagues at your grade level the twelve characteristics of a quality word study program in a quality literacy program. Evaluate strengths in each area and prioritize short- and long-term goals.

2. Take a look at your classroom program and/or the school program. Ask:

❚ What components are in place?
❚ Are components missing?

3. Prioritize a list of areas that you want to find out about in order to enhance the quality of your program. Identify chapters in this volume that may help your specific goals.

4. Now, take a look at your schedule for teaching the language arts. Ask:

❚ Is there time for several kinds of reading and writing?
❚ Where will word study fit?
❚ How can you make changes that will provide for better-quality sustained time?
❚ What resources or assistance will you need?

5. Make a timeline and an action plan to achieve these goals.

Becoming a Word Solver

When we teach children to read and write, we give them the gift of powerful language processes, which they can use to communicate with others and to expand and enhance their understandings of themselves and their world. Achieving the goal of literacy, inevitably, means teaching children the strategies for recognizing and writing words. We call this process *word solving* because it involves the reader or writer in active investigation of the underlying principles that govern how letters, sounds, and words work together to communicate meaning in our written language.

Word Matters is about teaching a cognitive process for solving words—recognizing them, taking them apart, putting them together—in the service of meaningful reading and writing. It is about helping children develop a system of thinking about how words work through powerful word study across the curriculum.

When we talk about word solving, we are describing a dynamic process in which the learner actively investigates how words work. Word solving is not just word learning. Its power lies in the discovery of the principles underlying the construction of the words that make up a written language. The children, for example, may learn some words that hold personal meaning (for example, their own written names), but then they will begin to build a network of understandings around the word, connecting it to other words. Soon, they will discover some generalities, making it possible for them to use particular knowledge in more general, strategic ways. For example, children might learn some words such as *mother*, *the*, and *with* as they encounter the words frequently in reading and writing. They might simultaneously notice that *t* is often coupled with *h*, and every time this coupling occurs, the letters are connected to the same sound. They can use this information in writing words such as *them* or *brother*. Similarly, they might use their knowledge of the *er* that they hear and see at the end of the words *mother* and *sister* to solve other words. We call word solving an *inquiry process* because it involves not only becoming familiar with and studying words, but also putting that information to use in pursuit of word recognition and spelling in a variety of reading and writing contexts.

We also recognize that word solving is related to the child's building a vocabulary of known words in reading and writing. Knowing words goes beyond word recognition or word spelling. While children are studying words, they are also exploring word meaning and the connections between words. Word study thus involves an expansion of the words that children know and an enrichment in the ways they know them. In the first years of word learning, children bring a listening vocabulary to reading and writing. The words they know in oral language enhance their literacy learning; indeed, the greater their oral vocabulary, the easier it is for them to learn new words in written language. Later, their vocabulary will greatly expand through their reading, so much so that as adults they will know and be able to read many words that are not a regular part of their spoken vocabulary.

We focus the content of this book on word solving because:

❚ Word solving is essential for efficient, effective reading and writing.

❚ In planning instruction, teachers need a foundation of knowledge about the language system, oral and written, and the strategies that competent word solvers and users have.

❚ Skill in word solving is sometimes difficult for readers and writers and requires teacher instruction and assistance.

❚ Many children do not possess the broad set of strategies for word solving required to enjoy the reading and writing of text.

❚ Children who have not had the opportunity to develop a deep understanding of the alphabetic system may have difficulty developing independence in literacy.

What is the connection between word solving, phonics, and spelling?

The word-solving process is at the heart of the instructional areas that we call *phonics* (letter-sound relationships) and *spelling* (the orthography of words). *Phonics* means different things to different people. We use *phonics* to refer to letter-sound relationships in read-

ing and writing, not to describe a particular method of teaching or approach to reading instruction. Phonics and spelling are interrelated processes; both involve readers and writers in using, analyzing, and solving words. Using letter-sound relationships, or phonics, helps children solve words in reading and writing. Phonics is extremely important but not sufficient in and of itself. Since only about half of the words in the English language are phonetically regular, readers need a wide range of language knowledge and strategies to solve words. In the writing process, children write words letter by letter or part by part as they spell, using not only letter-sound relationships but an understanding of how words look and how they mean.

In this book, we will use the term *word study* to refer to the body of knowledge that includes phonics and spelling. Word study involves a range of instructional activities and experiences that a teacher designs to support children's development of word-solving skills.

When we talk about teaching phonics, we refer to ways to help children acquire this body of knowledge about the oral and written language systems and to help them use the knowledge in a reading and writing process. There are many different ways to use phonics knowledge, and our language arts curriculum provides many opportunities for children (1) to become familiar with symbols such as letters, their related sounds, and the way they work in words; and (2) to use this information in a variety of ways. In all curriculum areas, such as science or mathematics, there are opportunities to help children learn new words and understand how they work. In writing, children also use a variety of strategies to spell words as they express their ideas in written language. Both phonics and spelling involve children in solving words—figuring out how to read or write them. Again, *word solving* describes the processes readers and writers use to take words apart and to build them; *word study* describes the teaching and learning experiences designed to help learners build understandings about how letters, sounds, and words work.

What does it mean to be a word solver?

In classrooms that brim with exciting reading and writing opportunities, we see word solving in action all the time. Here are three examples in three different kinds of learning contexts. All three examples represent opportunities for the kind of teaching and learning that enables children to become competent word solvers.

Example 1: Reading

During a guided reading lesson, David, a first grader, was reading aloud this sentence in a story:

There was only one dog left.

He read, "There was," and paused, looking at the word *only*. As the teacher was observing, she said, "What do you know that might help?" David said "on" as a first attempt at the word. He paused again, looking closely at the word, and said, "my . . . only" (pronounced like *lie*). He then said "only!" and finished the sentence accurately. This example shows that David knows how to take words apart while reading by attending to the parts that can help him get closer to the accurate word. Also, he performs these operations without losing the meaning of the story.

David's teacher reinforced his efforts by saying, "I like the way you worked that out."

Example 2: Writing

During writing workshop, the teacher presented a minilesson encouraging children to spell unfamiliar words by saying the words slowly and thinking of parts they know that might help. Marcia, another first grader, was writing a story about a trip to her grandmother's house.

To write the title, Marcia first wrote My quickly and easily. She then paused and said the word *grandmother's* slowly. Then, she said "grand" slowly several times as she wrote *gr* on her paper. Next, she said "and" and quickly wrote that part of the word.

"I know the word *mother*," she said, and wrote it in without stopping. Finally, she said the whole word *grandmother's* again and added an s. Marcia was learning how to put a word together using letters and sound relationships along with important words and pieces of words that she knows. In a later conference with her teacher, she learned how to put an apostrophe before the final s.

Example 3: Word Study

Raphael, age seven, was sorting a group of words, all of which end with *ed*. Figure 3-1 shows his completed sort.

As he wrote his words, Raphael was discovering that sometimes you add *ed* to words to make the past tense; sometimes the *ed* sounds like a *t*; sometimes the *ed* sounds like a *d*; and sometimes the *ed* sounds like a word part, *ed*. More generally, he was learning that endings may function the same but sound different in English pronunciation.

Why is word solving important?

Flexible, efficient word solving is an essential aspect of both reading and writing processes. Reading is a meaning-making process that involves using several different sources of information in a coordinated way. We know that readers bring their prior knowledge of language, of the world, and of print to every text they read. Ultimately, readers must read words, recognizing them quickly and using that information in the smooth construction of meaning. Sometimes, readers slow down, analyzing a word that is unfamiliar. When they do, they use many sources of information. But most competent readers can take words apart "on the run" while reading fluently, with little noticeable pausing.

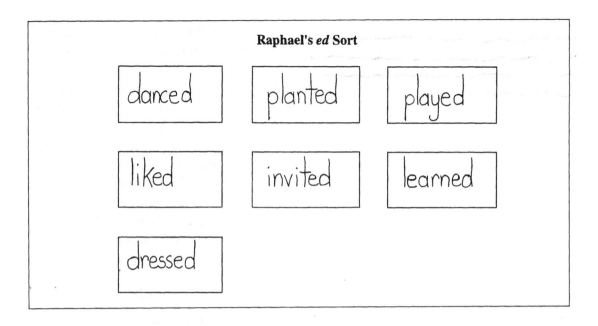

Raphael's *ed* Sort

danced   planted   played

liked   invited   learned

dressed

FIGURE 3-1   Word Sort

Writing is a process of communicating meaning that involves the mechanics of forming letters and words. Writers compose their messages with knowledge of the meaning and language systems, and, at the same time, write those messages letter by letter, word by word, arranged sequentially in space on a surface. All of these actions are coordinated smoothly by the competent writer, who needs to give little attention to word solving and writing and can focus on meaning. Word construction also happens "on the run," although there are times when writers have to slow down, think about a word, or, perhaps, check it for spelling or form.

It is obvious that word solving serves communication in written language; it is not an activity unto itself. It is meaningful because of the way it serves the reader or the writer. Word solving is an important part of the meaning-making process.

Letters, Sounds, and Words: A Framework for Teaching and Learning

A balanced approach to literacy education will provide for many different ways of learning and using reading and writing. We recommend at least two and a half hours of integrated language arts time each day, time in which teachers and children can plan activities ranging from reading aloud and literature discussion to small-group reading instruction and independent reading and writing.

We present the following framework (Figure 3-2) as a conceptual tool for thinking about the way we can attend to word solving within this balanced literacy curriculum. We recommend using this framework as a tool for planning and analyzing teaching.

The instructional model in Figure 3-2 guides us to think about a range of learning contexts that create the broadest range of learning possible. The teaching actions within each context are based on careful observation of children and what they understand about letters, sounds, and words. We recognize that many children discover critical understandings about the way written language works as they are immersed in enjoyable print experiences; but many others need explicit teaching to develop specific knowledge, fluency, and flexibility as they read and write new texts. We present the learning contexts in three categories; we define and briefly describe each in the following section. More complete descriptions and

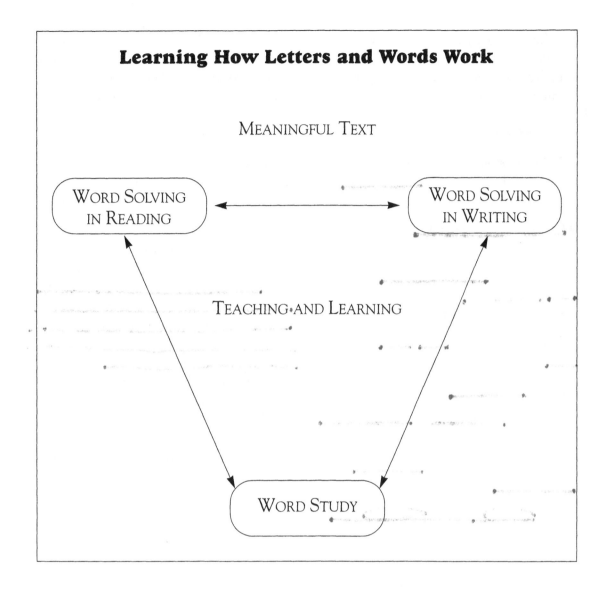

Learning How Letters and Words Work

MEANINGFUL TEXT

WORD SOLVING
IN READING

WORD SOLVING
IN WRITING

TEACHING AND LEARNING

WORD STUDY

FIGURE 3-2   Learning How Letters and Words Work

explanations of each learning context follow in chapters in this book.

1. Reading
Reading involves encountering an organized body of print and engaging in the process necessary to gain meaning from the text.

Read-Aloud Time
As you read aloud to your students, you demonstrate that reading is a meaningful, purposeful activity. At the same time, you use read-aloud time to help children develop their language, extend their world knowledge, and develop new ways of thinking about text and illustrations. Children gain implicit knowledge of the syntax or structure

of written language and expand their vocabulary. Reading aloud is an essential component of a rich literacy/language curriculum.

Shared Reading
Shared reading is another highly supportive instructional context. Here, you and the child read together from an enlarged text (a book, song, poem, or chart), which may contain repeating words throughout. With support, children are able to orchestrate their reading behavior, learn about the conventions of print, and focus on some words that they will learn. In a first reading of a shared-reading text, there is little "decoding" (analysis of words using letter-sound rela-

tionships). Shared reading is, however, an excellent transition tool to help children gain valuable understandings about the reading process and how it works.

During shared reading, the teacher can help children:

❚ Build up a store of quickly recognizable words (which we refer to as *known words*) and draw attention to the features of words.

❚ Find known and unknown words within a text.

❚ Give explicit attention to words, word parts, letter clusters, and letters as the opportunity arises in the text.

❚ Enjoy and attend to sound, rhyme, and the flow of language.

❚ Notice letter patterns within words.

❚ Attend to punctuation and capitalization as they shape meaning.

❚ Attend to words that are written in a particular way because of what they mean.

❚ Find interesting or new vocabulary words.

Guided Reading

Guided reading is an instructional context in which a teacher actually shows children how to read and supports them in processing novel texts. The goal is to help readers develop and use effective strategies for processing increasingly difficult levels of text. To engage your students in a guided reading lesson, you would follow this process (also see Fountas and Pinnell 1996):

1. Call together a small group of children who are similar in their reading development.

2. Select a text that is "just right" for the group of students—that is, not too easy and not too difficult.

3. Introduce the text in a way that helps the children read the text for meaning, while solving problems as needed.

4. Listen and observe while each student reads the entire story or a section of a much longer text softly or silently, not trying to stay in concert with others; you may occasionally intervene briefly to support an individual student's reading.

5. Revisit the text with your students to examine some aspect of the text related to understanding, interpreting, strategies, or word study.

The literacy program, through guided reading, must ensure that each child, every day, reads a text that is within his control, given the strategies and knowledge he currently has, yet one that also offers enough challenge to allow him to build and strengthen the reading process. Successful problem solving builds a reading system for children because they must figure out new words by various means while holding the meaning of the story in their heads.

During guided reading, you may make deliberate word-related teaching moves:

❚ When introducing stories, call children's attention to aspects of individuals words— beginnings, endings, middles, or letter clusters.

❚ During or following reading, draw children's attention to how to take words apart—use letter-sound relationships, letter clusters, parts of words.

❚ Following the reading, incorporate writing to help children analyze words; use an easel and chart paper, a white board, a pocket chart with sentence strips, or individual notepads.

❚ Select examples to teach for effective word-solving strategies involving visual information in combination with meaning and language structure.

❚ Help students practice checking and using the print information while reading "on the run."

▮ Give students a chance to use what they have learned in the focused experiences.

Independent Reading

We want all children to be able to do some reading that is largely unsupported by an adult, beginning with very simple books and increasing in complexity and difficulty as their reading skills grow. Independent reading requires independent word solving.

In all the contexts for reading mentioned here, you'll want to strike a balance. Sometimes you will do the reading for children and make it easy for them to acquire new ideas and language structures. Sometimes you will explicitly demonstrate a process. Sometimes you will confirm children's attempts and illuminate examples in a way that helps them apply knowledge in other contexts. As you prompt, reinforce, demonstrate, and explicitly teach principles, you encourage children to practice behaviors for themselves.

2. Writing

Language Experience

Writing and reading are parallel and complementary processes. Learning in one area helps children learn in the other area. We sometimes serve as the scribe for children, writing for them as they dictate their experiences and ideas. Writing for children is most frequently used when working with beginners (kindergarten or first grade), but even for older children the teacher may act as a scribe to demonstrate important aspects of composition, sentence construction, or punctuation. We call this *language experience*, and it offers an opportunity for teachers to demonstrate the writing process.

Shared Writing

Through a process called shared writing, the teacher also serves as a scribe but invites children to collectively compose a text that they can read again and again. These texts, created by the group, are ideal material for shared reading, which, again, is an ideal context for learning about the conventions of print.

Interactive Writing

Interactive writing is another group experience that increases children's participation in the act of writing and helps them attend to the details of letters, sounds, and words while working together on a meaningful text. The teacher and children compose a text together. It can be anything—a list of things to do, a retelling of a familiar story, a letter, a story. Then they write the message, one word at a time, with an emphasis on saying each word slowly and thinking how to write it. Sometimes, children go up to the chart and contribute letters, groups of letters, or words that they know. Teachers of children who are just beginning to learn about letters, sounds, and words may find that embedding children's names in a composition can be a powerful support tool.

Interactive writing provides texts for shared reading. It offers many opportunities to help children focus on how to construct words.

During interactive writing, children's attention is directed to aspects of words, for example, how words are segmented into sequences of sounds, and perhaps how words are constructed letter by letter or in parts. You may help the children in the following ways:

▮ Say words slowly, sounding out in a smoothly blended way, to analyze the sounds and use this information with the children to write the words and/or to check them.

▮ Say words slowly to analyze sequences of sounds with the children.

▮ Give explicit attention to words, word parts, letter clusters, and letters (spelling patterns).

▮ Ask children to think about how some frequently occurring words look.

▮ Relate a word to other words children know (names and high-frequency words).

❚ Generate words, derive words, and make links between words and word parts and among sets of words.

We find that when children are given a chance to write on their own, they use the skills and strategies that they have been taught in interactive writing.

from experience

Writing Workshop

During writing workshop, teachers can provide minilessons on every aspect of writing that writers need. You are always thinking about what children need to learn how to do as writers and what instruction or experience you can provide to help them develop as effective writers. Then, children write with your and their classmates' help. Such experiences lead to independent writing, the goal of all writing instruction.

Independent Writing

During independent writing, children construct words, hear and record sounds, use known words to get to words they don't know, and notice parts of words. You can

support children's word solving by planning for these instructional experiences:

❚ Create a word wall (selected words placed on a classroom wall and organized alphabetically or by some other principle) and word lists that are easy to access and handy for reference.

❚ Invite children to use personal word banks (their own collections of known words), word rings (useful words on a ring), and writing folders that include useful words or a personal spelling dictionary.

❚ Teach children, explicitly, to use the strategies for constructing words that they learned in interactive writing.

❚ Help children check their spelling during writing conferences and minilessons, and show them, using their own words as examples, how to produce new words from parts they know.

Teachers strike an instructional balance in writing. You demonstrate, interact,

These are seeds from foods we eat.

melon seeds   watermelon   lemon seeds   tangerine seeds   apple seeds

mango seed

cucumber seeds   acorn squash   peach pit   pepper seeds   sugarsnap peas

FIGURE 3-3   Example of Interactive Writing and Language Experience

promote, reinforce, and explicitly teach principles. Children also learn and discover much on their own as they work on written language. Their learning, in other words, is embedded in their reading and writing. As part of a focused learning experience, you may encourage children to notice particular aspects of written language out of context from the whole text they are reading or writing, a process that may reduce the complexity for the learner. Afterward, it is always best to return to the text and apply the new knowledge within the text.

3. Word Study

Word study involves focused attention to words and word elements, with the goal of helping children become excellent readers and writers. Again, word study is defined as an instructional process that involves the learner in an investigation of words. The result is "word solving" in reading and writing. Focused experiences in word study include many different instructional contexts. Here is a short list; we'll explore each in chapters in this book:

▌ Using word charts and word walls as resources and references.

▌ Using letter books.

▌ Making words with letters and letter clusters.

▌ Letter sorting and word sorting.

▌ Using dictionaries and word books.

▌ Making word webs.

▌ Using an editing or proofreading checklist.

▌ Participating in cooperative learning activities that center on words and their sounds, visual features, and meaning.

▌ Learning about how to study words.

Each of these instructional activities involves direct lessons from you, the teacher, as well as independent practice by students.

We emphasize the need for focused word study for the following reasons:

▌ Some children will not learn to attend to important understandings within embedded experiences or even from brief, explicit teacher demonstrations during those experiences. They need even more direct attention and repetition of important principles as well as much practice with them.

▌ Some children will discover on their own the necessary principles of how words work, but most will not.

▌ Studying our language is valuable and interesting in its own right, especially when students move into more complex word study.

▌ Word study contributes to decoding in reading as well as to spelling in writing.

▌ Word study provides a way for teachers to be systematic and organized.

▌ Word study does not take much teacher time. You provide a short, focused teaching session and then make provisions for children to work on their own, usually in an ABC or word study center. This activity is followed by a whole-group sharing or reinforcement of the learning.

In this chapter, we have described a framework for thinking about a comprehensive word study program. Our goal is to help children become active word solvers who can recognize words, take them apart or put them together, know what they mean, and connect them to other words—all directed toward reading and writing continuous text.

Word solvers are active and they pursue word learning for a purpose. Achieving this goal will require much more than lessons on how words work. The framework we propose involves word solving across many literacy contexts during a school day. In some settings, students will be directed by the teacher to examine some aspects of words; in others, they will be investigating words for themselves. In their studies in content areas of the curriculum, students will meet new words; they will discover words through reading high-quality children's literature. And, throughout the day, they will be putting their knowledge of words to work as they write and read.

Word solving is not something that can be located and isolated on a specific point on a lesson plan. Words make up our language and, inevitably, are part of almost every educational experience. Sometimes it is appropriate to bring words to children's attention and sometimes we would not want to interrupt learning by focusing, for example, on how to take a word apart. Nevertheless, whenever children are using language—oral or written—they are learning something about the use of words. The framework we propose combines direct and integrated approaches across a language-based curriculum.

Suggestions for Professional Development

1. If you are already making time for both integrated (within reading and writing) and focused lessons on letters, sounds, and words, you are ready to analyze what you are now doing and work to make it more effective and efficient. Take a look at the program that you currently provide for helping children learn about letters, sounds, and words. A good way to start is to examine your lesson plans or your daily schedule for a one- or two-week period of teaching. With a partner, review your teaching. Ask:

- ❚ Do I plan opportunities for teaching about letters, sounds, and words within reading and writing instruction?
- ❚ Do children have a chance to use knowledge about letters, sounds, and words in their own reading and writing?
- ❚ Have I set aside a brief time for focused lessons on letters, sounds, and words? Are the lessons followed by application, practice, and sharing time?
- ❚ What kinds of lessons am I providing?
- ❚ How am I determining the content of my lessons?
- ❚ How well are the children applying the knowledge they've gained in ABC center activity and minilessons to their own reading and writing of text?

2. Meet with colleagues at your grade level and at other grade levels to share your responses. Discuss ways that you can strengthen your teaching of word solving throughout the day.

CHAPTER FOUR

A Dynamic Classroom Environment for Word Solving

A First-Grade Classroom

Children learn best by using what they know in active, purposeful ways. Let's follow Quanisha through her morning of active learning in her first-grade classroom. It's October, and Quanisha has multiple opportunities to explore and interact with print.

Quanisha's classroom is full of resources for learning about letters and words. In one corner is a reading wall filled with a variety of colorful food wrappers arranged by letter for children to read. The children have collected these items from home. The other walls are filled with song charts, poems, and story retellings illustrated by the children. Several charts on one wall display the names of every child in the room—an alphabetically organized chart of first names, a helper's chart, labeled cubbyholes, a story with children's names in it, an attendance chart, restroom tags, etc. Quanisha can walk around the room and find her name nine times. Her name is written on her artwork, and her photograph and name are also on the door.

Quanisha's classroom has many books of all kinds. Rows of brightly colored books face front along the edges of the bookcases. Inside one bookcase are pots and baskets of books organized and labeled by categories.

The collection includes ABC books, folktales, word books, family books, books about animals, books about songs, books by author Lois Ehlert, and many more. In other tubs are some little books that are easy enough for Quanisha and her friends to read independently.

Every day, Quanisha hears stories read aloud by the teacher. The words she hears bring her pleasure and enhance her understanding of the world; reading aloud also expands her listening vocabulary. She may begin to use the words she hears. When she meets them in her own reading and writing, their familiarity will be a tremendous advantage.

Every day, Quanisha reads simple stories on her own or with a reading partner. Many of these stories she has read before, but they still offer opportunities for her to attend to different features of words every time she reads. She is learning many ways to solve words, such as using beginning letters and word parts. Now she can read many familiar words quickly and automatically because she recognizes them. She is also able to make connections between words she knows and those that she does not. For example, she figures out the word *then* by noticing a part, *the*, that she knows very well.

Another daily activity for Quanisha is a small guided reading group (see Figure 4-1) where she meets with her teacher and is introduced to a new story that offers new challenges. Her teacher is helping her learn how to be sure that the words she reads not only make sense but look right and sound right. In the guided reading lesson, there are many chances for the teacher to show Quanisha how to solve words as she reads for meaning.

Writing, too, is evident in the classroom. There is an organized writing center where children can find the materials they need to make their own books and write whatever they want. Quanisha has her own writing folder and word dictionary. In this classroom, children write every day for themselves, but they also participate in group writing. Around the room are many examples of group or interactive writing that children have produced with their teacher's assistance.

Writing for a variety of purposes is always a part of the day. Quanisha works with her teacher in a group situation, interactive writing, to coproduce a text that will become reading material. Teacher and children work together to compose and then write, letter by letter, word by word, a message, an informational piece, or a story. Working out the words provides an opportunity to learn about letters and sounds and how words are constructed. For example, when Quanisha contributed the *qu* for the word *quiet* in the children's retelling of *Farm Concert* (Cowley 1990a), linking it to her own name, the teacher pointed out to the children that *q* is always followed by *u* in words.

Sometimes Quanisha's class is involved in shared writing, in which the teacher and children compose the message together as the teacher acts as a scribe. Here, the teacher often thinks aloud to help children notice something important about words. For example, Quanisha's teacher was writing the word *son*, and she said, "I need to write an *o* in the middle of *son* so that readers will know that we do not mean the sun in the sky."

In Quanisha's own writing, she has many opportunities to solve words. She can write about twenty high-frequency words, such as *to*, *me*, *the*, and *I*, quickly and easily.

FIGURE 4-1   A Guided Reading Lesson

For words that are new to her, she can write many consonant sounds and usually knows where to place a vowel even if she does not get the accurate one for every word. She is using endings like *s* and *ing* regularly, and thus she is rapidly expanding the number of words she can write.

Quanisha is constantly solving words in her reading and writing, but she also finds it interesting to study and work with words. In the word study center, for example, she likes to take words from her own word book and make them with magnetic letters, an example of an activity she undertook on her own. There are also more structured events. Each day, Quanisha has an assigned task to complete that gives her practice in working with letters or words. Her teacher takes a few moments to teach a lesson about letters or words, and then shows children how to engage in an activity at the word study center that day. These activities are designed to

help young children manipulate the parts of words and practice some aspect of word making or analysis.

The opportunities for Quanisha to be a word solver are numerous. As she engages in reading and writing and in planned word study activities, she builds her understandings of how words work.

Creating a Classroom Environment that Supports Effective Word Solving

The physical environment of the classroom creates an important context for learning about letters and words. Quanisha's first-grade classroom is an example of a well-organized environment for word learning. In this section, we provide descriptions of materials and approaches drawn from our observation of many effective primary classrooms. With the exception of approaches to learning letters (which are particularly designed for

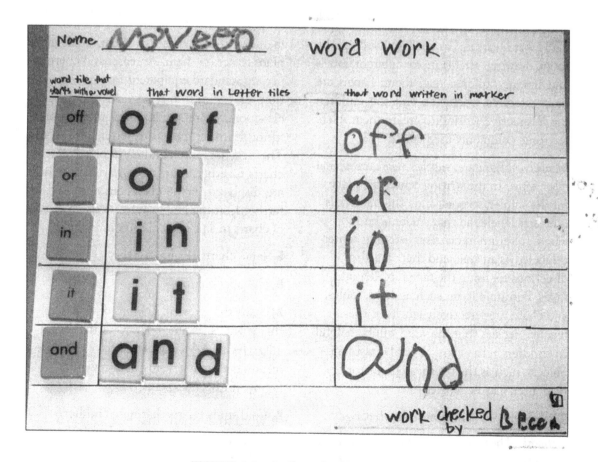

FIGURE 4-2   An Example of Word Work

kindergarten and first-grade classrooms), most of the materials and activities we describe can be adapted for readers at a variety of achievement levels.

Children use the environment and its references and resources to support their learning. In a literacy-rich classroom, the walls are filled with print resources for children to use in an interactive way. Displayed materials help children understand that they can use resources to solve their own problems independently. Most of the time, when young children have a problem in writing or reading, it involves a word that they do not know or cannot work out. References can help, but the children must know how and when to use them.

Labels

A label consists of one or a few words on a card placed on or below an object or a spot in the classroom. Clear labels help the children and the teacher know what is in the classroom and organize the work. Labels can also contribute to literacy learning, especially word learning, as you move around the room drawing attention to different labels and having children read them. Labels are most effective when you and the children use interactive writing to create them. Here are some commonly used labels:

❚ *Labels on furniture, supplies, work areas, and other items.* In the writing center the place for the stapler, scissors, and other materials is clearly labeled so that students know where to return items. The listening center is labeled as an area, and there are also directions for using the tape recorder and tapes. Furniture items such as desks, tables, and chairs are selectively labeled if the teacher decides that the word will be helpful to children in the class. Special classroom objects, such as the overhead projector or computer, may be labeled.

good for org.

❚ *Labels on wall murals and other displayed artwork.* These labels help viewers recall the objects or characters. A story map of *The*

Three Bears has labels for each bear and for items in the house (such as the *middle-sized bowl of porridge*). Kindergarten children sometimes draw pictures of themselves and label them with their names or parts of the body. Science projects, such as a study of plants, may include artwork and labels.

❚ *Labels on classroom job charts, journals, and other notebooks.* These labels, containing children's names and the function of the document, are used to designate ownership and responsibility. Baskets with different folders are also labeled so that materials are kept in order.

❚ *Labels on supplies and materials.* Baskets, pots, and plastic tubs of books are labeled to help the readers find books they can read, books they like, books by their favorite authors and illustrators, and books on topics they want to explore.

Interactive Word-Learning Charts

People of all ages use charts to get ideas down on paper so that everyone can see them, remember them, organize them, and make plans to act on them. An easel and chart paper are standard equipment for any organization or business meeting. In the primary classroom, charts are essential tools in organizing learning related to letters and words. The teacher and children typically create charts together in an interactive way. These are displayed in the classroom and used for further learning and as references. Examples of charts in a primary classroom include:

❚ Name charts (Figure 4-3).

❚ Alphabet charts.

❚ Charts that present all kinds of word lists—theme words (Figure 4-4), words that begin alike (Figure 4-5), words that have the same meaning, rhyming words, action words, family words, and so on.

❚ Word study charts that help children attend to aspects of words and ways that words are connected.

FIGURE 4-3   Name Chart

FIGURE 4-4   Example of a Theme Chart

❚ Charts with rhymes, songs, and poems that the teacher and children read together and that create a context for noticing and learning about letters and words.

❚ Charts with stories and messages that the teacher and children have created through interactive writing.

Typically, in literacy-rich classrooms, almost every inch of wall space is covered with learning charts, although when space is limited, they are sometimes stored on an easel where they can easily be flipped over for consultation.

Interactive Word Walls

A word wall is a designated section of a classroom wall that is devoted to the display and study of words (Figure 4-6). Cunningham (1995) has written extensively on the use of word walls. Word walls can be designed for a variety of purposes, depending on the grade level they are used in. A word wall for very young children might simply be a group of words they know; but soon, the word wall becomes a resource and teaching tool. Children learn to use exemplar words on the wall to derive new words. Thus, the word wall is one of the first references primary children learn to use.

Book Resources

The materials on charts and the classroom walls serve as references and resources for the group. But it is obvious that as children develop their literacy skills, they will need many more resources than it's possible to place on the walls. In fact, wall resources stimulate learning and provide exemplars. Book resources are available to provide more comprehensive information and to promote in-depth study. Part of the word study curriculum involves teaching children how to use these book resources. Here are some of the resources that primary classrooms need:

❚ Picture dictionaries.
❚ Word dictionaries for beginners.
❚ Rhyming dictionaries.
❚ Word books.
❚ Glossaries and thesauruses (at the beginning level, for use in upper-primary grades).
❚ Alphabet books (from simple to complex).
❚ Books with tongue twisters and other kinds of word play.

We have provided an extensive list of alphabet books and books about word play in Ap-

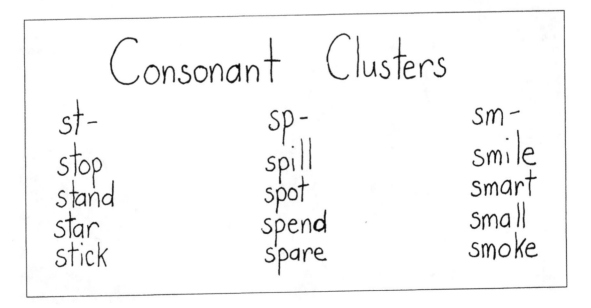

FIGURE 4-5   An Example of a Word Chart

FIGURE 4-6   A Word Wall in a First-Grade Classroom

pendixes 1 and 2. Use them to create baskets of books to support a rich language-based classroom.

A Word Study Center

A center specially designed to promote letter and word study is an integral part of the classroom environment. A word study center includes manipulative materials, books, and other resource materials about words. For example:

❚ Alphabet charts.
❚ An easel with a magnetic board.
❚ Magnetic letters—several different sizes, colors, and styles.
❚ Individual letter books (see Fountas and Pinnell 1996).
❚ A Magna Doodle magnetic drawing board.
❚ ABC stickers and pictures.

❚ Pipe cleaners, straws, Wikki Sticks, and other material for forming letters.
❚ Letter and word tiles.
❚ Letters made of different materials, such as foam, felt, sandpaper, wood, rubber.
❚ Alphabet letter games, phonics games, and word games.
❚ Letter and word stamps.
❚ Words on cards ready for sorting (see Chapter 13).

Figure 4-7 shows materials organized for a word study center. Children rotate to a table at the center according to a schedule and complete assigned activities. The activities often involve hands-on manipulating of letters, words, and word parts and sometimes a written follow-up such as making a list in the word study notebook (see Chapter 14).

The activities in the center provide

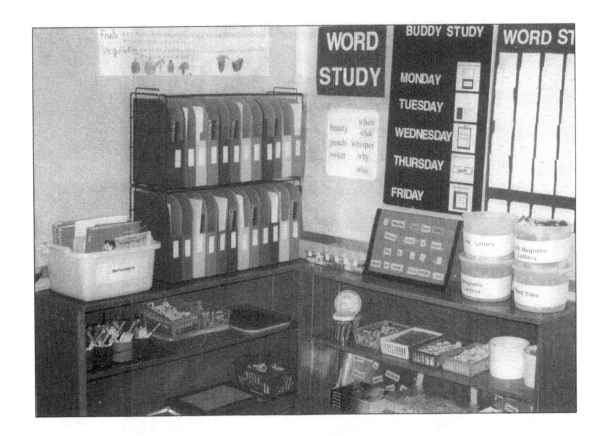

FIGURE 4-7   A Word Study Center

practice for students and also enable them to discover principles about how words work. The word study center is used in a highly organized way, with activities coordinated with the overall curriculum for learning about letters and words. Here are some suggestions for working effectively with a word study center:

❚ Place resources in the word study center for a specific purpose.

❚ Conduct a brief, focused lesson on a principle that children will explore later on their own in an assigned word study center task. This lesson often takes place at a morning community meeting. A minilesson might involve making a chart of *ed* words, placing words with like pronunciation in the same column. Another minilesson could involve a demonstration of sorting the words according to their sound.

❚ Use the white board, magnetic board, pocket chart, or magnetic letters on the chalkboard or easel to demonstrate word-solving principles in the lesson. Be clear and explicit and show each step using magnetic letters, cards, or writing, so the students will understand their assigned task.

❚ Design practical activities so your students can apply principles. Explain and demonstrate to your students the assigned activities in the word study center; for example, to learn about *ed* endings, children will need to sort the words themselves and then write the list in their word study notebooks. Place written directions at the center to remind students of the tasks' steps.

❚ After the lesson, give children time to work with the new principle or principles. After sorting the words a couple of times, children will discover new principles on their own and begin to come up with their own examples. They can share their discoveries at the community meeting.

▋ Refer to your overall curriculum guides for phonics or spelling as a resource to determine what aspects are important. Keep in mind what your students know and what they need to know. If you are working on a principle that is too difficult for students to understand, they will not be able to apply their learning and the time will be wasted. (See discussions of multilevel learning in Chapter 2.)

▋ Notice as much as you can about whether students are really able to perform the tasks successfully in the ABC or word study center.

▋ Reteach the lesson if needed.

▋ At the end of work time, invite one or two children to share their work at a community meeting. Bring closure by reinforcing the learning and sometimes by adding more words to the chart.

▋ Put an exemplar on the word wall and/or display the chart in the room. Remind children to refer to it to help them think about the word or words like it.

▋ Sometimes, you will need to work briefly in a small group with children who had difficulty with the task.

▋ Encourage children to collect more examples that fit the particular principle they are exploring, for example, more *ed* words that double the letter (*patted*) or sound like *t* (*jumped*).

A dynamic classroom environment provides a variety of resources and activities that make word learning interesting and rewarding. You will learn more about effective materials as you create your own dynamic classroom environment with your children.

Suggestions for Professional Development

1. Take a look at your classroom environment as you have presently organized it for literacy instruction. Gather a group of colleagues in your classroom and ask them to analyze the environment using the last section of this chapter.

2. Use a clipboard and write notes as a response to the following questions:
   - ▋ What kinds of resources are on the classroom walls and display areas to help children think about and learn about words?
   - ▋ What kinds of references and resources are available for children to use?
   - ▋ How is print displayed and featured in the various areas of the room? Is there potential for independent word study?
   - ▋ In what other ways do you draw children's attention to letters and words?
   - ▋ Is there a word study center? If not, what materials can you gather to create one?
   - ▋ Are lists of words posted on the wall that are related to areas of the curriculum such as science or social studies? Is curriculum-related vocabulary part of active word study?

3. After the analysis, generate ideas about enriching the environment to provide more support for word study and to capture children's interest in letters and words.

4. Repeat this process in your colleagues' classrooms.

Interactive Word Walls and Charts

Teaching children concepts related to letters and words begins with active learning. In the last chapter we described the classroom environment and the materials and resources that support letter and word learning. No matter how attractive the learning environment, no matter how well-stocked it is with good materials, the program will be ineffective without good teaching. In an effective word-learning program, teachers and children:

■ Engage in learning conversations about the words and letters included in the various charts and wall displays.

■ Work together to construct charts and displays of words and develop them over time.

■ Investigate important principles rather than simply memorize individual letters or words.

■ Build learning over time by using the present knowledge base to connect to new learning.

■ Find learning about letters and words interesting and exciting.

■ Work, as much as possible, at a level of success.

Meeting these criteria is a challenge for primary teachers. They must learn to carefully sequence activities and match the levels of activities to children's levels of development. Interactive word walls and interactive word charts provide a rich context for active, ongoing learning that meets the needs of many different children.

For much of the time, the teacher will work with the entire class of children but will strive for multilevel learning possibilities within the activity. For example, in creating an interactive writing chart, some children might notice and talk about the component parts of a word while others notice initial consonant sounds. The interactive learning that surrounds word charts and word walls also lends itself to brief lessons for small groups of children who need extra support. Teachers can work with smaller groups for five minutes or so, taking a closer look at a chart, reteaching principles, examining aspects of letters or words that the rest of the class already understands, and/or adding more to a chart so that the children's learning is deepened.

Interactive Word Walls

A word wall is a systematically organized collection of words displayed in large letters on a wall or other large display place in the classroom (Cunningham 1995). (See Figure 5-1.) We refer to an *interactive word wall* here because we want to emphasize the role of this resource in active learning. It is a tool to use, not simply display. In our view, word walls are designed to:

▮ Support the teaching of important general principles about words and how they work.

▮ Foster reading and writing.

▮ Provide reference support for children during their writing and reading.

▮ Promote independence on the part of young students as they work with words in writing and reading.

▮ Provide a visual map to help children remember the connections between words and the characteristics that will help them form categories.

Word walls are designed to promote group learning and to be shared by a classroom of children; however, word walls also work for individual students. In the chapter on writing workshop (Chapter 16), a personal word wall sheet for children to use in their own work is described. A reproducible version is provided in Appendix 50.

Based on our classroom research, we have developed general guidelines for working effectively with word walls:

▮ First, talk with the children about the word so they develop a network of understanding and an interest in the word before it is displayed on the wall. Engage the children in a conversation, inviting them to talk about the features they notice, and point out additional characteristics of the word. Attend to how words sound, look, mean, and are connected to other words.

▮ Place words on the wall *while* children are learning the principles they illustrate.

▮ Write words in large, clear print that is easily viewed from all angles of the classroom.

▮ Create a visually cohesive wall so that the viewer perceives it as a collection of words and it is obvious how the words are organized.

▮ Write the words on cards. Some teachers choose to cut those cards in a shape that shows the configuration of the word. At this point, we lack concrete evidence that such "word shape matching" makes a difference and do not recommend it.

▮ Place a row of alphabetically organized library pockets along the bottom of the wall (this is especially helpful with emergent writers). In the pockets, place the word cards. If a student finds it difficult to copy the words from a distance, invite her to take the word card to her seat, copy the word, and return it to the pocket.

Let's think about a possible interaction that might take place when working with a word wall. For the word *because*, you might discuss such features as:

▮ *Because* has two parts—clap them!
▮ There is a part at the beginning that is the same as *before* and *began*.
▮ There is an *s* near the end and it sounds like a *z*.
▮ There is an *e* at the end that you don't hear.
▮ The *au* sounds like the *o* in *hot*.
▮ *Because* is a word that tells the cause or reason for something.

After the conversation, you might:

▮ Encourage the children to use *because* in a sentence.

▮ Ask the children to examine *because* closely.

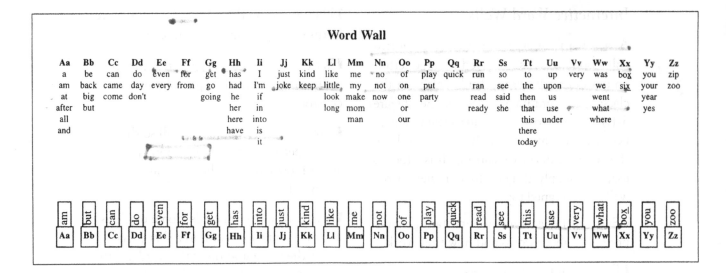

FIGURE 5-1   Word Wall with Library Pockets

❚ Ask them to share what will help them remember how to write it.

❚ Show them where it is going to be placed on the wall.

❚ Remind them to check *because* on the wall when they want to use it in their own writing to make sure it's spelled correctly.

❚ Remind them that when they want to write a word that sounds like *because* at the beginning, they can use the first part of the word.

A word wall is not just a display of words, nor is it simply a way to teach a list of individual words. A word wall is a dynamic teaching tool. The word wall changes often in accordance with the teacher's goals. The teacher removes words that are no longer needed because children know them, and adds words for particular purposes to extend children's understandings.

Word walls are most effective when (1) every time a new word is placed on the wall, you call attention to the word and help students understand how it works; and (2) you continue to help children connect with displayed words to extend their learning.

As you select words for a word wall, you should consider the following and choose:

❚ Words that children use in their group or independent writing and that are important for children to know, such as *the, was, were, went, going.*

❚ Words that many children use in their own writing and have difficulty spelling, such as *dinosaur, they.*

❚ High-frequency words, beginning with the easier ones and progressing to the harder ones, such as starting with *I* and *a*; moving to two-letter words such as *to, me, it, in, is, am, at, go, no, an, my, he*; then moving to three-letter words such as *and, the, can, him, her, had, his, but, for, not, you,* and *was*; then moving to four-letter words such as *that, said, have, they, with, your, this, then,* and *like.* (The lists of high-frequency words in Chapter 9 and Appendixes 4 and 5 will be useful resources for selecting words.)

❚ Words children request often, such as *grandma, basketball, school, because.*

❚ Words that serve as exemplars of spelling patterns or frequently occurring letter sequences, such as:

❚ Letters or letter clusters at the beginning or end of words, such as *stew, stop, list, nest.*

▮ Words with vowel combinations, such as *about*, *bear*, *bread*.

▮ Words with particular beginnings or endings, such as *working*, *writing*; *happy*, *sticky*; *quickly*, *quietly*.

▮ Words that are contracted, such as *can't*, *won't*, *isn't*.

The difficulty of high-frequency words is not simply based on the number of letters. The difficulty has to do with the complexity of the letter patterns and the regularity of the letter-sound relationships in the word. The frequency of occurrence is also a factor. For example, *the* and *was* do not represent easy spelling patterns, but they appear so frequently in all kinds of texts that children readily become familiar with them.

When you teach a spelling lesson, you will want to place a word on the word wall that illustrates the principle you are helping children to learn, including:

▮ Both phonetically regular and irregular words: *cat*, *fun*; *laugh*, *tough*.

▮ Words that are related in special ways: words that sound alike but are spelled differently (*to*, *two*; *no*, *know*); words that mean the same but are spelled differently (*pretty*, *beautiful*; *plump*, *chubby*); and words that are spelled alike but pronounced differently for different meanings (*wind*, *wind*; *present*, *present*).

You can use a variety of other media to work with a word before adding it to the word wall. Try magnetic letters on a chalkboard, magnetic letter tiles, a white board or chalkboard, letter cards, or an easel with chart paper and colored markers. You can use them all effectively to show:

▮ The letters and letter clusters in the word.

▮ How to build another word like the one for the word wall by changing a letter or word part.

▮ How to divide the word into syllables.

▮ How to add endings or prefixes to make another word.

In selecting words for the wall, it is important to recognize the many different ways words can be analyzed. For example, we might think about letter-by-letter construction and relationship to sound patterns.

Another way to think about words is by attending to parts such as onset and rime (see Chapter 8 for more information). In this case, teachers emphasize the beginning letter or letter cluster before the vowel (the onset) and the rest of the word (the rime). Taking words apart or constructing them using onset and rime is one way children can see parts in words. Sometimes we have called sets of words that have different onsets and the same rime *word families* or *phonograms* (for example, *hat*, *cat*, *rat*, *fat*, etc.). There are other ways to look at words, and we should be careful not to direct children's attention to a limited way of analyzing words by overattending to word families. Children, in fact, will become "pattern detectors" and discover many different ways to look at word parts. They may look at syllables such as *o-pen* and *o-ver*. They may create new words by changing the ending letter (*hid*, *him*, *his*), by changing the middle letter (*cat*, *cot*, *cut*), or by adding letters (*the*, *they*, *them*). Our goal is to help them develop a variety of flexible ways to notice and use word parts.

Exemplars of words on the word wall become the foundation for helping children think about how to use a word they know to get to words they want to solve. An interactive word wall, for example, might be used in the following ways:

▮ Engaging the children in decision making about what words go on the wall.

▮ Involving children in deciding what words can come off the wall.

▮ Making continual links among words while engaging children in instructional activities such as shared reading, interactive writing, and guided reading.

❚ Promoting word games using the words on the wall (for example, the teacher provides "clues" and children guess the word, or the children provide clues for each other to identify a word).

Different kinds of word walls include:

❚ A word wall of first and/or last names.

❚ A word wall of theme words (for example, all words related to the study of the ocean).

❚ A compound word wall.

❚ A contraction word wall.

❚ A homophone word wall of doubles (*one, won*) and triples (*buy, by, bye* or *to, two, too*).

❚ A "reading wall," which is made up of a collection of similar objects (such as food wrappers and containers) organized according to each letter of the alphabet. In the case of the food wrappers, children can also sort the items on this wall into food groups, into categories evaluating the health contribution of each food, etc. A list next to the wall can show an alphabetized list of each particular food name for children to read.

❚ A general word wall that includes a variety of words useful to the class.

You will want to keep an ongoing list of words or word principles to use in planning for word wall activities. You can generate such a list as you observe the children at work in writing and reading or look at the products of the children's writing. If you are new to word walls, have some linguistic principles in mind as you observe your students. Our chapter on language (Chapter 6) and the word lists in Appendixes 4 through 33 will provide helpful information to guide thinking. Also see our lists of high-frequency words in Appendixes 4 and 5.

Charts

Charts are used in many different ways to facilitate letter and word learning. In a clear, well-organized, and attractive way, teachers place print items on charts and work with children to use them as references. Some examples are described here, beginning with charts for early learning and progressing to a more complex use of charts.

Charts for Letter Learning

There are many varieties of alphabet charts. In Appendix 3, we include a simple chart that you can enlarge into a classroom chart. We recommend using individual versions of the chart in student writing folders and placing several of the enlarged charts around the room for classes of children who are just learning the alphabet letters and the letter-sound relationships. Here are some ways to use the alphabet linking chart:

❚ Read the chart *Aa-apple, Bb-bear, Cc-cat,* etc.

❚ Read every other box.

❚ Read only the letters.

❚ Read only the words.

❚ Read only the vowels.

❚ Read only the consonants.

❚ Identify the pictures.

❚ Ask one group to read the vowels and another group to read the consonants.

❚ Invite one group to read the letters and another group to read the associated word.

❚ Encourage the class or group to sing the chart.

❚ Cover some letters with Post-its, ask for predictions, and then remove the stickers.

For children who are beginners, we prefer simple, uncluttered alphabet charts. Many alphabet charts and friezes are works of art and will delight children who already know the features of letters and can name them.

Charts for Word Learning

Many charts contain words grouped in categories to help children develop new understandings. Of course, much letter and letter-sound learning takes place as children investigate these word charts. Here are some examples.

Name Charts

For kindergarten and first-grade children, some of the most powerful teaching occurs as the teacher and children interact with a name chart. A name chart is any kind of chart that presents the names of the children in the class. Typically, initial charts list only children's first names, but later, name charts may be expanded to include surnames and may also include the names of people in the school building the children know (for example, the principal or the music teacher).

Figure 5-2 provides an example of a name chart made on tag paper. It can also be made with card strips in a pocket chart.

Work with the name chart is highly interactive. For example:

▮ Make the name chart together with the children. Children acquire a beginning orientation to their names on the chart and learn what to look for (first letter, ending, etc.).

▮ Invite children to find names that begin or end with a certain letter (*Mary, mom*).

▮ Have the class say names to help write a new word with a particular sound in it (*Pat, apple*).

▮ Ask children to search for a name to find out how to write a letter during group writing exercises.

▮ Ask children to refer to names that help them write a word part (*Andy, and; Charles, chop*).

dif. color

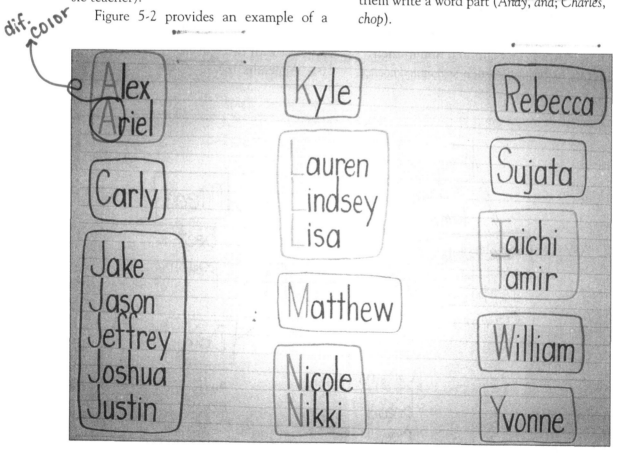

FIGURE 5-2   Written Name Chart

■ Point out a word that the children have written that is in some way like someone's name (*Gary, carry*).

■ When new children enter the class, add their names to the chart and compare to other names.

All of these actions require conversation. You will want to talk with your students and explain what they are doing and why. These actions may also call for explicit teaching and demonstration.

Word Study Charts

Examples of the kinds of word charts that engage children in word study include:

■ Theme words, such as family words (*mother, aunt, sister, uncle, brother, father, grandfather*), ocean words, transportation words, and so on.

■ Theme words in categories, such as the four food groups (Figure 5-3).

■ Words we love. A chart is filled with favorite words that children find in their literary experiences, such as *bommyknocker*

from *The Hungry Giant* (Cowley 1990b).

■ Palindromes, which are words that can be spelled in either direction (*mom, I, madam, Hannah*).

■ Portmanteau words, which are words shortened from two words (*brunch—breakfast and lunch; motel—motor and hotel; smog—smoke and fog*) (see Appendix 33).

KEY↓

★ ■ Word webs that show relationships among words (see Figure 5-4). ★

■ Strong verbs that help to make writing more interesting (*pounced, screamed, scampered*).

■ Words with a specific letter sound, such as the sound of *f* in *fat, phone, cough, off, fall, rough*.

■ Words with one syllable (*dog, box*).

■ Words with two syllables (*carton, paper*) (see Appendix 16).

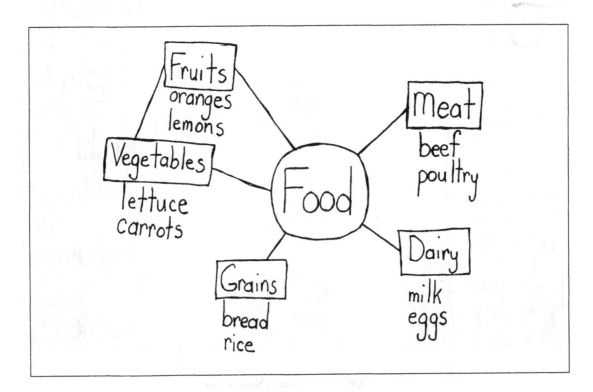

FIGURE 5-3   Food Word Web

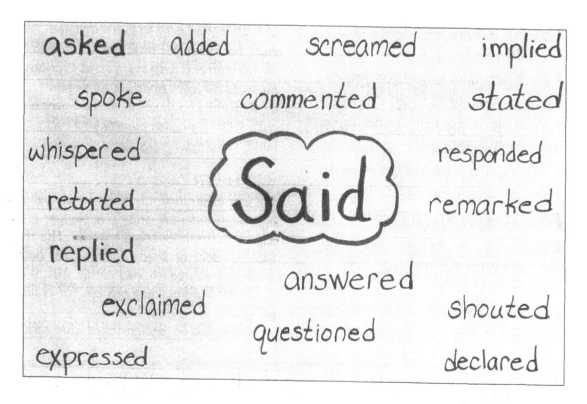

FIGURE 5-4 "Said" Word Web

Words with "o"						
-o-	-oy	-oi-	-ou-	-oa-	-oo-	-oo-
not box top	toy boy	foil coin	house mouth loud	soap boat coach	look good foot	boot hoop food
-o-e	-o-e	-or	-ow	-ow	-oll	-oll
love some none	rope cone slope phone	or for	how cow now	know row low	doll	toll roll
-ould	-ought	-ough	-ough	-o	-o	other
would could should	bought thought fought	cough trough	rough enough	to do	so no go	people through

FIGURE 5-5   Words with "O"

■ Words that rhyme (*book, look*) (see Appendix 15).

■ Words with silent letters (*make, knee, write*) (see Appendixes 14 and 17).

■ Words with double letters (*mitten, carrot, happen*) (see Appendix 11).

■ Lists of spelling "demons" (see Appendix 28).

■ Lists of tricky words for children in the class.

■ Words with a specific sound, such as the sound of *e* in *bed* and words with *o* (see Figures 5-5 and 5-6).

■ Lists of *hink pinks, hinky pinkies, and hinkety pinketies*. The three sets indicate the number

of syllables that must be in the rhyming pairs. For example, a hink pink for an insect on your carpet is a *rug bug*; a cranky person on a sofa is a *couch grouch*. A hinky pinky for someone who shouts in the basement is a *cellar yeller*. A hinkety pinkety for a sticky building is a *flypaper skyscraper*.

Word Ladders

We can create a word ladder by changing one or two letters and/or removing and adding letters from specific words. The resulting ladder of words demonstrates how words are related to each other but also shows the word-building process. An example follows in Figure 5-7.

Once you've demonstrated this tech-

Words with the Sound of "e" as in bed					
-et	-ead	-en	-em	-ed	-ess
Pet get	head lead spread bread	hen when	gem them stem	red bed fled wed	mess dress less
-end	-est	-ench	-eg	-eft	-ell
end spend	nest rest west chest vest	bench French	leg beg	left theft	fell well yell swell
-edge	-ealth	-aid	-ever		
edge pledge	health wealth	said	ever never clever		

FIGURE 5-6   Words with the Sound of "e" as in *Bed*

nique and worked on it with a group of children, they can continue to add to existing word ladders and make many more of their own.

Word Stairs

A word stair is similar to a word ladder in that each word is related to the word before. However, in this case you must use the last letter of the word to start the next word on the stair. These are sometimes called word vines or word snakes. You can use graph paper to structure this activity and can specify the number of letters that children may use (see Figure 5-8).

Reading Charts

Many of the charts teachers use have words and letters embedded in a text. Children read the message, poem, or story on the chart, but teachers have many other opportunities to draw attention to letters, spelling patterns, and words. These charts are sometimes created through interactive writing and are read using a shared reading approach. Children can later read the charts individually as part of independent work time. Here are some examples of the kinds of reading charts that are useful in the classroom environment.

■ *Charts with songs, chants, rhymes, and poems provide engaging, predictable text.* Participation in shared reading of this kind of text helps children become more aware of the sounds of the language, thus developing phonological awareness. In addition, children can attend to many different aspects of words, such as words that start the same (alliteration) or that rhyme. Because the children read the material many times together, the features of the words are visually more available to them. Masks, Post-it Notes, or highlighter tape are often used to find and notice words or word parts in the text.

■ *The stories and other messages that students produce through language experience (interactive or shared writing).* These can be

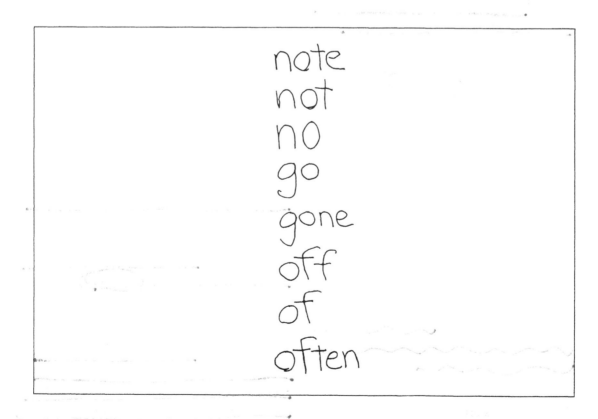

FIGURE 5-7   Word Ladder

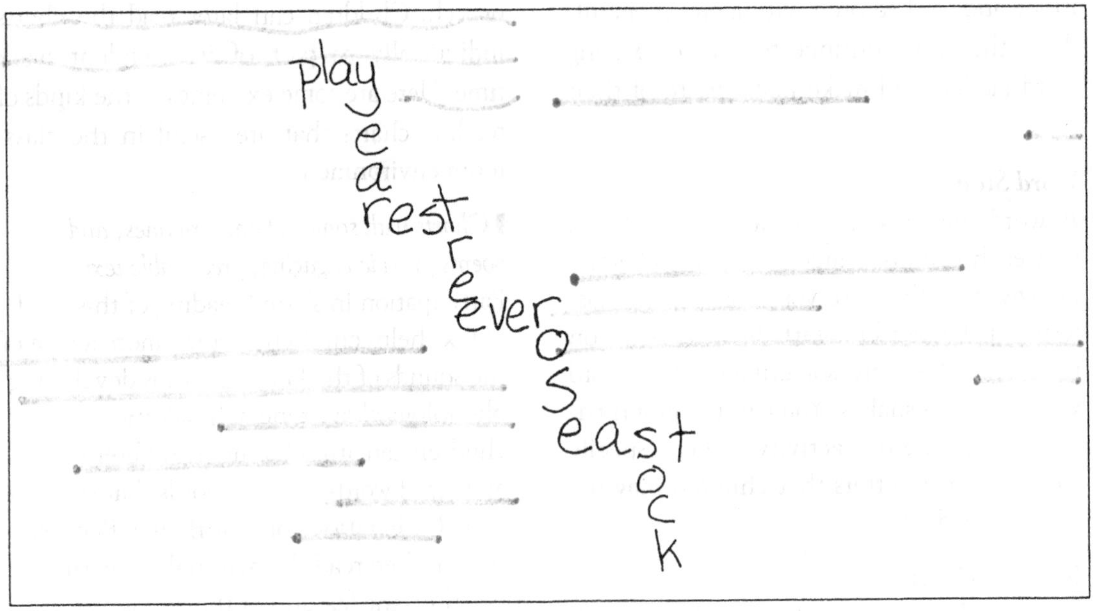

Word Search/Find

play
e
a rest
r
e ver o
s
e ast
o
c
k

FIGURE 5-8 Word Stair

read again and again. Teachers can use their students' own writing interactively to promote word and letter study. Sometimes, teachers laminate charts so that children can use wipe-off markers or crayons to circle or underline letters and words on charts. These materials are especially effective because children work together to compose the message and, in interactive writing, to write it together. Thus, they are working with a text that they already know quite well.

▌ *Children's art.* Either individual pieces or group projects such as wall murals or story maps are often accompanied by a written text that the children have composed. They can reread this material and use it for word study.

There are several ways that you can help children attend to features of words within story or message charts. These include locating, circling, underlining, or highlighting words such as the following:

▌ Words that start like children's names.
▌ Words that start or end alike.
▌ Words that have some of the same parts.

▌ Particular high-frequency words.
▌ One-syllable and two-syllable words.
▌ "Describing" words (*pretty*, *blue*, *fast*).
▌ Compound words.
▌ Words that begin with letter clusters (*sp*, *str*).
▌ Interesting words.
▌ Words that have the same meaning.

Working Documents: A Dynamic Concept

While the word walls and word charts we have described here provide an attractive, visual display in the print-rich classroom, their function extends far beyond an aesthetic one. Teachers don't preplan and make attractive charts to decorate the room; our word walls and charts are *working documents* created by the teacher and children together. We could not, for example, prepare all the charts for the year and then use them sequentially. While the general plan and the principles repeat year after year, the charts reflect the unique thinking of any one group of children: the examples they discover, the order in which they produce them, the way they organize them. The appearance of the charts and word walls will reflect ongoing daily use as children add words to them. When we recognize our word walls and charts as working documents that change and develop over time, we realize that they are also a living record of the teaching and learning that has taken place in our classroom program.

Suggestions for Professional Development

1. Work with a group of grade-level colleagues to create a list of ideas for interactive word charts.

2. Discuss your observations of children and select one kind of word chart that would be appropriate to extend their learning.

∎ Try out the word chart over a week of instruction. Then, get back together with grade-level colleagues to share the results. Bring your chart if possible,

or take a walking tour of each other's classrooms. As you discussed words and how they work with your students, which aspects did they focus on and learn? How words sound? How words look? Meanings of words? Other learning?

∎ What did you learn about your students' knowledge? How did you extend it?

3. Repeat the activity for an interactive word wall.

∎ At a follow-up session, share the words that you selected to put on the word wall over a two-week period. Discuss why each word was selected, particularly what aspects of the word children noticed, and what opportunities you discovered to use those words during reading and writing.

dif Int= dif words

Understanding Language and Words

In this section we explore word solving, an aspect of language worthy of our thoughtful consideration because, as teachers, we must understand *why* we make the decisions we do. We ask ourselves:

■ What do children know about words?
■ What do they need to know?
■ How do children learn to solve words?
■ How do they use that knowledge in reading and writing?

The answers to these important questions underlie our work and our decision making in teaching. There is no "set" curriculum, no script that enables us to respond to the children in a way that recognizes where they are, what they know, and where they each need to go in learning. Only by developing our own theories about literacy learning—admittedly incomplete—and honing our observation and assessment skills can we meet the needs of our students. In this section we provide the foundational understandings about language, letters, and words that children use to solve words. We also address the ways in which teachers engage in the assessment and teaching cycle.

What Teachers Need to Know About Language

At the heart of literacy is a language process in which children use what they know about the language they speak and connect it to print. Classrooms must be rich in opportunities for children to use language for different purposes. We are simultaneously helping children expand their oral language capabilities while we work with them on the understandings needed for literacy. Later in this book we will explore in depth children's development of early understandings about literacy as well as the processes related to learning about letters, sounds, and words in the reading and writing processes. Teaching decisions to support student learning must be based on knowledge of the individual children, knowledge of the reading and writing processes, and knowledge of the linguistic system. We would not explicitly teach complicated linguistic concepts to children, but, as teachers, we need a thorough understanding of language systems ourselves. We include this chapter as a reference and resource. We invite teachers to reflect on the implicit knowledge of language that we all have as speakers of a language.

As we begin, think about our language as a system for verbal communication. For the moment, forget about reading, writing, and the skills that go with learning them. Think about what we know and can do as users of a language. As speakers, we have acquired a vast and complex body of knowledge; we know and use a complex system of rules to generate oral language and to understand each other. For example, as speakers of a language:

■ We recognize sequences of sounds, made with the mouth and tongue, as units of meaning (words and parts of words). We have huge speaking vocabularies of words that carry and convey meaning in our language.

■ We know how to put those words together in sentences, using the rules of grammar.

■ We know how to change those sentences around in many ways, according to the rules of the language; with the words and rules we have, we can generate an infinite number of sentences.

■ We interpret and bring meaning to words, sentences, and larger units of text.

Characteristics of Language

Most of the examples in this book focus attention on English as a language system, but we present in the following section some characteristics that are true of *all* languages.

Language is governed by rules.

If a group of people existed on an isolated island and spoke a language that had never been written down and that no one in the world had ever heard before, outsiders who wanted to understand the island people would try to learn the words and their meanings but, more important, would try to discover the "rules" of the language. All languages have complex systems of rules by which people can generate an unlimited number of phrases, sentences, and longer texts. By this system of rules, we do not mean correct "grammar" rules that we all studied in school. We mean the unconscious knowledge we have of the way words and parts of words go together to make meaning clear. For example, if we take the following list of twelve words and put them together in a sentence, there are several possibilities that every reader of this book would recognize. First, here's the list:

the
big
with
only
green
the
a
river
slid
crocodile
into
ripple

Some possible sentences are:

With only a ripple, the big green
crocodile slid into the river.
The big green crocodile slid into the
river with only a ripple.
The big crocodile slid into the green
river with only a ripple.
The green crocodile slid into the big
river with only a ripple.

Sentences like the following would be grammatically correct but would not sound "quite right" to us as speakers of the language:

The big green crocodile slid into a river
with only the ripple.
A big green crocodile slid into the river
with only the ripple.

A sentence like the next one would also be grammatically correct in terms of the sentence structure but not quite right in terms of meaning. There is a conflict in meaning between the words *only* and *big*.

The green crocodile slid into the river
with only a big ripple.

The processes we use to generate and evaluate sentences come from our unconsciously held sense of the rules of the system of language.

Language is purposeful and is learned through use.

Through these rules, we communicate meaning and we accomplish a wide range of tasks. Language, if it is anything, is functional. Very young children learn that they can accomplish their own purposes through using language. They can get what they need or control others. They can state their questions and try out ideas. The words and the syntax are there for the purpose of communicating meaning and influencing others. By using the language, language users are learning more about how it works.

Language varies in many ways.

We all recognize and enjoy the fact that there are great variations in the ways people talk. Of course, every person has his or her own particular language characteristics. Certainly, we can recognize the voice of a friend or family member on the phone without an announcement of the caller's name. But groups of people also share language characteristics. A person from Boston generally will sound quite different from a person born and raised in Alabama. We can recognize people from our own neighborhoods because of accents! Differences are reflected in the pronunciation of words, choice of words, sentence structure, and expressions. Let's explore some of the ways in which language varies:

❚ Children and teenagers talk differently from adults and adults tend to talk differently when speaking to children.

❚ People from different socioeconomic groups may vary in the way they use language and the way their language sounds.

❚ People from different sociocultural groups may use different varieties of a language, including specialized expressions that mark the "in group."

❚ There are specialized ways of talking that are work-related (which we notice at "company" parties).

❚ There are differences in the ways the same people talk when they are at home with their family, with friends in a social circle, at church, at school, or at work.

Here are some terms related to language variation:

❚ An *idiolect* is an individual person's unique way of talking—the qualities that make it possible to recognize someone's voice in the next room.

❚ A *dialect* is a regional variety of a language. English dialects are mutually intelligible; the differences are actually minor.

❚ A *sociolect* is a dialect that is associated with a particular social group.

❚ A *register* is a way of talking that is associated with a particular context (such as church or school).

Language variation is a fascinating subject and a rich resource in the classroom. As teachers, it is important for us to recognize that language variation is simply a part of life. Our role is to listen to children, really

hear them, and understand their meanings. Sometimes teachers are concerned about what they may consider to be "ungrammatical" language, meaning that the student is not using the English we use at school or hear on the evening news. In this case, we want to expand students' language, but constant correction will not have the desired effect; it will only cause the language user to become silent. As we enjoy rich, lively conversations with children and immerse them in reading and writing, we can expand their language resources without silencing them.

All varieties of a language have complex rules of grammar and are vehicles for communicating complex ideas.

In the United States and many other countries, social class is marked by language differences. Some varieties are considered more "acceptable" than others because higher economic classes use them. These "acceptable" varieties of English, also known as *standard English*, are not inherently *better* than other variations in terms of expressing ideas. In fact, some features that once were associated with dialects or sociolects are regularly used by all of us for emphasis in expressions. For example:

"No way!"
"Been there, done that!"
"How's it goin'?"

Research has shown that when children have varied experiences and interact with many different groups, they expand their language capabilities. Many adults can use two or more different dialects to communicate in different circumstances. For children whose home language is different from "standard English," the teacher's role is critical. We work hard to honor their home language while we help them expand their language knowledge and skills. In this way, we give them the best chance of success in school and our society.

That goal is not accomplished by constant and public admonition but by engaging them in learning conversations. Another extremely valuable tool for expanding language is literature. Reading aloud to children not only offers models of written language but provides a foundation for discussion that will lift and expand language capabilities. As children learn to read and write themselves, they will acquire new structures, new vocabulary, and new ways of talking.

There are important differences between spoken and written language.

Written language performs special functions in our society. With written language, people can record ideas and information so that they can remember them and hold them up for reflection and analysis. Language, when written, is designed to communicate across time and space. Oral language possesses important features such as intonation, expression, and gesture. That's not true of written language. However, written language has other features such as a special syntax (dialogue) and punctuation. While these features of written language help readers understand the meanings of what they read, the features are a challenge to beginning readers who are trying to understand the complexities of reading and writing.

What are the components of our language system?

In order to describe language, linguists have defined and described three systems that are interrelated. It is useful for teachers of literacy to think about these three systems in order to more fully understand the variety of language resources that children use as they are working to become literate. We will describe them here and define some of the more common terms that are used to talk about language.

The semantic system: What does language mean?

Language was created by human beings to communicate meaning. While we can also convey meaning in other ways—for example, through gestures and visual images—language is our primary way to communicate with others and understand our world. You may have used the expression "you're arguing about *semantics*," meaning that the parties in disagreement are bickering over the connotation of particular words rather than real issues. While *semantics* actually has a broader meaning than the expression implies, it accurately captures the focus as the *meaning* of words. The system that linguists study when they work to understand meaning is called the *semantic system*.

Learning a language includes learning the units that represent meaning. Our words appear in streams of sound that we make with the tongue, mouth, and teeth. Our ears process the sounds and our brains sort them into meaningful units. Usually we think of the words of the language (the lexicon) as the units of meanings; actually, each unit is smaller. We call the smallest unit of meaning the *morpheme*, which cannot be divided. The combination of morphemes to form words is the *morphology of a language*. The system of meaning is sometimes called the *morphological system* because the morphemes are the building blocks of vocabulary. We have internalized rules about how morphemes go together in words and in strings to form meaningful phrases and sentence units. It is important for teachers to know about and pay attention to morphemes because these building blocks are the basis for some ways of analyzing words—that is, taking them apart in reading or constructing them in spelling.

A morpheme may be a single word: *home, dog, cake*. A word may be made up of more than one morpheme: *homesick, underdog, cakewalk*. Morphemes like *home* are called *free morphemes* because they stand alone as units of meaning. Other morphemes may represent units of meaning but do not stand alone. Think about the *s* on *homes*. It adds meaning to the word, but by itself it has no meaning. Units like *ing, ed, pre,* or *un* are *bound morphemes* because they must be used with words. Still, they are extremely important in our language. They add meaning or they change the meaning or the case of the word. In our language, there are *derivational morphemes*, which change the grammatical category: *wash* and *washable*. There are also *inflectional morphemes* that do not change the grammatical category: *fast, faster, fastest*. When you know the language, you know the morphemes, and you know how to form new words from these elements. It is obvious that when readers work on words, they are using their knowledge of free and bound morphemes.

When we speak, there are no "visual" spaces between words. As a beginning reader once said to us, "Hey, why can't I hear the spaces when I talk?" It's true. There are no spaces in talking. There are pauses for emphasis, of course, but these certainly do not occur between each word. Yet we have a psychological knowledge of a word and/or of the morphemes that communicate meaning.

Here are some morphemes—see how many words you can form using each of them.

run
be
ing
er
eat

Did you add endings that changed the grammatical category of the word (for example, *run* to *running*)? If so, you used derivational morphemes. We can represent morphemes in multiple ways: by a single sound, /s/;[1] by a syllable, *est*; by more than one syllable, *crocodile*; or by no sound at all—like the plural of *sheep*.

When we think about the words, or lexicon, of a language, we can think of many different categories of words. The parts of speech—nouns, verbs, adjectives, adverbs, and so forth—represent one kind of category. Here are some others:

■ *Homonyms* are words that sound the same but have different meanings (*hear, here*). *Homophones* are words that sound the same but are spelled differently and have different meanings (*meat, meet*). They are one type of homonym. A second type of homonym is the *homograph*. Homographs are words that are spelled the same but sound different (*read, read*).

■ *Synonyms* are words that have different sounds but the same meaning (*chair, seat*).

■ *Antonyms* are words that have different sounds and opposite meaning (*cold, hot*).

■ *Compound words* are words that are made up of two or more other words (*playground*). A speaker of a language can usually figure out the compound word by knowing each of the words included; but compound words are not always the sum of the parts: *egghead*.

■ *Multiple-meaning words* are those that mean something different depending on the ways they are used (*run*—home run, run in your stocking, run down the street, a run of bad luck).

■ *Idioms* are phrases with meaning assigned to the whole unit (*raining cats and dogs*). The meaning of idioms is complex; nonnative speakers, initially, find it difficult to understand idioms. As with compound words, idioms are not always the sum of their parts.

These examples illustrate how complex and varied the semantic system is. It is not a matter of simply learning individual words (or *lexical items*) and their definitions. In fact, children do not simply learn a collection of words when they learn language, although that is part of the learning. They learn an entire rule-governed system that will allow them to generate an infinite number of expressions that they have never heard before.

You cannot distinguish sharply between

---

[1] A symbol presented within two slash marks refers to the phoneme or sound.

the structure of words and the structure of syntax. Morphology and syntax are interrelated. If we understand language as a sequence of morphemes (some combined into words), we also understand that there are rules by which these sequences are structured. In essence, we cannot separate the units of meaning of our language from the rules that govern the ways in which these units are strung together. All elements combine to help us communicate. In fact, the study of meaning in language, or semantics, includes the analysis of meanings of words, phrases, sentences, discourse, and whole texts (Harris and Hodges 1995, 230). Consider the following sentence:

It's too cold to start.

How many interpretations of this sentence can you make? The grammatical structure and the several meanings of the words create an ambiguous sentence. We instantly recognize that this sentence represents multiple meanings; it might refer to a car that is stalling on a cold day or a hike postponed because of the weather. Sometimes ambiguity is the source of humor, as in the Amelia Bedelia (Parish) series: Amelia "steals" a base by actually taking it home. Just as the single surface structure "It's too cold to start" can have several different "deep" structures or meanings, we can express the same meaning in several different structures. For example, we can say "Tessie wore the dress" and "The dress was worn by Tessie." Knowing the many different ways meanings can be represented in written texts and knowing different ways to interpret the written language one reads is the essence of comprehension. We always want our young readers to search for meaning, make and confirm predictions, and ask "Does what I'm reading make sense?"

GOAL:

The syntactic system: How are words put together?

In the previous section we discussed the structure of language, that is, the rules that govern the ways in which morphemes and words work together in sentence patterns. That system of rules is called the *syntactic system*—which is not the same thing as the "rules for proper grammar," but involves the principles we all know and use in order to produce and understand language. Every regional dialect or variation of a language is highly rule-governed. When children learn language, they learn this system of rules. In fact, they actually use rules to put words together from the very beginning. Think about young children ages one to three. At first, they might learn one word, like *Mama* or *bye-bye*, and use it singly. But very soon they begin to put one, two, and three words together, and they do not do so randomly. For example, a child would say "Go bye-bye," but not "Bye, go, bye." The child would say "more juice" rather than "juice more."

Researchers who have studied children's language have called them "little linguists," because it seems that they are constructing a "grammar" at each stage of language development. Remarkably, they will have mastered most of the syntactic rules of the language by about age five, a phenomenal accomplishment. Indeed, children all over the world, speaking many different languages, seem to follow very similar (although not identical) patterns of development. For this reason, linguists have concluded that language has some genetic basis; that is, language abilities, to some extent, "unfold." But linguists also recognize that interaction with others is essential to language learning. It seems that young children have the inherited ability to reconstruct language for themselves if they have the opportunity to hear it and to interact with other speakers. They learn the words of the language and their meanings and they learn the rules required to put together an infinite number of sentences in whatever language they speak.

Syntactic awareness is the knowledge of grammatical patterns or structures; *syntax* is the study of how sentences are formed and of the grammatical rules that govern their formation. A special kind of syntactic awareness is related to written language. We have previously talked about young children acquiring the ability to "talk like a book." For example, four-year-old Phillip, while looking at *Goodnight Moon* (Brown 1947) says, "Goodnight mouse, good night little house. . . ." Of course, Phillip is not reading in the sense that he is tracking the words or even attending to print, but he is doing something very important. He is reproducing the syntax of written language because he has internalized the structures. He knows that there are slightly different rules when you are pretending to read. Clay (1991a) has identified "talking like a book" as an important step in learning to read.

The phonological system: How is meaning communicated through sounds?

The *phonological system* refers to the sounds of the language. When we talk, our voices produce streams of sounds, and those who are listening to us do something remarkable. Listeners construct a message from the streams of sounds, "sorting" those sounds into words and sentences that have meaning. Remember that there are no "spaces" between words when we talk. Linguists have identified single sounds as *phonemes*. A phoneme is not the same as a letter of the alphabet, but, obviously, phonemes and letters are related. *Dog* has three phonemes (sounds) and three letters; *cake* has three phonemes and four letters; and *eight* has two phonemes and five letters. Actually a phoneme such as /t/ is a category for several sounds people make that are only slightly different from each other. For example, the /t/ in *letter*, in *top*, and in *list* are very slightly different in sound, but they are enough alike that we categorize them all as /t/.

When teachers study the phonological system, it is wise to become knowledgeable about several linguistic terms, which often arise in professional discussions of beginning reading instruction.

❚ A *phoneme* is a category of speech sounds.

❚ *Phonetics* refers to the scientific study of speech sounds—how the sounds are made vocally and the relation of speech sounds to the total language process.

❚ *Phonics*, as it is related to reading, uses a small portion of the body of knowledge that makes up *phonetics*.

❚ *Phonemic awareness* or *phoneme awareness* is the ability to hear sounds in words and to identify particular sounds.

When we detect differences in the way people speak, often these differences are related to the phonological system. All varieties of English, for example, are closely aligned to the way speakers sound. Most of our words are mutually intelligible, but we enjoy slightly different pronunciations. Consider four people, one from New York, one from Texas, one from Iowa, and one from Georgia. How might each pronounce these words?

> Mary
> car
> wash
> going
> idea

Words are made up of sequences of phonemes. In any given language, there are phonological rules about which sounds can be combined with, precede, or follow other sounds. For example, which of the following words are possible in English?

> larp
> jzylp
> ferette
> idylp
> senite
> berzon
> gnoste
> femerolle

To English speakers, some of these words are easy to pronounce and could be English words, but others are nearly impossible. Yet, all of these sound combinations are possible in some languages. We might even decide that words like *ferette* are possible in English but have an origin other than English. As it turns out, all of these words are nonsense words. As we approach tasks such as these, we are using our implicit knowledge of the phonological system of English.

In a sense, all young children are aware of the phonology of language because they can understand and use the sounds of language. That is, they can speak and listen. But when literacy educators and researchers refer to the terms *phonemic awareness*, *phoneme awareness*, or *phonological awareness*, they mean that children can hold up language and its sounds to conscious observation. Children who possess *phonemic awareness* can, for example, respond to rhymes or alliteration and produce these language features. Young children love to repeat old verses such as "Pease Porridge Hot" and, in the process, they build an internal feeling for the sounds of language.

Phoneme awareness means that children can tell when words start like other words or end like them. They know that words are made up of sequences of sounds and they can hear the sounds in words. All of this happens in oral language. Parents and teachers take advantage of young children's delight in word play. This natural human tendency to enjoy the sounds of language works to children's advantage as they play with and manipulate words. Nursery rhymes and songs bring sounds in words to children's attention.

As we consider spoken language, we can categorize the sounds of the language. There are several categories of sounds, including the following:

❚ *Consonants* are speech sounds made by partial or complete closure of the air flow which causes friction, making a sound in varying amounts.

❚ *Vowels* are speech sounds made without stoppage or friction of the air flow.

Phonological awareness involves several different ways of breaking up and analyzing words. One way is a phoneme-by-phoneme analysis that requires separating the word into individual sounds. Words also can be divided by the following:

❚ A *syllable* is a minimal unit of sequential speech sounds composed of a vowel sound or a consonant-vowel combination. A syllable always contains a vowel or vowel-like speech sound.

❚ Words of one syllable may be broken into an opening part, usually consisting of a letter or cluster of letters, and an ending part. The opening part (or the letters before the vowel-bearing part) is called the *onset*, and the ending part (containing the vowel) is called the *rime*. Words with more than one syllable may be broken into phonological units (like syllables) and then into onsets and rimes. For example, onsets and rimes are indicated in the words below.

str-ing
l-ike
b-oy
c-at
sh-out
f-oot b-all
n-o
cr-y
tr-ee
pl-ay
m-o t-el

Rime is not the same as the commonly used word *rhyme*, but there is a relationship. If two words have identical *rime*, such as c-at and b-at, then they also rhyme or sound the same at the end. Sound sequence analysis, syllable analysis, and onset and rime analysis represent three ways that words can be broken into parts. Writers and readers probably use all three as they learn how words work.

The orthographic system: How is written language constructed?

Our focus in this book is children's development of literacy—reading and writing, specifically the development of a word-solving process. If we are concerned about literacy, then we must also be concerned about the oral language system, the foundation of literacy. But written language offers new challenges to the young learner. As teachers, several terms are relevant to our knowledge base.

■ The *orthographic system* is the spelling system of the language.

■ A *grapheme* is a letter or cluster of letters that represents a single phoneme.

■ The *grapho-phonic* relationship refers to the relationship between the oral sounds of the language and the written letters or clusters of letters.

■ A *phonogram* is a phonetic element represented by graphic characters or symbols. In word recognition, a graphic sequence composed of a vowel grapheme and an ending consonant grapheme (such as *an* or *it*) is often called a *word family* (see Appendix

15). Spelling patterns are complex. For example, one sound (the phoneme /f/) may be represented by many different letters (*off, cough, Christopher, soft, sophomore*).

The orthography of the language not only involves the relationships between the sounds and the letters but it also involves the spelling patterns of written words. We compose messages, sentences, and longer texts in oral language, keeping in mind the way written language is constructed, and map them out as written language. This process is not necessarily sequential; it is cyclical as we think and write at the same time. In reading, we discern the print on the page and connect it to our knowledge of oral language—the sounds related to letters but also to larger units such as syntactic patterns. For both processes, the oral language system is the foundation.

Figure 6-1 places components of the lan-

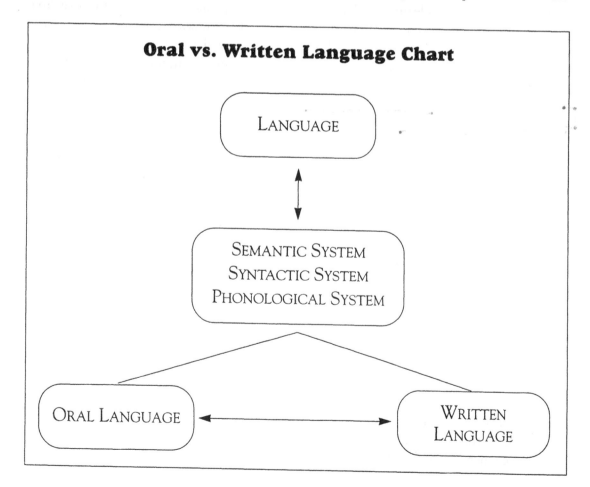

FIGURE 6-1   Oral vs. Written Language Chart

guage system in a visual arrangement to help us think about language, its meaning structure and sound system, and the relationship to written and oral language.

Knowledge of language is useful information for teachers of literacy because reading and writing are language systems. We have said that learning language is, to an extent, "natural." Literacy requires a different set of understandings. Some scholars claim that reading is not "natural" because we lack a tendency to "absorb" reading and writing. After all, not every person learns to read and write even when exposed to print in a literate society. But we argue that literacy is highly related to language; indeed, a strong familiarity with the systems of language is an important strength for young children as they meet the challenges related to interpreting print.

Clearly, there is much to teach and learn. Children need to learn to look at letters in print (graphemes) and tell one from another, to discern spelling patterns, and to map sounds onto letter patterns. Although this learning varies from child to child, much of it depends on an instructional program in the primary grades. You will discover that children's knowledge of the semantic, syntactic, and phonological systems of language provides them with a helpful background for understanding the complexities of becoming literate.

Suggestions for Professional Development

1. Explore young children's knowledge of the language systems by collecting several samples of writing from kindergarten or first-grade children, by taking running records, or by simply listening to several young children read simple texts. Ask yourself:

■ What is the evidence that children are aware of the phonological system and the connections to the orthographic system? (In writing you might see, for example, that children are representing sounds with their corresponding letters even though the spellings might not be accurate. You might also see some evidence of knowledge of spelling patterns. In reading, you might observe error patterns that indicate children are noticing the first letter of a word or some part of a word.)

■ What is the evidence that children are using their knowledge of language structure or syntax? (In writing you might observe children composing messages as they string words together in phrases or sentences even though the words are not fully formed or spelled accurately. The children are able to use these messages, nonetheless, to communicate. In reading, you might see error patterns that indicate children are predicting what a text will say from their knowledge of syntax. Of course, you will want them to compare their meaning with the print, but syntax is a powerful predictor in reading.)

■ What is the evidence that children are bringing meaning to reading or writing? Gaining meaning is the purpose of both reading and writing. As you analyze their writing samples, can you determine whether children are communicating a meaningful message? What words are they selecting and using? In reading, is there evidence that children are using meaning in several ways:

  ■ To determine whether what they read makes sense.
  ■ To predict meaning in reading.
  ■ To compose a meaningful message for writing.
  ■ To keep the message in mind (evidenced by rereading) while engaged in writing words letter by letter.

Building on Early Learning

W hen children enter the world of written language, they are guided by their knowledge of oral language and the ways in which they use it to communicate with others and to make sense of their world. Indeed, we cannot emphasize this understanding enough: learning to read and write begins with oral language. Here are some of the important principles that children develop as they use oral language:

■ Certain sounds are part of the language the people in my world speak, and other sounds are not.

■ Sounds and clusters of sounds have meaning and can be used for communication.

■ Language is made up of words that have meaning, and these words have boundaries, even though the boundaries are not always clear for every word.

■ Words are strung together to create messages, and they follow each other in an orderly, structured, rule-governed way.

■ The voice can be used to stress words—to convey emotion and meaning.

Of course, these understandings are not explicit. While children understand them implicitly, they are not consciously aware of them nor can they articulate them. Nevertheless, these understandings are powerful and form the foundation for early literacy learning.

As they learn written language, children are learning the complex ways that these understandings are mapped onto print. They are also developing additional sets of knowledge that have to do with written language, the way it is structured and organized, and the way it represents meaning.

Early Understandings About Written Language

As children experience written language at home or at preschool/kindergarten, they begin to develop some early understandings about the relationship between oral and written language. At first, their concepts are somewhat primitive, yet they represent complex learning at an early stage (Figure 7-1).

In the left column we have listed some experiences that children enjoy, often with adults; on the right are some key understandings that children develop through these experiences. For years, child develop-

Early Understandings Related to Print	
Learning Context	**Some Key Understandings**
Hearing and saying rhymes, jingles, poems, and songs.	• Language is enjoyable in the way it sounds. • Sounds can be repeated over and over in rhymes and songs. • Some words are like other words in the way they sound.
Hearing stories read aloud.	• Hearing written language is an enjoyable experience. • You can have high expectations of written language; that is, it's going to mean something. • When a story is read again and again, the same message is heard over and over (written language is constant). • Written language sounds different from the way people talk (it has syntactic structures and special words). • The story you hear goes with the pictures you see. • Pictures represent meaning that will help you understand the story.
Listening to stories while looking at pages of print.	• When you read, you hold the book a certain way and turn pages from the front to the back. • When you read, you look at the print (the marks on the page). • The marks on the page contain some letters that appear over and over, and some letters have similar features (such as lines and circles).
Sharing the reading of a familiar story with someone.	• When you read, you go from left to right across the page and also from top to bottom. • A word is represented by a group of letters; there is space between words. • One spoken word matches one written word on the page. • The punctuation tells you some action to take, such as stopping (period) or raising your voice (question mark).
Reading (or "pretending to read") for yourself.	• By looking at the pictures and going through the book, you can tell the story and produce some of the language. • You handle the book the same way every time (front to back, turning pages).
Watching someone write.	• When you write, you make marks on a page of paper. • Some marks appear over and over and have similar features. • When you write, you make your marks from left to right and leave spaces. • When you write, you use letters.
Writing for yourself.	• When you write, you make up something to say—a message or story. • Then, you create pictures and marks (scribbles or letters) to represent it. • When you write you put marks on the page in some kind of order (eventually learning to place print from left to right).
Noticing signs and print in the neighborhood streets, shops, and other areas.	• Writing tells us where something is and/or what it is. • Signs use letters to communicate meaning. • The features of letters are the same every time you see them. • The order of letters in signs is the same every time you see them.
Seeing your name, starting to write your name, and connecting it to other understandings.	• Your name is a word that is always the same wherever it appears. • Your name can be written or made with letters. • Your name starts like, sounds like, or ends like other words that you know. • The letters in your name are the same letters that appear in other words.

FIGURE 7-1 Early Understandings Related to Print

ment experts and educators have urged parents to read to their children. As children hear stories read aloud, they begin to internalize many of the characteristics of written language. However, reading aloud to children provides no "magical guarantee" that they will learn to read on their own. Some children who seldom hear stories read aloud acquire literacy quickly, while others who have had rich read-aloud experiences find reading and writing difficult. Reading aloud will not ensure early success in literacy learning, but it will increase the chances that children will have high expectations of print and expand their language knowledge. There are many different understandings that merge in the development of literacy.

It is wise to provide varied experiences to support young children. In addition to reading aloud, caregivers, preschool teachers, and kindergarten teachers can help children develop early understandings in an enjoyable way by inviting children to join in shared reading of stories and rhymes, talking about print in the environment, and promoting a range of writing activities. At first, children may only understand that language is somehow connected to the "marks" on a page, but in time they will begin to give these "black blobs" greater attention.

Reading must be a mysterious process to the young child, who cannot tell just by looking what people are really doing when they read. It is a little easier to see the mechanical aspects of the writing task, but not the thinking that goes with it. When adults share reading and writing with children in a way that they can to some degree participate, aspects of the task become clearer. Then, when adults support children in their first approximated versions of reading and writing, still more is learned. As children gain experience, they start to refine their understandings about the visual features of print—the letters and some first words (like *Mom, stop,* or *love*) that they have encountered over and over again.

By sharing the task and trying it for

themselves, children get a feel for the motor aspects of reading and writing—the movement from left to right, for example. Throughout all of these experiences, children are also learning something very important about written language—it has purpose and meaning. Building high expectations of print means more than learning about the mechanics of the process. Early reading and writing experiences must be connected in the child's mind with enjoyment and accomplishment. We want children to understand that books are a source of enjoyable stories, delightful nonsense, or rhythm and rhyme. We also want them to recognize that they can use written messages to communicate or to record important information (like telephone messages, letters to relatives, or grocery lists).

Some of the child's first written attempts might simply be to experience the power of making marks on paper rather than for real purpose or communication, but children can learn that adults prize this writing and expect it to mean something. Soon, young children are using written language to communicate, often creating their own greeting cards, lists, notes, or labels (Figure 7-2).

Some children depend on school for the activities that help to develop these early understandings. Many parents believe that their job is to feed, clothe, and love their child, while it is the school's job to develop literacy. Indeed, some parents are afraid of doing the wrong thing in teaching literacy at home. However, all of the contexts listed in the left column of Figure 7-1 represent a number of activities that volunteers, classroom assistants, and parents can do with individual children to support their journey to literacy success. ☺

Letter Learning

The chart in Figure 7-1 outlines some general principles that children derive from experience with written language in many contexts. Within those experiences, they are also learning about letters and how to use

FIGURE 7-2   Young Child's Label

them. Let's focus for a moment on the very important area of letter learning.

There is much to learn about a letter. For example:

❚ The letter name.

❚ The formation of the letter (the physical movement that creates the shape).

❚ The sound the letter represents alone.

❚ The sound the letter represents when it is located in a word with other letters.

❚ The features of a letter that make it different from every other letter.

❚ The direction that the letter must be turned in order to preserve its name (b and d; m and w).

❚ The relationship of the letter to known words (such as names).

As children learn and use written language, they build networks of information around letters, and they learn "how to learn" letters. When they have gathered a larger body of general information about letters, they learn, for example:

❚ There are a limited number of letters (twenty-six in all).

❚ Some letters are tall and some are short.

❚ Some have circles; others have tunnels.

❚ Some have lines that cross through them.

❚ Some have tails, dots, or curves.

❚ When you look at the alphabet, the letters come in a certain order (A, B, C).

❚ Some letters appear together more frequently in words.

❚ Some letters are doubled in words.

❚ There are different types of letters (capitals and lowercase; consonants and vowels).

❚ Letters may be large or small, different colors, and different styles, but you can still tell what the letter is by looking at the special features.

Letter knowledge is basic to literacy. Most important for children is their recognition of the features of the letters and then their ability to make the connection between letters and sounds. Children do not need to know the names of the letters to use them in reading and writing; however, most educators believe that letters names are useful because they assist children in identifying letters and they give teachers and children a way to talk about letters. Recognition of the visual features is key; the child's ability to look at print or to notice the unique features of each letter when it is embedded with other letters in a word will be important in the reading process. As Clay (1991a) has said, "A child must be able to distinguish what makes a letter different from every other letter before he can attach a sound to it." Looking at letters and groups of letters is the beginning of early letter-sound learning.

Early Word Learning

While children are learning letters and developing concepts about how print works, they usually begin to acquire a few words that they can recognize when they encounter them in print. A child does not need to know all the letters—or even very many letters—for the first word learnings to occur. Of course, the first word learned is usually the child's name, or a word with emotional connections, such as *love*, *Dad*, or *Mom*. Children may learn words as they sign their names on a greeting card or as they encounter a frequently occurring word in any meaningful context (such as the grocery store, a restaurant, or in many readings of a favorite story).

When children try to write their own stories, sometimes they try to represent these known words in an approximated way. Through early exploration of words, children learn that:

❚ Words are made up of one or more letters.

❚ The twenty-six letters in different combinations can make words.

❚ A letter or letters represent sounds in words.

❚ Some letters can make several different sounds.

❚ Some sounds may be represented by several different letters.

❚ A word is always spelled the same (uses the same letters in the same order) wherever it appears.

❚ Words are written from left to right.

❚ Words have white space on either side.

❚ Words often appear with other words (again, from left to right with spaces in between) in a way that makes a meaningful message.

❚ Words can be connected together in the way they look or sound.

❚ Words have some of the same letters or parts as other words.

❚ Some letters never go together in words (*xb*, *sb*).

Children may recognize high-frequency words in reading or may produce them in their own writing. For any given child, the two groups of words may not be the same, although there is likely to be some overlap.

The processes of word learning are different for reading and writing. In reading, children are looking for the features and the letters that help them recognize a word and say it. In writing, however:

To put . . . messages down in print [children are] forced to construct words, letter by letter, and so [they become] aware of letter features and letter sequences, particularly for the vocabulary [that they use] in writing again and again. These words become part of [the] writing vocabulary, the ones that [the child] knows in every perceptual detail. (Clay 1975, 2)

Much of the early word learning in reading and writing has little to do with the use of precise letter-sound connections. Children are building *visual* knowledge of words; however, once words are used in reading and writing, they can serve as powerful examples to children. The letter-sound relationships within them are more available because, at this point, the child has already attended to and used some of the information.

Writing experiences help children gain control of words and build into their knowledge the letter-sound associations of the language. Many of the frequently used words do have regular spelling correspondences. Once children have acquired a word like *can*, for example, they can use it as an exemplar to figure out other words with the same phonogram (*an*) or that have the same features (*cap, cat*). According to Clay (1991a), "by the time the list of core words a child controls grows to about forty, the writer controls most of the letter-sound associations . . . plus the most frequent and regular spelling correspondences" (244–245).

Simultaneous Learning of Word Features and Early Strategies

Word learning, letter learning, and learning about how print works are related bodies of knowledge. No one area is a prerequisite to any other. In fact, children who are involved in literacy experiences are learning in all three areas simultaneously. They are also able to put together some of their understandings as they first begin to read and write very simple texts. For example, Tanya reads a simple book, *Balloons* (a Keep Book). (See Figure 7-3.)[1]

The text offers language that is accessible to Tanya; the meaning of this simple story is clear to her from the beginning. She reads, pointing to each word. Figure 7-4 shows how Tanya read two pages. The checkmarks indicate accurate reading.

Tanya reads accurately, pointing to each word, moving her finger from left to right. This behavior shows that Tanya is using her understanding that print is read moving in one direction and that readers match spoken words with written words. She is coordinating the motor aspects of reading, using the hand as a support until her eyes can take over the process. She recognizes some words she knows—*I* and *a* (her "known words"); these words serve as anchors for her reading. She knows that the written message is constant and that when she sees these two words she should be saying them. If Tanya's matching gets "off track," noticing the words she knows can call her back.

Tanya also knows that the illustrations provide some help in figuring out the words. She does not know the word *balloon*, but she sees a balloon in the picture and says the word. She might, with the help of an adult, be able to check the word by saying *balloon*, listening for its beginning sound, and checking the word for a sound-letter match.

What about the color words? Tanya knows the word *red* in isolation, but no other color words. And, since the illustrations of this book are in black and white, she is not able to make use of the information from the picture. The answer is probably found in Tanya's understanding of the meaning of this simple book and her knowledge about how it "works." The book is all about colors, which gives Tanya a more limited set of words to work with; that is, she is looking for color words and can use her knowledge of first letters and their sounds even though that knowledge is quite limited. She is successful on most pages. In this example, Tanya shows that children can begin to behave like readers even if they have not fully completed their knowledge of the letters and sounds. Clay (1991a) contends that:

> Children do not need to learn all the symbols in the writing system *before* they can proceed to reading stories. On the contrary, once they have learnt a few letters they usually have a procedure for learning letters and they can learn the remainder while writing and reading. (263)

---

[1] This book is intended to be used with teacher assistance. See Chapter 20 for a description of Keep Books.

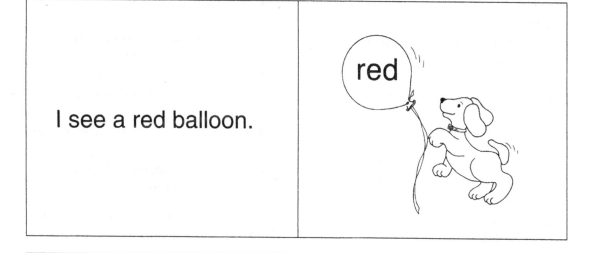

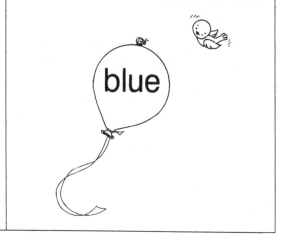

FIGURE 7-3 *Balloons*

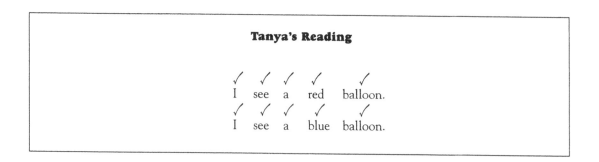

Tanya's Reading

FIGURE 7-4 Tanya's Reading

In this chapter we have explored the range of knowledge that children acquire and organize in the course of early learning about written language. Taken altogether, it is complex and multifaceted. Amazingly, most children acquire these basic understandings easily when they are given the right kind of teaching and support. Sharpening our own awareness of the kinds of knowledge children need to develop will help us to be sure that our letter- and word-solving curriculum does not neglect any important area. In fact, the chart in Figure 7-1 might be a good beginning guide for designing preschool and kindergarten programs that support early letter and word learning.

Suggestions for Professional Development

1. Working with colleagues, look for evidence of children's early learning about letters, sounds, and words. First, examine the greeting card created by four-year-old Chris (Figure 7-5). The message says, "Happy birthday Grandma, love Chris." You may find it difficult to find this message at first, but keep trying. Every letter is there!

2. Now look at a different writing sample, from six-year-old Justin (Figure 7-6). What does this sample show that he knows about letters, sounds, and words in the written language?

3. At a follow-up meeting, bring samples from children in the preschool or kindergarten class in your school. Examine the writing samples, asking questions such as the following:

- Is the child using letters or letterlike shapes?

- Are there strings of letters? What are they?
- Are there double letters or other conventional uses of letters?
- Are letters written left to right?
- Do any of the letters represent consonant or vowel sounds?
- Does the child use space in an attempt to define words?
- Is there any evidence of knowledge of high-frequency words?

You may also want to collect and talk about examples of children's early reading behavior.

4. Revisit the example of Tanya's reading of *Balloons*. What does Tanya know about reading?

5. Select a caption book similar to *Balloons* and read it one or more times to a child in kindergarten who cannot yet read conventionally.

6. Ask the child to "read" the story to you. (Most children will readily read the book either with accuracy, pointing as they do so, or with approximation. Accept what the child does and notice what happens.)

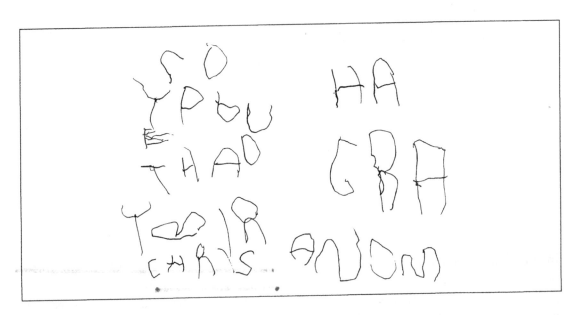

FIGURE 7-5   Chris's Writing Sample

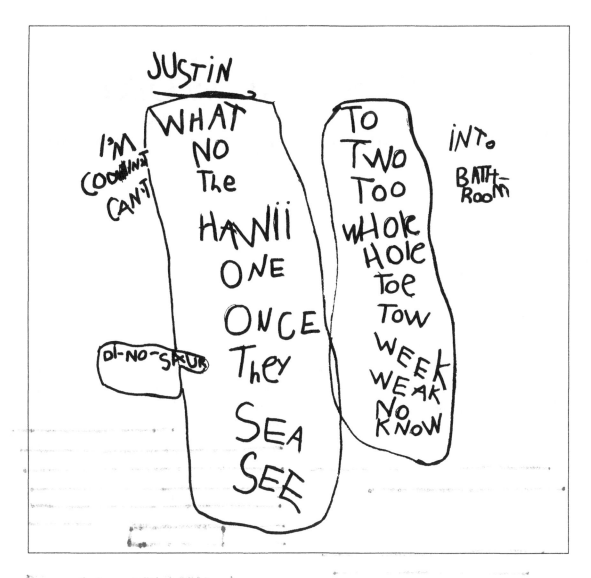

FIGURE 7-6   Justin's Writing Sample

7. Discuss your experience with colleagues, using the following questions:

- Did the child handle the book correctly (front up and turning pages)?
- Did the child engage with the print or just use the pictures while "remembering" the story?
- Was there evidence that the child knows how to go from left to right in reading?
- Did the child use the illustrations?
- Was there evidence of some words the child knows and recognizes quickly?
- What did the child notice about print?

What's in a Word?

Phonological and Orthographic Awareness

*P*honological and *orthographic* are technical words often used by teachers and researchers to discuss important areas of knowledge related to becoming literate. As we discussed in Chapter 6, phonology refers to the sounds of language and orthography refers to the print. *The Literacy Dictionary* (Harris and Hodges 1995) provides the following definitions:

> Phonological awareness is awareness of the constituent sounds of words in learning to read and spell.
> Orthographic awareness is awareness of the symbols in a writing system.

We are interested in phonological and orthographic awareness because these sets of knowledge, used together, are key elements of word solving. Of course, reading is not just about using phonology or orthography, or even both. Reading requires using phonological and orthographic information in a coordinated and integrated way within a larger processing system that encompasses language aspects. As teachers of reading know well, a child can read a page of text using letters and sounds with just about 100 percent accuracy and yet not know much about what was read. And, as kindergarten and first-grade teachers know well, many children approximate reading by producing "booklike" language in response to the illustrations in a familiar text but give little attention to print. While that behavior is an important early step in learning to read, ultimately we want every child to develop an effective reading process that involves attending to and processing information from various sources, both written and oral language, simultaneously.

Being phonologically *aware* means becoming sensitive to the sounds of the language. Sensitivity to sounds begins early and probably occurs about the same time that children begin to notice and experiment with the orthography of language. Learning in one area supports learning in the other. We have discussed the powerful role of rhymes and poems in helping children become sensitive to sounds. Phonological awareness is further stimulated as children move into early learning about reading and writing.

Writing

Early writing is a particularly powerful context for children to become more aware of the sounds in words, learn to look at the letters and the spelling patterns, and make connections between the two. Writing workshop, interactive writing, and independent writing are all contexts that help children learn how to make the connections between the phonology and orthography of the language. You can encourage children to say words slowly, thinking about the sounds. Demonstrate the process but invite children to say the words as well. At this stage, children need to feel the production of sounds in their mouths. Saying words slowly prompts children to make the first connections to letters as they begin to learn the series of movements to form the letters into words.

It is important to teach children how to say words as accurately as possible; variant pronunciations will interfere with spelling. This doesn't mean you correct everyday pronunciation of words; that would have a detrimental effect. All of us pronounce words in a casual way, reflecting our local and regional origins, rather than the careful way we might pronounce words in order to spell them correctly. Explain to children that everyone, when writing, says words very carefully so that they can hear as many sounds as they possibly can. Have children practice this skill themselves.

Young writers need to think about:

❚ The sequence of sounds in the words (how they sound and feel in the mouth when spoken).

❚ How sounds they hear are related to letters they can write (how letters look and how they are written).

One process appears to strengthen the other.

In interactive writing, teachers prompt children not only to say words slowly but to break streams of speech sounds into individual words, and then, sometimes, to break words into syllables for recording.

Reading

Children learn to read by engaging in the reading process in all of its complexity. With their attention focused on constructing meaning as they read, good readers match their thinking with that of the author in some way (Clay 1991a). As they read they use their knowledge of the world (semantic) and language (syntax) along with their understanding of the alphabetical symbols (visual/orthographic) and their sounds (phonological) to make predictions. Readers check on themselves to be sure all the cues match. If there is a match, readers continue to process the text; if there are mismatches, young readers stop and work to pick up more information before reading on. Readers are constantly checking their predictions of what they think the text will say with the letters on the page. As readers learn more efficient ways to access visual information in the text, the visual processing strategies require less and less attention and the readers become increasingly fluent in processing text.

Children need to use phonological information in the reading process simultaneously with other sources of information. Children who are aware of sound segments such as phrases, words, syllables, rhymes, letter clusters, and individual sounds have developed phonological awareness and can use this knowledge to connect their oral language with the written language as they read. The development of this sound awareness is necessary in order for readers to understand that print represents speech (Adams 1990; Clay 1991a; Goswami and Bryant 1990; Stanovich 1994).

Children develop an understanding of rhyme and can hear syllables at an early stage, but analyzing a word into all of its individual sounds comes later. Between these time periods children can often divide a word into beginning consonants and the vowel-bearing unit (b/all, st/ep). Good readers use not just the sounds connected to individual letters but phonological information from several levels of language. They can provide phonological information for letters, letter clusters, syllables, prefixes, suffixes, root words, and phrases. When they read they can analyze words letter by letter or in larger units such as letter clusters, which are often more efficient (Clay 1991a).

Some General Principles About Word Solving

There are more than half a million words in the English language. These words are made from twenty-six graphemes (letters) that represent between forty-four and fifty-three phonemes (sounds), depending on how words are pronounced. For example, the letter *a* has seven different sounds (as in *father*, *eat*, *plate*, *away*, *car*, *air*, and *fall*). The alphabetic system is very efficient because it allows us to generate so many words from just a few symbols. That capability also makes the system quite complex. Competent readers and spellers have some general understandings about this complex system. For example:

❙ They have a systematic understanding of how words work rather than just a collection of known words.

❙ They don't simply memorize lists of words but learn how to think about words.

❙ They use phonics but go beyond letter-sound relationships to attend to how words look and how they communicate meaning.

Our goal as teachers is to enable children to become competent word solvers—to be able to:

❙ Take words apart while reading to understand.
❙ Put words together (spell) while writing to communicate.

The chart in Figure 8-1 describes what word solvers know and can do in reading and writing. The inventory of knowledge listed here includes beginning understandings such as letter recognition as well as the complex ways that words solvers operate on words.

Ways of Solving Words

There are several broad strategies that readers and writers use as they learn about how words work in the written language system. It is helpful here to use a simple rubric—*how words sound, how they look, how they mean, how they connect,* and *how more can be learned about them*—as we consider this knowledge span. That is, readers and writers use:

❙ *Phonemic strategies:* how words *sound* and the relationships between letters and letter clusters and phonemes within words (*cat, make*).

❙ *Visual strategies:* how words *look*, including the clusters and patterns of the letters in words (*bear, light*).

❙ *Morphemic strategies:* how words represent *meaning* through the combination of significant parts or morphemes (*happy, happiest; run, runner, running*).

❙ *Connecting strategies:* similar words can be used to solve unfamiliar words through *analogy* (knowing *she* and *out* helps with *shout*).

❙ *Inquiry strategies:* using materials as references and resources (dictionaries, thesauruses, etc.) to *learn more* about words.

Relying on analogies between words enables readers and writers to make leaps in learning as they use phonemic, visual, and morphemic strategies to solve words. Goswami and Bryant (1990) found that once children have some words they can read and/or spell, they can think of words or parts of words they know that sound the same, look the same, or mean the same to take a word apart.

How Words Sound

Word solvers use letter-sound relationships.

Readers use their knowledge of the relationships between letters and sounds to take words apart while reading. Spellers use this same body of knowledge as a guide for constructing

Competent Word Solvers: What Do They Do?	
Solving Words in Reading	Solving Words in Writing
In reading, competent word solvers: • Discriminate letter symbols in print quickly. • Recognize whole words as units. • Use word parts. • Use letter-sound relationships in flexible ways. • Use knowledge of known words to get to unknown words. • Sound out words by individual letter or by letter clusters. • Use base words to analyze parts. • Analyze words left to right. • Check on their attempts by using letter-sound relationships and word parts. • Use partial print information in combination with meaning and language information. • Use the information about words in coordination with the meaning and language of the text. • Use references and resources to learn the meaning and exact pronunciation of new words for which they can approximate pronunciation. • Try new words. • Notice letter patterns.	*In writing, competent word solvers:* • Form letters easily and quickly. • Write the sounds they hear in words. • Write a large number of known whole words quickly and easily. • Listen for and use word parts to construct words. • Use letter-sound relationships in flexible ways to construct words. • Use knowledge of known words to write new words. • Write words letter by letter, checking on the letter-sound relationships. • Write words left to right. • Check on words they have written to be sure they look right and represent accurate letter-sound relationships. • Use partial information along with references and resources such as word lists and dictionaries. • Keep the composed message in mind while attending to the details of word construction. • Try new words. • Know that every word has at least one vowel. • Know that every syllable has at least one vowel. • Think about base words. • Have ways to remember some tricky words.

FIGURE 8-1   Competent Word Solvers: What Do They Do?

words as sequences of letters. This strategy is especially effective when solving words that are phonetically regular or almost regular.

It is useful to think about some of the features of letter-sound relationships. When young children first begin to represent sounds in writing words, they are likely to use consonants, which are more regular than vowels. Children can feel the production of consonants in the mouth; making the sounds stops the air flow. Say the following words and feel the lips stop the air flow to make consonant sounds:

foot
mom
jump
sweet

Vowels, on the other hand, tend to be "lost" in the mouth. For example, say:

owl
at
eel
island

It's harder to "feel" the production of the vowel sound. Moreover, vowels are greatly influenced by the letters surrounding them. For example, try:

fall
far
pain
day
at
along

caught
ache
ax
was

When readers decode words using a left-to-right sound analysis, they produce the sounds in the order of the letters related to them. This process is commonly called "sounding out" words, and it is frequently taught in reading instruction. There are limitations to teaching sounding out as the *only* strategy for solving words in reading because the "chunks" or meaningful parts of words and spelling patterns are also quite helpful to the proficient reader. In other words, proficient readers *can* work out a word letter by letter, but the process seldom happens this way while reading text. The proficient reader may say the first part or notice some aspect of the word and suddenly solve it using these larger "chunks." A totally unknown word may require more visual analysis than a known word. Further, it is rare for a reader to sound every letter before actually figuring out what the word is. In spelling, writers produce the sequence of letters that is prompted by the sounds (in sequence) in the word they are producing.

In English, there is not a one-to-one regular letter-sound correspondence for all words. So, while phonetic strategies work for about 50 percent of our words, the skillful word solver needs to use a wider range of strategies for words that do not have exact letter-sound correspondence.

How Words Look

Word solvers use visual strategies.

Word solvers go beyond the sound-letter strategies to use patterns of letters. In our language, there are permissible patterns or clusters of letters that represent sounds. For these patterns of letters, for example *ough*, individual letters and their related sounds are not evident. The entire cluster is connected to the sound as a whole. Some are

fairly simple and common patterns, such as the underlined parts in the following words:

rain
bell
game
snow

Other letter sequences are complex and rarely used. For example:

often
delicious
excuse

How Words Mean

Word solvers use the structure of words and their meaning to spell and/or pronounce a word.

This type of strategy could be called a "morphemic" strategy because the word solver is using knowledge of word parts—free morphemes (like *run*) as well as bound morphemes (like *ing*, *s*, and *ful*). (For a discussion of morphemes, see Chapter 6.) Here are some examples of words that can most efficiently be solved by knowing parts and what they mean:

removable
heard
can't
jumping
sunshine

How Words Connect

Word solvers use what they know about words to figure out new words.

Where possible, readers and writers use the largest chunks of information they can. They constantly search for connections between what they know about words and what they are trying to figure out. The use of analogy is the ability to manipulate and think about words. What is known in one area is used in another area. For example, a reader who is trying to figure out an unfamiliar word like *troll* while reading *The Three Billy Goats Gruff* might recognize that the first part of the word is like *try*, a known word, and that the last part ends like *tell*, another known word, but *troll* has an *o* in the middle. The reader might even know the word *roll* or use analogy to figure it out. Drawing upon all of this knowledge would enable the reader to analyze *troll* and read it accurately. One second grader, Nathan, substituted *droll* for *troll* the first time he encountered it in the text. When he saw it the second time, he first said *droll* and then corrected to *troll*. We cannot know exactly what was going on in his head, but we can hypothesize that he was looking at the last part of the word, as well as the *r*, during his first encounter but later noticed the *tr* cluster. It is very possible that known word parts helped him in this complex problem solving.

Analogies can lead readers astray if they think that the process is one of "looking for little words in bigger words." How would it help a reader, for example, to notice the *me* in *some*? The strategy is to use parts of words, usually drawn from what is well known, and to link them together in new ways. A more productive analysis of *some* is to think of a known word, such as *come*, and to use the last part (*ome*) and attach the *s*.

doesn't always work!

Sometimes it backfires when we impose adult logic on children. We can encourage them to try different strategies, and we can discuss and model efficient strategies so they have a repertoire, but we should always notice what they are noticing. Often children approach word solving in idiosyncratic ways that reveal their growing hypotheses. For example, if a beginning reader is trying to figure out the word *got*, there are several strategies that will work. The reader might predict the word from the structural context of the sentence. But, a reader using sound analysis might sound it letter by letter, or might think of the known word, *not*, and change the first letter. The reader might think of the known word *go*, which is part of *got*, and then work toward *got*. Even though *go* does not have the same vowel sound as *got*, it gets the reader closer to the word. We have observed evidence that children use all of these strategies in word solving. We should not narrow the approaches for children but constantly open up new ways of thinking. (See Figure 8-2.) Competent word solvers have a large repertoire that they draw from and use flexibly.

FIGURE 8-2   Magnetic Letters

Instead of using the smallest parts—the graphemes and their associated phonemes—word solvers frequently use larger parts: syllables or onsets and rimes. Goswami and Bryant (1990) found that the easiest sound pattern for children to hear is a whole word, then syllable parts, and then individual letters. They proposed that there might be an intermediate step, onset and rime, between hearing syllable breaks and hearing the individual letters. The larger parts are easier to hear, and these researchers suggested that many children figure out words by using the break between the first part of the word and the rest of the word, as in:

c-at
str-ing
str-eet
t-o d-ay

Wylie and Durrell (1970) identified thirty-seven of the most common phonograms in the English language. They are listed in Figure 8-3 with the phonograms or rimes underlined. It is obvious that many of these words can be sounded out letter by letter; others have visual patterns that children might recognize. All can be divided into onset and rime.

If you know the words *bring* and *joke*, then you can use the parts to write or read *broke*. To us, this research simply confirms that children are seekers of pattern (Moustafa 1997). The more they know about how the language works and the more they manipulate it in different ways, the more flexible and efficient they become as word solvers.

How Word Solvers Learn More About Words

Word solvers use proofreading skills, study methods, and reference materials to learn more about words and how they work.

Using reference materials such as dictionaries, word lists, personal dictionaries, thesauruses, glossaries, and computer spell checkers helps readers work in an independent way to expand their own knowledge of words. Some of the very first resources for primary children are the charts, labels, and word walls they see in their classrooms (see Chapter 5). Later, they will be taught how to use alphabetical order and to discover information in more sophisticated reference books such as dictionaries and thesauruses. These resources will increase their ability to

---

Thirty-Seven Most Common Phonograms

back	meat	nice	clock	duck
mail	bell	stick	joke	rug
rain	crest	wide	shop	jump
cake		light	store	junk
sale		ill	not	
game		win		
plan		line		
bank		bring		
trap		think		
crash		trip		
cat		fit		
plate				
saw				
stay				

FIGURE 8-3   Thirty-Seven Most Common Phonograms

attend to definitions, multiple meanings, root words, guide words, alternate spellings, pronunciation, syllabication, and etymology. They also learn how to locate an error and work at correcting it, and how to use a variety of processes for learning new words.

Making Learning Multidimensional

We have described five different ways of solving words. Of course, these are not discrete, separate paths to word solving. Good readers and writers combine approaches, moving swiftly from one to another as they notice productive information. Furthermore, there are probably several hundred more ways of solving words than we have described here. We have merely presented these categories in a way that helps us, as teachers, talk about the behaviors that we observe. We can never know precisely what is going on in the complex activities of the brain, but we can support productive behaviors if we know what to look for. It helps us as teachers to understand the linguistic system and the probable categories of information that young writers and readers are using. Our challenge is to offer support in varied, rich ways so that children become flexible readers and writers who have a broad repertoire of effective strategies to bring to the process.

Phonological and orthographic knowledge is key to becoming an effective word solver. As described in this chapter, using this knowledge is a complex process in itself; however, we also must understand that phonological and orthographic analyses are situated within a language context—meaning and language structure also play a part. We are indeed lucky that our language is so redundant, with many sources of information to draw on in deciphering the written word. In everyday terms, good word solvers just use everything in connection with everything else. And, as teachers, we are glad that they do so and we work to support them.

Suggestions for Professional Development

To examine the ways in which your students use phonological and orthographic information for word solving, observe them at work. To learn how children approach the solving of words using these two systems alone, you will need to work with words in isolation. As you observe your students, you will learn more about the way children use phonological and orthographic knowledge, but you will not see the complex process in action as children read a text. So, you will want to follow this assessment with an informal observation of reading and writing behavior.

Reading

1. Select several children in the middle or end of first grade and present a list of words for them to read. Use a list of high-frequency words or a graded word list available in your school. You might also use the Ohio Word Test (Clay 1993a).

Observe the way children read the list of words, and record their responses. The accurate responses and, more important, the attempts will provide useful information. Afterwards, ask the children, "How did you know how to read that word?" Record their responses and share them with colleagues. Discuss the following questions:

- ❚ How did children use what they already knew?
- ❚ What connections did they seem to be making?
- ❚ What evidence was there of using the strategies described in this chapter: *how words sound, how they look, how they mean, how they connect,* and *how more can be learned about them?*

Writing

2. Ask the same group of children to write the same list of words you had them read. Watch them as they try to spell the words. Note nonverbal and verbal behaviors. Note their accurate representations; note their

close attempts. Afterwards, for each word, ask them, "How did you know how to write that word?"

Then, with colleagues, discuss:

■ How did children use what they already knew?

■ What connections did they seem to be making?

■ What evidence did you see of the strategies described in this chapter: *how words sound, how they look, how they mean, how they connect,* and *how we can learn more about them?*

Word Study: Investigating Letters and Words

Some of the most difficult decisions in teaching entail finding the right balance in the instructional program. As teachers, we might ask ourselves: How much should I show children and teach them directly? How much should I let them discover for themselves? How can I be sure they are learning what they need?

When it comes to learning about letters, sounds, and words—crucial elements of literacy learning—the questions become especially pointed. We know that children learn about words through writing and reading. This learning is perhaps the most important and the most effective because as they read and write in the service of meaning, children are simultaneously learning *why* the information is helpful to them.

Powerful learning also occurs in the focused experiences for word study. A three-pronged program, with attention and good teaching for word-solving skills in reading, in writing, and in word study experiences ensures that children not only are exposed to the critical understandings and skills but have a chance to learn and use them in many contexts.

As we plan and implement effective word study, we are guided by two key considerations: (1) the components of the reading and writing processes, including foundational understandings related to letters and words; and (2) the skills and knowledge of the particular children we are teaching. In Chapter 9, we discuss in a general way what children need to know about letters and words—those important understandings that are necessary for fluent, competent reading and writing. As teachers we have found it helpful to keep in mind this "big picture" so that we can be systematic in planning instruction and create benchmarks against which to measure progress.

We must keep in mind the particular children we are teaching. Good word study is not about following a recommended sequence. It is about the children we work with—where they are and where they need to go next. In Chapters 10 and 11, "Assessing What Children Know" and "Word-Solving Strategies: Organize to Teach," we discuss ways that teachers can assess children's strengths as a basis for planning effective word study experiences. The remaining chapters in Section 3 present a variety of active, multi-level, practical approaches to word study, from early learning about print and sounds to the active inquiry involved in word exploration to a practical system for word study.

What Children Need to Know About Letters and Words

Effective word study takes place within the context of a classroom where language is in constant use. Children use writing and reading for a variety of purposes and they also wonder about aspects of words—why they are spelled the way they are, what they mean, how they are related to each other. The word investigations that children engage in are interesting and fun. Enjoyment, motivation, and interest are essential for effective word solving.

Keeping in mind students' interest in and enjoyment of word solving, we outline the essential elements of a word study curriculum (Figure 9-1). In the next section, each component is expressed as a body of knowledge and skill that contributes to a child becoming a highly effective literate person.

Goal 1: Children need to understand how to look at and use the features of print.

Looking at print involves visual perception of letters both by themselves and in combination with other letters to make words. The perceiver of print is required to use detailed information in order to differentiate one letter from another. As we described in our chapter on early learning (Chapter 7), children need to learn the distinctive features of a letter—what makes that letter different from every other letter. For example, differentiating m, n, u, and w requires noticing some fine details.

At the same time, we recognize that reading and writing are not about the simple recognition of individual letters. Readers and

---

Core Goals of a Word Study Curriculum

As readers and writers, children need:
- Knowledge of how to look at and use features of print.
- Knowledge of a large core of high-frequency words.
- An understanding of simple and complex letter-sound relationships.
- The ability to notice and use patterns in words (how words sound, look, and mean).
- The ability to use a repertoire of word-solving strategies.
- Skill in using references, resources, and proofreading.

FIGURE 9-1   Core Goals of a Word Study Curriculum

writers need to recognize and use letter information that is embedded in words, while words are embedded in sentences, and so on. Letters in clusters form patterns that competent readers and writers use as units. So, while we are helping children learn about letters, we are also thinking about how they can notice and use these clusters and patterns.

First, let's talk about the letters and what children need to know. There are fifty-two symbols in the alphabet (upper- and lowercase forms for each of the twenty-six letters). Children need to learn that:

❚ Letters have features such as sticks, curves, circles, tails, and tunnels.

❚ Orientation is an important feature of a letter. For example, it matters whether a letter is upside down or turned the wrong way because it could become a different letter.

❚ There is a specific way to form a letter using the hand and motor skills.

❚ A letter has a name.

❚ Each letter has two forms (upper- and lowercase).

❚ A letter is connected to a sound, and it may be connected to more than one sound in combination with other letters.

❚ When connected to other letters, a letter becomes a unit of sound like a word or a piece of a word.

❚ A word is made up of a series of letters clustered together with space on each side.

❚ A letter is a form on its own, but a word can have one letter or two or more letters.

❚ Letters are organized left to right when they make up a word. Letters in words are always organized the same way (words are constant).

Not only do children need to develop this knowledge, but they need to use this knowledge quickly and automatically while they are reading and writing. Fluent readers have a swift, automatic perception of the visual forms they are processing, so their atten-

tion is freed to focus on meaning. But for emergent readers, who are just beginning to see print as something different from the world around them, the process of learning involves looking at the details. Fluent writers form the letters (or strike keys) to make words and sentences without constant attention to the hand movements. They are thinking of the message and have an automatic program of action to produce the symbols. Efficient programs of action for forming letters are an essential part of literacy instruction for emergent writers.

Goal 2: Children need to develop a growing core of words that become part of a reading and writing vocabulary.

Many of these "core words" will be high-frequency words that occur often in oral language and thus occur often in reading and writing. These high-frequency words are useful because:

❚ Emergent readers use the limited set of words they know to "anchor" their reading—to help them monitor the way they are reading a text.

❚ As readers learn more, having many words that are quickly recognized helps to move the reading along so that problem solving is not necessary on each word; fluency is supported by a large number of easily recognized words.

❚ Being able to write a small group of high-frequency words quickly without conscious attention helps young writers produce longer and more meaningful messages; they keep the momentum going because they do not have to slow down to puzzle out every word.

When children know how to look at the features of the letters, it becomes easier for them to learn how to recognize a word. The first words children learn, besides their names, are very easy. For example, kindergarten children might develop a core of words like many of those in Figure 9-2.

why 25?

Twenty-Five Easy High-Frequency Words		
a	he	no
at	in	see
an	I	so
and	is	the
am	it	to
can	like	up
do	me	we
go	my	CHILD'S NAME

is this still the standard?

you?

FIGURE 9-2   Twenty-Five Easy High-Frequency Words

Our goal is that by the end of kindergarten children will know these twenty-five words along with a few specialized words they have encountered. Many children will know more words; some may know an equal number but have a slightly different repertoire. The precise collection of words does not have to be the same for every child. Kindergartners should learn what a word is and have some great examples on which they can draw for new learning. In addition, they will have many words of personal interest and know how to use those words and others to write messages and stories in a correct or partially correct way. Just as important, these words become resources that will help them write other words. In a literacy-rich kindergarten, it is typical for children at the end of the year to be able to write twenty to thirty or more words. In the process, they are learning "how to learn" words, a system that will support additional learning. ✓

Every time children learn a word they may be learning more about the process. Sometimes children simply want to write a word for a particular purpose (like *banana* or *Power Rangers*), and that will be part of the learning as they produce their own stories and messages. While it is not necessary for all children to learn every one of the listed words, they should acquire a consistent core of high-frequency words. Our word list is "high utility" because the listed words are useful to children in multiple ways. To summarize:

▮ Children learn the words that they need to produce their own messages. Some are high-frequency words; others hold personal interest for a particular child.

▮ Systematic instruction is needed to help every child learn a core of high-frequency, high-utility words. *(occuring + used often)*

By the end of first grade, children should be able to write fifty to one hundred words quickly and accurately and to use their knowledge of spelling patterns to produce many more words, which may be correct or nearly correct. Teachers may want to consider the list shown in Figure 9-3 as they assess their first graders' knowledge of spelling.

→2-4× more words than in K.

The list in Figure 9-4 contains one hundred high-frequency words. Teachers have found this list useful as a chart to check children's word knowledge. Those words that children still cannot read and write should be acquired in second grade.

Most of the words in the list are not nouns. They are, in fact, the kinds of words that appear in many different sentences and texts, regardless of the content. In addition to these words, children will learn many "content" words that are related to the topics that they read and write about. For example, they may use family names, animal words like *cat* and *dog*, or names of places such as *zoo* or *school* in their writing. Additionally, you will find children adding endings (like *s*). They will use parts of words to

Fifty High-Frequency Words for Grade One

a	him	that
all	his	the
and	I	their
are	if	then
an	in	there
at	is	they
be	it	this
but	me	to
came	my	up
for	of	was
from	on	we
go	one	went
got	out	were
had	said	with
have	saw	you
he	she	your
her	so	

FIGURE 9-3   Fifty High-Frequency Words for Grade One

write other words (like *get* or *pet*). This list does not by any means represent a first grader's full repertoire, but is simply a powerful resource for further learning.

In second grade, you will help children expand the core of words to include more and more difficult high-frequency words. This learning will continue throughout the grades. In Appendix 5, we provide a list of five hundred words that you can use as a resource for selecting appropriate high-frequency words at every grade level. Words that children use frequently and need to learn how to spell will be a focus of spelling instruction.

It is important to note that the lists of words that a child can write and read will not be precisely the same. Early on, children can read and write many of the same words; how-

ever, as children become more proficient, the reading vocabulary will grow much faster than the writing vocabulary. Still, wide reading exposes children to how words look, making it easier for them to learn to spell. The two areas, reading and writing, are complementary. Children who read a great deal learn more about how words look in print.

Goal 3: Children need to develop knowledge of sound-letter relationships.

Our language is communicated through sounds (or phonemes) that we make with our mouth, tongue, and teeth and that communicate meaning to our listening audience (see Section 2). Phonemic aware-

One Hundred High-Frequency Words for Grade One

a	house	see
about	how	she
after	I	so
all	if	some
an	in	than
and	into	that
are	is	the
as	it	their
at	its	them
be	just	then
because	like	there
been	little	these
but	look	they
by	make	this
came	man	to
come	many	two
could	may	up
day	me	us
did	mom	very
do	my	was
down	no	we
for	not	went
from	now	were
get	of	what
go	off	when
going	on	which
got	one	who
had	other	will
has	our	with
have	out	would
he	over	you
her	put	your
him	said	
his	saw	

FIGURE 9-4   One Hundred High-Frequency Words for Grade One

ness means that a child must become sensitive to the sounds of the language, to the sounds within words, and to the feel of words in the mouth when they are spoken. In other words:

❙ Children need to know that words are made up of sequences of sounds.

❙ They need to be able to tell when a word sounds like another word in some way (starts the same, ends the same, or rhymes).

❙ They need to hear the unique sounds that are blended when we say a word.

❙ They need to say and hear the sounds in words.

❙ Children need to hear individual sounds, syllables, onsets and rimes, word parts, and whole word units.

When children can hear sounds, they can then connect them to the graphic symbols we call letters. That process is called phonics. When we investigate written language and literacy development, we discover the sometimes simple and sometimes complex relationships between the letters and sounds as they make up words. When children can say words slowly and record the corresponding sounds, they can produce most of the words that have regular correspondence (such as *got* or *can*). They can also produce many other words as approximated spellings that come increasingly close to conventional spelling and demonstrate their growing knowledge of letter-sound correspondence. For example, Figure 9-5 is a writing sample that Emma, a kindergarten student, produced in early spring. In conventional spelling, her message would read, "Doctor Payzant spoke in the microphone. I got my

picture taken with Daddy and Doctor Payzant."

Emma spelled the words *I*, *got*, *the*, *with*, *in*, and *my* accurately. Her attempts at other words show her grasp of the relationships between letters and sounds (for example, MIKROFON for *microphone*). She represents all of the sounds in *doctor*, *microphone*, *picture*, *taken*, *Daddy*, *spoke*, *doctor*, and *Payzant*. Moreover, these sounds are in the correct sequence. It is easy to see that Emma is moving forward in her writing ability. As she moves into first grade, her repertoire of words that she does not have to work out using letters and sounds will multiply. Also,

FIGURE 9-5 Emma's Writing Sample, Early Spring

she will begin to create categories of words that let her use larger patterns of regular letter-sound correspondence. Writing is an instructional context within which children can learn a great deal about letters and their related sounds. We see here the evidence of Emma's growing knowledge base.

We also see evidence of letter-sound knowledge in children's early reading behavior, but there are qualitative differences in what is required in writing and reading. Through writing, children learn to analyze all of the sounds in a word in sequence and record them to represent the word as fully as possible. At first, in early reading, children can use partial information in a checking and monitoring process. They generally use letter-sound information in coordination with other sources of information. For example, a child who reads *mom* for *mother* in one of the first reading books may be using some letter-sound information, notably the first letter of the word, in connection with picture information. Let's look at another example. The text says "I see a rabbit," but Jonathan reads, "I see a bunny." Then he stops, looks at the word, says "bunny," and returns to the beginning of the line, this time reading it accurately. In this way, he uses letter-sound information to cross-check.

We could infer that Jonathan predicted *bunny* but then noticed a mismatch based on his beginning knowledge of letters and sounds, and was able to choose another word that fit. Granted, the choice was limited and easy, but it enabled him to use what he knew. Moreover, he was performing in this way without having full and complete knowledge of all the letters of the alphabet and their related sounds. While still acquiring the essential body of knowledge about letters and words, he was behaving like a reader and, in the process, learning more. He was using visual and sound information in pursuit of meaning. Children do not need to learn all the symbols in the writing system *before* they can proceed to reading stories. Once they have learned a few letters they

usually have a procedure for learning letters, and they can learn the remainder *while* writing and reading (Clay 1991a, 263). Note that letter learning is still necessary—letter learning, reading, and writing proceed all together. Early reading and early writing help children use and extend their knowledge of letters and sounds.

> **Goal 4: Children need to develop an understanding of word patterns— how different letters and groups of letters represent sound and meaning in the orthographic system.**

In this section we outline the kinds of patterns that will be useful for children to learn and use in spelling and reading. We provide some basic examples here; extensive lists are found in Appendixes 4 through 33.

Understandings About Consonants

As discussed in Chapter 6, consonants are easiest for children to learn because they are more regular in letter-sound correspondence and because of the way they are made in the mouth. The consonants consist of all the letters except for the vowels. Consonants can come in different places in a word. Initial and final consonants are easier for early learning. A sampling of words that begin and end with each consonant can be found in Appendix 6.

Often consonants are found in clusters, especially at the beginning and ending of words. A consonant cluster is two or three letters (each with its own sound) that are blended together. Some examples include *store*, *crystal*, and *rest*. Of course, very few of these clusters appear frequently in all positions.

Often the consonants are grouped in cluster families, as shown in Figure 9-6.

If we look at the words with consonant clusters, we could have quite a discussion of the ways clusters are used. Here are some important understandings about consonant clusters:

Groups of Consonant Clusters

s clusters: *st, sp, sn, sm, sl, sc, sk, sw* and *spl, str, spr, scr, squ*

l clusters: *bl, cl, fl, gl, pl*

r clusters: *br, cr, dr, fr, gr, pr, tr*

FIGURE 9-6 Groups of Consonant Clusters

▌ Like single consonants, a *consonant cluster* can be the onset of a word, like *spr* in *spring*.

▌ Referred to as *consonant digraphs*, sometimes two consonant letters represent one sound that is different from either of the sounds alone. Examples are: *cheese*, *where*, *shoe*, *this*. The sounds related to these four consonant clusters are unique.

▌ There are two common sounds for *th* (*thought* and *this*); there will always be exceptions for pronunciation of words with all consonant clusters (for example, *charisma*).

▌ The sound of *f* can also be represented by two other consonant clusters, *ph* (*phone*, *photograph*) and *gh* (*cough*, *laugh*).

▌ Sometimes consonants are doubled, as in *little*, *runner*, *summer*, *puffin*, *dress*, *bell*.

▌ The sound of *k* can be represented by a *c* or a *k*, as in *car* or *key*.

▌ Sometimes clusters of consonants may be referred to as *final digraphs* (a letter cluster at the end of a word), such as *ck*, *nk*, and *ng*. (See the list in Appendix 10.)

▌ *C* and *g* make two sounds, as in *car*, *face* or *giraffe*, *get*.

▌ Sometimes consonants are silent, as in *knowledge* or *wrap*. (See the list in Appendix 17.)

▌ *Qu* sounds like *kw*, as in *quiet*.

Understandings About Vowels

Vowel sounds in words are represented by the letters *a, e, i, o, u, and sometimes y*. Also, clusters of vowels and consonants in larger spelling patterns may represent vowel sounds, such as the *ow* in *cow*, or the *igh* in *light*, or the *ea* in *meat*. Every syllable in a word has a vowel sound. Often, these vowels are referred to as *short* or *long*. The sounds really have less to do with length and more to do with articulation in the mouth. What children really need to learn is the sound patterns that these vowels represent when they are combined with different letters.

Several different spellings may be associated with each vowel sound. For example, the *o* sound can be represented in the following ways: *caught*, *hot*, *yacht*, *saw*, *thought*. Vowels are particularly sensitive to different pronunciations in different geographical regions. A complete list of vowels in different combinations is provided in Appendix 15: Phonograms.

Vowel combinations are often referred to as *vowel dipthongs* or *vowel teams*. Children can learn how to look for these patterns through a variety of word study activities; they can also notice them as they use the word study system (see Chapter 14) and as they engage in writing.

Vowel Combinations

Often, vowels appear with an *r*, such as in *corn*, *car*, *her*, *first*, *burn*. In these examples, it is easy to see that when the vowel is combined with an *r*, the sound is different from other sounds associated with the vowel. Sometimes people refer to an "r controlled" vowel when explaining this difficult letter combination (see Appendix 13: Words with Vowels and "r").

There are many vowel patterns such as

oo in *look* or *moon*; *ow* in *snow* and *cow*; *ei* in *eight* or *ceiling*; *ea* in *bread* or *meat*; *ee* in *feel*; *oa* in *boat*; *ay* in *day*; *ie* in *pie* and *receive*. These vowel patterns are very complex, and the sounds they make in words are related to the other letters they are with. Writers and readers need many experiences working with words so that they are not only thinking about letter-sound relationships but also noticing how words look. They can then build up an internal knowledge of the clusters of vowels that are related to sounds.

One useful rule is related to the "silent *e*," which is another example of how vowels change in sound correspondence depending on the letters they are with. Consider these structures: *făt*, *fate*; *cut*, *cute*; *pet*, *Pete*; *kit*, *kite*; *hop*, *hope*. You will find many of these kinds of words on our phonogram list. The rule here is obvious to the sophisticated language user: when there is a silent *e*, the vowel says its own name. That silent *e*, in fact, changes the sound of the vowel. Lists of words with various vowels and vowel combinations are provided in Appendixes 12, 13, and 15.

Phonograms

Vowels may be combined with each other to form the vowel sound of a word (*bread*). Vowels can be combined with consonants to make a unit of sound that is part of a word and called a *phonogram*; for example, *ake*, *at*, *am*, *it*, *in*, *ade*. A phonogram is not always a complete syllable; it will usually need an initial consonant or consonant cluster to make it a syllable or word. Sometimes phonograms are called rimes or word families (see Chapter 6). The rime is the rest of the word following the initial consonant sound.

Phonograms and rimes have been used in literacy instruction for several hundred years and are still considered useful. Some phonograms are more useful than others. There is some variation in opinion, but a limited set of thirty-seven phonograms are considered the most common in English (see Wylie and Durrell 1970, and the list pre-

sented in Chapter 8). Phonograms also appear in many multisyllable words.

In Appendix 15, we provide a comprehensive list of phonograms; the thirty-seven most common are marked with an asterisk. We suggest focusing on the "high utility" phonograms, the ones that are associated with the most words. When children want to write a word, for example, they can think of a word that "sounds like that." We do not recommend teaching long lists of word families. A single example or two will lead children to construct many other words. (We do recommend these phonograms for interactive word charts as described in Chapter 5.) It is useful to teach vowel combinations as parts of words rather than in isolation.

Open and Closed Syllables

An open syllable is one that ends in a vowel. In syllables that are open, such as the first one in *ho-tel*, the vowel sound is usually long. The vowel is usually short when it is surrounded by consonants (as in *mat-ter*). Children need to work with many different kinds of syllables. These sophisticated understandings are built slowly over several years of experience and are eventually useful to children in breaking up long, multisyllable words. We provide a list of multisyllable words in Appendix 16.

Understandings About the Structure of Words

The structure of words and their construction relates to what writers and readers understand about meaning. In this section we explore different kinds of words that function in our language in different ways. They reflect the way words are "put together" to create meaningful structures through which we communicate.

Sometimes structures are added to base words; sometimes words are shortened or changed in some way; sometimes words are grouped for comparison because they have to do with the reader/writer's ability to understand or communicate meaning. These word structures are not simply different patterns to memorize. They are connected to meaning. Here we present some of the useful word categories for building children's understanding of how to read and write words. A few examples are provided for each. Comprehensive lists for each category are included in Appendixes 18 through 33.

Contractions

Children use many contractions in oral language and in reading and writing. They need to understand underlying principles for contractions as well as the visual pattern. A contraction is one word made from two longer words. Some letters are omitted and replaced with an apostrophe. Examples are:

> *I am = I'm*
> *do not = don't*
> *cannot = can't*
> *I will = I'll*
> *we would = we'd*
> *it is = it's*
> *will not = won't*

We provide an extensive list of contractions in Appendix 18.

Compound Words

Compound words are two whole words that are combined to make a new word. These compound words may be simple (*into*) or more complex (*everywhere*). Compound words may be derived from the meaning of the words combined (*blackbird*) or change the meaning completely (*brainstorm*). Some examples of compound words are:

1st grade

snow + bound = snowbound
air + plane = airplane
some + time = sometime
after + noon = afternoon

You'll find an extensive list of compound words in Appendix 19.

Affixes

In our oral language every day we make additions to base words that add meaning. We add clusters to the beginning of words (called *prefixes*) and to the ends of words (called *suffixes*). Sometimes these additions change the type of word (for example, from noun to verb), and sometimes they do not.

Prefixes are letter groups added before a base word or root. Prefixes generally add to or change the meaning of the word. Understanding the meaning of a prefix is a great advantage to students when they encounter them in reading or want to use them in writing. In fact, combining root words with a large variety of prefixes will enable them to effectively understand many words. Some examples of prefix use are shown in Figure 9-7, and a more extensive list is in Appendix 21.

Suffixes are letter groups added to base words at the end. Frequently, they are associated with change of tense or meaning. There are some frequently used word endings that are very useful for children to learn about during the first years of school, as shown in Figure 9-8.

There are several principles or rules for adding endings to words, but only a few are

Prefixes		
Prefix	Meaning	Example
re-	again	rewrite replay
un-	not	unhappy undesirable
bi-	two	bicycle bicentennial

FIGURE 9-7 Prefixes

Suffixes		
Ending	**Examples of Words with Endings**	
- s	like, likes	walk, walks
- er	run, runner	happy, happier
- est	calm, calmest	long, longest
- ed	play, played	want, wanted
- ing	come, coming	sit, sitting
- less	care, careless	hope, hopeless
- ly	week, weekly	careful, carefully

FIGURE 9-8   Suffixes

useful to children learning to read and write. There are listed below.

1. *Most words.* Simply add the ending to most root words. For example, *walk* becomes *walks, walked, walking.*

2. *Words ending in e.* When a word ends in silent *e,* drop the *e* when adding an ending that begins with a vowel. For example, *hope* becomes *hoping, hoped.*

3. *Words ending in y.* Change the *y* to *i* when adding an ending unless the ending is *ing.* For example, *carry* becomes *carried* or *carrying.* **carries**

4. *Words ending in a single vowel and a consonant.* Double the final consonant before adding an ending that begins with a vowel. For example, *stop* becomes *stopping, stopped.*

Synonyms and Antonyms

Synonyms are words that have the same or almost the same meaning: *gift* and *present; bother* and *annoy; fix* and *repair; look* and *see.* Antonyms are words that have opposite or nearly opposite meanings: *old* and *young; tall* and *short; hard* and *soft; fat* and *thin; never* and *always; new* and *old.* We provide sample lists in Appendixes 23 and 24.

Homonyms

Homonyms are words that sound the same but have different meanings (*reed, read*). There are two types of homonyms: homographs and homophones.

Homographs are words that are spelled the same but differ in meaning and origin. For example, *bat, bat; ball, ball; fly, fly. Present* and *present* are examples of words that are spelled the same but have different meanings and are pronounced differently. When homographs are spelled the same but pronounced differently, they are called *heteronyms.*

Homophone means "same sound." These are words that sound the same but look different and have different meanings: *here, hear; break, brake; buy, by, bye.*

You'll find lists of homographs and homophones in Appendixes 25 and 26.

Plurals

A plural is a form of a word that means more than one. Plurals are always nouns, and they signal a change in the verb form that follows. The structure of a plural usually includes a base word and a plural ending. Sometimes the spelling changes the spelling of a base word. Figure 9-9 includes some generalizations that will help children understand the formation of plurals. We have provided a summary list of plurals formed in different ways in Appendix 27.

Possessives

The possessive form of a noun indicates ownership of something. Forming possessives usually means adding a morpheme to a noun form. Two ways to form possessives are:

■ Add an apostrophe and an *s* to a noun form.

Forming Plurals

Add s.
Add s to most words to form the plural (*car, cars*). Also add s to words ending in the vowel *y* (*monkey, monkeys*).

Add es.
Add *es* to words that end with s, ss, sh, ch, x (*box, boxes*).

Change f to v.
Change f or *fe* to v and add *es* to words ending in f or *fe*.

Change y to i.
Change y to i and add *e* to words ending in y preceded by a consonant.

Change spelling.
Some words change their spelling to form the plural (*mouse, mice*).

Spelling stays the same.
Some words are spelled the same in both the singular and plural forms (*sheep, sheep*).

FIGURE 9-9   Forming Plurals

❚ If the word ends in *s*, simply add an apostrophe.

Clipped Words

"Shortcut" words or "clipped" words (Sittonn 1995) exist in the language as people shorten forms for greater efficiency. It will be interesting to children to look at the long and short forms of many commonly used words, such as:

> auto for *automobile*
> bike for *bicycle*
> burger for *hamburger*
> champ for *champion*

Abbreviations

Many words in the language are formally abbreviated. Often, these abbreviations are so common that children do not realize the full form. They provide interesting content for word study. For example:

> Mr. for *mister* or *master*
> Dr. for *doctor*
> St. for *street*
> Ave. for *Avenue*
> Rd. for *road*

Mrs.?
Ms. = Miss
Abs. = absent
Ln = Lane

Syllabication

A syllable is a word part that includes a vowel sound. When we pronounce a word, some syllables are stressed and some are unstressed. A large number of words have more than one syllable, and some have many.

Awareness of syllables helps children realize there are parts of words, take words apart while reading, pronounce words in reading, construct words in spelling by thinking of the different parts in sequence, and use hyphenation. Some useful understandings about syllables are listed in Figure 9-10.

Greek and Latin Word Roots

Many words in the English language are derived from Greek and Latin. These roots, which have meaning, help readers greatly in understanding new words. For example, the root *aqua* means *water* in Latin. We have a group of words that utilize that root: *aquarium, aquanaut, aquatics,* and *aqua* (a color). All of these words have something to do with water. The root *port* means *to carry*. Here are some variations: *portable, transport, porter, export, import, portfolio.* When children learn

---

Understandings About Syllables

- Words have parts that you can hear.
- Some words have just one part and others have more than one part.
- You can clap and count the parts of words.
- Every syllable has a vowel sound.
- Usually, endings and prefixes are syllables in themselves.
- When you add a prefix, the spelling of the root word doesn't change (*reread*).
- When a word has two consonants in the middle, divide the syllables between the consonants (*bet-ter*).
- Syllables ending with a vowel have long vowel sounds (*ho-tel*).
- Syllables ending with a consonant have short vowel sounds (*mat-tress*).
- When a word ends with *le*, the consonant preceding it joins the cluster to make a syllable (*trou-ble*).
- Letter clusters such as *th, ch, wh, sh, ck, nk*, and *ng* usually stay together in a syllable.
- Affixes and endings are syllables that have meaning.

FIGURE 9-10 Understandings About Syllables

---

about word roots or word origins, they gain important strategies for vocabulary development. We provide a sampling of Greek and Latin word roots in Appendixes 31 and 32.

Words for Fun and Curiosity

There are many groupings or combinations of rhymes and syllables in words that build understanding of how words work. Some categories follow:

■ *Hink pinks.* The phonogram list (see Appendix 15), since it is a list of rhyming words, will be a useful resource in creating hink pinks, which we described in Chapter 5.

■ *Words that sound like they look.* Onomatopoeia is an aspect of poetry because the words are "borrowed" from the sounds in the environment. Some examples are *screech, chirp, buzz, whiz, roar, whoosh* (see Appendix 30).

■ *Words from names.* Our language is full of words that have their historical roots in the name of a place or of a person who had some kind of significant influence. Examples include *teddy bear* from Theodore Roosevelt; *sandwich* from the Earl of Sandwich; *cologne* from Cologne, Germany; *pasteurize* from Louis Pasteur. *HUH?*

■ *Portmanteau words.* The words combine parts of two other words, such as *squiggle* from *squirm* and *wriggle* (see Appendix 33).

To summarize the categories of letter-sound relationships, using patterns, and meaning categories, a list follows in Figure 9-11.

Spelling Rules and Principles

There are many spelling rules, but only a few are truly useful. Invite children to look at words and derive a principle or rule; don't ask them to memorize a rule that has little meaning. Seven useful spelling generalizations that apply most of the time are shown in Figure 9-12.

Lots of tools for their toolbox.

Goal 5: Children need to develop the ability to use a repertoire of word-solving strategies. TRUE.

Children need to develop useful ways of thinking about words so that they will know how to approach them. Remember, word solving is about learning how to connect words in ways that generate more word knowledge. Word learning will be useless unless children can use the information while writing and reading (See Chapter 13).

Understandings About Words

1. High-Frequency Words
2. Letter-Sound Relationships and Patterns
   - Consonants
     Consonant Clusters
     Consonant Digraphs
     Alternative Sounds
   - Vowels
     Long and Short
     Vowel Combinations
     Two Sounds of oo
     Vowels with r
     Silent e
   - Phonograms
   - Open and Closed Syllables
3. Word Structure, Word Meaning, and Other Categories
   - Contractions
   - Compound Words
   - Affixes
     Inflectional Endings
     Prefixes
     Suffixes
   - Synonyms
   - Antonyms
   - Homonyms
   - Plurals
   - Possessives
   - Clipped Words
   - Abbreviations
   - Syllabication
   - Greek and Latin Word Roots
   - Other
     Hink Pinks
     Words from Sound
     Words from Names
     Portmanteau Words

FIGURE 9-11   Understandings About Words

Goal 6: Children need to develop skill in using references, resources, and proofreading.

Children need to develop a "habit of mind" for knowing *when to check* and *how to check* on themselves in reading and writing. First, they need to know how to locate errors they make; then they need to have the skills to work toward a solution. These actions must be increasingly independent. Depending on the teacher to identify misspelled words in writing or correct one's oral reading is highly inefficient and will not result in competence in reading and writing. At first, of course, the teacher is the young child's best resource, but even from the beginning we should encourage self-monitoring or self-checking. The critical proofreading skills are:

∎ Locating errors or noticing when words don't look right.

∎ Using knowledge of how words sound, look, and mean to correct errors.

∎ Using references and resources to correct errors.

Useful Spelling Rules
Qu Rule Always put a *u* after *q*.
Syllable Rule Every syllable has a vowel or *y* (*hot, mitten, sky*).
Two Sounds of *c, g* Soft *c* or *g* is usually followed by *i, y,* or *e* (*city, cygnet, cent; magic, gym, gem*).
***Ei* or *ie* Rule** Write *i* before *e* except after *c* or when sounds like *a* as in *neighbor* or *weigh* (*piece, eight*).
Silent *e* Rule When a word ends in silent *e*, drop the *e* when adding an ending that begins with a vowel (*like, liking*).
Adding Endings to Words that End in *y* Change the *y* to *i* when adding an ending to a word that ends with consonant *y* (unless the suffix is *ing*) (*party, parties; party, partying*).
Adding Endings Double the final consonant of a word that ends with a single vowel and consonant before adding a suffix that begins with a vowel (*stop, stopping*).

FIGURE 9-12   Useful Spelling Rules

■ Knowing when and how to ask for help from an "expert" if word solving is not effective.

After noticing mismatches and errors, readers need the kinds of skills and resources they can use to solve their problems. On a highly sophisticated level, this would mean using a dictionary to spell or pronounce words, using a thesaurus to find different meanings for words in order to improve a text, or using a computer's spell check program. In Chapter 5 we described interactive word walls and word charts, which serve as some of the first easy references and resources that children can use. The purpose of these charts and walls is to develop children's skills in using references and resources. If children are to become independent, they need to know:

■ Letter names and alphabetical order.
■ How to categorize words in groups so that they can apply word-solving principles.
■ How to look words up in personal dictionaries, on word walls, and in beginning dictionaries.

More sophisticated dictionary skills include:

■ How to use guide words in dictionaries to quickly find the words on the page.
■ How to read the different kinds of information in an entry.
■ How to use the pronunciation guides in the dictionaries.
■ How to read a list of definitions and select the one that fits best.
■ How to use synonyms and antonyms as given in dictionary definitions.
■ How to read the symbols indicating parts of speech.
■ How to use the accent marks to pronounce words.
■ How to recognize where to divide syllables.

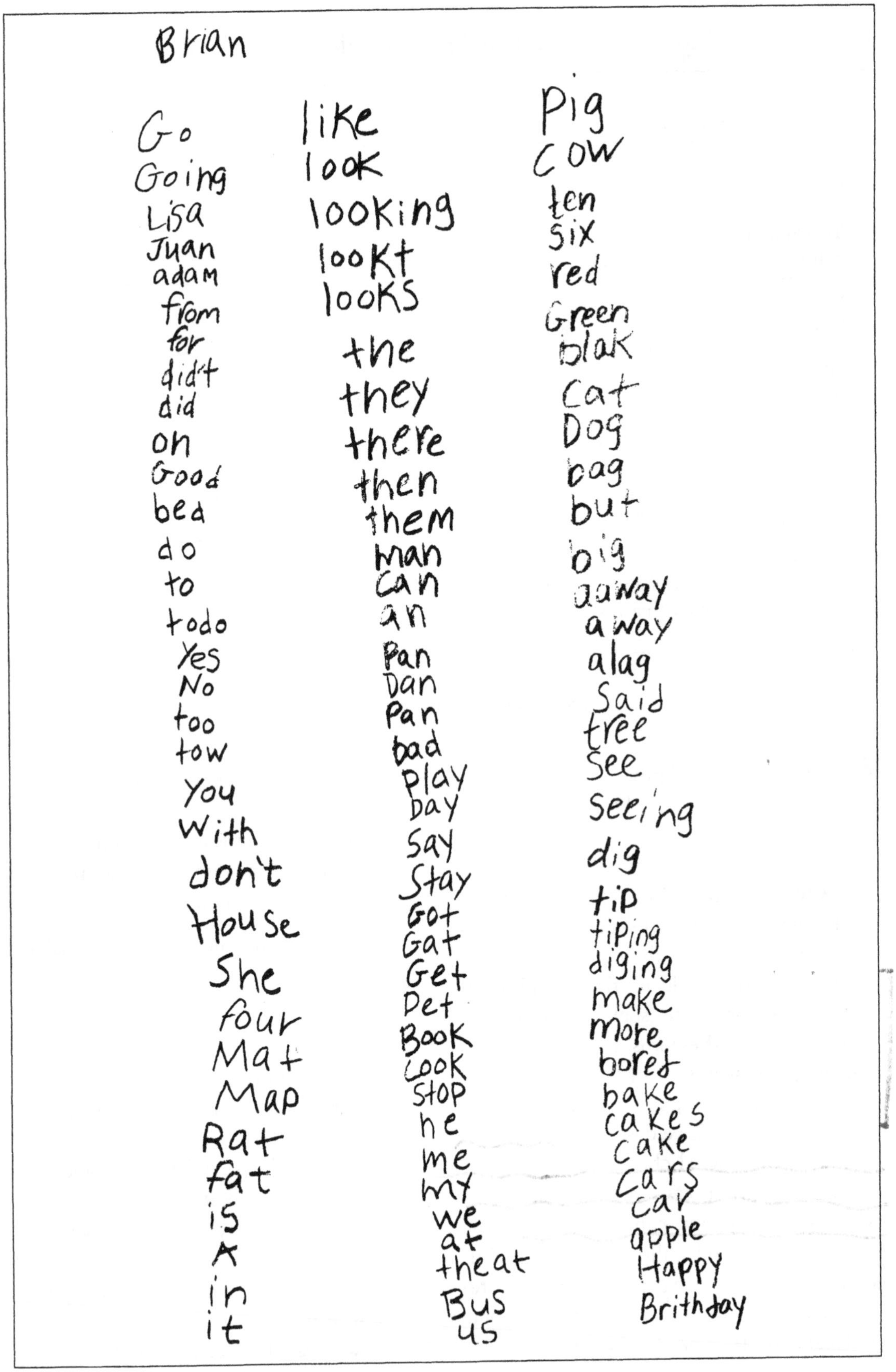

Brian

Go	like	Pig
Going	look	Cow
Lisa	looking	ten
Juan	lookt	Six
adam	looks	red
from		Green
for	the	blak
did't	they	Cat
did	there	Dog
on	then	bag
Good	them	but
bed	man	big
do	Can	away
to	an	a way
todo	Pan	alag
Yes	Dan	Said
No	Pan	tree
too	bad	See
tow	Play	seeing
You	Day	dig
With	Say	tip
don't	Stay	tiping
House	Got	diging
She	Gat	make
four	Get	more
Mat	Det	bored
Map	Book	bake
Rat	Look	cakes
fat	Stop	cake
is	he	Cars
A	me	Car
in	my	apple
it	we	Happy
	at	Brithday
	theat	
	Bus	
	4S	

FIGURE 9-13   Brian's Writing Sample

Moving from Content to Instruction

In this chapter we have outlined the complex body of knowledge that readers and writers acquire and use in their work. In word study, it is more important for children to be able to categorize words and to come up with their own examples than it is for them to memorize and be able to repeat a set of rules. Words have meaning, structure, and features that distinguish them. "Knowing" a word has many dimensions. Our goal is to help children build that deep, flexible knowledge of the linguistic system.

Suggestions for Professional Development

1. After reading this chapter, talk with colleagues at four grade levels—kindergarten, first, second, and third. Consider:

- ❚ What understandings do the children in your class or school generally develop by the end of the year?
- ❚ What are your predictions about their understandings given an expanded program of word study that invites children to play with words and enjoy extensive experiences in reading and writing beginning in kindergarten?

Set some goals for expectations by the following year.

2. Review some of the concepts listed in this chapter. Consider the following:

- ❚ Are there any principles or categories that are relatively new to you or that you had not thought about for some time?
- ❚ Try thinking of some of your own examples for each category. This activity will help you in planning minilessons for your students.
- ❚ Think about how readers and writers would use these understandings.

3. Analyze the writing vocabulary assessment (Clay 1993a) for Brian (Figure 9-13).

- ❚ Analyze Brian's writing, considering each principle of learning listed in this chapter—high-frequency words, letters and sounds, word structures, and categories of meaning.
- ❚ What is Brian showing that he knows?
- ❚ What does he almost know?
- ❚ What does he need to know next?

Assessing What Children Know

In Chapter 8, we described what competent word solvers do in reading and writing. Our students in elementary classrooms are at various levels of expertise on their way to achieving effective literacy. Their levels of understanding are the result of previous experiences and opportunities. Each child is working to understand and use a common language and a common set of understandings about words, but each will have a unique knowledge base and a unique journey toward that goal. As teachers, we are working with groups, and we need to know where most members of the group are so that we can plan and manage instruction. At the same time, we must keep in mind that children are learning as individuals, and we will need records of the particular understandings that those individuals have developed.

How do we understand what children know about letters and words? We observe children in both formal and informal contexts. Much of the observation is embedded within instructional classroom activities, a process that helps teachers who have limited time for assessing the knowledge of individuals. Even though the observation is embedded, it is still systematic. Teachers need to have a classroom assessment plan that includes the systematic collection of data on what children know about letters, sounds, and words. The assessment plan leads directly to instruction.

Key Areas for Assessment

As we consider assessment, our goal is to enable children to acquire fluent, phrased, accurate reading for meaning and conventional spelling as one aspect of effective written communication. The following are key areas for assessment.

Attitudes Toward Word Learning

▌ Do children engage actively in word solving?

▌ Do children demonstrate an appreciation for the importance of conventional spelling?

▌ Are they interested in words?

▌ Do they discover and communicate new learning in word study areas (for example, adding new words to ongoing word charts or finding the historical origins of a word)?

▌ Are they persistent in working on words when they encounter difficulty in reading or writing?

▌ Do they work at solving problems?

Vocabulary and Word Meanings

■ Is there evidence that their speaking vocabulary is growing?

■ Do they show interest in learning new words?

■ Do they show evidence of noticing new words and searching for their meaning?

■ Do they have strategies for figuring out the meaning of unfamiliar words when they meet them in oral language and reading?

■ Is there evidence that they are learning that words have a range of meanings, both alternative definitions and the fine shades of meaning that are related to context?

■ Do they have a growing body of words that they know how to write? To read?

■ Do they try to use more interesting words as they write even if they are unsure of the spelling or precise meaning?

■ Do they have a growing body of words that they use in context with appropriate meaning? (use correctly)

Core Knowledge of Letters, Sounds, Words, and Word Patterns

■ Do they know the names of the letters?

■ Do they have control of a body of high-frequency words in reading and writing?

■ Do they know basic relations among sounds and letters or letter clusters?

■ Do they know a large number of spelling patterns?

■ Are they able to analyze the sequence of sounds in a word?

■ Do they understand the way groups of letters are formed to make patterns and communicate meaning?

■ Do they understand that the way words are spelled communicates meaning?

Ability to Use Effective Strategies for Word Solving

■ Can they use information about letters, sounds, and words to notice an error and work at correcting it?

■ Can they use information about letter-sound relationships to solve words in reading and writing?

■ Can they use letter patterns and letter cluster patterns in word solving?

■ Can they use what they know about words to figure out new words? build

■ Can they apply useful principles and rules in word solving?

■ Can they use information from letters and words as part of a smooth, fluent process of reading for meaning?

Study Strategies

■ Can they use a range of study methods that are effective in learning spelling (for example, "Look, Say, Cover, Write, Check" or "Have a Try" [see Chapter 14])?

■ Do they demonstrate expertise in using classroom charts and references?

■ Can they use proofreading skills in order to produce conventionally spelled written products?

■ Can they assess their own knowledge and identify areas of need?

It is even more important to assess how children work on words to solve them during reading and writing for many purposes. By gathering information about strategies, we can assess children's progress toward effective, efficient systems for solving words in reading and writing. This information also helps us make the instructional decisions that will support the children's expansion of skills.

Effective assessment of word-solving ability:

❚ Is multifaceted, involving many different ways to observe children working with letters or words.

❚ Includes information about how students work with words in isolation as well as how they work with letters and words in the context of reading and writing.

❚ Involves the learner so that students learn to assess what they have learned, what they need to learn, and how they will engage in new learning.

❚ Informs teaching by revealing what students know, partially know, and don't know.

❚ Includes procedures that are an ongoing, integral part of instruction as well as more formal, structured procedures that are not part of teaching.

Here are two strands of assessment that represent ways to address these five key areas:

1. *Ongoing Observation.* It is an integral part of the teacher's role to observe children throughout the instructional day and to notice significant reading behaviors or aspects of children's written products that indicate learning. Sometimes teachers will take observational notes that inform their teaching and contribute to the ongoing record on the child.

2. *Performance-Based, Systematic Assessment Tasks.* There is a time to use systematic, planned tasks that are designed to gather information about particular aspects of children's growing word knowledge. Performance-based assessment may involve observation, but represents a more formal, structured experience in which the tasks are standardized. Standardization of the procedure creates a reliable assessment situation that is more objective than daily ongoing observation. The goal is to get a picture of what the student can do independently. Usually, the teacher does not actively teach during a performance-based assessment, but may make teaching points after the neutral observation.

Within both formal and informal contexts, we are always asking two questions: (1) What do children know and control relative to letters, sounds, and words? (2) What do they need to know? We need an ongoing inventory of the content that children have mastered or nearly mastered. This information will help us as teachers in the following ways:

❚ We can relate their knowledge to a continuum of typical progress.

❚ We can plan specific lessons that will serve the group as a whole or small groups effectively to move them forward in knowledge.

❚ We can adjust interactions to meet individual needs because we know where children are in their development of word knowledge.

❚ We can ascertain when children have acquired knowledge of many examples in any given area (for example, recognizing alphabet letters, using possessives, or forming plurals), and we can plan activities that will "tidy up" or solidify knowledge and deepen children's understanding of a basic and useful principle.

In Figure 10-1 we present lists of different assessments that we have found useful in gathering information relative to children's attitudes, core knowledge, strategies, and study skills. In the next section we will describe each of these tools.

Observation

One way to gather data is by observing children reading and writing in the multiple contexts of a balanced program. Effective assessment is an integral part of instruction. The true measure of whether children have developed an efficient processing system is

Tools for Assessing Word Solving		
	Reading	**Writing**
Attitudes	Informal Observation Self-Assessment· Process Interview	Informal Observation Self-Assessment Process Interview

Core Knowledge	Informal Observation
	Reading Conference
	Running Records*
	Miscue Analysis**
	Informal Reading Inventory
	Fluency
	
	Self-Assessment Using Checklists and
	  Questionnaires
	Letter Identification*
	Concepts About Print*
	
	Word Reading Tests
	  Word Test*
	  High-Frequency Words
	  Features Lists
	  Graded Word Lists
		Informal Observation
		Writing Conference
		Analysis of Student Work
		
		Self-Assessment Using Checklists and
		  Questionnaires
		Hearing and Recording Sounds in Words*
		Writing Vocabulary*
		Dictation Tasks
		Spelling Tests
		  High-Frequency Words
		  Features Lists
		  Developmental Spelling Tests
		  Graded Word Lists
		  Error Analysis
		  Word Tests

Strategies	Informal Observation
	Reading Conference
	Running Records*
	Miscue Analysis**
	Informal Reading Inventory
	Fluency Assessment
	Process Interview
	Self-Assessment Using Checklists and
	  Questionnaires
	Letter Identification*
	Concepts About Print*
	
	Word Reading Tests
	  High-Frequency Words
	  Features Lists
	  Graded Word Lists to Read
		Informal Observation
		Writing Conference
		Analysis of Student Work
		
		Process Interview
		Self-Assessment Using Checklists and
		  Questionnaires
		Hearing and Recording Sounds in Words*
		Writing Vocabulary*
		Dictation Tasks
		Spelling Tests
		  High-Frequency Words
		  Features Lists
		  Developmental Spelling Tests
		  Graded Word Lists
		  Error Analysis

Study Skills	Informal Observation Self-Assessment Process Interview Reading Conference	Informal Observation Self-Assessment Process Interview Writing Conference

*Clay (1993a) **Goodman, Watson, & Burke (1987)

FIGURE 10-1 Tools for Assessing Word Solving

the extent to which they can solve words "on the run" while reading and writing.

Observational assessment of word solving within reading, writing, and independent activity is valuable because it:

❚ Provides an understanding of children's hypotheses about how the written language system works.

❚ Shows children's risk-taking in reading and writing.

❚ Provides evidence of children's understanding of letter-sound relationships.

❚ Shows evidence of children's knowledge of visual patterns in words.

❚ Provides knowledge of children's store of high-frequency words.

❚ Provides evidence of children's repertoire of strategies for solving words in reading and writing.

❚ Provides evidence of children's understanding of word meanings.

❚ Provides evidence of children's ability to notice and correct errors.

❚ Provides information about what would be appropriate to teach—that is, what children need to learn next.

There are many different contexts for this informal, ongoing observational assessment. Here we present several examples of instructional contexts and the kinds of assessment that might take place alongside instruction.

Reading

Observational assessment may take place in several different reading contexts, *even* when you are reading aloud to children and they are not actually reading themselves. In reading aloud, for example, we might assess:

❚ Children's interest in language and words.

❚ Children's attention to words and how they sound as well as their ability to

pronounce words (for example, as they join in while the teacher rereads favorite books) that are initially unfamiliar.

❚ Children's ability to acquire new vocabulary.

In shared, guided, and independent reading children are, to various degrees, reading for themselves. These instructional activities provide a rich setting for the observation of behaviors that offer evidence of word learning. In each of these three settings, the support level is different, but we are still watching for behavioral evidence of children's ability to identify and use:

❚ Letters and words.

❚ The patterns in words, including letter-sound relationships, letter clusters, and word parts.

Shared Reading

Shared reading is a highly supported situation. Using an enlarged text, the teacher and a group of children are reading in unison. There are many opportunities to quickly assess what children know about letters and words and how they are beginning to use this knowledge to locate words, search, and check on themselves in reading. Shared reading moves along quickly, but teachers can build in quick assessment techniques such as having children locate known and unknown words, or masking or highlighting words or parts of words to see how the group of children approach the task of predicting and checking. Individual children may be asked to perform some tasks as a natural part of group reading. All of the behaviors noted are significant as they add to our knowledge about how a group of children or an individual child is approaching the reading task.

Guided and Independent Reading

In guided and independent reading, we have a chance to observe what the child can do individually. Guided reading always involves an orientation to the book or introduction to a story. You might introduce some unfamiliar words, such as new vocabulary or those that might be difficult to pronounce. In either case, you might demonstrate some word-solving strategies, such as taking words apart to show the children how they can work out pronunciation. Then, you'll want to observe the way children use this information when they come to that word in the story.

Even when children are reading silently, you can ask individuals to read aloud just for a few minutes while you take observational notes and check on their oral reading and fluency. The readers' oral production of the text is closely associated with their thinking about and understanding of the passage. You can use the same assessment process during independent reading when children are rereading familiar books, trying new books that are easy for them, or trying books of their own choice because of interesting content or class projects.

A good reason to listen to oral reading is to check on the fluency of the reader. The reader's oral production of the text is seen as closely associated with her thinking about and understanding of the passage. Several important systems contribute to fluency, including:

▮ Fast, automatic word recognition that allows readers to move beyond preoccupation with decoding and turn more of their attention to comprehending the text and enjoying the reading experience.

▮ Fast, automatic word solving when the reader sees an unfamiliar word.

▮ Processing the text in a meaningful way.

▮ Awareness of the way oral and written language sounds when read aloud.

▮ Fast, automatic decoding of words.

Another good reason to hear children read aloud is to observe for evidence of a growing reading vocabulary. We sometimes think of a reading vocabulary as the words that a beginning reader can recognize or figure out and a writing vocabulary as the words they can write with accuracy or with close approximation. Young children's speaking vocabularies grow rapidly and far exceed the reading and writing vocabularies. At first, when reading aloud to children you may notice how they take on new words, puzzling out the meanings. Later, as children learn to read more, they may encounter words that they do not actually know from their speaking vocabulary. Listening to children read aloud is a good way to check on whether they understand the meanings of the words they are reading. Mispronouncing a word while "sounding it out" or taking it apart can signal either that the reader has not truly connected the word to one in her speaking vocabulary or that she does not know the word. In either case, your support will help.

Teachers who are accustomed to taking running records sometimes find that they are making quick notations of their observations based on their considerable practice in noticing reading behaviors. We characterize this process as "taking a running record in our heads." Over time, this observation helps to build a picture of the reader's competence in word solving.

Writing

In writing contexts we can gather information about how children construct words by using their knowledge of letters and related sounds, patterns in words, and word parts. After all, a written message must be constructed word by word, letter by letter. Writing provides a context within which children are motivated to attend to the details and patterns of written words.

Shared Writing

In shared writing, you can serve as a scribe while your students participate in composing the message and reading and rereading it. Even though individual children are not writing, you can note:

❚ What aspects of letter and word construction children are noticing and commenting on.

❚ The patterns that children notice in words.

❚ The high-frequency words that they recognize.

For example, as one teacher was writing the word *they*, a child said, "That word looks like *the*." Children also frequently notice that words are connected to their own names.

Interactive Writing

In interactive writing, you make a more deliberate attempt to draw children's attention to aspects of constructing words. For example, a kindergarten teacher might link the word *an* to Andrew's name or *stew* to Steve's name.

Also, in interactive writing children go up to the easel or chart and "share the pen," writing selected letters and/or words and parts of words. This action helps you draw attention to word elements, and it also provides an opportunity to watch different children while they are engaged in word construction. Since the message created in interactive writing is intended to be read again and again, and because you are there sharing the task, the final spelling of words is standard.

Interactive writing enables you to explain to your students why spelling matters and to informally assess their growing concern for spelling words. It enables you to assess what words children know how to write quickly and easily, how they use letter-sound relationships, what patterns they have attended to and control, and what strategies help them think about what they know and figure out new words. Teaching and assessment are intricately intertwined during interactive writing because you are constantly working at the "edge" of children's knowledge.

Independent Writing

Independent writing occurs in writing workshop as well as in various writing activities across the day. For example, children may write in science study, social studies, or mathematics. Writing provides another opportunity for ongoing, informal assessment. Here, children are writing on their own. At first, very young children will only approximate writing and many words may represent temporary constructions. As writers become more experienced, they will spell most words in a standard way, but if children are expanding their writing and spelling abilities, they will deviate from standard spelling as they try new words.

As children are using more difficult words in their language, there will still be a percentage of words that they are learning about. You'll find their partially correct responses very useful in assessing the strategies they are using to construct words. Over time, you will expect a higher and higher percentage of words to be spelled correctly. Two kinds of informal assessments are related to children's writing.

1. To learn how they work at solving words, observe them while they are writing. For example:
   ❚ Do they notice when something doesn't look right, cross it out, and try another way?
   ❚ Do they say words slowly as they try to write letters that correspond with the sounds?
   ❚ Do they write some words quickly and easily with accurate spelling?
   ❚ Do they form letters in a fluent, efficient way?

2. We can examine the written products to determine:
   ❚ Are the letters in manuscript or cursive writing formed correctly so that they represent the intended symbol?
   ❚ What are the words that the child can spell in a standard way? Is this body of words growing?
   ❚ What sound-letter relationships does the child know?

▌ What patterns or word parts does the child know?

▌ Does the child understand basic principles?

▌ Does the child understand the word form that represents his correct meaning (for example *there*, *their*)?

Written products help us understand children's current hypotheses about how the written language system works. Children's attempts to spell are not random but systematic. They become one of the most important sources of information for assessment of phonics and spelling. Sometimes teachers save and analyze not only the final product a student prepares but several drafts to make inferences about the processes students are using.

Revisions matter!

Word Study

Observing children's behavior while they are involved in a variety of word study activities helps us learn how they work with words without the supportive context of extended text. In word study activities children are focusing in on words, talking about them, analyzing them, sorting them, connecting them to each other, taking them apart, and building them. Observe *what* they are noticing, correcting, and linking, and also the speed at which they are processing the information.

Word study activities involve inquiry and discovery processes in addition to practicing and applying principles. Word study also involves teaching children to use references and resources, including charts, classroom reference materials, library resources, and technological resources such as computer spell check and thesaurus programs.

Self-Assessment

Self-assessment is an important aspect of any learning process. For children, self-assessment:

▌ Promotes independence.

▌ Provides more immediate feedback than the usually delayed teacher evaluation.

▌ Offers an opportunity to respond constructively to a problem they discovered themselves.

▌ Supports their ability to talk about what they do well and what they have difficulty with.

These four values were identified by Johnston (1997):

▌ Promotes student ownership of the process.

▌ Increases student investment in learning.

▌ Provides information that the teacher might not pick up by assessment alone (such as insights into students' thinking).

▌ Increases motivation because students are involved in goal setting.

Self-assessment tools include checklists, such as:

▌ Editing checklists.

▌ Reading checklists.

▌ Checklists of known words or word patterns.

▌ Questionnaires, in which students provide oral or written responses to questions about their interest in words, what they know, what they do well, what they want to learn to do.

Process Interviews

One of the best ways to find out how students are thinking about words and how words work is simply to ask them. The process interview is a conversation or oral discussion that you can use to gain insights about a reader's or writer's attitudes, strategies, and skills. The process interview is more appropriate to use with older students since very young children are usually able to do much more than they can articulate. You can administer a written checklist or questionnaire prior to the process interview and use it as a basis for the session, or you may use a blank checklist or questionnaire as a general guide for conducting the oral discussion.

Questions asked in the process interview are open-ended and invite the child to respond and to offer information. Teachers often construct their own process interview questions based on what they value in their own word study programs. Some questions one teacher used for second-grade students are listed in Figure 10-2.

Reproducible forms for the process interviews are included in Appendixes 35 and 36.

Conferences

A conference is a short conversation between a teacher and an individual student about the child's attitudes, knowledge, strategies, and skills as a reader or writer. The goal of the conference is to observe children's processes, confirm their strategies, and teach them

spc. not broad.

something new. A conference (as opposed to a process interview) is usually focused on a particular piece of writing or something the child is reading that day. But, you can gather other information as part of the conference.

For example, you might take a running record as part of the conference or look at a child's reading list. You might look at a child's list of "words to learn" and help the child add words to the list. You can also use process interview questions as part of a reading or writing conference. In fact, one or two process interview questions will build up useful information about students' thinking as they work with words. Additionally, you might take a few moments of the conference to set learning goals with the child. This combination of techniques is important for efficiency. Guard against taking on every assessment process as a separate and time-consuming task. You may be left with little time to teach!

Process Interview -- Reading Name: _Jan_

Date: _5/28/98_

What do you do when you come to a word you don't know how to read? What else do you do?

I look at the parts, sound some out, until it makes sense with the other words.

What were some tricky words for you in reading today? What made them hard to figure out?

Some of the long words that I don't know how to say.

If you were teaching a kindergartner how to read words, what would you do? Anything else?

I would tell them to look at the word, and to look at the different parts, to try to put them together until the word makes sense going with the other words.

How can you get better at reading new words?

Once I find out how to say words, I can try to read them over to make sure I know them.

Process Interview -- Writing Name: _Jan_

Date: _5/28/98_

What do you do when you come to a word you don't know how to write? What else do you do?

I say it slowly to myself, think about the parts, and try to write the sounds.

What are some words that are tricky for you? Why do you think they are hard?

The two words which/witch and the three words there/their/they're. I get them all mixed up.

How do you learn to write new words? What else do you do?

I remember how they look, practice writing them, and look up the correct spelling in a dictionary if I'm not sure.

If you were teaching a kindergartner how to write words, what would you do? Anything else?

I'd teach him how to say the sounds, find parts, and add missing letters.

How can you get better at writing new words?

By finding the correct spelling and practicing.

Why is correct spelling important?

So others will know what I am trying to say.

FIGURE 10-2 Process Interview: Reading & Process Interview: Writing

Running Records

A running record (Clay 1993a) is a tool for coding, scoring, and analyzing a child's behaviors while the child is engaged in oral reading of continuous text. Clay has developed a standardized system that enables teachers to serve as objective recorders of reading behaviors. The record provides both quantitative and qualitative information.

For example, in the running record in Figure 10-3, the quantitative information on Peter shows that the book *Tiger, Tiger* was easy for him. This indicates a level in the range (90–100 percent) that supports reading for meaning with some opportunity for reading work.

quant.

Peter read the text with 96 percent accuracy. He made six errors but self-corrected four of them. The qualitative information provided in the record indicates that Peter was using meaning and language structure as strong sources of information to help him read this simple text. His attempts at words, as analyzed by the teacher using meaning, structure, or visual information, identify the probable source of the error. We also note that his reading was choppy and word by word, indicating some qualitative information relative to fluency.

Specifically relative to word solving, we note that he was consistently using visual features of words in coordination with meaning. In other words, Peter was checking one kind of information with another or coordinating several different kinds of information. For the most part, he noticed when the words he said didn't "look right," and he tried to fix them. Twice he substituted *sleeping* for *asleep*, an error that indicates he uses several sources of information to read the text. Since the error is one that made sense,

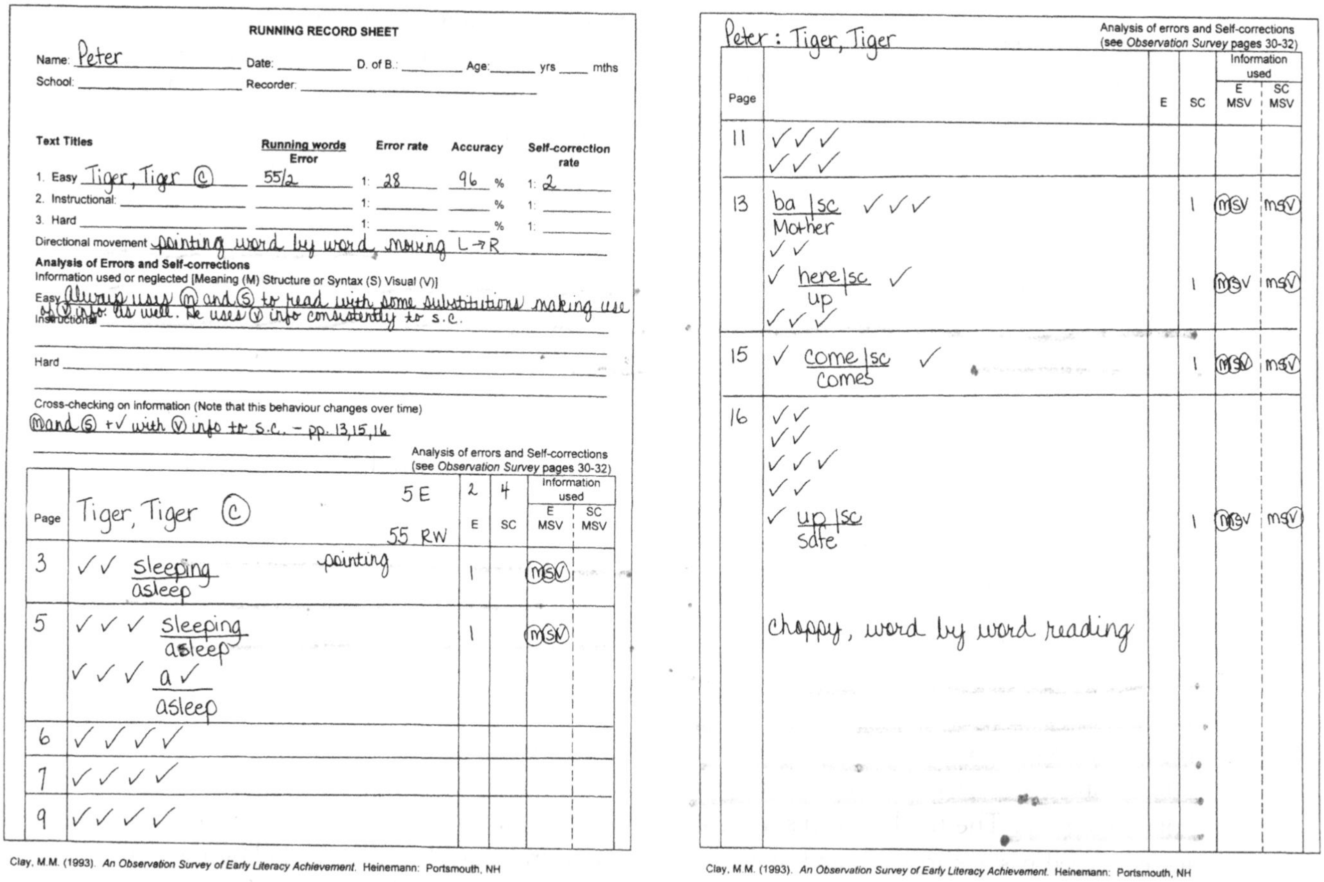
RUNNING RECORD SHEET

Name: Peter Date: ____ D. of B.: ____ Age: ____ yrs ____ mths

School: ____ Recorder: ____

Text Titles	Running words Error	Error rate	Accuracy	Self-correction rate
1. Easy Tiger, Tiger ©	55/2	1: 28	96 %	1: 2
2. Instructional:		1:	%	1:
3. Hard		1:	%	1:

Directional movement: pointing word by word, moving L→R

Analysis of Errors and Self-corrections
Information used or neglected [Meaning (M) Structure or Syntax (S) Visual (V)]

Easy: Always uses Ⓜ and Ⓢ to read with some substitutions making use of Ⓥ info. as well. He uses Ⓥ info consistently to s.c.

Instructional:

Hard

Cross-checking on information (Note that this behaviour changes over time)

Ⓜ and Ⓢ +V with Ⓥ info to s.c. – pp. 13, 15, 16

Analysis of errors and Self-corrections (see *Observation Survey* pages 30-32)

Page	Tiger, Tiger © 5 E / 55 RW	E (2)	SC (4)	Information used E MSV	SC MSV
3	✓✓ sleeping / asleep (pointing)	1		ⓂⓈV	
5	✓✓✓ sleeping / asleep; ✓✓✓ a ✓ / asleep	1		ⓂⓈV	
6	✓✓✓✓				
7	✓✓✓✓				
9	✓✓✓✓				

Clay, M.M. (1993). *An Observation Survey of Early Literacy Achievement*. Heinemann: Portsmouth, NH

Peter: Tiger, Tiger

Analysis of errors and Self-corrections (see *Observation Survey* pages 30-32)

Page		E	SC	Information used E MSV	SC MSV
11	✓✓✓ ✓✓✓				
13	ba | sc / Mother ✓✓✓; ✓✓; ✓ here | sc / up ✓; ✓✓✓		1	ⓂⓈV	MSⓋ
			1	ⓂⓈV	MSⓋ
15	✓ come | sc / comes ✓		1	ⓂⓈⓋ	MSⓋ
16	✓✓ ✓✓ ✓✓✓ ✓✓ ✓ up | sc / safe		1	ⓂⓈV	MSⓋ

choppy, word by word reading

Clay, M.M. (1993). *An Observation Survey of Early Literacy Achievement*. Heinemann: Portsmouth, NH

FIGURE 10-3 Running Record of Peter's Reading of *Tiger, Tiger* initially Peter did not stop to correct it. By the time the word appeared on the third page, he noticed something about the feature of the word *asleep*. Saying *a*, he then read the word accurately. The record reveals that Peter was learning to take words apart while reading for meaning. The record enables teachers to see not only what sources of information the child is using, but also how the child tackles the information.

The running record is not about word reading alone. The real value is in how the reader is using sources of information in a process. This process is described in the summary statement at the top of the record. On easy text, Peter was:

Go Peter!

✓

■ Using meaning and language structure in reading.

■ Noticing when something was not quite right.

■ Making use of visual information to read and to self-correct.

Peter's teacher could comment positively on his efforts to notice print and use visual information. She would record some comments about processing to keep in mind when introducing stories to his group and interacting with him in guided reading.

Miscue Analysis

Miscue analysis is defined as a formal examination of miscues, the reader's unexpected responses to a text, as a basis for determining the strengths and weaknesses in the background experiences and language skills of students as they read (Goodman, Watson, and Burke 1987). We provide a sample of a complete miscue analysis in Chapter 17.

Informal Reading Inventory

An informal reading inventory is a graded series of passages of increasing difficulty used to determine students' strengths, weaknesses, and strategies in word identification and comprehension. The teacher marks a preselected, typed passage to score and analyze a child's reading and then asks the child to retell and/or respond to a series of questions.

Running records, informal reading inventories, and miscue analyses yield many similar types of information about word reading.

As stressed earlier in our discussion of guided reading, fluency is an important aspect of a reader's ability. The rate and fluency of the reading is a good indicator of the reader's ability to quickly solve words, among other skills. For a more detailed discussion of fluency and a useful rubric for assessing fluency, we refer you to Fountas and Pinnell (1996), page 81. Also, see Chapter 18 in this volume.

Letter Identification Tasks

In a Letter Identification task (Clay 1993a), the child is asked to identify the printed upper- and lowercase letters and typeset *a* and *g*. Children may respond by saying the name of the letter, saying the sound the letter makes, or identifying a word that starts with the letter. Each of these different responses tells us something important that the child knows about the letter as well as the child's preferred ways of thinking about letters. It may reveal letter confusions as well as knowledge of some letter-sound relationships. It can also indicate that a child is looking at distinctive features of letters. For example, a child who says *m* for *n* or *h* for *n* is evidently looking at some of the features of the letters. The substitution is not random, and that information helps the teacher know what to help the child attend to. Figure 10-4 is a sample Letter Identification test, showing Katy's fast processing and accurate letter recognition. Katy showed some confusion with the letters *g* and *r*.

The Concepts About Print Assessment

The Concepts About Print Assessment (Clay 1993a) measures a variety of concepts about print during the reading of a small book. The context is close to an authentic task but the assessor asks questions that activate the child's use of current knowledge about the conventions of print. Several items in the assessment are of interest to our examination of letter and word learning, including the concept "that there are letters, and clusters of letters called words, that there are first letters

LETTER IDENTIFICATION SCORE SHEET

Date: 6-10-97

Name: Katy   Age: 6 yrs. 2 mons.   TEST SCORE: 52/54

Recorder: D. Powell   Date of Birth: 4-15-91   STANINE GROUP:

	A	S	Word	I.R.		A	S	Word	I.R.
A	✓				a	✓			
F	✓				f	✓			
K	✓				k	✓			
P	✓				p	✓			
W	✓				w	✓			
Z	✓				z	✓			
B	✓				b	✓			
H	✓				h	✓			
O	✓				o	✓			
J	✓				j	✓			
U	✓				u	✓			
					a	✓			
C	✓				c	✓			
Y	✓				y	✓			
L	✓				l	✓			
Q	✓				q	•			
M	✓				m	✓			
D	✓				d	✓			
N	✓				n	✓			
S	✓				s	✓			
X	✓				x	✓			
I	✓				i	✓			
E	✓				e	✓			
G	✓				g	✓			
R	✓				r	•		P	
V	✓				v	✓			
T	✓				t	✓			
					g	✓			
26			TOTALS	**26**			TOTAL SCORE	**52**	

Row for q shows P in I.R. and r shows † in I.R.

Confusions:

p   t
q   r

Letters Unknown:

— ✓s up to corresponding capital (H) before answering

Comment:

"letters"
hesitates on 'h'
moves L→R across lines pointing to each letter
most letters were named without hesitation

Recording:

A	Alphabet response: tick (check)
S	Letter sound response: tick (check)
Word	Record the word the child gives
IR	Incorrect response: Record what the child says

Clay, M.M. (1993). *An Observation Survey of Early Literacy Achievement.* Heinemann: Portsmouth, NH

FIGURE 10-4   Katy's Letter Identification Score Sheet

and last letters in words, that you can choose upper- or lowercase letters, that spaces are there for a reason" (Clay 1993a, 47).

Word Reading Tests

There are many different kinds of word reading tests. Generally, a word reading test pro-

vides a sampling of reading vocabulary in a category. Clay (1993a) writes, "A word test cannot describe a child's integrated system of reading behaviors because this can only be observed on continuous text" (54). Nevertheless, teachers can use word reading tests effectively to assess:

■ A child's ability to read some words quickly and without attention.

■ A child's ability to read high-frequency words.

■ A child's ability to use spelling patterns.

■ A child's willingness to attempt unknown words and be persistent in the effort.

■ A child's ability to use letter-sound knowledge in attempts at unknown words.

■ A child's ability to use a range of strategies in attempting to read isolated words.

■ A child's ability to use letter clusters or word parts.

■ A child's ability to break words down into component parts.

■ A child's ability to categorize words by component parts or according to meaning units.

■ A child's ability to build a reading vocabulary.

The real value of a word test is not simply in the words the child knows but in the information revealed by the child's attempts.

Tests of High-Frequency Words

Clay has developed a word test that is widely used for first graders. This list has many high-frequency words sampled from those that children have had the opportunity to encounter in reading texts. Children are asked to read them in isolation and their attempts are noted (see Figure 10-5). In this example, Katy shows the ability to recognize eleven words, makes three attempts that are visually similar, and self-corrects one attempt.

On this word test, children approach single words in isolation without the support of meaning or predictability in text. Their attempts at words provide information about their ability to recognize features of letters and words and to take them apart.

Teachers can construct other tests of high-frequency words sampled from the lists

we provide in Appendixes 4 and 5 or from the reading series or collection of books used at the school. Note that the word test is valid only after children have had a chance to learn about words in many literacy contexts.

Features Lists

As children grow in their knowledge of words, it may be useful to construct specialized word lists, perhaps with your colleagues, to assess their knowledge of particular features of words. These may include such features lists as words with particular rimes or phonograms, words with letter clusters, or a sampling of contractions or homographs.

Grade-Level Word Lists

Lists of words that include a sampling of reading vocabulary organized for each grade level provide a way to track student progress along an expected path. There are many lists of words by grade level that you can use to assess approximate reading level. These include tests such as the Botel Word Recognition Test and the Slosson Oral Reading Test.

Tools for Assessing Word Solving in Writing

Many of the tools listed in Figure 10-1 may be used in both reading and writing (for example, informal observation, process interviews, and conferences). Several other tools are related specifically to assessing word solving in writing.

Analysis of Student Work

To assess students' growing ability to write words and to solve words in writing, some of the best information comes from analysis of student work. In a literacy-rich program, students are writing all day for many different purposes. You will have many samples of a great variety of work. Save these products to document progress, and analyze them to determine how your students are approaching words. Several samples of writing are analyzed in Chapter 16; for each sample you review, you might ask:

```
APPENDIX 1                    OHIO WORD TEST SCORE SHEET

                                              TEST SCORE    12 /20

Date: 6-10-97

Name: Katy                    School: Mason

Recorder: D. Powell           Classroom Teacher: Ms. Shelton

Record incorrect responses.
Choose appropriate list of words.    ✓ (Checkmark) Correct Response    • (Dot) No Response
```

	LIST A	LIST B	LIST C
Practice words	can ✓	in	see
	and ✓	ran	big
	the ✓	it	to
	pretty party •	said	ride
	has ✓	her	him
	down •	find	for
	where there	we	you
	after •	they	this
	let •	live	may
	here ✓	away	in
	am I'm	are	at
	there ✓	no	with
	over ✓	put	some
	little ✓	look	make
	did ✓	do	eat
	what went	who	an
	them that/sc	then	walk
	one ✓	play	red
	like ✓	again	now
	could •	give	from
	yes ✓	saw	have

Clay, M.M. (1993). *An Observation Survey of Early Literacy Achievement*. Heinemann: Portsmouth, NH

FIGURE 10-5   Katy's Ohio Word Test Score Sheet

■ What words does the student know in every detail as evidenced by conventional spelling?

■ To what degree does the formation of letters (handwriting) represent conventional forms?

■ What knowledge of spelling patterns is evident in the student's attempts at unknown words?

■ What knowledge of letter-sound relationships is evident in the student's attempts at unknown words?

The analysis of students' written work can provide important information about students' word solving and word learning, including children's skills in:

▮ Writing high-frequency words.

▮ Using content-related words (*leaves*, *photosynthesis*, *dinosaur*).

▮ Putting together multisyllable words, including compound words.

▮ Dividing words at the ends of lines.

▮ Representing common spelling patterns as well as those that are more rare and difficult.

▮ Using the inflectional endings that are appropriate to signal plurality or tense.

▮ Using prefixes and suffixes.

▮ Varying words to make a text more interesting (for example, using synonyms).

▮ Using the sounds of language to put words together in interesting ways (for example, using alliteration).

Hearing and Recording Sounds in Words

Clay (1993a) devised five sentences, each of which contains letters representing thirty-seven phonemes. The sentence is read to the child, who tries to write the words. This task is not designed to measure accurate spelling; rather, the interest is in the child's ability to hear the sounds in words and record letters that represent them. Hearing and Recording Sounds in Words is a test of phoneme/grapheme awareness (see Figure 10-6).

As shown in this figure, Katy was able to record all thirty-seven phonemes. Most of the words are spelled correctly, and one can hypothesize that she almost knows the word *coming*.

Writing Vocabulary

In Clay's (1993a) writing vocabulary task, children are asked to write all of the words they know how to write. First, the assessor suggests that children write their own names,

and then prompts children to think of words that they know how to write. This assessment is not simply about the number of words a child can write accurately. We also acquire invaluable qualitative information about the child's approach to word writing. For example, the writing vocabulary assessment gives us information about:

▮ Children's knowledge of their own writing inventory (since they are thinking of the words they know).

▮ The way one word leads children to think of another, revealing connections between words.

▮ Children's use of phonograms and spelling patterns.

▮ The ease and fluency with which children write words.

▮ Children's use of endings to make several words from a root word.

In Michael's writing vocabulary (see Figure 10-7), we can see he has many different ways of getting to the words he wants to write. He began with his name and then wrote another name he knew. He wrote simple, high-frequency words in the first column but seemed to connect them because of similar patterns (*in*, *is*, *it*; *there*, *here*). After writing *look*, he wrote several more words that end the same way. He added *s* to *book*, making another word, as well as *ing* and *ed* to *play*. He wrote *good* and then thought of *go*, perhaps noting their similarity visually. He wrote *you* and then *your*. Beginning with *into*, he went on to write two other forms of the word *to*, which he wrote instantly because he knew them. He didn't have to stop to construct the words by thinking about the sounds and letters. He added *d* to *see* to produce *seed*. He made one attempt that resulted in inaccurate spelling, *Ttat* for *that*, and we hypothesize that this error was the result of hurrying or simply not noticing. After all, Michael certainly knows how to use the letter cluster *th*, as evidenced in his spelling of

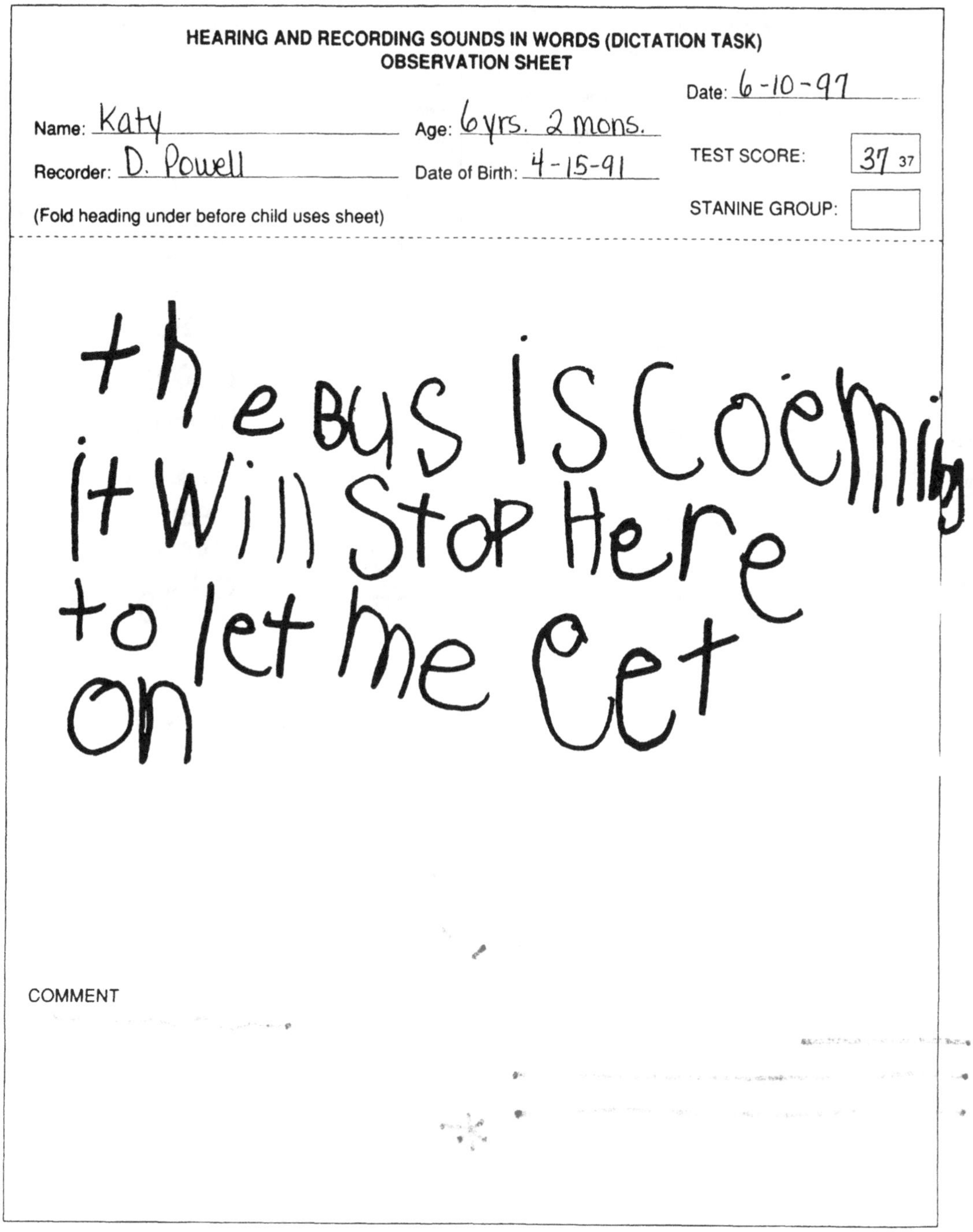

HEARING AND RECORDING SOUNDS IN WORDS (DICTATION TASK)
OBSERVATION SHEET

Date: 6-10-97

Name: Katy   Age: 6 yrs. 2 mons.

Recorder: D. Powell   Date of Birth: 4-15-91   TEST SCORE: 37 37

(Fold heading under before child uses sheet)   STANINE GROUP:

- -

the BUS IS Coeming
it Will Stop Here
to let me eet
on

COMMENT

Clay, M.M. (1993). *An Observation Survey of Early Literacy Achievement.* Heinemann: Portsmouth, NH

FIGURE 10-6   Katy's Hearing and Recording Sounds in Words Observation Sheet

there, they, and *then.* It is obvious that Michael, even as a first grader, has a dynamic process for making connections between words. He produced fifty-nine accurately spelled words within a ten-minute period, so he was working with some ease and fluency.

A writing vocabulary test like this one does not take the place of observation while children are writing their own messages and stories. We want to know how children approach the writing of extended text; however, writing words in a standardized task

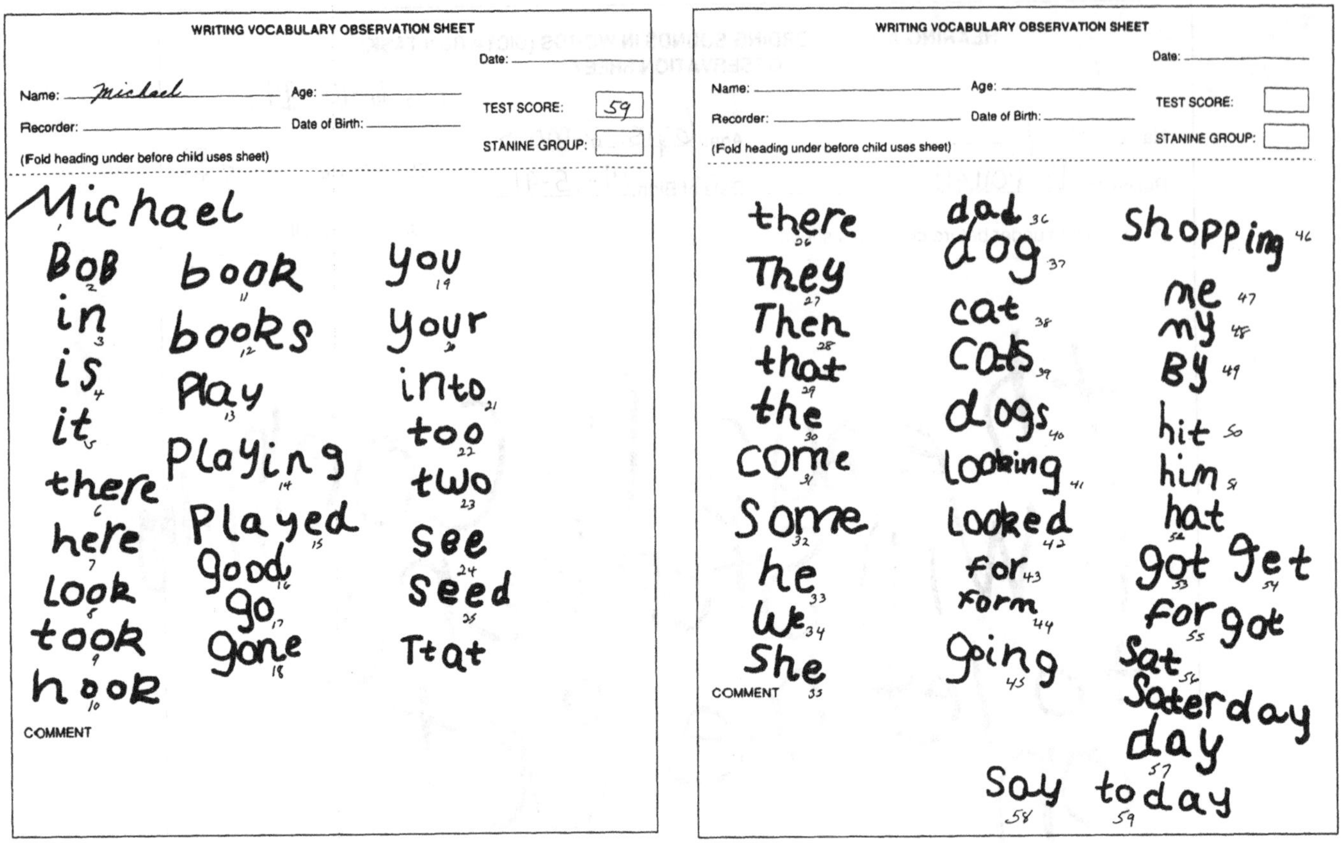

Clay, M.M. (1993). *An Observation Survey of Early Literacy Achievement*. Heinemann: Portsmouth, NH

FIGURE 10-7   Michael's Writing Vocabulary

like this one shows us what children control and almost control as they build a word-solving system.

Dictation Tasks

The Hearing and Recording Sounds in Words test is one example of a dictation task. Children are asked to try to write a message which is first read in its entirety and then dictated to them word by word. The message contains thirty-seven phonemes. Scores reflect the number of phonemes represented with an appropriate letter. You can construct your own sentences that contain a variety of letter-sound patterns as a way of assessing children's phonemic awareness and spelling skills by simply making up a sentence or two containing all thirty-seven phonemes.

Another type of informal dictation task is the daily edit. The teacher dictates a sentence or two to the class. Each child writes the sentence and checks for spelling and punctuation. Then one child writes the sentence on the board and the class gives feedback. Children can share their attempts at words and the teacher can reinforce good strategies.

Error Analysis

If we only look at children's spellings as "right" or "wrong," we are missing some very valuable information. We have said that young children approximate spellings as they are learning the phoneme-grapheme system. As they learn more about words, these phonetic approximations disappear. But spellers who write most words accurately are still learning new principles about spelling. Their errors reveal their current understanding and help us make good decisions about teaching. Here is one way to use children's errors constructively:

■ Every two or three months, analyze the errors of each child, using an Error Analysis chart (Figure 10-8).

∎ Use a writing sample that has been read over and edited by the child.

∎ Make notes or put a check in the columns indicating areas of need.

∎ Look for patterns in the columns.

∎ Conclude what underlying principles or patterns the child needs to learn how to use and what the child needs to learn about how words work.

A reproducible version of the Error Analysis chart can be found in Appendix 52.

Spelling Tests

Spelling tests may be teacher-constructed and tailored to the school or district curriculum. In general, spelling tests follow the same principles as the word reading tests described earlier. They may focus on high-frequency words or words with special features. There are graded word lists that accompany spelling or basal series. In our description of a word study system (Chapter 14), we pro-

pose a process for identifying words for children to learn that is individualized and reflects the need for core understandings. Spelling tests provide much more than information on which words are spelled right or wrong. They show what children understand about letters and words. For example, one child spelled the word *you* as *u*, while a second child wrote *yuo*. These spellers have very different understandings.

Developmental Spelling Test

A developmental spelling test designed by Gentry and Gillet (1993) is simple and easy to administer yet powerful in the information it provides about young children's growing ability to analyze words. Ten words, drawn from the research on children's invented spellings, are called out to the children, along with a sentence including the word. Teachers ask the children to attempt to write the word, and their responses are categorized by their level of spelling development. When teachers are able to identify

Error Analysis

Date	Word	High Frequency Words	Consonants: Initial, Final, Cluster, Digraph	Vowels: Long, Short Vowel Patterns *y* as a Vowel	Contractions, Compounds, Plurals	Base Words and Affixes: Prefixes, Suffixes, Inflectional Endings	Homophones Homographs	Other: e.g. Letter Form, Letter Order, Silent Letters
5/98	ther/their	their					there/their	
	cood/could	could		−ould				
	wokt/walked			−alk		add ed		
	runing/running					double consonant and add ing		
	haveing/having	having				drop e and add ing		
	playd/played					add ed		
	nifes/knives		Kn		plural			silent K
	wus/was	was						
	wusnt/wasn't	wasn't			contraction			apostrophe
	cant/can't	can't			contraction			apostrophe
	laft/laughed			−augh		add ed (t)		
	askt/asked					add ed (t)		
	cot/coat			−oat				
	sop/soap			−oap				

FIGURE 10-8   Error Analysis Chart

the stage, they can focus on teaching that helps move the child forward.

Making the Assessment Plan

In the previous sections we described a variety of assessment tasks. Some might be ongoing and used daily; others represent regularly scheduled tasks. For example:

1. Ongoing tasks would include the informal assessment that takes place every day as well as the collection of students' work for later analysis. Having systems for storing products and systematized ways of recording anecdotal notes will support this process. Another way that even informal observation is sometimes made more systematic is to have a brief list of children to "notice" each day, rotating the list so that you are sure to observe every child during the week. This does not mean, of course, that other children and their significant behaviors would be neglected, but only that no children would be consistently ignored.

2. Regularly scheduled assessment tasks would be those that are connected to instructional plans, such as the word study system described in Chapter 14 or the system for taking running records described in this chapter. The word study system requires the collection of spelling data once each week. A guided reading system might involve collecting an official running record on each child every two or three weeks, with informal observations and lists of books read in between.

For efficiency in assessment, it is wise to create a comprehensive assessment plan that includes several different kinds of assessment tasks. Working in grade-level groups or as a primary team is a good idea. Making a plan has several advantages, including:

■ Clarifying for administrators and others the variety of procedures you are using and what you are measuring relative to children's word learning.

■ Illustrating what children are expected to know about letters, sounds, and words.

■ Making it easier to analyze the time to be devoted to assessment. (If the plan is too extensive, it could impinge on instructional time.)

■ Creating a rigorous process for evaluating the effectiveness of the teaching and the curriculum.

As you consider your assessment plan, keep in mind the following characteristics. Effective assessment plans for measuring students' word-solving skills will:

■ Include both ongoing assessments and regularly scheduled assessment tasks.
■ Address both reading and writing contexts to assess word solving.
■ Be organized along a time line for the school year.
■ Be supported by systems for recording and organizing information.

Connecting Assessment with Instruction

Making sure that children acquire the letter, sound, and word knowledge they need is a challenge for teachers, especially when we consider the complex body of information presented in Chapter 9. A traditional approach is the construction of a scope and sequence of skills and concepts along a grade-level continuum. It is necessary to have in mind what children need to know and to establish expectations at various points in time. That "big picture" helps us know where to start and where to go. But a major factor in instructional decision making is *where children are* in their learning about letters, sounds, and words; they don't all simply move along the same path.

Figure 10-9 presents a summary of characteristics for five levels of word-solving knowledge and skills. They are presented in a rubric so that you can begin to place stu-

Analysis of Word-Solving Skills

Description	Key Behavioral Indicators	Instructional Implications
1. Beginning The beginning word solver is becoming aware of the sounds in words and some visual features of print, usually a letter in his/her name.	• Repeats words and identifies a few sounds. • Recognizes own name (or part of it) in writing. • Notices print in the environment. • Responds to stories and sometimes notices print.	• Rhymes, songs, chants • Work with names (charts songs, poems) • Shared reading • Reading aloud • Interactive writing • Language experience/shared writing • Independent writing
2. Emergent The emergent word solver understands that words are made up of sequences of sounds, can connect some sounds with letters, and recognizes a few high-frequency words.	• Notices and can identify some sounds in words. • Notices when words sound alike. • Recognizes own name and can write part of it. • Recognizes a few easy high-frequency words. • Uses letter names to represent some sounds in writing. • Knows how to read and write a few high-frequency words. • Notices print in the environment. • Knows the names and/or sounds of some letters—mostly consonants and some dominant vowels.	• Rhymes, songs, and chants along with shared reading • Work with names (name charts, name puzzles) • Guided and independent reading of easy books with some high-frequency words • Word study of consonants and simple regular dominant vowel patterns • Interactive writing with emphasis on linking to names, building high-frequency words, and hearing and recording sounds in words • Use of word wall for names, some high-frequency words, and easy word patterns
3. Early The early word solver knows many sound-letter/letter cluster relationships and patterns. Writes and reads using the letter-sound relationships he knows and acquires more in the process.	• Hears and writes many dominant sounds in words, particularly consonant and dominant vowel sounds. • Looks at and writes most letters easily. • Knows the names of the alphabet and related sounds. • Reads and writes a small core of high-frequency words. • Writes many words using consonant sounds and easy-to-hear vowel sounds.	• Word study with emphasis on exploration of connections between words and regular spelling patterns • Interactive writing with emphasis on hearing and recording sounds in words, on making connections between words, and on word construction • Guided and independent reading of early books with moderate picture support and a wider range of high-frequency words and letter patterns • Minilessons and conferences in writing workshop • Reading books with less support and solving new words using regular spelling patterns and connections to known words along with other sources of information • Use of word wall
4. Transitional The transitional word solver knows consonant and vowel patterns and relationships between letters, letter clusters, and sounds and is moving from reliance on regular letter-sound	• Hears most sounds, including harder-to-hear vowel sounds. • Writes letters and many letter combinations easily. • Indicates in spelling the understanding that there is a sound in each syllable. • Reads and writes a larger core of	• Word study with emphasis on categorizing words, making connections between words, and word construction using onsets and rimes, beginnings and endings • Word study system (Chapter 14) • Minilessons and conferences in writing workshop • Guided and independent reading of texts

FIGURE 10-9   Analysis of Word-Solving Skills

correspondence to spelling patterns and how groups of letters represent sounds. Uses this information to take words apart and check on his reading and to construct words in writing.	high-frequency words and many words that are of personal interest or related to content study. • Reads and writes some easy two or three-syllable words. • Reads and writes words with simple endings. • Notices and uses simple word patterns (*like*, *bike*). • Writes and reads some words that depart from regular spelling patterns; tries alternative representations for words.	with longer, more complex sentences, many high-frequency words, and many words to figure out using letter-sound relationships and connections between words • Some shared or interactive writing as part of a minilesson • Use of word wall
5. Self-Extending The self-extending word solver has a broad base of information and uses letter-sound patterns, analogy, and a range of information flexibly in reading and writing.	• Uses a variety of strategies to spell words. • Spells many/most words in standard spelling. • Notices misspellings and is able to try various representations to self-correct. • Reads and writes a large number of words accurately, quickly, and automatically. • Uses generalizations and principles to figure out new words when meeting them in text. • Reads and writes many multisyllable words. • Proofreads and edits written products.	• Word study emphasizing more complex spelling patterns, working with many different categories of words, making words using morphological components • Word study system • Minilesson and conferences in writing workshop • Guided and independent reading emphasizing fluent reading of longer and more complex texts with little picture support, as well as the expectation to solve multisyllable and irregular technical words • Use of word wall
6. Advanced The advanced word solver understands the variety of rules and principles of how words work, as well as how to use historical roots to derive meaning, and has a sophisticated knowledge of words, including base words and inflections, root words and their meanings, and the historical origins of words.	• Demonstrates understanding of rules and principles of how words work by categorizing words and providing examples. • Manipulates base words, changing different parts to make new words. • Uses inflections, plurals, affixes correctly. • Uses root words to derive meaning of words. • Is interested in words and uses knowledge of words, their origins, and histories. • Reads accurately, with fluency and smooth, usually unobservable, word solving. • Writes fluently, attending to meaning, writing many words accurately, making attempts at others, and employing proofreading skills to edit the piece.	• Word study with emphasis on connecting words by meaning, structure, and a variety of other ways as well as the study of word origins • Minilessons and conferences in writing workshop • Word study system • Writing workshop with more emphasis on composition, editing, proofreading, and publishing • Guided and independent reading of more complex texts with specialized content vocabulary and many multisyllable words • Use of word wall

FIGURE 10-9 Analysis of Word-Solving Skills, *continued*

dents within a broad band around which you organize your instruction.

This sample rubric represents the thinking of teachers who had been working for some time on the development of benchmarks for progress in reading, writing, and word study. It is a practical tool for thinking about children across the grades. Any such tool requires testing with students, conferring with colleagues, and adjusting so that judgments are reliable and communication is helpful.

Suggestions for Professional Development

1. Work with grade-level colleagues to construct a beginning assessment plan for your school.

   ▌ Look at the chart on page 107 of this chapter, and be sure that you know

   each of the assessments offered as examples in this chapter.

   ▌ In place of the process assessment tasks we recommend, you may want to select assessments that are commonly used in your school or district.

2. Create a word-solving assessment plan that meets the criteria outlined in this chapter.

3. Test your word-solving assessment plan for part of the year and meet again to evaluate progress. Ask:

   ▌ Are you getting the information you need to guide instruction?

   ▌ Is the plan manageable?

   ▌ Were you able to implement all aspects of the plan?

Word-Solving Strategies

Organize to Teach

Observation of behavior is the key to powerful teaching. Children's behaviors reveal their understandings about word solving. Observation that focuses on the quality of behavioral response will inform the teaching program. Direct, explicit teaching is effective only if it meets the learners where they are. And, explicit teaching of how words work is essential, including all the complex and interrelated knowledge about letters and sounds that words entail. That means that observation and teaching must come together.

How do teachers help children become word solvers?

Quanisha, described in Chapter 3, was actively involved every day in learning and using literacy. Word solving and word exploration were part of the rich language and literacy curriculum that she experienced. The teacher played a critical role in creating the classroom environment, planning for Quanisha's active learning, and interacting in powerful ways to promote learning. Helping children become competent word solvers requires thinking through the role of the teacher and the role of the learner in the classroom literacy program. Many of the essential elements of these roles are described in Figure 11-1.

As described in the chart, the teacher's role is multifaceted. Teaching children to be word solvers is not a simple matter of providing a lesson every day, although that might be part of the approach. Teachers provide models, demonstrate, give feedback, explain, and encourage children to solve words in many different ways throughout the school day.

Teachers' actions have a profound effect on how children engage in word solving. Beyond lessons and practice, we want children to actively search for ways to solve words in writing and in reading. Once they understand how to use resources in the classroom, we want them to initiate their use and work independently. And, we want them to be conscious of themselves as powerful users of words.

We know that young children will not spell or read every word perfectly (and all learners, even adults, occasionally encounter literacy tasks that they find challenging). We want our students to view their every problem solving attempt as learning and to move toward the goals of conventional accuracy. That means they need to be active

Roles in Teaching and Learning About Words

Teacher Role	Learner Role
• Provides a quality, organized environment.	• Uses materials independently and works in an organized way.
• Has an understanding of the alphabetic system.	• Is developing an understanding of the alphabetic system.
• Has an understanding of the strategies competent word solvers use.	• Is learning to use a variety of strategies for word solving.
• Schedules time for teaching word-solving strategies.	• Uses learning time well in word-solving activities.
• Shows interest in words and language.	• Demonstrates curiosity about words and language.
• Links reading and writing.	• Makes connections between words in reading and writing.
• Demonstrates reading and writing for a variety of purposes.	• Uses reading and writing for a variety of purposes.
• Encourages learners to take risks.	• Takes risks.
• Emphasizes positive aspects of learners' attempts.	• Is aware of own strengths and knowledge about letters, sounds, and words.
• Promotes peer interaction and support.	• Works with and supports others in word solving.
• Helps learners understand the importance of effective word-solving strategies.	• Understands the importance of effective word-solving strategies.
• Helps learners understand the importance of conventional spelling.	• Understands the importance of conventional spelling and works toward it as a goal.
• Teaches learners how to use classroom resources such as charts, lists, and dictionaries.	• Uses classroom resources effectively.
• Integrates vocabulary from other areas of the curriculum.	• Attends to and uses vocabulary across the curriculum.
• Systematically observes and documents the learner's reading and writing.	• Participates in collecting samples of learning such as lists of known words, keeps records of own progress, and self-evaluates.
• Uses information from observation to inform teaching.	• Is aware of own knowledge as a resource in solving words in reading and writing.
• Provides careful teaching of strategies for word solving individually, in small groups, and with the whole class.	• Participates actively in whole-class, small-group, and individual instruction.
• Values approximations in reading and writing as evidence of learning.	• Uses own knowledge to make attempts and sees attempts as a way to learn; engages in active word solving work.
• Teaches within reading and writing experiences.	• Attends to new understandings in reading and writing experiences and solves words in pursuit of meaning.
• Provides focused experiences to expand learning.	• Engages in and learns from focused experiences including practice in word solving.
• Teaches children how to check on themselves as word solvers.	• Checks on self as a word solver.
• Demonstrates a consciousness for careful word solving throughout the day.	• Proofreads work in writing and checks on errors in reading.

FIGURE 11-1   Roles in Teaching and Learning About Words

word solvers even when they are working independently. They need to check on themselves while reading, for example, noticing mismatches and making information fit. They have to proofread their work in writing, noticing potential errors and finding ways to solve the words.

In classrooms where children are learning a great deal about letters and words, they are active users of language. They engage in reading and writing for a variety of purposes throughout the day. They have many encounters with print, and all literacy activities are surrounded by and supported by talk. The rich oral and written language experiences provide a foundation for understanding the importance of words and making connections between words. The enjoyment and engagement that children bring to their oral and written language prompts word investigation on multiple levels and enhances the study of words.

Principles of Effective Word Study Teaching

In this section we describe very specific approaches to teaching children how words work. It is important to remember that even this extensive list does not describe the entire word study program. Word study goes on in many contexts throughout the day. Sometimes it is in the context of reading and writing; sometimes it is within a focused lesson. Word study is active; it involves children in an investigation through which they make sense of the way written language works. The following are seven ways of teaching about words and how they work:

1. Provide direct and explicit teaching of strategies and principles to the whole group, to small groups, and to individual students in conferences; base decisions about grouping on the needs of children and the principles you have in mind.

2. Demonstrate specific principles and then engage children in making, sorting, and creating charts or webs of principles and generalizations.

3. Place an example on the word wall or list examples on charts and lead the students in a discussion of how this word is related to other words on the wall or other charts once you have taught important principles and patterns in whole- or small-group instruction.

4. Follow whole-group instruction with an application of concepts and principles or strategies using manipulative and/or reading and writing activities.

5. Set up a variety of learning investigations for small groups or partners at a word study center or for individuals at desks or tables; again, it is the teacher's decision based on the nature of the task and the needs of the particular children involved.

6. Bring to closure whole-group, small-group, partner, or independent application with a group meeting in which students report on their understandings and discoveries about words.

7. Draw children's attention to powerful examples within the context of language—reading and writing—helping to solidify the new principles.

The chart in Figure 11-2 summarizes the cycle of observation, teaching, student application, and teacher reinforcement. As the chart indicates, you will be able to evaluate the effects of teaching by continuous observation of student behavior in reading, writing, and word study activities. The information gained guides your teaching.

Teaching Within a Word Study Curriculum

In this section we concentrate on the combination of specific teaching approaches that make up a word study curriculum. These approaches are "nested" within the broader framework of reading and writing. Teachers

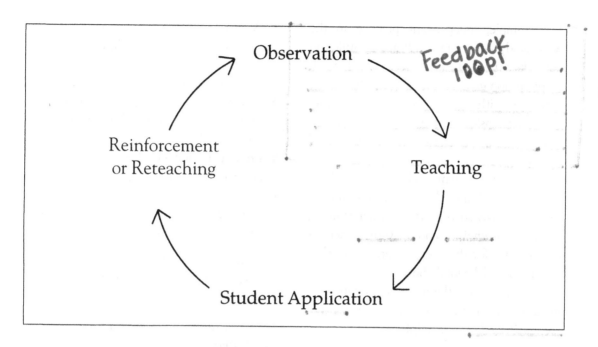

FIGURE 11-2   Teaching and Learning Cycle

not only demonstrate specific word-solving principles in explicit minilessons, they point them out again and again across the reading and writing tasks of the language arts block. We can categorize these specific teaching approaches into three broad areas (see Figure 11-3), which we will describe more fully in this chapter.

Varying Contexts for Teaching and Independent Work

There are two contexts in which children can learn about letters, sounds, and how words work:

1. In a *direct instructional* context, you are working with individuals or small groups selected for particular characteristics, strengths, and needs, or with the whole

class. The instruction may take different forms. Sometimes you are demonstrating and explaining an aspect of word study; at other times you may guide children as they work at a task designed to help them discover something about words or practice skills.

2. In an *independent work* context, children may work individually at their own desks or tables. At other times, they may work at centers, either alone or in cooperative learning with other children.

Moving from one setting to another, you can guide children and direct their attention as they explore basic concepts related to how words work. We find that one word study experience naturally follows another.

Teaching Approaches: Three Broad Areas

- Knowledge of an ever-increasing core of high-frequency words
- Knowledge of letter-sound patterns
- Knowledge of a variety of strategies for solving words

FIGURE 11-3   Teaching Approaches: Three Broad Areas

For example, independent practice in the word study center may follow a minilesson with the whole class, while a related small-group session gives a few children either some extra help with the concept or explores something more basic that they need in their learning. Follow-up sharing sessions reinforce and extend concepts presented in minilessons.

The management goal for the teaching is to "mix and match" the contexts and the teaching goals so that order is maintained, teaching is efficient and powerful, there is opportunity for discovery of principles that will be useful beyond the exercise at hand, and children have the maximum chance for meaningful practice so they can deepen their knowledge of principles.

Materials

For effective word study, a classroom must be very well equipped with appropriate materials. Figure 11-4 is an extensive list that we call a "tool kit." Some materials are teacher-made; others are purchased.

We recommend preparing and using materials in a way that supports children's independence. For example, place multiple copies of open-ended word study sheets (see Chapter 14) where students can take them as they need them. Or, have students complete their written word study activities in a word study notebook, which helps in collecting and saving work over time.

It is very important that materials are organized and accessible within the classroom. Each time a new material is introduced, create a minilesson to teach children the specific routines for using it. Each type of material (such as handwriting notebooks, dictionaries, clipboards, highlighters) should have a specific place so that children know precisely where they are and can take them out and put them away.

We also recommend that teachers organize their own word study notebooks—perhaps a three-ring notebook with dividers. In the notebook you can place:

■ The six goals of the word study program.

■ A set of comprehensive word lists and word patterns (see Appendixes 4–33).
■ A list of minilessons (Appendix 34).
■ Assessment information on children.
■ Prompts to support word solving (see Figure 18-10).
■ Prompts to help children make connections (see Figures 18-3, 18-4).
■ The list of benchmarks for progress (see Figure 20-1).
■ Other individually developed materials.

This notebook will be a constant resource for planning lessons and reflecting on instruction.

Using Minilessons Within a Structured Work Plan

Minilessons focus on the skills and strategies children need to become good readers and writers. These brief, powerful instructional sessions may be conducted with the entire class, a selected small group, or individuals with specific needs. In designing minilessons, keep in mind the repertoire of skills and understandings students, in general, need to know, as well as the strengths and needs of your particular students. The best source for minilessons is observation of children's writing and reading behavior. A minilesson is a focused instructional session designed to:

■ Create interest in written language.
■ Introduce children to any aspect of word or letter study.
■ Extend understandings of any aspect of word or letter study.
■ Demonstrate an important principle that children may use in many different ways.
■ Teach particular items of information that children will use in strategic ways.
■ Create a climate of inquiry regarding words and how they work.

A minilesson is most effective if only one aspect of word study is well taught—avoid covering several topics in a lesson. Another way to extend the learning in a minilesson is to use ongoing materials, such

A Tool Kit for Teaching About Letters, Words, and How Words Work

Writing Surfaces
Chalkboards and erasers (for individual students)
White "wipe off" board and markers
Chart paper and colored markers
Steno notebooks
Paper on clipboards
Magna Doodle (A magnetic drawing board and pencil that can be purchased at most toy stores.)

Writing Tools and Materials
Highlighter pens and tape
Clipboards
Post-it Notes (different sizes)
Markers, pencils, pens

Manipulative Materials and Games
Magnetic letters (all colors and sizes)
Alphabet letters (made of felt, foam, rubber, cardboard, or plastic)
Cookie trays or stove burner covers (for individual children to use with magnetic letters to make words)
Letter books (See Fountas & Pinnell [1996] for reproducible letter books.)
Published ABC books of all kinds (see Appendix 1)
Index cards for word sorts
Word tiles (ceramic, plastic, or cardboard) for whole words and word parts
Pictures of all kinds to sort
Hinged, sliding, and window masks (for shared reading)
Alphabet stamps
Word games
Handwriting notebooks (individual student copies)

Resource and Reference Materials
Table-top pocket charts or cardboard desk "tents" (for group reference)
Word cards to put on the word wall
Pocket charts
Alphabet linking charts
Pictionaries, dictionaries, glossaries, thesauruses
Lists of high-frequency words on cards, around coffee cans, in folders, and other places
Handwriting charts (wall and individual)
Franklin speller and speaking Franklin spellers

Other Materials for Word Study System
My *Spelling Dictionary* (individual student copies)
Teacher word study notebook (see Chapter 14)
    Word lists: high frequency, words by pattern (see Appendixes 4–33.)
    Lists of minilessons
    Assessment information on children
Forms for word study system (in trays): Look, Say, Cover, Write, Check; Have a Try; Make Connections; Buddy Study; Words to Learn
Word study notebooks (in baskets)
Study flaps
Pocket charts for word sorts

Other
Handwriting notebooks (individual student copies)

FIGURE 11-4   A Tool Kit for Teaching About Letters, Words, and How Words Work

as the interactive word charts and word walls described in Chapter 5. Here is a basic structure for using minilessons in a language arts block. We think in terms of three steps: minilesson, application, and sharing.

Step One: Minilesson

■ Provide a short, focused lesson to illustrate a principle, strategy, or understanding about letters or words.

■ Demonstrate with magnetic letters or word parts by manipulating letters, tiles, or cards, or by writing on a board or an easel.

■ Engage the students in the writing or manipulating if appropriate.

■ Talk with the students about what they are noticing or want to remember.

■ Show several examples and review the learning by making a chart with an example.

■ Invite children to generate more examples for the collection.

■ Put an exemplar on the word wall for reference.

■ Explain and/or demonstrate the word study center activity or independent assignment that the students will be expected to complete.

Step Two: Application
Students:

■ Engage in individual, partner, or small-group experiences at the word study center.

■ Manipulate letters, words, or word parts, or a form of writing that supports learning (for example, making a web, chart, or list).

■ Talk about the words with a partner or group.

■ Work at their own desks or tables rather than a center in the classroom, but the work must be active, and it is best to make some provision for interaction.

Step Three: Sharing

■ Review the principle or strategy by inviting students to share their examples or written work.

■ Arrange for review and sharing within the language arts block or at the end of the morning or afternoon.

■ Place a summary chart on the wall and/or review the exemplar on the word wall.

A comprehensive list of minilessons is provided in Appendix 34.

Using a Word Study (ABC) Center for Independent Work
The word study center is an organized place in the room that provides for independent practice following a minilesson on spelling or phonics principles. For young children, you might want to call this an "ABC center." Many of the materials listed earlier are used in the word study center, but materials are not the only feature of the word study center. To ensure meaningful learning at centers, a carefully structured plan is required. See the guidelines listed in Chapter 4.

Varying the Planning for Independent Work
It is important to remember that the goal of the structured word study plan is not to "do" the word study center, it is to provide for application of principles. Some teachers feel uncomfortable implementing work at centers, particularly if they or the children have not had much experience in this kind of independent work. We advise opening center work gradually, teaching the routines very carefully, and observing and interacting with children during their first experiences. The process of learning to work in centers may take several weeks or longer. You do not have to wait until children are using centers skillfully and independently to get started with some independent word study work.

The chart in Figure 11-5 suggests an overall structure for planning word study activities. As indicated on the chart there are

Structure for Instruction in Word Study	
Instructional Component	**Options**
Minilesson An explicit teaching session on letters, words, and how they work. A minilesson may include manipulating letters, making group charts, and referring to a word wall.	Community Morning Meeting or Writing Workshop Minilesson or Small-Group Teaching
Application Activity An engaging process of hands-on activity with manipulative materials and/or writing.	Center Work or Whole Class Activity or Partners or Independent
Group Share May include group chart and word wall exemplar.	Whole Class or Small Group or Partners

FIGURE 11-5   Structure for Instruction in Word Study

many options you will want to consider for minilessons, application activities, and sharing. Each can be accomplished with the whole class, groups, or individuals; the location of the activity also can vary.

Many of the activities that we will suggest in the next few chapters can be accomplished in several different settings, including the word study center. After a minilesson in which students have seen the task demonstrated and have been engaged on some level, consider the following possibilities:

▌ Use a workboard and ask students to visit the word study center sometime during the language arts period and perform the task, incorporating some kind of writing that provides evidence that they have completed the work (such as the word study notebook).

▌ Provide materials at students' tables or desks and involve the whole class at once in the application of principles, perhaps allowing students to work with partners or in triads, while you observe and give feedback.

▌ Rotate small groups of students into the word study center on a set time schedule and check with each group as they finish the task.

▌ Provide activities and materials for each student, working independently at a desk or table, asking them to complete the assigned task within a set time frame (for example, by midmorning or the end of the morning).

Using Time in a Word Study Program

There are two ways to think about time in a word study program. First, we have to think of the way word study will work over the course of a week or several weeks. In the sample plan in Figure 11-6, we have outlined a week's work. The second column describes the weekly class lesson using a word study center and sharing. The third column, the Buddy Study System, is described in Chapter 14.

The plan indicates that a systematic word study system is part of the weekly schedule and that activities in the system vary over the days. The purposes of a word study system are to provide continuous, systematic teaching of principles and strategies as well as to meet the differing learning needs of children. A comprehensive word study system is described in detail in Chapter 14. This efficient process engages students in daily focused learning experiences

		Class Lesson (strategy, pattern, or principle)	Buddy Study System*** (core words and personal words)	Writing
	Reading			Writing
Monday	Read Aloud Shared Reading Guided Reading Independent Reading	• Minilesson* (Strategy, Pattern, Principle) • Exemplar on Word Wall • Word Study Activity** • Sharing	Choose, Write, Build, Mix, Fix, Mix	Shared Writing Interactive Writing Writing Workshop Independent Writing
Tuesday	Read Aloud Shared Reading Guided Reading Independent Reading	• Review Strategy, Pattern, Principle • Word Study Activity** • Sharing	Look, Say, Cover, Write, Check	Shared Writing Interactive Writing Writing Workshop Independent Writing
Wednesday	Read Aloud Shared Reading Guided Reading Independent Reading	• Review Strategy, Pattern, Principle • Word Study Activity** • Sharing	Buddy Check	Shared Writing Interactive Writing Writing Workshop Independent Writing
Thursday	Read Aloud Shared Reading Guided Reading Independent Reading	• Review Strategy, Pattern, Principle • Word Study Activity** • Sharing	Make Connections	Shared Writing Interactive Writing Writing Workshop Independent Writing
Friday	Read Aloud Shared Reading Guided Reading Independent Reading	• Summarize Strategy, Pattern, Principle • Review Exemplar	Buddy Test	Shared Writing Interactive Writing Writing Workshop Independent Writing

Word Study System (table title)

*A minilesson may be taught one or more times per week.
**This can be a whole-class, small-group, or word study center activity for one or more groups daily.
***Day 2, 3, and 4 activities can happen in any sequence.

FIGURE 11-6   Sample Weekly Work Plan for Word Study

related to their individual learning needs and at the same time expands the knowledge base of the whole class. It provides for open-ended high-level work on how words work. The system includes both explicit teaching and student ownership and responsibility.

We also have to plan and manage time on a daily basis. There are many demands on instructional time, and one of the most pressing problems is to "fit" everything into the time allotted for language arts. It is essential to have at least two and a half to three hours for reading, writing, word study, and other areas of the language arts. Remember that word study includes both phonics and spelling. Figure 11-7 contains two sample work plans for a school day. In Chapter 14, we provide further suggestions for time planning, along with a description of the comprehensive word study system.

These sample work plans are intended to be examples only. Every teacher has to consider her own schedule and the time available. Word study is only one part of

[handwritten annotation: This is not attainable 1) too structured 2) what about all of the other parts to the day??]

Sample Daily Work Plan 1

8:45	Read Aloud
9:00	Shared Reading/Interactive Writing
9:15	Handwriting Lesson and Practice
9:25	Class Lesson on Word Study
	Word Wall Exemplar
9:35	Whole Class Word Study Activity
10:05	Group Sharing Word Study
10:15	Guided Reading/Independent Reading
	Buddy Study System: Partners
	Work Board Literacy Activities
11:35	Writing Workshop: Minilesson, Conferring, Sharing
12:30	Lunch
1:15	Math
2:15	Science/Social Studies
3:00	Dismissal

Sample Daily Work Plan 2

8:45	Buddy Study System: Partners
9:00	Read Aloud
9:15	Interactive Writing/Shared Reading
9:30	Handwriting Lesson and Practice
9:40	Writing Workshop: Minilesson, Conferring, Sharing
10:40	Centers and Guided Reading
	Centers, e.g., Word Study
	Poem Box
	Buddy Reading
	Listening Center
	Browsing Boxes
12:00	Lunch
12:45	Science
1:30	Math
2:30	Social Studies
3:15	Dismissal

FIGURE 11-7 Two Sample Daily Work Plans

the language arts curriculum, and it must be organized so that time is not taken away from reading and writing. The purpose of word study is to contribute to reading and writing skill and to create excitement about words—not to deaden the curriculum by too much practice on isolated items. Finding a good balance requires effective use of time and good organization in addition to good planning for lessons. With those challenges met, word study can greatly enhance learning in the literacy curriculum.

Suggestions for Professional Development

Use this time to get organized for word study.

1. *Time.*
   ▮ Examine your schedule and plan when you might provide minilessons, application, and follow-up.
   ▮ Create a one-week schedule. As you get started, it might be a good idea to stick to the same weekly time schedule for a few weeks.

2. *Materials.* Looking at the tool kit list,
   ▮ Consider the needs of your students. Select the materials you will need to support a word study program.
   ▮ Take an informal inventory of materials that you already have in your classroom and/or that are available in the school.
   ▮ Identify essential materials for getting started and create an active plan to acquire what you need.

3. *Space.* Looking at your classroom area,
   ▮ Identify a space where you can provide minilessons. Students should be able to see as you work on an easel or board. The children might be sitting at tables or on the floor, but they should have enough space to be comfortable, especially if they are using materials.
   ▮ Identify places to store word study materials so they can be kept in order and be easily accessible. If necessary, acquire containers such as plastic tubs or covered cardboard boxes.
   ▮ Identify a place for a word study center and begin to design it.
   ▮ Look for wall space to display charts and words. Backs of shelves and filing cabinets also work well.

Teaching for Print and Sound Knowledge

handwritten note: clear handwriting

Acquiring Print and Sound Knowledge Through Varied Activity

By the end of kindergarten, we expect that our instructional program will have supported children in their early learning of important concepts about print and sounds in the language (see Chapter 19 for kindergarten benchmarks). In a dynamic literacy program that includes word study, children will:

■ Have a network of clear understandings about letters—how they look, their names, and that they are related to specific sounds made with the mouth.

■ Know how to look at print—identify the features that distinguish one letter from another, know how space is used to define words, use left to right directionality, and identify punctuation and other important aspects of print.

■ Have established the alphabetic principle—know that words are made up of sequences of sounds, identify some sounds in words, and connect them to letters.

■ Be able to form many letters in writing (most with ease and fluency).

■ Be able to form letters that are legible and reflect the essential features of a letter so that others can read it.) *handwritten: → important*

■ Have a small body of high-frequency words that they can read, write, and use to monitor in reading and to create messages in writing. *handwritten: ✓*

These early learnings give children a wealth of knowledge as they enter the more formal literacy curriculum that usually exists in our first-grade classrooms. In the section that follows, we list and briefly describe nine instructional actions that help children develop print and sound knowledge. Each of these activities may be accomplished in whole-group, small-group, or individual instruction at a word study center as described in Chapter 11. *handwritten: ✓*

Picture Sorting

It is useful for kindergarten and primary teachers to have a large number of pictures categorized for sorting. Children can help to collect pictures from newspapers and magazines. The pictures are then glued onto cards for sorting. Another good source for lots of pictures is phonics and spelling workbooks.

Sorting pictures is useful for very young children because it requires them to focus on the sounds of the words. To sort pictures, children must think of and say the names of the objects and search for ways that those words sound alike or different.

The activity is different from a worksheet in which children must have the precise name of the object in the picture and get it "right" or "wrong." Picture sorting is more active and open in nature. Children can find pictures that start with, end with, or in some way represent a certain sound, and they can say the sounds as they sort. Pictures can also be used in a more exploratory way as children discover several different ways to put them into groups. Some of the basic ways to sort pictures are by:

▮ Beginning sounds.
▮ Ending sounds.
▮ Medial sounds.
▮ Number of syllables.
▮ Rhyming words.

Letter Sorting and Matching

In letter sorting, children organize letters and match them according to various characteristics. They can use magnetic letters on a table or on a metal surface such as a magnetic chalkboard. It is sometimes useful to have children working with the letters on both vertical and horizontal planes, because then they can see the forms of the letters in different ways. Many other kinds of letters can be used, for example, letters printed on cards, stiff felt letters, rubber or plastic letters, and so on. We think it is useful to have many different sizes and colors of letters so that children can see the same features across a variety of letters. For beginners, it is helpful to have letters that are cut out so children can feel the shape rather than just see it on a card. The whole idea is for children to develop fast letter recognition and to become flexible with that knowledge. For example, in Figure 12-1, there are many different forms of the letter g.

Readers who use the alphabetic system know that while there are quite a few variations in size and shape, these letters are all g. Those readers can even deal with the considerable variation involved in the g that is used in printed text; they know what to look for in order to identify the letter.

Letter sorting focuses children's attention on the letters in several important ways by:

▮ Helping them attend to the important features that distinguish one letter from another.

▮ Giving them practice in saying the names of the letters.

▮ Contributing to their ability to form letters by familiarizing them with the features.

▮ Giving them practice perceiving letters when they are with other letters.

At first, it is a good idea to encourage children to simply play with and explore the letters without specific assignments to sort them or make words. Exploration helps them discover features on their own and make connections between letters and what they know about words, (even if that knowledge is limited.) Children can make their names or find some of the letters in their own names and the names of friends. They can reproduce words by building from a model some of the simple words that they are meeting through reading and writing.

Children can sort letters in the following ways:

▮ Letters in my name and letters not in my name.
▮ Letters in ABC order.
▮ Letters of different colors.
▮ Letters of the same size or different sizes.
▮ Letters made from different media.
▮ Upper- and lowercase letters.
▮ Letters with tails (y, p).
▮ Letters with circles (o, a, d, p).
▮ Letters with sticks (p, b, l, m).
▮ Letters with tunnels (h, m, n).

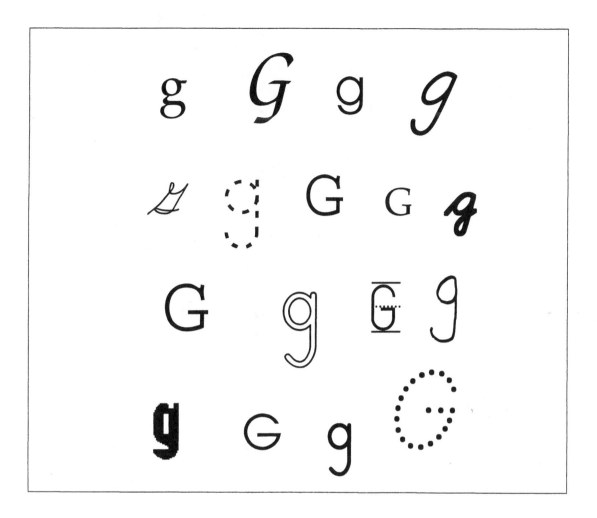

FIGURE 12-1   Letter Features: A Variety of Gs

▋ Letters that are tall (*h, l, f*).

▋ Letters that are short (*c, u, a, n*).

▋ Letters with lines that cross through them (*t, f, x*).

▋ Upper- and lowercase letter pairs (*Aa, Bb*).

▋ Letters with the same upper- and lowercase forms (*Xx, Ss, Yy*).

▋ Letters with a dot (*i, j*).

▋ Letters with curves (*n, m, e, f*).

▋ Letters with slants (*x, y*).

▋ Letters with two parts that are symmetrical (*W, w, M, m*).

▋ Vowels (*a, e, i, o, u*).

▋ Consonants (all letters except *a, e, i, o, u*).

After children have become accustomed to the process of sorting letters, they will think of new ways to sort them.

Alphabet Linking Chart

An alphabet linking chart is an alphabet chart with clear pictures, letters, and words that children use as a reference. An example is shown in Figure 12-2 (see Appendix 3 and also Fountas and Pinnell 1996 for a reproducible version of this chart).

This chart can be enlarged to make wall charts; students can have smaller copies in their writing folders. They can use the chart to do any of the following:

▋ Read every other box.

▋ Read only the letters.

▋ Read only the words.

▋ Read only the vowels.

▋ Read only the consonants.

▋ Read the pictures.

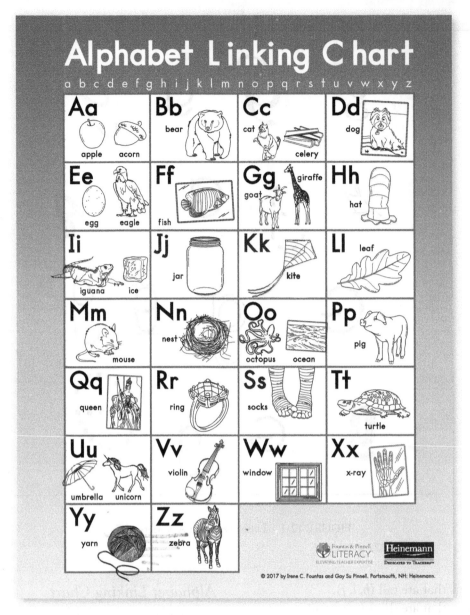

FIGURE 12-2   Alphabet Linking Chart

❚ Read the vowels as a group while another group reads the consonants.

❚ Sing the chart as a class or group.

❚ Make predictions of letters the teacher has covered with Post-its.

Alphabet Books

ABC books are a useful reference and learning tool for kindergarten or first-grade children. We recommend providing a variety of ABC books in the book corner, the ABC center, the writing center, and many other places in the classroom as well as utilizing them in word study activities. The books provide numerous opportunities to engage children in the following:

❚ Reading letter names.

❚ Matching letter forms in the book with plastic letters.

❚ Developing new letter-sound associations.

❚ Using magnetic letters to match the words that are associated with each letter, and then checking constructions against the words in the book.

❚ Making a class alphabet book or individual alphabet books using a pertinent theme.

❙ Making individual letter books (see Fountas and Pinnell 1996).

Letter Books

As children are just beginning to make the connections between letters and sounds, it is helpful to have little books that focus on one letter (Figure 12-3).

On the front of the book is the letter in plain type, and on each page of the book is a clear picture of something that begins with the sound of that letter. The word naming the object in the picture is written below it. The child can "read" through the letter book by simply saying the name of the letter on the cover and then naming each picture. These books have several advantages:

❙ The child is saying and hearing a series of words that begin with the same sound, thereby developing phonemic awareness.

❙ The child has the opportunity to notice the visual features of the letter on the front cover and at the beginning of each word.

❙ The child has numerous opportunities to connect letters and sounds.

❙ The child is building a repertoire of examples of words that begin with the sound associated with a particular letter.

If you would like your students to have their own collection of letter books, directions and reproducible masters for eight-page letter books for each alphabet letter are included in *Guided Reading* (Fountas and Pinnell 1996).

Letter books may be placed in the ABC center, adding one or two at a time as the letters are brought to the children's attention. They may also be included in children's personal book collections.

Name Charts

At first, literacy learning is highly personal. There is no more important word to a child than his own name. Kindergarten teachers especially use children's names as a starting point. First-grade teachers who are working with children who have limited experiences with print also find children's names to be an effective starting point as well as a resource for more complex kinds of word study. First- and second-grade teachers find name charts with first and last names very useful resources for making links to read and write new words. The elements of word analysis are often contained in names, such as *er* endings and *st* and *ch* letter clusters. The name chart is an important resource for classroom work (see Figure 12-4).

For beginners, the chart will display children's first names, but later charts may have both first and last names. The chart may be made in a pocket chart (a hanging chart with folds or "pockets" where cards may be inserted for display) or a wall chart. Usually, names that begin the same are grouped together, but several different configurations (for example, ending sounds,

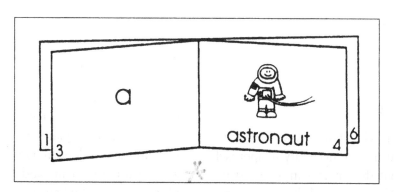

FIGURE 12-3   Individual Letter Book *Aa*

FIGURE 12-4   Name Chart

double letters, or letter clusters) are possible as children become more familiar with all of their classmates' names. The name chart is a constant reference as the teacher works with the whole class or small groups in interactive writing. In addition, children can use the name chart for word study:

■ "Reading" the name chart (or several different charts) using a pointer.

■ Finding names with particular features (such as words with er as in Peter).

■ Writing their own names and the names of friends.

■ Making their own names and the names of friends with magnetic letters or letter cards.

Name Puzzles

For children who have very low letter knowledge, it may be necessary to approach learning about their names in a very structured way. We have found the name puzzle (Figure 12-5) to be especially effective.

The child's name is written on a strip of paper and then cut up, letter by letter. The letters should be large enough to clearly see and manipulate (about two inches tall). The letter pieces are placed in an envelope. The child's name is clearly written in black letters across the top of this envelope in about the same size as the puzzle letters. The envelope makes a surface upon which the child can make the name. At first, children who do not know the letters in their names can use the print on the envelope as a model, creating the name underneath.

After a while, challenge the child to cover up the model and then check with it after she has put her name together. Eventually, she can make the name without the model, and you can add her last name to the puzzle. Children can also try putting together the name of a partner. You can ask your students to place a particular letter back in the envelope, requiring them to find a letter using its name and searching for its visual features. We have found that by using the name puzzle every day, kindergarten

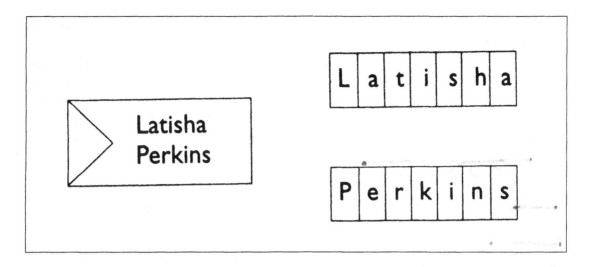

FIGURE 12-5   Name Puzzle

children quickly learn the letters in their names. They:

▍ Learn very well a few examples of letters so they know *how* to look for distinctive features.

▍ Acquire examples of letter-sound relationships (for example, the first letter of their name or a dominant consonant).

▍ Learn that the sequence of letters in words is important.

▍ Learn that a word is constant—that it is made the same way every time. ✓

▍ Learn that a word is displayed as a cluster of letters with space on either side.

▍ Acquire a known word that can be a constant reference point as they learn other additional words.

Songs, Chants, and Rhymes

Rhythmic language provides opportunities for children to hear similarities and differences in sound patterns. In our literary heritage there are a variety of jump rope jingles, chants, and rhymes that help children not only attend to sound patterns but to learn the alphabet and vocabulary associated with particular sounds and letters. An example is "A, my name is Alice," a jump rope jingle that explores a variety of words for each letter.

We should not neglect the classic "alphabet song" that many children learn. The musical version of the alphabet makes it easy to remember what letter comes next, and children enjoy singing the song. Of course, there may be a few misconceptions as children approximate, but by singing it frequently and sometimes pointing to letters on the ABC chart while doing so, they will gradually systematize knowledge.

Letter Formation (Handwriting)

Another way to help young children learn about the important features of letters is to invite them to write letters for themselves. Letter writing and teaching will certainly happen within the context of word and message writing during interactive and independent writing, but there is also a place in the word study curriculum for short, directed attention to handwriting. Assuming efficient movements in handwriting helps children feel how the letter is formed. It helps fix the features of the letter in the child's mind and visual memory so that it can be identified. There are some more important reasons for handwriting instruction.

As teachers and children in kindergarten and first grade concentrated on the constructive aspects of composing and writ-

143

ing messages (and rightly so), handwriting may have been neglected. We do not like to see children inefficiently "drawing" letters. That makes their writing less fluent, and spelling may be seen as poor simply because they do not know how to make their writing legible. Attention to helping children acquire smooth, efficient movements in handwriting is essential. Writing must be:

■ Legible, with letters conforming to standard features so that the words are decipherable.

■ Organized in lines with space.

■ Produced with some fluency so that the writer does not have to tolerate too much mechanical difficulty.

Figure 12-6 shows a basic handwriting chart, which can be reproduced on cardboard and given to each child. In addition, the charts can be displayed around the classroom for reference. If your school uses a different style of letter formation, you should make a chart corresponding to that style.

A System for Handwriting Instruction
To learn letter formation in manuscript or cursive, all children should have their own handwriting notebook. Take a composition notebook with about fifty pages and cut it in half using a paper cutter so that the pages are short and children can easily use them for brief periods of practice. On the front, write *My Handwriting Book* (see Figure 12-7).

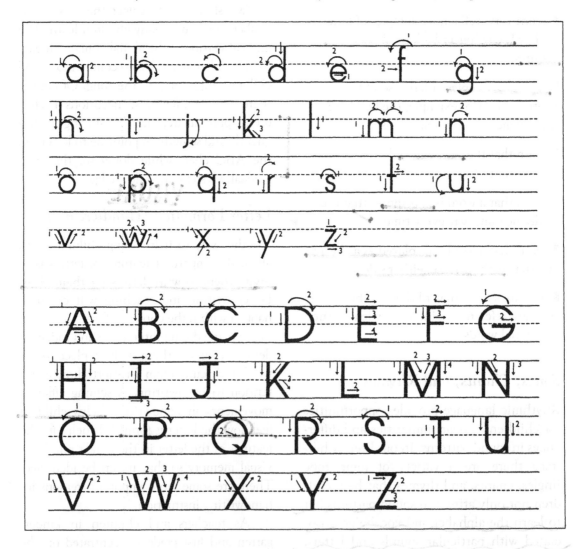

FIGURE 12-6   Letter Formation Chart

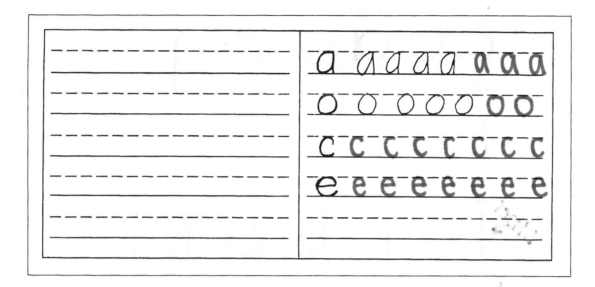

FIGURE 12-7   Sample *My Handwriting Book*

Children work in the handwriting notebook after a brief demonstration by the teacher. We call this the "five minute" handwriting lesson. Teachers spend a few minutes demonstrating or reminding children of the letter. The introduction or review of the letter might include one or more of the following, but should be brief:

■ Make the letter in the air.

■ Make it on the rug.

■ Make it in large form on the chart paper or on a Magna Doodle.

■ Brainstorm words that start with this letter so that children have an association.

You can easily manage the system. One teacher cut cereal boxes in half, covered them, and wrote *Handwriting Books* on the side. For a class of twenty-four, she used four boxes—red, blue, yellow, and green. The colors helped the children quickly find their individual books among the books in the box. Each child knew the color of the box in which his notebook was placed.

These boxes were placed in the middle of each of the class tables. Children could go to the table, find their own books, practice the letters as directed, and then go on to another activity. Alternatively, the children may use these books at their desks, but it is best to keep them in one place so:

■ The books are well organized and preserved for use.

■ You can easily examine them to check children's progress.

■ You can quickly write a letter at the beginning of a line to provide individualized handwriting assignments in each book.

In the child's book, make an example of the letter at the beginning of the line so the child has a clear model and knows to practice that letter. Sometimes teachers stay with a group of letters that are formed similarly before going to another grouping, sometimes mixing the letters within that grouping. Figure 12-8 is a suggested grouping of letters that are made in similar ways.

Start with lowercase letters and then individualize by noticing the letters with which some children or individual children are having difficulty. With that information, plan the handwriting minilessons to review those letters. Or, take individual children's

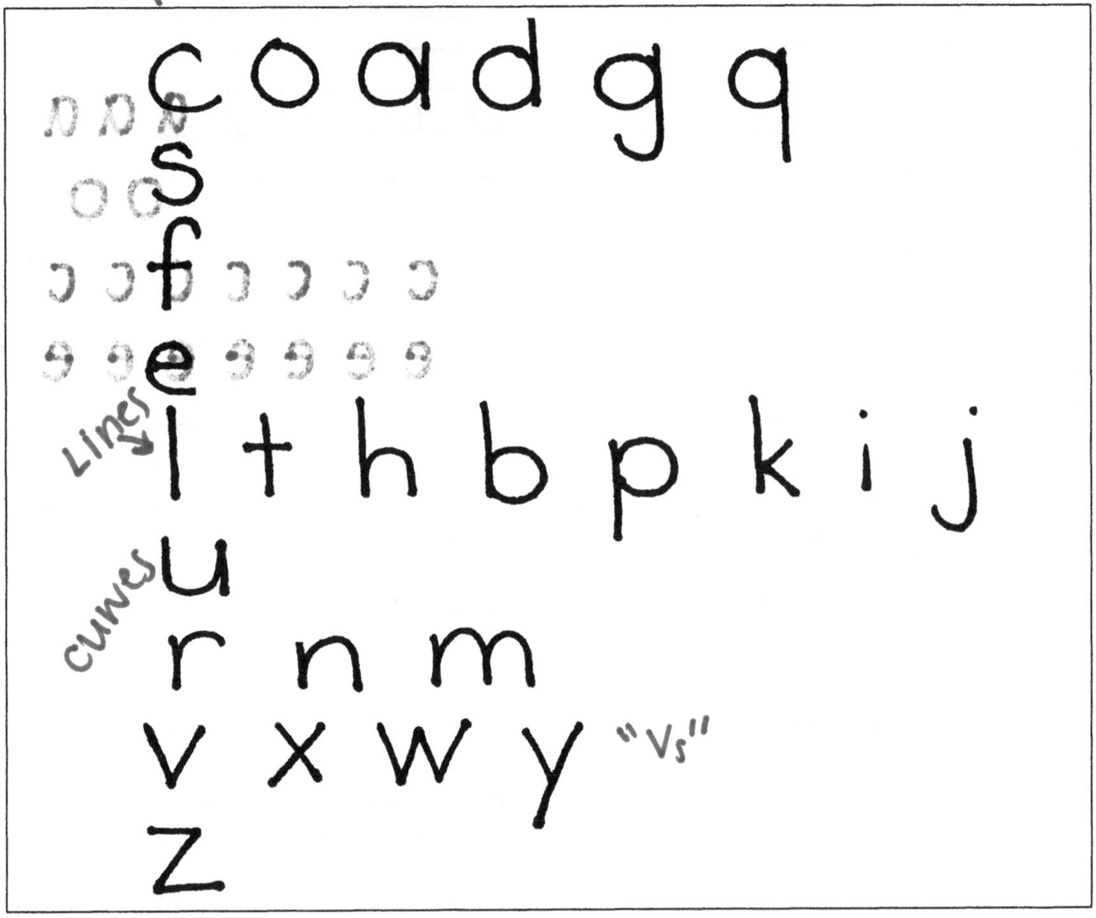

circles

Liners

curves

c o a d g q
s
f
e
l t h b p k i j
u
r n m
v x w y "Vs"
z

FIGURE 12-8   Letters Made in Similar Ways

handwriting books and write in the letters for them to practice today. Then, when they open their books, they practice the letters indicated. When one handwriting book is filled up, the child gets another one. After letter writing is well established and fluent, handwriting practice on individual letters may not be needed.

For letters that have been introduced and practiced:

▌ Have children write some words, perhaps the high-frequency words they are starting to use in interactive writing, or words from the weekly spelling minilesson (see Chapter 14), so they can learn to arrange letters within words with good spacing.

▌ Move to writing a simple sentence that has one word with that letter in it so they can write in proportion with other letters. For example, for k, try "I like ____."

Working with Handwriting over Time
We recommend that this handwriting practice be accomplished in kindergarten and first grade. In kindergarten, the handwriting will generally be accomplished through interactive writing and more informal exercises rather than in the smaller notebooks, but it is important to help young children learn how to form letters from the beginning. Big motor movements will be helpful. Here are some ways to help kindergartners get started with efficient ways of forming letters:

▌ Show children how to form each letter by explaining the process out loud as you write it. For example, for h, say, "pull down, up, and over," or for a, "pull back, around, and

write in sand

down." Invite children to talk out loud as they form the same letter.

❚ Have children in the whole group make the letters in the air and on the rug or table several times, talking out loud about the motions.

oooo!

❚ Create "rainbow letters" by demonstrating a selected letter on a large piece of white chart paper with a pencil or thin black marker. Invite children to go over the letter with crayons of different colors. If each child adds three colors to the letter, much practice in the movement of letter formation will have taken place and the result will be a large letter with a "rainbow like" effect for one child to take home.

ooh!

❚ Let children write letters on paper with colored markers, in sand on a cookie tray, with a thick wet paintbrush on a chalkboard (dip the brush in water), on a Magna Doodle or magic slate—anywhere the children can write.

❚ Create a space along the chalkboard for children to write. It's easy to create several little "booths" by simply drawing lines for one child to write letters and words. Many children have not had the opportunity to work on a chalkboard and find the experience exciting. Also, it helps for children to write on a vertical plane in addition to the writing work they do at tables.

❚ Let children trace letters using stencils or plastic forms.

You may introduce handwriting notebooks whenever you decide that children have enough knowledge and control to practice some letters within a more confined space using markers or pencils. That might happen for a class or small group of children by the end of kindergarten and certainly by the beginning of first grade. The notebooks

will be useful in first grade up to the point that children have very good control of movement in letter formation.

In a later grade, you will want to use the system to help children learn cursive writing. The goal throughout the grades is to be sure that children can make legible letters as they write words, and legibility and fluency become even more important as children are spelling longer words and writing longer pieces. There are several good handwriting systems. We encourage teachers to refer to the particular handwriting charts used in their own schools.

In this chapter we have explored ways of supporting children in critical early learning about sounds and print. The learning activities mentioned here take place alongside wide experience with reading and writing. Children produce their own writing, sometimes using standard spelling of easy high-frequency words or their names, and sometimes approximating spelling as they experiment with letters and sounds. Also, children participate in shared reading and reading easy "caption" books with natural language patterns so they can get the feel of reading and develop early concepts about print (see Chapter 7 on early learning). It is not necessary for children to know all of the letters and the sounds or to be able to write, sort, or use letters in any other way before they have a chance to try out early reading and writing skills for themselves. In a literacy-rich classroom, reading, writing, and word study accompany each other simultaneously.

Remember:

Suggestions for Professional Development

1. Gather a sample of writing from a small group of kindergarten children who you think are similar in their development of knowledge about literacy. Analyze the samples, asking:

❚ What does this child know about print concepts—spacing, directionality?

■ What does this child know about letter formation (handwriting)? (If possible, have some information from observation of the child who produced the sample.)

■ Are letters formed in efficient ways?

■ Where is improvement needed?

■ What does this child know about letter-sound relationships?

2. Based on the observation of the children's writing, plan two minilessons, one on looking at print and one on handwriting. Include the minilesson focus, active involvement, application, and follow-up sharing.

Word Explorers

Teaching Strategies that Promote Active Inquiry

As children become more familiar with print, our word study program should help them expand and refine their knowledge of letters, sounds, and words. Children develop word-solving strategies throughout the primary grades. They engage in active inquiry as they encounter new words, take them apart, and investigate them inside and out:

■ They learn to make connections between words in many ways. Our ultimate goal is to help children develop a way of thinking about words. Sophisticated word solvers make connections between the words they know. They use the component parts, the spelling patterns, and the meanings of known words to derive the meaning, spelling, or pronunciation of unfamiliar words. For young children, the first connections may be very simple, but increasingly complex connections become possible as the child learns additional words.

■ They continuously expand their repertoire of high-frequency words. Children build knowledge of high-frequency words as they encounter them in reading and as they use them again and again in writing. They also build word knowledge as they work with words in word study activities such as those described later in this chapter.

■ They build knowledge of letter-sound connections from very simple to complex relationships. Learning one letter for one sound, they begin to see that more than one letter can make a single sound and that there are patterns of letters that represent sounds.

■ They learn the common spelling patterns of the language. In our language there are definite rules for the way letters follow each other. For example, in English we simply will not see a word that begins with *tl*, but we will see many that begin with *sl*. As children become more familiar with the way words work and build up a repertoire of known words, they will internalize the basic patterns that are possible. The brain is a pattern detector as well as a rule applier. When a reader or writer sees a word, the pattern is noticed and applied in other circumstances.

■ They learn to recognize and use morphemic elements of words. As we explained in Chapter 6, morphemes are the basic meaning units of language. They are, in a way, building blocks that readers and writers use to figure out unfamiliar words and to build new ones. Morphemes like *some* and *body* or *one* may be strung together to make compound words. Or, morphemes like *s* and *ing* may be added to other morphemes to add meaning. The spelling of words is intimately connected to the meaning of words in very logical ways that children will discover as they work with words in our word study curriculum.

As we indicate in Chapter 19, "Establishing Benchmarks for Progress," we would expect that all of these understandings and strategies will be in place by the end of second grade and will be expanded and used flexibly by the end of third grade. In Figure 13-1, Jackie, a third-grade teacher, summarized these strategies with her class on a chart.

Prompting for Word-Solving Strategies

A basic way to extend word study is through a combination of minilessons and practice of various kinds. Throughout the process, teachers can prompt and remind children to use what they know in strategic ways.

The conversations that take place during teaching make the particular activities powerful. Because teachers' language prompts children to use effective strategies, we call this kind of conversation "teaching for strategies." We can show and demonstrate examples that illustrate principles about how words work. We present the structure and organization of minilessons in Chapter 11. But we also need to work with children as they apply principles. So, we precede our list of approaches and activities with some suggestions for interacting with children.

Teacher-Child Interactions to Support Word Solving

The word study curriculum highlights techniques and strategies that children can easily learn to help them solve words. Some of these approaches involve techniques, such as saying the word slowly, that prompt the kind of in-the-head thinking that is required. You may want to make a list with the children of ways they can help themselves solve words. This list, perhaps added to over time, could remain on display in the classroom as a reminder. Figure 13-2 is a chart

Strategies for Solving Words
Sound   You can read or write some words by thinking about the sounds   (*man, dog*).
Look   You can read or write some words by thinking about the way they look   (*the, pie*).
Mean   You can read or write some words by thinking about what they mean   (*unpack, two, sandwich*).
Connect   You can use what you know about a word to figure out a new word   (*tree, my—try*).
Inquire   You can use materials to learn more about words   (list, dictionary, chart, computer).

FIGURE 13-1 Strategies for Solving Words

Good Spellers . . .

- look for patterns
- look for word parts
- try several ways to write a word
- write sounds in words
- write a vowel in each word and in each syllable
- think about words that sound the same
- think about words that look the same
- check to see if words look right
- think about what words mean
- practice words
- use a dictionary to check
- look for words in the classroom
- ask someone if they can't figure it out

FIGURE 13-2   Good Spellers . . .

[handwritten: reminders; key]

that was used in one classroom to remind children of the range of effective strategies.

Such a chart can be used in group instruction and referred to in individual conferences. The list is designed to prompt actions such as the following:

1. Say the word slowly; listen to the sounds; write the sounds in order, with each sound represented by one or more letters.

2. Clap syllables; listen for the sounds in syllables; write the word, syllable by syllable, making sure that each syllable has a vowel or y.

3. Think about how words look; try several different patterns; and think of other words with that pattern.

4. Think about what the word means (this may help in finding a pattern that works). *[handwritten: connect]*

5. Think of other words that are like this word; try using parts of other words and putting them together to make the different parts of this word.

[handwritten: notice how this is the LAST action on the list]

6. Check the charts on the wall and the dictionary.

7. Ask for help.

Teaching How to Make Connections Between Words in Word Study

It is important to use manipulative letters or write on an easel to demonstrate looking at and using similarities and differences in words. The questions in Figure 13-3 will guide students to make links between and among the words they know once they have been taught how to make these connections. The goal is for them to focus on sounds, letter patterns, and meanings of words. They learn that when they know something about a word, they can use that knowledge to figure out the sounds, letter patterns, or meanings of many other words. When teachers promote this kind of thinking in minilessons and other teaching throughout the day, students will attend to "linking" or making connections, learn to manipulate letter and sound parts, and learn more about how words work.

Making Connections to Solve Words

- Do you know other words that start with the same letter or letters? (*steep, stairs*)
- Do you know words that end with the same letter or letters? (*rest, west*)
- Do you know words that have the same middle part? (*coat, float*)
- Do you know other words that rhyme? (*do, new, blue*)
- Do you know other words that have the same number of parts? (*tomato, magazine*)
- Do you know other words that sound the same but look different? (*to, two*)
- Is there a word that can sound different but is spelled the same? (*read, read*)
- Can you add letters to the front of the word to make a new word? (*and, stand*)
- Can you add letters to the end to build a new word? Can you add more? (*care, careful, carefully; go, going; to, too, today*)
- Can you change the letter or letters at the front to make a new word? (*string, thing*)
- Can you change the letters at the end to make a new word? (*track, trash*)
- Can you change the vowel or vowels to make a new word? (*and, end; get, got*)
- Can you change one syllable to make a new word? (*Jell-O, jelly; with compounds: someday, someone; with contractions: didn't, wasn't; with endings: littler, littlest*)
- Can you change one or two letters to make a new word? (*next, nest*)
- Can you take away or add one or two letters to make a new word? (*stand, and; air, chair*)
- Can you use part of the word to make a new word (*spring, spray; day, gray*)
- Are there other words that mean the same or almost the same? (*turquoise, aquamarine*)
- Are there words that sound the same but look different? (*wood, would*)
- Is there a word that looks the same but sounds different? (*present, present*)
- Can you add *s* to the word to make another word? (*pen, pens*)
- Can you make the word a plural form? (*life, lives*)
- Can you join the word with another word to make a new word? (*in, inside*)
- Can you add *d, ed,* or *ing* to the word? (*hoped, started, standing*)
- Can you shorten the word by removing parts (or lengthen the word by adding parts)? (*automobile, auto; remove, move; breakfast, fast*)
- Are there other words that can be made from the base or root word? (*move, movement, moving, removed, movable*)

FIGURE 13-3   Making Connections to Solve Words

The questions can be used in minilessons, games, or partner activities. Select the ones that are appropriate for your students.

Prompts to Support Word Solving During Reading, Writing, and Word Study Activities

One of the most effective ways to draw children's attention to words is to prompt them to notice particular aspects of words *while* they are reading or writing extended text. In this way, they learn that what they know can be used in many ways to figure out what they do not know. They analyze words—taking them apart in reading and constructing them in writing—in the service of meaning. The text always has to make sense, and we figure out words so we can make meaning for ourselves. Children will learn that many of the same prompts they use to solve words during reading and writing can also be used when they are focusing on word study at a center, with a partner, or independently.

In Figure 13-4 we list some of the prompts that might be used in reading, in writing, and in word study. In Chapter 18, we illustrate word-solving prompts during reading.

We have found that concise language such as the examples in our lists of prompts is more effective than long explanations that interrupt the process. We have to

Scaffold

Prompts to Solve Words in Reading and/or Writing
To help the student notice errors: You noticed what was wrong. Find the part that's not quite right. Check to see if that looks right. Where's the tricky part? (after an error) Underline the tricky part. Get a good look. There's a tricky word on this line. What did you notice? (after hesitation or stop) What's wrong? Why did you stop? Do you think it looks like _____? Were you right?
To help the student problem-solve words: Did you write all the sounds you hear? Did you write a vowel in each part you hear? There are two vowels together in the middle. What could you try? What do you hear first? Next? At the end? Write the ending. What's that like? Listen for the first part. Next part, last part. It starts like _____. It ends like _____. Listen for the ending. Look at the parts. There are _____ letters. What do you know that might help? Do you see a part that can help? Do you know a word like that? Do you know a word that starts with those letters? Ends with those letters? What's that like? Think of what the word means. Is it like another word you know? What other word do you know like that? What letter do you expect to see at the beginning (or end)? Do you see a part that can help? What could you try? Look for/write a part you know. There's a silent letter at the beginning. Try it.

FIGURE 13-4   Prompts to Solve Words in Reading and/or Writing

To help the student notice errors and fix them:
Does it look right?
One more letter will make it look right.
That sounds right, but does it look right?
You only have one letter wrong.
It starts like that. Now check the last part.
I like the way you worked that out.
That's one way to write it. Is there another way?
You made a mistake, can you find it?
You wrote all the sounds you hear. Think about how that word looks.
Something wasn't quite right.
You're nearly right.
You almost got that. See if you can find what is wrong.
You've got the first part (last part) right.
Try that again.
Try it another way.

FIGURE 13-4   Prompts to Solve Words in Reading and/or Writing, *continued*

do they know?

remember, though, that a *prompt* is just that—it reminds, arouses, or provokes a response. The meaning of this word implies that the response is there and the knowledge is there; the learner must simply be reminded. The following sequence of events might take place over time, but it is essential if any of the prompts are to be effective:

1. In a clear demonstration, usually within a minilesson, teach the children a response or connection that will help them (for example, that many words begin with clusters of consonant letters). Show several examples and have children generate examples. This lesson may result in beginning a list or chart for reference in the classroom and an exemplar for the word wall.

2. Design an application activity (such as sorting and/or writing or reading words with letter clusters and recording some of them in a notebook).

3. Following the application activity, bring the group together for sharing. Add student examples to the chart.

4. Reinforce the principle through explicitly pointing out word examples in reading and writing as the opportunities naturally arise. When children are looking for a word similar to the one they want to write, tell them that sometimes it helps to look at more than one letter at the beginning of a word.

5. Plan other minilessons and applications as needed.

6. When children demonstrate that they have a beginning understanding of the principle, teachers can use the prompt effectively during word study activities, in reading, and in writing. For example, teachers can say:

■ Try the first part.
■ Do you see a part that can help?
■ Write the first part that you hear.
■ Do you know another word that starts like that? Or, with those letters?

Application Activities for Word-Solving Discovery and Practice

Teachers can apply the principles and concepts that they address in lessons to many different instructional settings. Ideally, teachers and students will explore each word-solving principle in a variety of ways. In the following section, we list and define several different kinds of activities that we have found effective in helping children learn to solve words. Each is active and promotes inquiry and discovery on the part of the child. Many are multilevel; children can go beyond the particular activity to discover more.

Word Making

Word making can be accomplished with magnetic letters or with letter cards. Sometimes children record the words they make in a notebook. Children can build words in a variety of categories, such as:

- ▮ Names (first and last).
- ▮ Names that begin with the same letter or letter clusters (*Stan* and *Stevie*).
- ▮ Words in special categories (color words, animal words, number words, theme words).
- ▮ Words that rhyme (*mail*, *pail*).
- ▮ Words with two, three, four letters (*am, ant, make*).
- ▮ Words from a particular set of letters (making words from a set like *c, a, h, s, l, r, t*).
- ▮ Words from word parts (such as *ack, ame, tr, cr, sh, pl*).

- ▮ Words with one, two, three syllables.
- ▮ Words that start with a consonant or vowel (*dog, door; apple, ant*).
- ▮ Words that end the same (*track, duck*).
- ▮ Words that have the same vowel sound (*feet, meat, receive*).
- ▮ Words with a particular vowel (*cat, make, sail, board*).
- ▮ Words with silent letters (*lamb, comb, meat, knight*).
- ▮ Contractions (*I'm, wasn't, don't, didn't*).
- ▮ Compound words (*everywhere, something*).
- ▮ Words with prefixes or suffixes (*unfasten, removable*).
- ▮ Homophones (*aisle, I'll*).
- ▮ Words from the same root (*medical, medicine*).

Word Sorting

As children become more knowledgeable about letters, sounds, and words, a good activity for the word study center is word sorting (see Figure 13-5).

In this activity, children compare, contrast, and sort words according to specific features (Henderson 1990; Templeton and Bear 1992; Zutell 1996). Word sorting will enable students to form hypotheses, concepts, and generalizations about the properties of written words, and it will help them link new words to the familiar ones they can

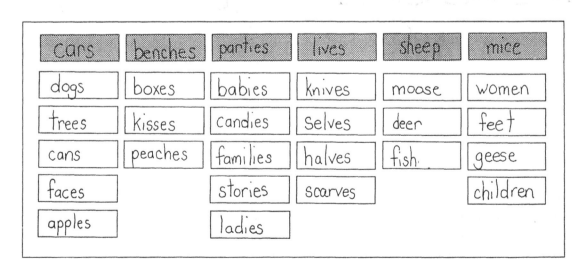

FIGURE 13-5   Word Sort: Plurals

already spell. There are two basic types of word sort activities:

1. In *closed sorts*, students are asked to find a specified feature in a group of words. For example, students can find words that have a silent *e* (*make, pile, cute*) or any other sound. In closed sorts, children are being asked to engage in deductive thinking.

2. In *open sorts*, students classify words according to shared features that they themselves discover. For example, students can find words that have an *ed* and learn that some of those words have a consonant that is doubled before the *ed*. In open sorts, children are being asked to engage in inductive thinking.

For children at all levels, it is important to talk about the words as they sort them because the dialogue promotes understanding and the internalization of principles. Here are some basic guidelines for sorting words:

■ Words can be sorted by how they sound. Word sorts for early readers would focus on using their knowledge of consonant and vowel patterns. Children can sort by initial consonants and move to ending and medial sounds. When asking children to sort words by vowel patterns or phonograms, use words that are highly regular phonetically and patterns that are common and reliable.

■ Words can be sorted by how they look. Start with simple patterns. Later, add more complex sorts—ones that do not sound entirely as they look. Use words with letter patterns that are more complex.

■ Words can be sorted by connections between meaning units. Word sorts can be constructed to help children discover word components and how they add to or change the meaning of words. Sorts can revolve around roots, inflected endings, prefixes, suffixes, contractions, compound words, and so on. Later, words can be sorted in much more complex categories such as homophones, homographs, synonyms,

antonyms. Word derivations and etymology can also be explored through word sorting, so it is an activity that can be used throughout the elementary grades as children work with words to uncover important linguistic understandings.

Word sorting is actually a mind-stretching and enjoyable activity. As teachers, it reminds us of the features of words and of what we know about the linguistic system. We encourage you to use the word lists in Appendixes 4 to 33 to create specific sorts that meet the needs of your students.

Figure 13-6 shows an example of a double word sort. This collection was sorted by how the ending sounds (*ed* as /d/ and *ed* as /t/), and then it was sorted by the way the word looks (whether a letter is doubled). Children have the opportunity to discover two kinds of rules within one set of words. Figure 13-7 on page 158 contains some other suggestions for constructing word sorts.

The categories are endless. Making lists in categories helps children attend to sound and letter patterns and move beyond regular, simple letter-sound correspondence. Children will learn how to identify complex patterns.

Word sorting may be accomplished in whole-class, small-group, or independent center work settings. It is important to demonstrate the process many times with children so they understand the task.

Word Searches

Word searches involve words arranged in a grid. Students search for particular words or any words that can be detected in the array of letters. There are many commercially produced word searches, but students will also enjoy making their own word searches to share with each other. They can include any words or specific categories of words, such as contractions or compound words. Using graph paper or the grid paper provided in Appendix 39, teach the students how to make a word search. Figure 13-8 on page 159 shows an example of a word search made by a second grade student. Children write their

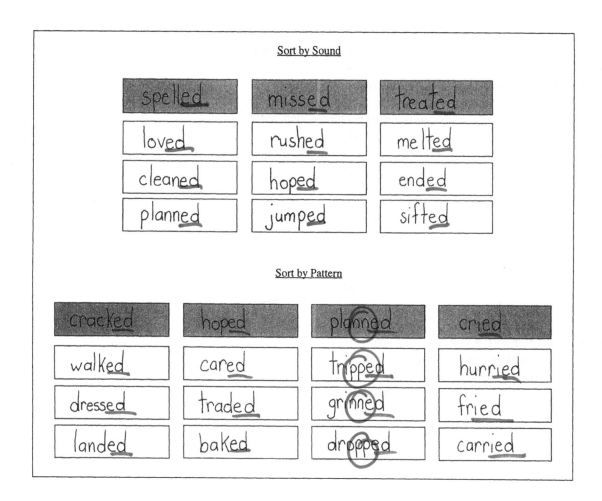

FIGURE 13-6 Two Word Sorts

good skill to develop.

words across, down, and diagonally, filling in as many spaces with whole words as possible. When the words are all written, they write any letters in the remaining spaces.

Crossword Puzzles

Crossword puzzles represent another way for children to attend to the spelling patterns and meaning of words. They will enjoy making their own puzzles, as shown in Figure 13-9 on page 160. Also, children can use letter tiles to plan crossword puzzles or word searches (see Appendix 40).

Have a Try

"Have a try" is a common study method. The writer writes a word, notices that it doesn't look quite right, and then tries it two or three different ways to decide which construction looks right. The technique is useful

because it requires writers to make attempts and check on themselves. You'll want to demonstrate this activity so that the children will attend to ways they can think about the task. The activity can be done on a sheet of paper folded in columns or on a blank form (see Appendix 37).

When children have written stories and are proofreading, they can circle some words they may have misspelled and try the word another way. This simple step fosters more self-correction behavior.

Words Around the Room

LOVE!

Using a clipboard, pencil, and a sheet of paper, pairs of children find words in specified categories (for example, words that begin with consonant clusters, compound words, words with similar endings, three-letter words, words with a particular sound, and so

Categories for Word Sorts

Categories related to sound or letter pattern
Words that begin/end with particular consonants (*mom, mix, or, path, with*)
Words that start/end with consonant clusters (*spring, clap, soft*)
Words with double consonants (*zipper, mitten*)
Words with two consonants that make one sound (*shoe, chimney*)
Words with a vowel sound as in *apple* (*cat, map*)
Words with a vowel sound as in *egg* (*pet, then*)
Words with a vowel sound as in *igloo* (*sit, lip*)
Words with a vowel sound as in *octopus* (*hot, top*)
Words with a vowel sound as in *umbrella* (*under, up*)
Words with a vowel sound as in *cake* (*late, cape*)
Words with a vowel sound as in *feet* (*meat, keep*)
Words with a vowel sound as in *kite* (*sign, fight*)
Words with a vowel sound as in *goat* (*rope, soap*)
Words with a vowel sound as in *mule* (*cute, use*)
Words beginning with a vowel (*under, over*)
Words ending with a vowel (*tuba, solo*)
Words with the same vowel sound (*play, mail, take*)
Words with vowel combinations (*cream, boat, soil*)
Words with a vowel and *r* (*corn, first*)
Words that rhyme (*mail, sail*)
Words with a letter that makes a particular sound (the *s* sound in *see* and *bus*, or *was* and *treasure*)
Words with silent letters (*make, seat*)
Words that can be paired with another word that sounds the same but means something different (*to, two; sail, sale*)
Words with one, two, or three syllables (*dog, rab-bit, to-ma-to*)
Words with an open syllable (*mo-tel, to-ken*)
Words with a closed syllable (*rob-in, cab-in*)

Categories related to structure or meaning
Words that have prefixes (*redo, unfasten*)
Words with endings (*smartest, looking, carried*)
Words with the same base (*write, rewrite, rewriting*)
Words that name people (*brother, friend*)
Words that name places (*home, yard*)
Words that are short or long (*to, remainder*)
Words in a category (*carrot, orange*)
Words that describe (*lovely, green*)
Words that mean the same (*fight, argument*)
Words that mean the opposite (*hot, cold*)
Words that can be pronounced two different ways (*live, live*)
Words that sound the same but are spelled different ways (*to, two*)
Words that are contractions (*haven't, wasn't*)
Words that are compounds (*someday, cannot*)
Words that have the same part (*fat, fatter, fattest*)
Word forms that are singular or plural (*calf, calves*)

FIGURE 13-7   Categories for Word Sorts

Word Search

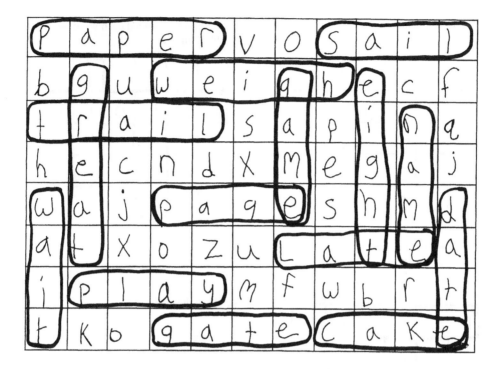

game   weigh   name

play   great   page

cake   Late   wait

Sail   paper   trail

eight   date   gate

FIGURE 13-8   Word Search

on). Alternatively, you can give children open-ended sheets that specify different types of words to find (see Figure 13-10 on page 161). Children can look on shared reading charts, word walls, and interactive writing pieces, and share their findings at the end of the day. This is an excellent way to review, practice, or consolidate learning.

Mnemonics

Mnemonics are systems or devices for remembering words. Children need to be able to think of them right away when needed. When children are learning how to think about tricky words in a minilesson, sharing, or as part of the word study system (see Chapter 14), invite them to share their

oooh I Love this idea.

Making a Crossword Puzzle

1. Put words into the squares.

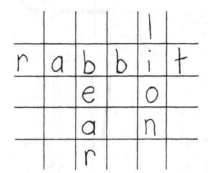

2. Make a box around each word with a thin black marker.

3. Number the words.

4. Write the clues.

5. Using plain white paper, trace the boxes and numbers.

Example of a child's Crossword Puzzle:

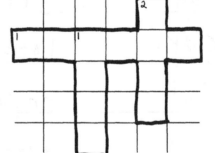

FIGURE 13-9   Making a Crossword Puzzle

clever devices. The best ones are those that children think of themselves. Some children have used these:

Mi-ssi-ssi-ppi
The *principal* is my *pal*.
A *piece* of *pie*
At-ten-dance

Friends to the *end*
Twice with *ice*

Twenty Questions and Other Games

Engage children in games that encourage word analysis as a whole-class, partner, or individual activity. Many word games are included in computer software. You can consult local

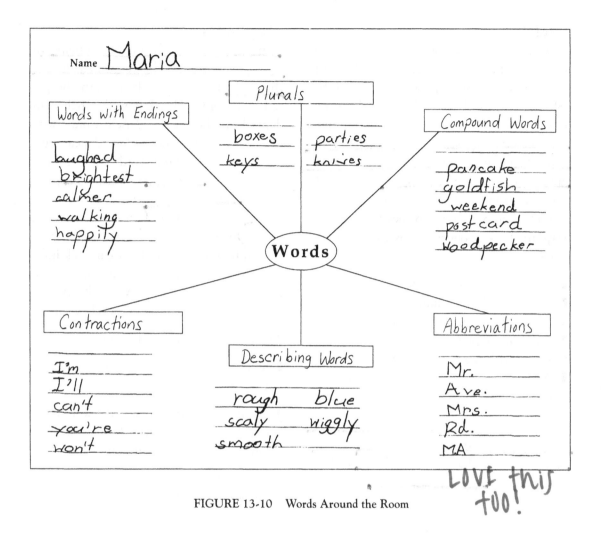

Name Maria

Plurals

boxes   parties
keys   knives

Words with Endings

laughed
brightest
calmer
walking
happily

Words

Compound Words

pancake
goldfish
weekend
postcard
woodpecker

Contractions

I'm
I'll
can't
you're
won't

Describing Words

rough   blue
scaly   wiggly
smooth

Abbreviations

Mr.
Ave.
Mrs.
Rd.
MA

LOVE this too!

FIGURE 13-10   Words Around the Room

software stores or catalogs for programs that will be compatible with your computer system. Other games are commercially produced.

A simple game that does not require additional purchase is "twenty questions." The procedure in the twenty questions game (it could be ten or any other number) is to have one child select a word and then ask children to pose *yes* or *no* questions. The word must be selected from a defined set of words, such as those on the word wall or on charts.

If the child doesn't guess the word by twenty questions, she writes or highlights the word and chooses another child. The goal is for the team to figure out the word as quickly as possible. Children can ask questions about whether:

❚ It is a plural.
❚ It has a prefix or suffix.

❚ It has one or more syllables.
❚ It has more than one vowel.
❚ It begins with or ends with a consonant or consonant cluster.
❚ There are silent letters in the word.
❚ It means the same or the opposite of another word.

Children will come up with many more questions, but they should avoid simply guessing precise letters.

Another game for studying word characteristics is to create a set of five to ten clues about a word. The student tries to locate as many statements about the word as possible. For example, *muffin* names something, has two tall letters in the middle, has two vowels, begins and ends with a consonant, has two parts, has three letters in each syllable, and rhymes with the name of a bird.

161

Word Webs

A word web is a way of beginning with one word and helping children make different kinds of associations. The associations can be related to the word root, to letters in the word, to patterns in the word, or to word meanings. Making word webs encourages children to make the kinds of connections we included in our list of prompts on page 152. Figure 13-11 shows an example of a word web on synonyms that children refer to when they write. Some ways to think about words as the webs are made are:

❚ Words that sound the same.
❚ Words that have a similar part.
❚ Words that begin with the same prefix.
❚ Words in different forms.
❚ Words with the same base or root.
❚ Words that mean the same or almost the same.

Word webs can be interactive because once they are started and displayed on charts in the room, children can add spokes. They also can make personal word webs to include in their notebooks.

Word Origins

Knowing where words come from helps students learn why words are spelled the way they are. It also helps them learn the patterns of words. This knowledge helps students learn how to read new words, write new words, and understand word meanings.

Information about word origins is often provided in dictionaries, thesauruses, and other reference books. This area of word study is appropriate for late-elementary students. Students can select six or eight words related to a word root. They can seek information about each and write a set of clues for a crossword puzzle or write descriptions in their word study notebooks. They can:

❚ Find out what the word means.

❚ Find out where it is from (country or language of origin).

❚ Tell about its past (the way the word has evolved and changed over the years in meaning, spelling, and pronunciation).

❚ Talk about the root meaning and how it changes when prefixes or suffixes are added.

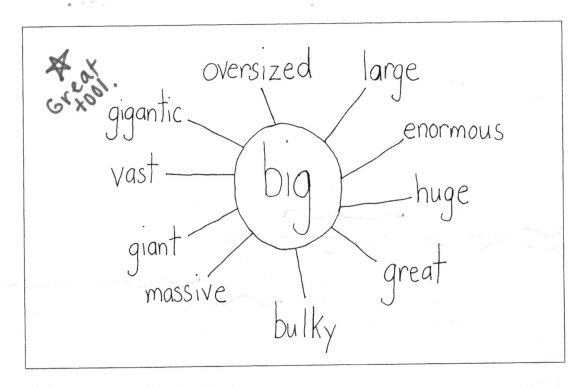

FIGURE 13-11   Word Web Example: *Big*

❚ Write sentences with the word.

❚ Make a list of other words like it.

All of these activities are part of an organized system for word study. They represent ways to apply principles and/or discover principles that have been introduced through instruction that actively involves children in learning how words work.

Teaching Children to Use References and Proofreading Skills

We want students to learn the skills that will, ultimately, make them independent, effective users of written language. As others will not always be available to assist students in writing and reading, it's imperative that children understand how to use references and resources. Proofreading is a related skill—knowing how to check one's own work with possible assistance from references is part of becoming an effective reader and writer. We expect students to learn:

❚ How to read and check their own written work.

❚ How to search for information.

❚ How to use information to check on their own reading or writing.

❚ How to use specific resources such as word charts, word webs, and word walls, and, ultimately, dictionaries, thesauruses, and other references.

❚ How to use spell check programs and other tools on the computer.

Teacher-Made References and Resources

The Classroom Environment

Teachers have found many ways to create lists of different kinds of words for children to use as references while they read and write. You can use cardboard "tents" on a table; write or place words on each side so that children can easily see and use them. Or, you might form a small tent from a table-top pocket chart. Still another idea is to write high-frequency words on paper strips around cans that also hold markers and pencils (see Figure 13-12). All of these are reference tools.

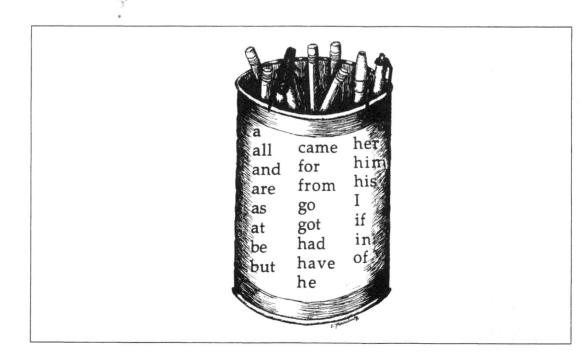

FIGURE 13-12   Can with Words

163

Teach children how to use these lists and encourage them to use them during reading and writing activities. Without specific teaching and encouragement, all of your work creating these references will be wasted. It is better to have a few good references that children really know how to use than many tools that they ignore or cannot use. For each resource you provide, create a minilesson to show children how to use it and encourage them to use it every day until they see it as part of the routine.

In Chapter 4, we provide many more examples of references and resources that will be available in the classroom environment. Descriptions of more individualized resources follow.

Personal Word Wall

A more personal list of words related to the alphabet letters can be placed inside children's writing folders for reference. As children are working on new words, the teacher or child adds the word to the chart for reference. We describe the personal word wall in Chapter 16 and provide a blank form in Appendix 50.

My Spelling Dictionary

A personal dictionary is a highly useful tool. When children can learn how to use the alphabet as an ordering system, teach them how to use a simple dictionary.

1. Give children a blank notebook in which you or the children have written the upper- and lowercase letter forms at the top of each page.

2. Provide useful high-frequency words on a sheet of paper that students can glue to the back or front cover, or some high-frequency word strips (Appendix 38) that they glue to each appropriate page. A third option is to have them copy a few of the high-frequency words that teachers select each day until they have many to use. Figure 13-13 shows a personal dictionary in which a teacher has glued word strips.

Students can add words they have learned in the word study system (see Chapter 14) to the dictionary pages on a designated day each week. Words from lists of frequently misspelled words or spelling demons may also be added. The use of a spelling dictionary should

	Tt	Tt
take	today	
than	they're	
that	try	
the		
them		
their		
then		
there		
they		
this		
time		
to		
too		
took		
two		

FIGURE 13-13   Pages of Personal Dictionary with Word Strips

begin in about second grade and continue through the years with increasing complexity.

Commercial Dictionaries and Other Word Resources

It is very important that students learn to use the resources, such as dictionaries and thesauruses, that are available in printed and technological forms. This work should begin with young children using pictionaries and very simple dictionaries. For children in the first two grades, remember that the resources on the walls (such as charts and word walls) are a way to teach them beginning dictionary and reference skills. Through using these clear, readily available materials that you and your students have created together, children learn essential skills such as categorizing a word, searching for it based on visual features, finding the word, and interpreting the information about it.

As children grow in their knowledge of words, they can use rhyming dictionaries and junior thesauruses that help them enrich their own writing and give it more variety. They can also use the computer and begin to use spell check programs. Finally, students learn to use adult versions of thesauruses (also available on computer) as well as dictionaries.

Dictionary Skills

Some essential skills for using dictionaries are listed below:

▌ Making a good estimate of the spelling of a word to have enough knowledge to search for it in the dictionary (first letter or letter clusters, first part, etc.).

▌ Using alphabetical order to find a word.

▌ Learning how to use the words at the top of each dictionary page to help find words.

▌ Learning whether words need to be capitalized by finding out whether they are proper nouns.

▌ Discovering divisions between syllables (signified by a black dot).

▌ Learning to pronounce the word using the pronunciation key.

▌ Learning what stress to place on a word when pronouncing it (signified by an accent mark).

▌ Learning the meaning of a word as explained in the text and sometimes extended through drawings.

▌ Identifying the part of speech of a word.

▌ Researching word origins (explained in some dictionaries). *(LATER)*

▌ Discovering synonyms and antonyms for a word.

Each of these dictionary skills can be the subject of minilessons and application. Fast, efficient use of the dictionary for many different purposes will take time and practice. This area of learning is most effective when it is more than an exercise. Students will be more motivated to use the dictionary if they are using this tool to enhance their own writing or reading or if they are engaged in finding out something interesting about words.

Thesaurus Skills

A thesaurus can help students add variety to both their oral and written expression. Teach children how to use a junior thesaurus, which is a simple form, and later an adult one. Teach them how to find synonyms and antonyms and engage them as partners to make two- or three-letter word choices for a specific writing piece.

Spell Check Skills

As students become more sophisticated with word processing, they will want to use the tools that are available to them, including the ability to check on the spelling of words. They need to understand that a spell check program is not the magic answer, nor is it simple to use. In order for the software to recognize a word, the word's spelling needs to be close to standard. The writer must select the actual words from several options. This means that the writer needs to know how words look to decide which one is correct. The computer makes no distinction between homographs. Using a spell check program requires fairly complex knowledge and will call for deliberate teaching.

Proofreading Skills

Children need to take responsibility for the accuracy of their own spelling. Proofreading becomes a habit, one that children internalize and automatically perform as they produce writing. Proofreading is a skill that enables children to locate their own spelling errors and use effective strategies to correct them. Children need clear demonstrations of how to look at the word and ask themselves if it looks right. Proofreading lessons may be conducted with the whole group, individuals, or small groups. Proofreading is best done when there has been a lapse of time between the writing and the proofreading so the writer can take a fresh look. Some techniques that teachers have used include helping children learn how to:

❚ Check to be sure all sounds and syllables are represented.

❚ Check to be sure that all syllables have a vowel sound or y.

❚ Underline or circle words that don't look right.

❚ Mark the part of the word that the writer is not sure of.

❚ Start reading at the end, looking at each word and asking whether it looks right.

❚ Use a ruler or a sentence strip to place under each line and read the words on the line from right to left.

❚ Circle words that don't look right and have another try above each one.

❚ Ask a partner to proofread the piece after the student has proofread it first.

Editing Skills

It is important to teach children how to check their responses. This action will foster independent self-correction behavior. In writing, students need to learn how to use a variety of strategies for self-correction. About once a week, particularly with more proficient spellers, take ten minutes to edit a paragraph. Select one or two paragraphs from a piece of writing (check with a student for permission) and place them on the overhead projector. With the class or a small group, share thinking about strategies to fix up the parts. This process works well as a minilesson.

We have explored three broad areas for word study—teaching for sound and print knowledge, teaching for word solving strategies, and teaching for the use of references and resources. These three areas generally imply a movement from easier learning to learning that is much more complex later in the primary grades; however, it is obvious that even very young children begin to develop word-solving and checking strategies as they use the simple references and resources in their classrooms. Teachers may design word study programs that incorporate all three of these elements at levels appropriate for the children they teach.

Suggestions for Professional Development

1. Meet with colleagues to study children's writing as a basis for teaching. Follow these steps:

❚ Collect two or three samples of writing from one child.

❚ Fold a paper in three columns.

❚ In the first column, make a list of the attempts at words not correctly written.

❚ In the second column, note the strategies the child can use to solve words.

❚ In the third column, note what the child needs to learn how to do.

❚ Repeat the process for different children.

❚ Discuss your analyses with colleagues. Talk about minilessons, individual conferences, and word study center activities that will assist this child.

2. Analyze classroom references. Collect the children's dictionaries you have in your classroom and others at your grade level. Analyze the resources, asking:

▮ Are they easy for children to read?

▮ Are they set up in a way that makes the information easily available?

▮ Is the size of print and formatting appropriate for the age group?

▮ Are the definitions easy to understand?

▮ Does the artwork contribute to or detract from the delivery of information?

▮ Do they contain the kinds of words that children at this age level need?

▮ Is the information presented in an interesting way?

▮ Is there opportunity for children to find out some interesting things about words (beyond simply spelling and definition)?

Then, collect other word study books such as thesauruses and apply the same criteria.

▮ Think about how some of the information can be made part of the classroom environment through interactive word charts and word walls.

▮ Plan a minilesson to use one of the dictionaries.

A Comprehensive Word Study System

Good spellers develop strategies that allow them to learn how to spell a large number of words, even those they have not attended to in formal instruction. They can do so because they have internalized a network of word-solving strategies, a few important principles, and many basic spelling patterns. And, they know how to apply the knowledge to an ever-increasing number of words. Teaching that emphasizes these strategies, principles, and patterns is significantly more effective than instruction that targets memorizing lists of words. In Chapter 11, we described the use of minilessons and word study centers with children in the primary grades.

In addition, we recommend that, beginning in second grade and continuing throughout elementary school, teachers implement a word study system that combines the spelling minilessons with buddy study. Depending on the group of children, some teachers may want to start using the buddy study system during the last half of first grade.

An effective word study system is part of a strong literacy program. We have designed a word study system that:

■ Includes a short, specific, focused class lesson during a morning class or community meeting followed by a short time for independent student application and practice. (This part takes place beginning in kindergarten and first grade.)

■ Follows a structured routine that is easy to implement and requires minimal teacher time.

■ Maximizes student engagement and responsibility for their learning.

■ Provides for cooperative learning.

■ Provides opportunities for multilevel learning.

■ Leads to the development of strategies for spelling.

■ Helps students learn both individual words and spelling patterns that can be generalized.

■ Values spelling as part of the writing process.

■ Provides for modification to meet individual needs.

In this chapter we describe our comprehensive word study system, materials needed, and suggestions for modification to meet individual needs. The system is highly structured to allow for efficient teaching and independent student learning; however, within the structure are many opportunities for flexible and open-ended thinking so that students can make the kinds of connections that will help them spell many words beyond the specific examples they are studying. We draw from two major sources of words for study:

■ We refer to the first source as *core words*. Teachers choose core words from their observations of the class in reading, writing, or engaging in other assignments in coordination with an understanding of the core knowledge and grade-level benchmarks (see Chapters 9 and 19). From these, we plan a weekly class lesson to teach a useful strategy, principle, or pattern. Words used in the lesson are the source for about half of the words children will study in a week.

■ We refer to the second source as *personal words*. These words, comprising the other half of the words for study, are drawn from children's personal writing and high-frequency word lists. Children are taught how to build a resource list of words they need to learn.

Prerequisites for Initiating the Word Study System

This approach to word study is systematic and organized, freeing you and the children to enjoy learning conversations about words. Advance organizing will help you implement the system. Some steps are included in the summary at the end of this chapter.

Forming Spelling Buddies

Since peer interaction is important to learning, our system is built on buddies working, talking, sharing, and checking on each other. Assign buddies to work together for a period of time, for example a month, two months, or even a quarter of the school year. Use your judgment and assessment information to form buddies similar in spelling achievement at a particular point in time. Alter the buddy combinations often enough to give children new learning relationships, to accommodate

changes in student achievement, or to improve learning as needed when specific buddies aren't working productively together.

Stephanie, a first-grade teacher, used the Spelling Buddies chart shown in Figure 14-1 to pair children each month. The chart is a strip of tagboard, with clothespins attached to show partner pairs. Although just three pairs are shown here, a classroom would typically have ten to fifteen pairs of buddies.

Implementing Cooperative Learning Techniques

A good word study system provides opportunities for children to learn from each other by discussing words and checking on each other's attempts. They can give each other immediate feedback and reinforcement during the process, and there is value in talking about words: the children are going beyond simple memorization. When children are working together, multilevel learning occurs in the classroom. Main Point.

Establishing a Routine for Learning

Our word study system has built-in routines. In fact, the first several weeks of implementing the system will include explicit instruction to help students learn how to use each routine in detail. Teaching continues until the students are independent. We provide a general plan for getting the routines for the buddy study system started once the class lesson (minilesson and word study center activities) is well under way (see Figure 14-2). You will need to adjust it to fit your students.

Some small groups or individual students may require reteaching. Students are taught how to select their words, so they can engage in the process independently. They see numerous demonstrations of the study methods. They learn how to use materials and how to check each other. Materials, such as pockets for spelling cards, clipboards, highlighter pens, trays of word study sheets, and baskets of word study notebooks are organized in the classroom to support independent learning.

Because there are routines, children become more efficient in using a framework

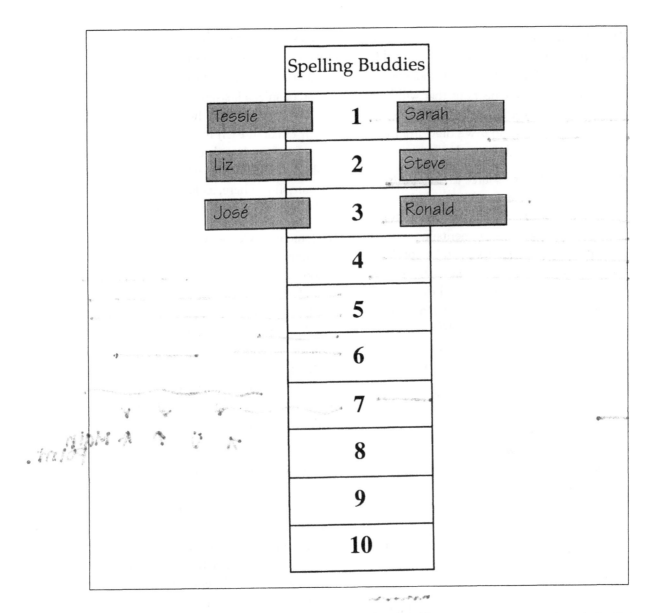

FIGURE 14-1   Spelling Buddies

Teaching for Strategies

When using the word study system with core words or personal words, children spend their time learning how to think about that guides them to notice and use effective learning strategies. The teacher can make better decisions about how to spend time and is able to work with individuals or small groups of children with similar needs. Cooperative learning is supported by a structured routine that makes the best use of instructional time.

words and applying what they learn in many different contexts. They are taught to use several different strategies for analyzing words and making connections between words. For example, for any given word, they might derive other words that it starts like, rhymes with, or means the same as. Making these connections focuses attention on patterns and principles that work across many words. For some words, children might find more connections through sound-letter relationships. For others, unique spelling patterns that do not represent one-to-one

Getting Started with a Comprehensive Word Study System

The following are small steps to teach the routines for both parts of the comprehensive word study system. These steps can be completed over several weeks. As you teach the routines, evaluate whether reteaching is necessary until a good standard of work and independence in each routine is achieved. Reteaching may only be necessary for individuals.

1. **A Classroom Lesson Followed by Application and Sharing**
   Implement a weekly minilesson, daily activity, and daily sharing structure until children have internalized the routines. This process includes teaching strategies, patterns, and principles, as well as routines: how to use and put away materials at the center, how to write in the word study notebook, and how to prepare to share with the group. It will also mean setting a standard for what is quality work at the center, helping children learn how to help each other, and helping them maintain a voice level that allows for others to focus on their work.

2. **Choosing Words**
   Teach children where to get a spelling card. Show them how to choose three or four *core words* from the weekly class lesson and how to write them carefully on a spelling card. Share several cards that show a name and words written clearly as examples of good work. Then show children how to place their cards on the word study board in the pocket that lists their name.

3. **Building Words**
   Teach children how to make the words several times with magnetic letters, emphasizing left-to-right construction. Consider a whole-class activity in which partners observe each other mixing and fixing words, and then have them evaluate how well their partners followed the steps. Show the *Choose, Write, Build, Mix, Fix, Mix* icon, place it on the buddy study workboard, and teach children how to put the magnetic letters away properly.

4. **Look, Say, Cover, Write, Check**
   With the three or four words from the class minilesson, teach the class how to use the study approach (page 176), and model using the study flap. Have spelling buddies observe their partners using the process and then give feedback to each other. Show the *Look, Say, Cover, Write, Check* icon and place it on the buddy study workboard.

5. **Buddy Check**
   Using the words from the class minilesson, teach students how to use the Buddy Check sheet. Demonstrate how to dictate a word to a partner, use it in a sentence, and say the word again. Teach them how to mark if the word is right or wrong, and how to have their partners try again. Demonstrate scoring and allow the students to practice. Collect the papers to review them carefully and give feedback to the whole group and to individuals. Show the *Buddy Check* icon and place it on the buddy study workboard.

6. **Make Connections**
   Teach the students how to write the words carefully at the top of the Make Connections sheet. As you first teach, you might want to have everyone use the same set of three or four words from the class minilesson. After the children list the words, demonstrate one way of making connections with each word (e.g., words that rhyme). Show the students how to write a string of connections in each box, for example, "*play* rhymes with *day, stay, way, clay*" or "*went* starts like *we, was, water, wall, west.*" After teaching different ways to think about sound connections, you can begin to introduce other ways of thinking about making links, for example, "*play* looks like *please, plow, stay, way*"; "*play* goes with *plays, playing, played, replay*"; "*play* means to have fun, to do things." Show the *Make Connections* icon and place it on the buddy study workboard.

7. **Buddy Test**
   Teach students how to date the page in their word study notebook. Then teach them how to dictate a word, use it in a sentence, and say the word as their partner writes each one. (When students have completed the test, collect the word study notebooks to correct the spelling of each student and to give feedback to children as needed.) Show the *Buddy Test* icon and place it on the buddy study workboard.

FIGURE 14-2   Getting Started with a Comprehensive Word Study System

8. **Week of Activities**
   Now that the children have learned to apply the buddy study system to *core words* from the class lesson, have them engage in the daily buddy study activities for a few weeks using the word study board. When they fully understand the daily routines using the words from the minilesson, you are ready to move to step 9.

9. **Developing a "Words to Learn" List**
   When the children have shown independence and quality work, teach them how to write *personal words* on their "words to learn" list in minilessons and in conferences during the writing workshop. As you read the children's writing, you will also want to put words on a stick-on note and have children write them on the list. Explain that this list will provide more words for the daily buddy study system.

10. **Pretest of High-Frequency Words**
    Give a high-frequency word test (Appendixes 4 or 48), and highlight all the words known by each child on the high-frequency word list kept in their writing folders. Teach children that the words that are not highlighted can be selected for study. Teach them to highlight the word once it is mastered on the weekly test. These words will also be part of the *personal words* to choose for from weekly buddy study.

11. **Choosing Words to Learn**
    Teach children how to put a check next to or circle the specific words chosen for the week from the "words to learn" and/or high-frequency word list. You are now ready to add *personal words* to the buddy study system.

12. **Adding Personal Words to the Spelling Card**
    The children are now ready to choose three or four *personal words* from their Words to Learn sheet and some *core words* from the class lesson, list them carefully on their spelling card, and place the card in the pocket on the buddy study workboard.

13. **Using the Buddy Study Workboard and the Word Study Center**
    Review the use of the buddy study workboard icons for daily activities and the use of the *ABC Center* icon for word study center activities.

14. **Evaluation for Reteaching**
    Evaluate the daily word study center activity and buddy study system to decide what reteaching may be necessary for the class, a small group, or individual.

FIGURE 14-2   Getting Started with a Comprehensive Word Study System, *continued*

letter-sound correspondences emerge. These words may have visual features for children to notice.

Children also define words, seek synonyms, link words to other words by meaning, and derive different forms of the word by adding morphological elements (such as *s, ed, ing,* or *able*). This process provides more context for the word and encourages flexibility as students attempt to use it. Finally, the system provides ways to record unique aspects of words, including those of special significance to the individual.

many ways to use

Selection of Spelling Words for Study

Many educators maintain that it is most effective to take spelling words for study from the errors children make in their own writing. After all, children will want to learn to spell those words that they need to use in writing, so this practice may increase motivation. When you look at a child's particular errors, you can learn the child's current hypotheses about how the alphabetic system works, and decide what needs to be taught. The error analysis technique described in Chapter 10 will help you understand children's spelling strengths and needs.

Children's writing is one good source for the words that will be part of spelling lessons. Inviting children to self-select their own spelling words enables them to know more about what they need to learn and gives them a sense of ownership. Moreover, using their own words in spelling encourages children to pay more attention to spelling while they are writing, and prompts them to strive for accurate spelling in future writing. Finally, this selection process takes into account individual differences.

On the other hand, basing a spelling program *entirely* on words from students' own writing has some limitations:

■ Selected words may not provide opportunities to apply all the useful strategies spellers need.

■ Selected words may not represent all of the important spelling patterns that children need to learn.

■ Children are limited to the words they use in their writing, possibly limiting the range of words they encounter.

■ It is difficult for the teacher to systematize spelling instruction if there are no common spelling experiences within a class.

As mentioned above, our word study system involves attention to two sources of words, *core words* and *personal words*. Core words are selected by the teacher to illustrate strategies, principles, and spelling patterns in the weekly class lesson. Personal words are words that children select from their own writing (personal and high-frequency words). They will select some words from an ongoing list of errors from their writing. Teachers provide resources to help children self-assess and guide their choices.

Core Words

You will need to design weekly minilessons to address the spelling needs of the class as a whole. From your observations of the children, from formal assessments, and from grade-level benchmarks or curriculum goals, design a weekly lesson that addresses the needs of the class as a whole. Refer to Chapter 9 for a description of what children need to learn and Chapter 19 for sample benchmarks. The list of spelling minilessons in Appendix 34 will also be useful. Use several

words as examples in the lesson and invite student examples. Put these on a board or chart and have children choose half of their weekly words from these.

Personal Words

You'll need to teach your students how to list words from their writing and how to choose words to learn from their "words to learn" list. As children choose from a resource list of words from their writing, you'll want to show them how to choose a group of words that may go together. For example:

■ *Looked, walked,* and *played* are words that end in *ed.*
■ *To, an,* and *at* are simple two-letter high-frequency words.
■ *Make* and *like* are words that have "silent *e.*"

To assist children, you can put a mark next to words on the list that will make good choices. Minilessons on word study choice are effective when you include them as part of the weekly word study teaching.

Since a growing core of high-frequency words is also essential, high-frequency word lists provide a good source of personal words for study. You'll want to show your students how to choose the easier high-frequency words before the harder ones from a selected list.

At the start of the year, give a pretest of twenty to one hundred high-frequency words using lists of words arranged by frequency (see Appendix 4). Depending on the grade level, you can test ten or twenty words per day for a week or two, and, using the one hundred-word list, highlight the words a child spelled correctly. Place the Words to Learn sheet (Appendix 41) in the child's writing folder or glue it inside the cover of a special notebook. For listing words to learn, a two-column steno book or the back of the word study notebook described later in this chapter works well. This list will be a good resource from which to make choices. When the words are exhausted, you might use the list of five hundred high-frequency words (Appendix 5) as another source. For young children, a goal is the ability to spell the one hundred most frequently used words by the end of second grade. Some children will not achieve that goal, so the lists can be passed on to third grade.

Number of Words to Study

We advocate selecting a limited number of words per week, approximately six to ten, for word study. The number may vary by grade level or according to the needs of specific children. Six words works well with first- and second-grade students.

Because the choice of words combines student selection with teacher expertise regarding essential understandings, some words (about half) are connected to the weekly spelling lesson and serve as exemplars of strategies, patterns, or principles. The children simply choose three to four of the words to study from the weekly spelling lesson and write them on their weekly spelling card. These words are powerful because they provide examples that students can apply to their learning of other words. The other three or four words are chosen from the ongoing personal resource list of words to learn. These words are added to the spelling card.

Review the choices for each child to be sure they are good ones and are spelled correctly, and initial the corner of the card as children are making their lists. You may prefer to teach the weekly minilesson on Friday, and give the children time to choose their words so they will be ready to start their word study work on Monday. This gives you time to review and initial the cards. Or you may provide the lesson on any other day, allowing a five-day cycle. As you coordinate word study and the spelling system, you will probably find that you are providing several of these brief, focused lessons in a week, sometimes revisiting concepts and principles and sometimes taking advantage of learning that comes out of reading and writing activities.

A Comprehensive Word Study System

We use a flexible weekly framework for organizing the study of how words work. The following section describes our word study system. It is comprised of two parts:

1. A class lesson on a strategy, principle, or pattern followed by a class activity or small-group rotation to a word study center. In a previous book, *Guided Reading: Good First Teaching for All Children* (1996), and in this book, we describe the word study minilesson, application, and sharing. The application activity is conducted at an ABC or word study center, and an "icon" on a workboard (a list of assigned activities for each group) is used. If you are using a workboard including an ABC center, you already have the first part in place and can simply add the second. It is common for kindergarten and first-grade teachers to implement the first part of the word study system only, using the minilessons and ABC center.

2. A buddy study system that engages students in daily activities for studying a specific list of words.

Let's explore the first part of the word study system. It includes a minilesson, followed by application and sharing. We describe a basic framework below.

Minilesson

From observations of the children's writing and work with words in the classroom, select strategies, patterns, and principles that most of the children need to learn and provide a whole-class minilesson to teach a particular concept. The goal is for children to glean new understandings and select an exemplar of the word to be placed on the word wall. Here are suggestions for the general procedure:

❚ Using magnetic letters, an easel, chart paper, or a white board, demonstrate useful ways of thinking about how a group of words is constructed and how the words sound alike, what they look like, or how they are related to other words. You might work with a group of words that illustrate similar features (*scream, steam, meat, please,* which share the *ea* in combination with different beginnings and endings); different forms of the same root word (*happy, happily, happiness, happier*); or words with similar letter patterns making different sounds in words (*owl, snow, know; how, now, mow*).

■ Provide a word and a few examples. You might construct it with magnetic letters.

■ Engage the children in a conversation about the words and help them notice their features.

■ Invite them to talk about the parts they will want to remember.

■ Invite the children to provide additional examples. You might invite them to the board to make the new words with magnetic letters.

■ Make a chart illustrating the principle or categorizing the words.

■ Put an exemplar on the word wall and remind children to refer to it as needed.

■ Have each child choose three or four words from the examples provided. These words become part of the individualized list the child will work with throughout the week as part of the word study system.

When the minilesson focuses on a procedure or other concept that doesn't involve specific words (for example, how to give a buddy test), have children choose words from their personal word lists.

Application Activities

Plan for activities at the word study center that will engage children in active manipulation of letters and word parts to practice and extend their learning of the strategy, pattern, or principle presented in the weekly lesson. The activities might include word building, word sorting, or making word ladders (Chapter 13) and provide a range of useful activities for letter and word learning for individuals or partners, or for use at a word study center. You might also include a

written task that is completed in the word study notebook (described later). You might plan one or more activities for the week, with small groups rotating to the word study center each day. Alternatively, students can engage in the planned activity as a class, simultaneously in small groups, or as partners.

Sharing Activity

At the end of the day, when the children have had time to apply the concept or when some children have worked in the word study center, invite a few children to share examples of the words they made. This sharing activity will reinforce the weekly lesson. Review once again the important understandings children should be thinking about when writing words like the word wall examples. Place the class chart on the wall for future reference. Repeat the sharing each day as more students work at the center.

Now let's look at the second part of the word study system—the buddy study system (see Figure 14-3).

Later in the chapter, we will explain in detail each of the open-ended activity sheets described in our buddy study system.

Day 1: Choose, Write, Build, Mix, Fix, Mix

Provide a clear, short, focused lesson on a strategy, pattern, or principle that students need. (A comprehensive list of minilessons is provided in Appendix 34; Chapter 9 provides an explanation of core knowledge; and Chapter 19 describes grade-level benchmarks). These lessons generally are provided to the whole class, but you may decide to work with half the class or a small group that needs some specific teaching. In the lesson share a variety of words and invite students to generalize the principle and provide more examples. You may write them on a chart or make them on a magnetic chalkboard. The children choose three or four of the class words for study and write them on the spelling card.

Second, each child *chooses* three or four words from his "words to learn" list and/or a

	Buddy Study System	
	Buddy Study Activities	Materials Needed

Day 1	Choose, Write, and Build Mix, Fix, Mix	• Spelling Cards (Word Study Board)
		 • High-Frequency Word List
		 • Words to Learn List
		    or
		    Words to Learn Listed at the Back of
		      Word Study Notebook
		 • Magnetic Letters

Day 2	Look, Say, Cover, Write, Check	• Study Flap • Look, Say, Cover, Write, Check Sheet • Highlighter Pen • Magnetic Letters
Day 3	Buddy Check	• Buddy Check Sheet • Clipboard • Highlighter Pen • Magnetic Letters
Day 4	Make Connections	• Make Connections Sheet • Highlighter Pen
Day 5	Buddy Test	• Word Study Notebook • Spelling Card (Word Study Board) • Clipboard • Highlighter Pen

FIGURE 14-3   Buddy Study System

high-frequency word list (explained earlier), and circles them or marks them with a colored dot. The child adds them to the spelling card. During the word-choosing time, circulate and initial the spelling cards in the upper-right corner to guide choices, to verify correct spelling, and to confirm good choices.

Using the card, the children make the six or eight words (number assigned by teacher) with magnetic letters, and then *mix* the letters and make the words two or three times. The construction of the words with letters from left to right helps children learn the exact sequence of the letters. It is important to insist on left-to-right construction because writing words well requires appropriate sequencing of the pattern.

Be sure to organize the letters for building so students don't spend long amounts of time finding letters. A box with small com-

partments for each letter, cupcake trays, or the rectangular box made with milk cartons used by Pat and Sue (Figure 14-4) are useful storage tools. You can also purchase clear plastic boxes with compartments. Place these in different parts of the classroom, in the center of tables, or at the word study center.

Day 2: Look, Say, Cover, Write, Check

Teaching "How To" Study Words
Simply having children write words many times is not sufficient to help them learn how to look at and study words. The instruction must be designed to help them know what parts of the word to notice. They need to make hypotheses about why words are spelled the way they are. Fitzgerald (1951), and later Horn (1954), described study techniques that have been

FIGURE 14-4   Letter Storage Box

proven effective over the years. Both talked about looking carefully at the words, saying them, visualizing them, writing them without a model, and then checking them. These repeated steps are more effective than writing words over and over in a rote way. Here is a step-by-step procedure that helps children learn how to study words effectively:

■ Take a paper with three or four columns (see Appendix 42).

■ Write the list of words in the first column.

■ Begin with one word. *Say* it and notice parts to remember.

■ *Look* closely at the letters to notice the visual details.

■ *Cover* the word with the fold-down flap (study flaps described on page 180) or a card so the previous column is not seen, and think about how the word looks (visualize it).

■ Say the word softly. *Write* it from memory in the next column.

■ Uncover and *check* it with the word in the previous column.

■ Repeat the process in the next column until the last column is complete.

■ If it is spelled wrong in the last column, add the word to the first column again and repeat the process.

This process places responsibility on students to focus on their own learning and check on themselves as they make progress toward more conventional spelling. Throughout the process, teachers give their students immediate feedback at their own level. You might want to make a sample chart with the children to remind them of the steps in the procedure. Following each step is an important aspect of our buddy study system.

On Day 2, each child uses a blank Look, Say, Cover, Write, Check sheet placed in

177

the study flap to complete the study task, following the process described. The child highlights parts to remember in the last column and makes words that were difficult with magnetic letters.

Day 3: Buddy Check

Buddies work together, dictating their words to each other, and checking each other's Buddy Check sheets. They place a check to the right of correct words and an X to the right of incorrect ones. (Appendix 43) Words that are misspelled in the last column on the sheet are made with magnetic letters.

Day 4: Make Connections

Making connections provides for an open-ended task that engages students in thinking about how words are related. The children write their words at the top, highlight parts to remember, and then make lists of words they can link to each word by focusing on how words sound, look, and/or mean (see Chapter 13). They can also use magnetic letters to assist in thinking about words to link. The task requires much teaching over a long period of time and needs to be adjusted to fit the grade and achievement level of the particular students. For example, first graders might focus on words that sound the same (rhyme or start alike) for a long time, while third-grade students might be able to work with words that sound alike, look alike, and mean the same.

Buddies work together on each of their sets of words using the Make Connections sheet. They can also use the word study notebook instead of the sheet, if desirable, using the same procedure of listing the words and writing strings of connections. (See Chapter 13 for suggested teaching points).

Day 5: Conduct a Buddy Test

Buddies test each other on the week's list. The buddy dictates each word and uses it in a sentence as the other child writes the word in the word study notebook. The children place their notebooks in a basket and the teacher corrects the test. This provides the teacher with feedback for future planning.

Words that children continue to misspell are made again with magnetic letters and remain on the Words to Learn sheet for future choice. The children then check off the words they've learned on the Words to Learn sheet, and/or highlight the ones chosen and learned on the high-frequency list. You will want to create the expectation that children will spell the words correctly in their writing.

Modifications of the System

The teacher who gets to know the strengths and needs of individuals can make good teaching decisions. Some children may need to work with fewer words at first; others may need a more challenging list. Teachers may need to shorten or extend daily activities to meet particular student needs. In any case, all children will need teaching and reteaching of every aspect of the system. The weekly system is summarized in Figure 14-3, but can be modified in many ways to achieve your goals. You may choose to assign the activities on different days, or assign different activities. What is essential is the teaching and learning of the routines, the emphasis on effective spelling strategies, and the independent learning the students adopt and handle.

Assessing Students' Progress in the Word Study System

The word study notebook and Words to Learn sheets provide evidence of learning over time. By observing students' performance on weekly buddy tests and noticing how they apply their understanding in daily writing, you can effectively prepare the class lesson, set a focus for an individual or small-group conference or lesson, and modify activities to ensure all children are making good progress in the instructional system.

Prerequisites for the Buddy Study System

Before beginning to teach the buddy study system, you will need to take these steps:

1. Make a word study board for the lists.

2. Make a buddy study workboard for weekly activities.

3. Make trays or piles of the reproducible sheets needed:
   ▮ Words to Learn (Appendix 41).
   ▮ Look, Say, Cover, Write, Check (Appendix 42).
   ▮ Buddy Check (Appendix 43).
   ▮ Make Connections (Appendix 44).

4. Make study flaps from file folders.

5. Make a box of blank spelling cards.

6. Make a word study notebook for each child.

7. Place clipboards, cans of highlighters, colored pencils, and trays of magnetic letters in a place for students to use.

8. Administer a pretest of high-frequency words, if appropriate.

9. Form initial spelling buddies and note them on a spelling buddies board.

10. Teach children how to select three to five words from their journals or story writing to begin to create a resource of words to learn. Have them write the words on their Words to Learn sheet.

Additional Minilessons for the Buddy Study System

Each material and activity will require teaching. Use your class lesson time to teach children how to add words to the Words to Learn sheet, choose words, mix and fix words, use highlighters, mark words right or wrong, score buddy study sheets, administer and score buddy tests, make connections, use the buddy study work-board, etc. See the list of minilessons in Appendix 34.

Tools for the Buddy Study System

The basic tools to implement the buddy study system are listed here with brief descriptions.

Basic Materials
Each student has a clipboard for daily use with blank weekly spelling cards and study sheets. Colored pencils and highlighter pens are available in a central place.

Words to Learn Sheet
Students keep a columned sheet (three to four columns) with an ongoing list of personal words from which to select for weekly word study (Figure 14-5 and Appendix 41).

These words are drawn from each student's writing. Either the student or the teacher places words on the sheet continuously. For example, you might ask the children to circle three to five words they may have spelled wrong in a piece of writing and to try spelling them again above each missed word. Then, you can collect the writing, write the correct spelling where needed, and tell the students to add the words to their Words to Learn sheet. Another option is for you to add words while conferring with individuals in writing workshop, or to assign some particular words to the whole class because they are all spelling them wrong. Further, you may write some words on a Post-it for a particular child at any point in the day and ask the child to add them to his list. Alternatively, the word study notebook, which is opened from the front to use for word study center activities, can be opened from the back cover and used to keep the ongoing list of words to learn. This choice gives the notebook two uses and eliminates the need for the list in the writing folder. Use what works best for your students.

Word Study Board
The word study board is a chart located on a bulletin board or other convenient display

Words to Learn					
(the)	✓				
(and)	✓				
but					
have					
went					
(can)	✓				
for					
from					
(get)	✓				
has					
like					
(my)	✓				
put					
said					
you					
(am)	✓				

FIGURE 14-5   Words to Learn Sheet

space in the classroom (see Figure 14-6). On the board, each student has a library card pocket, identified by his name, to store the weekly spelling card. The library card pocket is simply the paper holder placed in the back of library books to hold cards. Because these pockets have adhesive backs and hold blank three-by-five-inch cards nicely, we use them to create the word study board. You can quickly scan the board to be sure each student has completed a card with a list of words to study.

Spelling Cards
Students use blank index cards that will fit into the pockets on the word study board to write their weekly words to study (see Figure 14-7).

Look, Say, Cover, Write, Check Study Sheets
Since an effective study technique is an important routine, we have provided two blank,

reproducible sheets in Appendix 42. These sheets (Figure 14-8) are placed in study flaps.

Study Flaps
Prepare a manila folder to use with the study sheet (see Figure 14-9). (These folders are also available in colors.) One side of the folder is cut into three or four columns to provide a way to cover and uncover words while using the study sheet. If the word is spelled correctly in the second column, the child puts a check in the next column to indicate it doesn't need to be written again. This process applies to columns three and four as well.

Buddy Check Sheet
A Buddy Check sheet is designed to help children study words (see Figure 14-10). The child writes words dictated by his "spelling buddy." The buddy marks those right or wrong and scores the number written correctly on the first attempt in the first

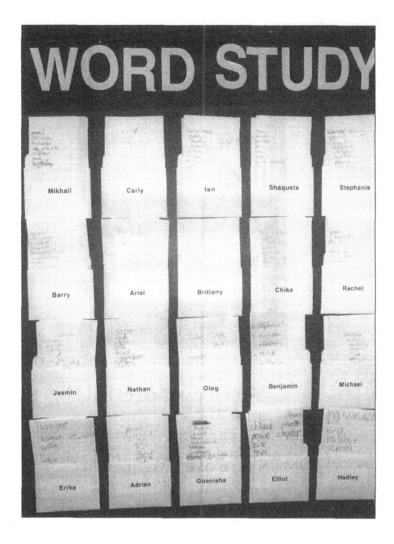

FIGURE 14-6   Word Study Board

column. If the child writes the word incorrectly in Column 1, he tries it again. The buddy indicates if the spelling is right or wrong, and the child uses the last column to write the word correctly. The child then highlights with a marker parts to remember, and makes the words spelled incorrectly with magnetic letters. Three versions of this sheet are provided in Appendix 43. Note that the more advanced one is two-sided.

Make Connections Sheet

One of the most important aspects of the word study system is the thinking that children engage in as they solve words. The Make Connections sheet (Figure 14-11

shows two examples) can be used for students to focus on one particular kind of thinking (e.g., words that start the same) or a combination of ways of making connections. With first-grade students, for example, you might stay with links to how words sound for many months. Two versions of reproducible Make Connections sheets are in Appendix 44.

Word Study Notebook

The word study notebook (see Figure 14-12) is a notebook for writing weekly tests and for assigned word study activities such as charts, word ladders, sorts, and so forth, that are linked to the weekly class lesson. As described, children can also use the notebook,

FIGURE 14-7   Spelling Card

Look, Say, Cover, Write, Check			
before	befor	before	before
because	becus	becaus	because
belong	belog	belong	belong
their	thier	their	their
they're	there	theyre	they're
there	ther	there	there

FIGURE 14-8   Look, Say, Cover, Write, Check Study Sheet

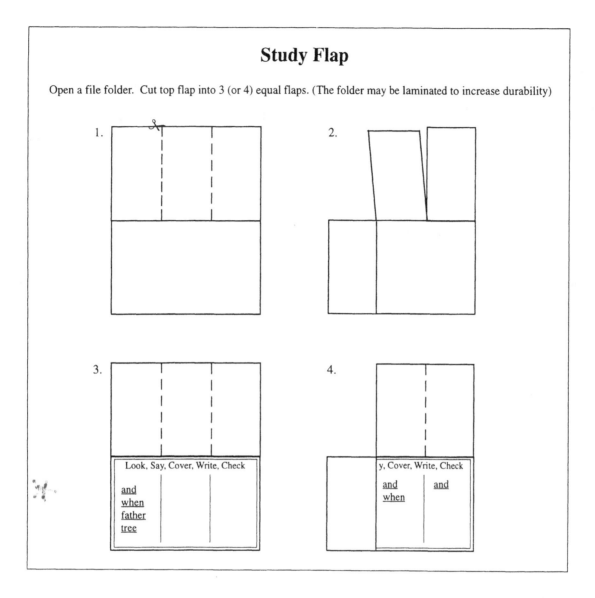

Study Flap

Open a file folder. Cut top flap into 3 (or 4) equal flaps. (The folder may be laminated to increase durability)

1.

2.

3.

Look, Say, Cover, Write, Check

and
when
father
tree

4.

y, Cover, Write, Check

and   and
when

FIGURE 14-9   Study Flap

starting from the back, to maintain a list of words to learn.

Using a Buddy Study Workboard

We are advocates of managed independent learning, in which students learn how to refer to a list of tasks and work independently and productively to achieve them. The board shown in Figure 14-13 includes several icons—simple clear pictures that signal a task. You can use a board such as this one to organize the second part of the word study system. (The icons to use with it can be found in Appendix 53.) You can assign the activities in varied order or change the specific activities. The goal is to provide a list that signals daily routines for partner and independent learning.

You can include the first part, the class lesson activity, on a general workboard (see Fountas and Pinnell 1996 for description and workboard icons). Alternatively, you can place the buddy study system icons (for example, Make Connections) on the general workboard so that all the children will engage in the activity on that day. It is important not only to work with the children over time to implement this comprehensive

Version 1

Name: Jeremy Date: 5/13/98

Buddy Check

1. Buddy reads your words to you and then checks them.
2. Try again if they were not right.
3. Use your list to write it correctly in last column, if it wasn't right.
4. Highlight or circle parts you want to remember and make the word with magnetic letters.

Word	**Try Again**	**Correct Spelling** [Highlight parts to remember and make the word with magnetic letters.]
and ✓		
wet	went ✓	
char	char ✓	shar (circled)
chest ✓		
chill ✓		
like ✓		

Score: 4/6 Score: 5/6

Version 2

Name: Jeremy Date: 5/13/98

Buddy Check

Words		Try Again		Correct Spelling
1. sad	X	said	✓	
2. thay	X	they	✓	
3. can't	✓			
4. spl	X	spel	X	spell
5. spot	✓			
6. spy	✓			
7.				
8.				
9.				
10.				

Score: 3/6 Score: 5/6

For words not right in the second column, what do you need to remember?
(Use a highlighter to mark parts you want to remember.)

spe(ll) → there are two ll's at the end, like fell

Version 3 (front)

Name: Jordan Date: 5/13/98

Buddy Check

Word	Try Again	Correct Spelling [Highlight parts to remember and make the word with magnetic letters.]
did'nt	didn't ✓	
once ✓		
affr	after ✓	
frend	freind	friend
playing ✓		
runing	running ✓	
carying	caring	carrying
was ✓		

Score: 3/8 Score: 6/8

Version 3 (back)

Write the words misspelled correctly; highlight parts to remember.	Tell why they were misspelled and what you will need to remember.
friend	i comes Before e, friends to the end"
carrying	douBle consonant in middle

FIGURE 14-10   Three Versions of Buddy Check Sheet

Version 1 (front)

Name: Paul   Date: 5/8/98
Make Connections
Write your words:

car   there   _____

corn   went   _____

first   have   _____

Make Connections . . .

__car__
car   rhymes   with   far, star, bar
car   starts   like   cat, children, came
car   goes   with   cars, card, carry
car   means   mobile

- -

__corn__
corn   starts   like   chair, come, cane
corn   goes   with   corner, core, cord, corny
corn   rhymes   with   born, thorn, worn
corn   means   crops, vegtible

Over→

Version 1 (back)

Paul

__first__
first   starts   like   fairytale, figure, fit
first   rhymes   with   worst, burst, cursed
first   means   number one

- -

__there__
there   starts   like   teacher, tought, their
there   rhymes   with   where, stair, hair, share
there   goes   with   they're, their
there   means   place

- -

__went__
went   starts   like   wherever, want, wonderland
went   rhymes   with   tent, cent, spent, sent
went   goes   with   want
went   means   gone

- -

__have__
have   rhymes   with   Ave,
have   starts   like   havent, hurry, hairy
have   goes   with   havent, behave, caves, having

Version 2

Make Connections

Name: Rosa   Date: 5-58-98

Write Your Words

Sounds Like [have some of the same sounds]		Looks Like [other words are spelled the same way]
swim meet swing sweep	Sweet	beet swim feet
peek pop wheel deal	peel	feel wheel
chest chair peak	cheek	peek seek
won her wind mother	water	never
but brother wetter	betten	wetter
swell sweat sister	sweater	better

FIGURE 14-11   Two Versions of Make Connections Sheet

185

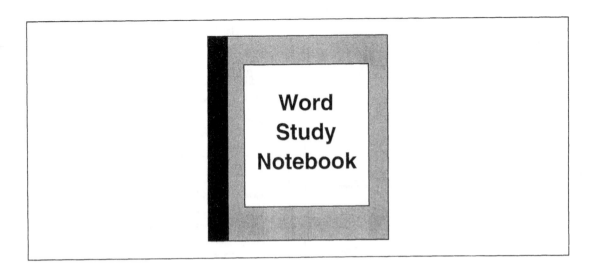

FIGURE 14-12   Word Study Notebook

FIGURE 14-13   Buddy Study Workboard

Dear Parents,

In our classroom this year, children will participate in many different kinds of reading and writing for a variety of purposes daily. Within these experiences, teaching and learning about phonics and spelling will be an important goal. ✓

This letter is to describe the word study system in which your child will participate and to suggest some ways you can help your child learn about letters, sounds, and words.

I will teach one or more weekly lessons or important spelling strategies and patterns that will be reinforced and applied each day. Each week the children will select six to eight words to learn and will write them on a spelling card. They work with magnetic letters to make the words, use a study method to learn words, engage in activities such as buddy checks and word linking, or give each other a buddy test on the last day of a five day cycle.

At home you can help your child learn by doing the following:

- Read books to your child, including rhyming books, song books, alphabet books.
- Enjoy rhymes with your child.
- Show interest in your child's word study activities by asking to see your child's weekly spelling words.
- Dictate the weekly words for your child to write (tell your child to try the word again if it's not written correctly the first time).
- Help your child notice the tricky parts of words.
- Help your child notice letter patterns, or how words are the same or different.
- Show pride in your child's attempts by noticing what is right about words, not what is wrong.
- Show interest in words as your child reads and writes, as you read aloud to your child, and as you notice words together in daily living activities.

You are an important partner in your child's learning. Please know that what you do to support your child's interest in and success with words will make an important difference in school. Please call me if you have any questions.

Yours sincerely,

Classroom Teacher

FIGURE 14-14   Parent Letter

word study system, but also to work across the grades with colleagues. When children have used the system in second grade, use in third grade will require much less teaching of routines.

It is also important to inform and educate parents. Some teachers have used the parent letter shown in Figure 14-14 to explain their word study program. You may wish to compose a similar letter to describe the particulars of your program, or invite the parents for a parent night to engage in the word study center and buddy study system

activities. In any case, informed parents will be able to support their children's spelling work in powerful ways.

Suggestions for Professional Development

1. Gather a group of grade-level colleagues. Have one person in the group bring a class set of writing samples or writing folders.

■ Take each folder and look for patterns in the words the child is spelling wrong. Make a list of errors and then discuss what the child *does* understand in each word. Then look for overall patterns, such as not representing all the sounds in a word, not using silent letters, and so on. Notice what strategies the child is using and what the child is neglecting.

■ Make some general statements about the children as spellers.

2. Make a list of three to five class minilessons that would be appropriate over the next several weeks to move the class as a whole forward in their spelling.

3. Take one of those minilessons and talk specifically about how you will demonstrate a principle or understanding you want to teach with magnetic letters, tiles, or a white board.

4. Share the routines you have established with the children in your word study center.

5. Bring a set of spelling cards from your class and discuss the patterns evident in the words the children have selected for study.

6. Talk about each daily activity from the buddy study system. Share the routines you have established and a sample of the student work included.

Inside Reading and Writing:
Learning About
Letters and Words

Children learn about letters, sounds, and word matters as they read storybooks, poetry, and letters from friends, and as they create their own written messages. That's where it counts. Teaching children to analyze some aspect of a word in a group lesson is useless if the same students cannot apply their knowledge while reading and writing continuous text. And, reading and writing must proceed with ease and fluency.

Many children will not know how to apply word and letter principles within the context of reading and writing unless you direct their attention to the information they need to use and show them how to use it. In Section 4, we explore how children learn to use their knowledge of letters, sounds, and words to read extended text—right from their first experiences as readers. The chapters in this section explore interactive writing and writing workshop as powerful contexts within which children not only learn about letters, sounds, and words but learn how to use what they know within the context of writing. Interactive writing is described as a group activity that makes the actual process of writing come alive for children as they participate in a demonstration of how it works. We discuss the interactive writing process and also describe shifts in teaching as children learn more about writing. In Chapter 16, Mary Ellen Giacobbe presents a discussion of how teachers can support word learning during writing workshop, a context in which children are learning to compose and write in their own voices.

Shared and guided reading are also explored as meaningful contexts within which we can help children learn to take words apart while reading for meaning. Two chapters focus on reading: Chapter 17 presents a discussion, with examples, of the powerful role of the observation of individual readers, and Chapter 18 describes how teachers can support word solving throughout the structure of guided reading lessons.

Interactive Writing

Developing Word-Solving Strategies

Whenever we write we are thinking of messages or texts that we craft into strings of words, all arranged according to the rules of our language. We have to hold this text in mind, all the time revising and extending it, as we write the words in a conventional left-to-right way. And there is a mechanical task—that of actually putting the words down on paper, using automatic movements of the hand, or typing them letter by letter onto the computer screen. During all of this activity, the eye brings information to the brain so that the construction of the written text can be monitored and revised as needed.

Some of the actions of writing are easy to demonstrate to young children; others are nearly impossible and the children have to figure them out for themselves through much exploration with writing instruments and paper. We believe that it will benefit most children to be involved in a supported writing context within which the way the process goes together can be demonstrated. Interactive writing provides this opportunity in primary classrooms.

A Description of Interactive Writing

Interactive writing is a teacher-guided group activity designed to teach children about the writing process and about how written language works. Working with the whole group or a small group, the teacher gathers children around an easel or other vertical plane on which the teacher will be writing. The physical setting may involve children sitting on a rug. Small groups sometimes sit on chairs in a circle. The goal is for children to be close to the teacher and to be able to quickly come up to the easel. All children must be able to see the writing easily, so teachers should work next to the easel, writing in dark markers and making clear letters.

Together, the teacher and children compose a message or text. They "share the pen": children write word parts or whole words; teachers fill in the rest. It may be any kind of written product. For example:

- A grocery list or list of things to do.
- A description of something children did or something they saw.
- The retelling of a favorite story.
- Labels for a mural or story map.
- A letter or note.
- A set of directions.

- A page of a book that the group is composing and writing together.
- A child's own story.

If the message is a long one (for example, a retelling of "The Three Little Pigs"), it may be composed and then written one sentence at a time. In this case, the previous sentence or sentences might be reread before composing the next one. Often this process is carried over several days, illustrating for young children how a writer comes back to something, thinks about it again, and then adds more text. Usually, for young children one or two sentences is plenty of work for a session of interactive writing.

Through interactive writing, you can demonstrate and engage children in virtually every aspect of the writing process, including:

- Composing a message or story.

- Using complex sentences and references to make the message coherent and clear.

- Describing characters, using dialogue, creating episodes, and writing beginnings and conclusions.

- Forming letters.

- Hearing sounds in words and constructing words using a variety of strategies.

- Using the full range of spelling patterns.

- Using punctuation in simple and more complex sentences.

- Selecting form to fit the function, such as letters, lists, narratives, and informational pieces.

- Connecting writing to reading, as when the interactive writing is drawn from literature experiences and is then reread.

What children learn in interactive writing they use in their own independent writing. Sometimes this group process is used to provide minilessons for writing workshop; at other times it is used to integrate literature and the content areas while at the same time learning about the writing process.

Interactive writing is a particularly powerful tool for helping children learn about letters, sounds, and words. In this chapter, we focus on word solving as a dynamic part of the interactive writing process, but we note that many other understandings about the writing process are developed as well. In fact, one of the advantages of interactive writing is that the children are focused on the construction of their message—recording an experience or producing their own story. The text is one that they will return to and read again and again with enjoyment. They are not thinking that this is a lesson on letters or words; rather, they encounter and use those elements in the service of real writing. Thus, the whole experience helps children understand the process.

Demonstrating Writing

An Example of Interactive Writing with Young Students

Let's take a look at an example of interactive writing to illustrate how teachers can support children by taking on some of the tasks in the complex series of behaviors required to produce a written message (Figure 15-1).

It is the first month of school for a group of kindergarten children. By now, most of the children have learned to write all or a part of their names and to recognize their names in several different contexts. The teacher, Beth, has worked extensively with a large chart showing the names of all the children in the room—reading the chart, finding particular names, and linking it to any piece of interactive writing the children produce. The children have also been putting together name puzzles—matching the cut-up letters of their name to the printed name on a big brown envelope.

The shared alphabet knowledge in the group is not great; a few children know all their letters but most are still working to develop knowledge of letter names and some sounds. Beth is emphasizing the lowercase letters, their names, and how to form them.

Trevor likes to play football.

FIGURE 15-1   An Example of Interactive Writing: *Trevor likes to play football*

In this example, they are writing about someone in the class as part of a "Getting to Know You!" wall. On the wall, each child has a photograph, a drawing, and a brief sentence describing themselves. The display develops over several days, the children returning to it each day to reread all the names and sentences. By now, each child can find her own name and is adding more information to her descriptive text. Eventually, these items will come down and be part of a big book that will be available in the classroom all year. Before composing, the children reread some of the sentences they have written about their classmates (Figure 15-2).

Today, the sentence is about Trevor. After stating the sentence they want to write about Trevor, the children construct it letter by letter, word by word. *To* is a familiar word for many children, and the teacher invites Tony to come up and write it quickly. Children also contribute the *p* in the word *play* and the *b* in the word *football*. The teacher has them clap the word *football* before they start to write it to hear that it has two parts. Each time they add a word, they reread the message while the teacher points.

At first glance, it may seem that interactive writing is a simple process of saying the words and having children come up to write words and word parts, but the teaching decisions are actually quite complex here. Beth's goal is to help these children become familiar with both letters and the nature of words. She decides to draw attention to several strategic *processes* that are important for these emergent readers to learn about:

∎ Using space to define words so the message is easier to read.

∎ Saying words slowly and listening for the sounds.

∎ Connecting new words to known words (in this case, names) to help us write.

∎ Remembering a known word (in this case, *to*) and writing it as part of a message.

∎ Rereading the message to help in remembering what we are writing.

∎ Remembering how to write certain letters by thinking of how they look or taking a quick look at a place where we know the letter is written (in this case, someone's name) and thinking of the movement needed to make it.

With this group at another time or with another group, the decisions might be different. For example, when all children know

193

An Early Example of Interactive Writing

Teacher:	We're going to write about Trevor today. Who can find Trevor's name on the chart? [Several children locate Trevor's name and there is a brief discussion about the fact that his name starts like Tara's name and Tony's name and has an *r* like Robert. The children spontaneously come up with these connections.] Trevor, would you tell us something about yourself? What would you like for us to write?
Trevor:	I like to play football.
Teacher:	That's something interesting! Can we say that sentence about Trevor and use his name?
Several children:	Trevor likes to play football.
Teacher:	That would sound good. Is that what we want to write? Everyone say it all together. [The children say the message several times and the teacher actually points to spaces along the chart paper. It is clear that they will not be able to write all the words on one line. She invites Trevor to come up and write his name and he does so. Then, they read his name again and say the whole message as a support for thinking of the next word.] That's right, the next word is *likes*. Let's write *like* first. Say *like* [demonstrating].
Children:	Like [they say slowly]. [They repeat this action several times and hands are up.]
Sharra:	I hear *k*.
Several children:	L.
Teacher:	You're right. It does have a *k* and it does have an *l*. Let's say it again. Which comes first?
Children:	Like. *L*!
Teacher:	John, would you like to come up and help us write *like*? And, Todd, can you hold your hand there to remind us of the space? [Todd places his hand after the word *Trevor* while John writes *l*.] It's just one straight stick down. Everyone make an *l* in the air in front of you! Pull straight down. Now, say *like* again. [Todd sits down.]
Children:	Like.
Stephanie:	There's an *i*.
Teacher:	That's right. There is an *i* next. We can hear it, can't we? John, write the *i*. It's like the *i* in Lisa [a name of one of the children] and the *i* in *is*, but it sounds different—a dot and then straight down. Now, John, Sharra says that there is a *k* in *like*. Everyone say the word again and listen to see if she's right.
Children:	Like. Yes! [John writes the *k*.]
Teacher:	Now we have to put another letter on *like* to make it look right. I'll put an *e* on the end. That's the word *like*. Let's read again.
Children:	[Reading]. Trevor like.
Sharra:	It's *likes*.
Teacher:	Yes, we wrote *like*. We need to make it say *likes*. Say *likes*. What can you hear at the end?
Several children:	S.
Teacher:	Sharra, can you put the *s* on quickly? It's the first letter in your name, isn't it? We don't need a space because it's part of that word *likes*. [She does it.] Now let's read it again.

FIGURE 15-2   An Early Example of Interactive Writing

and can write the word *to* fluently, Beth might decide just to write it herself to save time. If the word *like* were quite familiar, Beth might write it and invite children to think about the *s* on the end and to generate some other words that are similar. She would be careful not to focus on too many details in one lesson. That would be tedious and destroy the writing momentum. It's important for the lesson to move at a lively pace, keeping the message in mind. The interactions surrounding interactive writing are most effective when the examples brought to children's attention—those that children come up to the chart and write—have instructional value. The idea is not just to produce the message, but for children to learn something during the process that they can take away and use in their own writing.

In this example, the teacher also:

▌ Supported memory by acting as the "keeper" of the message, a particular combination of words that had meaning to everyone in the group. Any child who found it difficult to remember the message after some word solving could refer back to the teacher.

▌ Showed the children how to remember by having them repeat the message several times, think about it, and reread it while writing.

▌ Demonstrated word solving by modeling how to say a word slowly, think of the sounds in sequence, and connect words to other known words.

▌ Offered guidance in letter formation for the child who was writing and encouraged children watching to engage in the same motions.

▌ Provided a guide for placing letters and words on the page and for using space to define words.

▌ Reminded children that they knew some words that could be used to write a message.

▌ Showed children how to connect what they are trying to write with something they already knew (in this case, a name), and then reminded children to make connections.

▌ Built in the routine of referring to a class reference that would remain on the walls and, in the future, could be a resource to support children when they work independently.

An Example of Interactive Writing with a More Advanced Group

Figure 15-3 shows another example of interactive writing, this time with a much more advanced group of students. The teacher, Celia, and a small group of second graders were working on an interactive writing message connected to their study of the sea. The purpose of the writing was not word study, but these teaching interactions provide an example of how word study "echoes" through the curriculum. Through conversation with the students, Celia demonstrated the processes of noticing aspects of words and made connections between words. Soon, children will be initiating their own connections.

A Later Example of Interactive Writing	
Text:	We saw seagulls flying in the sky. We wrote what we saw in our naturalist book. We learned a lot about sea animals and their habitat.
Attention to words:	• The teacher drew attention to *seagulls* as a compound word, masking each individual word and having the children say it. • She asked them to look at *wrote* and said that there was a silent letter. The students came up with w and then looked at the word wall for more examples of words with silent letters at the beginning. They noticed *know*. • *Naturalist* was not an unknown word because they had been using it in connection with their study of the sea, but most children had not looked closely at the spelling. The teacher asked them to clap the word and used it as an example of how to work out a multisyllable word. • The word *learned* provided a chance to make a connection with the morning's minilesson (or words with the *er* sound) and to discuss how it fit one of the spelling patterns. Later, a card with *learned* was added to the word sort example. • *Habitat* was added to a list of words about nature study.

FIGURE 15-3   A Later Example of Interactive Writing

In word study, Celia's students had been focusing on words and word parts that sound the same but are spelled differently. Earlier in the day, Celia had provided a minilesson on this topic, illustrating it with the *er* sound. She placed four words—*her, earth, turn,* and *first*—in the pocket chart and demonstrated how to sort several more words under each. All words had the *er* sound with one of the four different spelling patterns. As an application activity, children were asked to sort a bank of words under the categories. They would revisit this word sort several times and eventually make a wall chart to which they could add more examples over time.

Later in the day, Celia gathered the group together and asked them to write some things they had learned in their study of the sea. The text the children composed for this interactive writing offered several opportunities for them to notice aspects of words. However, the *sentences were not composed simply to illustrate spelling patterns.* That would distort the message and undermine the purpose of interactive writing. But all sentences were composed of words that are rich in meaning and provide an endless number of examples to help children learn more about words.

The sentence this group of children composed was complex and related to the content; nevertheless, there were many opportunities for word solving. Words like *we, what, saw, our, lot, in,* and *the* were simply written quickly by the teacher. She used the opportunity of writing the message to draw children's attention to words and word principles that they would find useful in their own writing. The word work was intentional on the teacher's part but seemed incidental to the rich discussion of sea life, the composition of a message, and the rereading of the text.

Variations in Interactive Writing

We have said that interactive writing may be used for virtually every writing purpose, and it is helpful to children to see this variety in the authentic functions of written language. We also think it is helpful to young children to revisit their pieces of interactive writing again and again. It might take several days to produce a piece of writing; that process helps children learn how to carry a literacy event over several days.

Interactive Writing in Kindergarten

In the example in Figure 15-4, children in a kindergarten class were illustrating a mathematical process with graphics, comparing different numbers of responses to their survey on a trip to the apple orchard.

They first wrote the survey question using interactive writing. Discussing the wording of the question and then writing it helped every member of the class think how they would respond to the survey, which they did by printing an image of an apple in the appropriate column. It was easy for them to see which activity had more responses; later they would write a sentence about the results of their survey. In the sequence they wrote—"What did you like the best at the apple orchard?"—different children produced the *W* in *What,* the final *d* in *did,* the words *you* and *at,* the *k* and *e* in *like,* the *st* at the end of *best,* the *th* for *the,* and a few letters in *apple* and *orchard.* The focus here was on hearing and representing consonants and consonant clusters at the beginnings and ends of words. These children were using lowercase letters and a few known high-frequency words were known by participants in the group. The teacher will be working with them to hear more sounds in words and to gain control of a few more words like *the.*

Interactive Writing in First Grade

The next examples illustrate interactive writing in Kate Roth's first-grade class.

Retelling a Story

The first example, Figure 15-5 (page 198), shows one page that some first-grade children have written based on a story about the Three Bears. They had heard eleven ver-

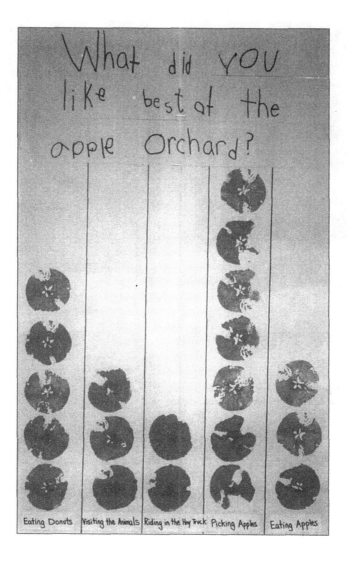

What did you
like best at the
apple Orchard?

Eating Donuts | Visiting the Animals | Riding in the Hay Truck | Picking Apples | Eating Apples

FIGURE 15-4 Apple Orchard

sions of the story and knew it well. Their story pretty much followed the traditional tale, but there were a few interesting variations (for example, the bears went for a bike ride).

One of the pages described what happened when Goldilocks saw and sat in the three chairs. The word *smithereens* provided the chance to work out a long word syllable by syllable, using sound-to-letter and letter-cluster correspondence, double letters, the *er* cluster, and the plural ending. More important, using this unusual word was fun. It gave the writers a voice.

On the last page of their story about the Three Bears, the children used dialogue and a conventional story ending (Figure 15-6).

The teacher had them listen for word parts in longer words, such as *jumped*. She made the decision to write a word pattern that they all knew (*jump*), but had a child put in the *ed* because they were focusing on endings. She wrote *out* and *the*. She had them clap longer words like *Goldilocks*, *window*, and *baby* before writing them. Writing this piece also offered the opportunity to teach about quotation marks, commas, and exclamation marks.

Recording Information

The next example (Figure 15-7, page 199) is an informational piece. Writing was used to label the parts of a skeleton as part of a study of bones.

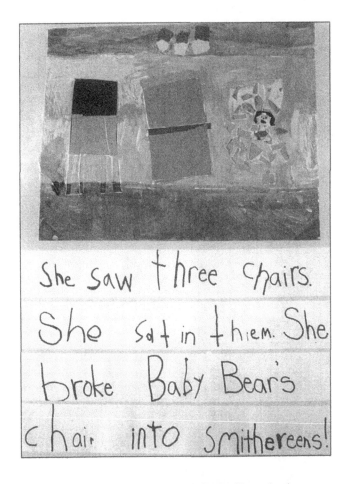

She saw three chairs.
She sat in them. She
broke Baby Bear's
chair into Smithereens!

FIGURE 15-5   *The Three Bears (Example 1)*

Goldilocks jumped out
the window and ran
home. Baby Bear
said, "Bye-bye!"
The End

FIGURE 15-6   *The Three Bears (Example 2)*

The labels were constructed by the group in an interactive writing session and then placed on the display. Here, writing performed a very different function than it did in the Three Bears example. Children had to think about individual words that were of a technical nature and use them appropriately. As far as attention to words, there was the opportunity to explore vowel patterns like the *ou* in *our*, the *ack* in *back*, and the *igh* in *thigh*. The children also talked about silent letters like the *gh* in *thigh*, the *l* in *calf*, and the *k* in *knee*. In addition, the teacher pointed out clusters at the beginning of words, such as the *sh* in *shoulder* and the *sk* in *skeleton* and *skull*. The *er* at the end of *shoulder* and *finger* provided another way to look at a word part. The children were also learning how to make a diagram with illustrations and labels.

An exploration of plants and roots is shown in the example in Figure 15-8. On this chart, the teacher made the decision to provide some of the writing herself, and the rest was produced through interactive writing.

The important thing about this text is the information it provides and the learning it represents. It is not necessary for children to participate in the physical writing of each letter of a text; that would be too tedious. Here, the teacher and children produced an informative text that everyone in the group could read and refer to. In the part of the text used for interactive writing, there were examples of words with double letters (*carrot*, *little*, *need*, *roots*), words with letter clusters (*plants*, *stem*, *bring*), and long, multisyllable (words still regular in letter-sound correspondence) that children could work out letter by letter (*nutrients*).

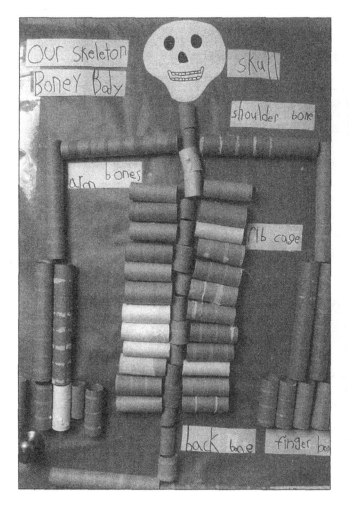

FIGURE 15-7   Skeleton

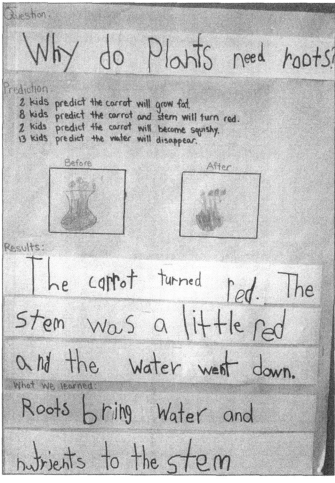

FIGURE 15-8   Plants and Roots

A Complex Text

The example in Figure 15-9 (page 200) shows a combination of sentences and labels on a chart reporting the results of a scavenger hunt. In the process of writing this report, children had to think about how to arrange the text so that readers would understand their experience. There were long words to work out (*triangle* and *rectangle*) and many words required an *s* ending. The *ar* at the end of *calendar* could be compared to *er* in *checkers*, showing another way to represent that ending. The cluster *qu* was evident in two of the words, providing an opportunity to discuss how those two letters always appear together. The abbreviation *t.v.* was also used, as well as two- and three-letter clusters (<u>blan</u>-ket; <u>placemat</u>; <u>screen</u>). Compound words such as <u>placemat</u> and <u>earring</u> made for an interesting discussion. Not all of this attention to words would take place during the writing of the text; some might emerge in rereading or revisiting it over time. The potential of the piece is in the rich learning conversations that take place around it.

Some Suggestions for Helping Children Learn About Words Through Interactive Writing

All of the previous examples illustrate children's word solving in the service of producing a meaningful piece of writing. Each piece is spelled conventionally for several reasons:

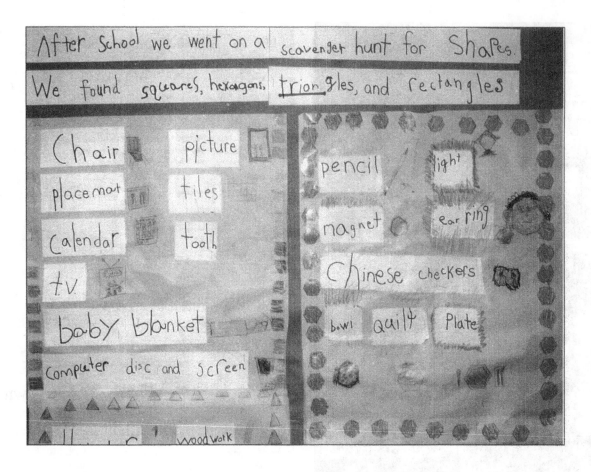

FIGURE 15-9 Scavenger Hunt

❚ The text is coconstructed. The teacher is right there, so that children make some of the contributions in a constructive way and the adult fills in the rest.

❚ The text will be a reading piece that will be used again and again in the classroom. It is important that reading texts be spelled conventionally.

❚ Spelling the words conventionally with the teacher's help illustrates the complex processes involved in spelling—that it goes beyond simple letter-sound correspondence. Conventional spelling helps children to go further in their understanding of spelling.

In the following section we present five suggestions for effective use of interactive writing to help children become word solvers. Each represents a goal to work for in teaching.

Work on the Edge of Children's Understanding About Letters and Words

Working on the edge of learning will take some time to accomplish. It is easy to get started in interactive writing, and we encourage teachers to try it out right away to get the feel of it. The first time you try it with a group of students, you will want to explain the task—that together with their classmates they are going to think about what to write and then write it on the piece of chart paper. The children should have a clear view of the easel and look in that direction. Building on an experience or a favorite story, you can decide with the children what sentence to write and proceed from there. In the process, you will learn a great deal about the children with whom you are working. Most of us have found that even young children can contribute a great deal during the writing of a message.

Using interactive writing in a powerful way requires reflection on teaching. It is difficult to develop skill in making the teaching decisions that will help children go further in their learning. Some general principles are to:

❚ Let children contribute parts of the message that they can produce but still need to practice a bit more.

❚ Write very familiar words for the children.

❚ Select for attention and conversation those patterns and structures that represent what children are just learning.

Teaching through interactive writing shifts as children learn more. It would be strange indeed if most second graders were asked to link beginning consonant sounds to their names! It would be equally inappropriate to ask kindergarten children to notice the *ear* in *learned* and compare it to *earth* and *turn*. Teacher decision making based on observation of children is the key to effective teaching through interactive writing.

Use Interactive Writing as a Resource for Studying Words

Most of the word construction learning in interactive writing takes place during the process of writing the text; however, many teachers have found it helpful to use the piece as a kind of laboratory for studying words. Revisiting a piece of interactive writing can happen right after a sentence has been written by a group of children or it could be part of a minilesson later. Reference may be made to a piece of writing as a resource to help produce another piece, thus modeling for children what we hope they will do in their independent writing.

Make Connections to Other Contexts in the Word-Learning Curriculum

Interactive writing provides an ideal setting for showing children how words are constructed in pursuit of producing a meaning-

ful message. The class is doing just what writers do—composing a message and then writing it word by word, letter by letter. In the process, they may have to slow down to think how to spell a word (and check it), and there are many strategies for doing that.

Through interactive writing and the independent writing that children do, word study comes together. It is beneficial to create what we have called "echoes" across lessons and literacy contexts. We have mentioned that interactive writing may be used in a minilesson for a writing workshop. That lesson may be connected to a word study activity (such as sorting or chart making) that the children have experienced earlier.

Beginning late in first grade, the word study system (described in Chapter 14) also offers good connections. Observation of children in interactive writing, for example, may yield some words that will be important to use as part of the word study system. Also, the weekly tests that children give each other as part of the word study system can reveal some words or kinds of words that might be good to emphasize as part of interactive writing.

All of these connections come through the natural redundancy and richness of all languages. When children are producing a large amount of written language, examples will always be available. It is up to us to have in mind the concepts and principles that are particularly powerful for our students *right now*. We plan some teaching actions (such as minilessons and application activities), and we take advantage of other teaching actions (such as recognizing opportunities in interactive writing).

Use a Combination of Demonstrating and Prompting Techniques

Interactive writing is a setting in which you can prompt and remind your students to use what they know in the service of producing a text. The technique will not be as powerful if you simply direct students the whole time.

Try using a combination of direct teaching, reminding, inviting, supporting, and specifically praising as you help students construct a message. A general guide is to prompt *after* you have taught a principle, concept, or item (word, letter, etc.). For example, if you want to prompt students to say a word slowly, thinking about how it might end, it's best to do so after you have explicitly demonstrated the technique with lots of support for students to practice it. It is not helpful to tell students to say a word slowly if they don't know what those instructions mean.

The list of prompts in Figure 15-10 provides some language that we have found to be useful during interactive writing. You would not use all of these prompts within a single interactive writing session. They are meant to represent a repertoire of specific language that can be useful when you select it based on your observation of the children and the opportunities possible within the text they are creating.

Work to Help Children Use the Understandings Gained in Interactive Writing as They Write for Themselves

The goal of interactive writing is fluent, independent writing with control of the conventions of text construction (sentences, paragraphs, and whole texts), spelling of words, and punctuation. We want our students to produce writing for many purposes, to be aware of various audiences, and to find their voices as writers, gaining control of conventions as they go along. It is not a matter of either being "creative" *or* producing accurate, conventionally punctuated text. Our job is to help students accomplish both, realizing that learning to write is a process that takes time. It will be essential to provide opportunities every day for students to write, and we want to make them independent in the process. A well-supplied, organized writing center, like the one shown in Figure 15-11 (page 204), is essential.

In this center, references and resources such as dictionaries and word lists are readily available. Handwriting charts are also there for students to refer to, and supplies are well organized and labeled. There are several different sizes of paper; some plain white paper has a box drawn for a picture at either the long end or across the page horizontally so that students get the idea of thinking about different kinds of formatting. Writing utensils of all kinds are organized and labeled.

In classrooms where much modeling of writing is provided through interactive writing and the minilessons of writing workshop, even young children write a great deal. Consider the example of Jessica's writing in Figure 15-12 (page 205). Jessica is a kindergarten student; it was January when she produced this piece of writing. For five months, she had had daily experience with reading and writing. Much of her writing experience came from interactive writing, although she had been writing a little for herself each day. The lessons in her classroom supported her growing independent control. The text says, "I like you, Ma. It makes me cry when you are fighting. You know why? Well, it's because you make me think you are going to be divorced and it makes me think you are having me live with somebody else."

The first response to Jessica's writing is to talk with her about the powerful and emotional ideas she is expressing. We would also notice that Jessica understands:

■ That there is something needed between words to show word boundaries.

■ How to form capital letters in conventional form.

■ That words are comprised of sounds that are represented by letters.

■ That words are comprised of letters that are written from left to right (MCS for *makes*; BTE for *body*; DVOST for *divorced*).

Prompting for Word Solving in Interactive Writing

During interactive writing: brief interactions

To teach for sound analysis:

- Clap the parts you hear.
- Listen for the parts.
- Listen for the sounds you hear in the first part.
- Say the word slowly. What do you hear first?
- Listen for the consonant sound at the beginning, at the end, in the middle.
- Listen for the vowel sound in the middle, at the beginning, at the end.
- Listen for the ending.
- Say the word slowly. How many sounds do you hear?
- Write the first sound you hear, the next sound, the last sound.

To teach for visual analysis:

- Does it look right?
- What would look right there?
- It's almost right. Add the ending.
- You're nearly right. Add a letter to make it look right.
- It looks like (another word they know).
- Think about how the word looks.
- Think about another word like that.
- Do you know a word like that? Do you know a word that starts (ends) like that?
- It sounds like that, but it looks different.
- There's a silent letter next.
- You need a vowel next.

After interactive writing: a brief period (two minutes at the most) to revisit and reinforce

- Which words did we write quickly without stopping to think about them?
- What's a word with two sounds (three, four, etc.)?
- What word(s) has more letters than sounds?
- Which words begin with consonants clusters? A vowel?
- What words have one syllable (two, more than two, etc.)?
- Which words have silent letters?
- Are there compound words, contractions, words with prefixes, endings, etc.?
- What word has parts that can be removed?
- What words sound exactly like they look?
- Which words have a tricky (interesting, hard, new) pattern (spelling)?
- What word is tricky (hard, new) for you to write? What will you want to remember about it?
- What's a new word you learned to write today?
- What words could be spelled another way but sound the same?
- What word has a special pattern (spelling) that shows what it means?

FIGURE 15-10   Prompting for Word Solving in Interactive Writing

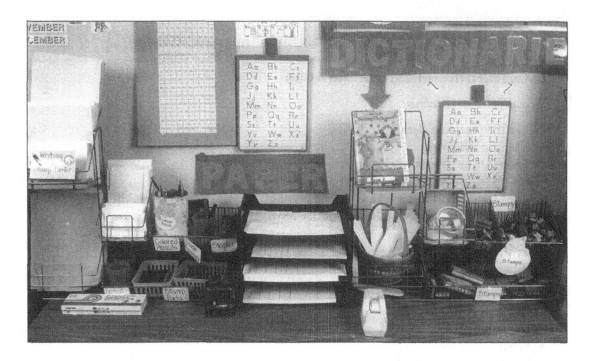

FIGURE 15-11   Writing Center

▌ How to represent lots of consonant sounds and many easy-to-hear vowels with letters.

▌ That known words should be spelled with conventional spelling—*I, me, at, to, be.*

▌ That the spelling of a word is constant and consistent (*you* is represented by *uo* six times).

▌ That words have silent letters (*e* at the end of *LEKE* [like]).

▌ That sometimes two letters are used to make one sound (*ae* at the end of *cry* and *why*).

▌ That the *th* sound is presented with two letters, *t* and *h* (*THK* [think]; *WTH* [with]).

▌ That letter names are sometimes related to sounds (*LS* [else]).

▌ How to hear syllable parts and represent them (*DVOST* [divorced]; *BTE* [body]).

▌ That consonants cluster together in some words (*CRAE* [cry]).

Jessica is still new to word solving. She largely uses phonics principles, but she is beginning to understand spelling principles. While she does not represent every sound, we can see that she is probing the complexity of the spelling process.

The real purpose of writing is to enable children to communicate in their own voices their messages to others. Jessica is well on her way to doing that. It is obvious that she needs much more instruction to bring her writing and word-solving skills to a proficient level. Our job as teachers is to help students develop word-solving strategies that will enable them to use and control the conventions of our written language. Interactive writing, with strong connections to word study, independent writing, and reading, is a way to help young children gain this power.

Suggestions for Professional Development

1. Select a small group of children with whom to try out interactive writing. Don't begin right away. Instead, gather some

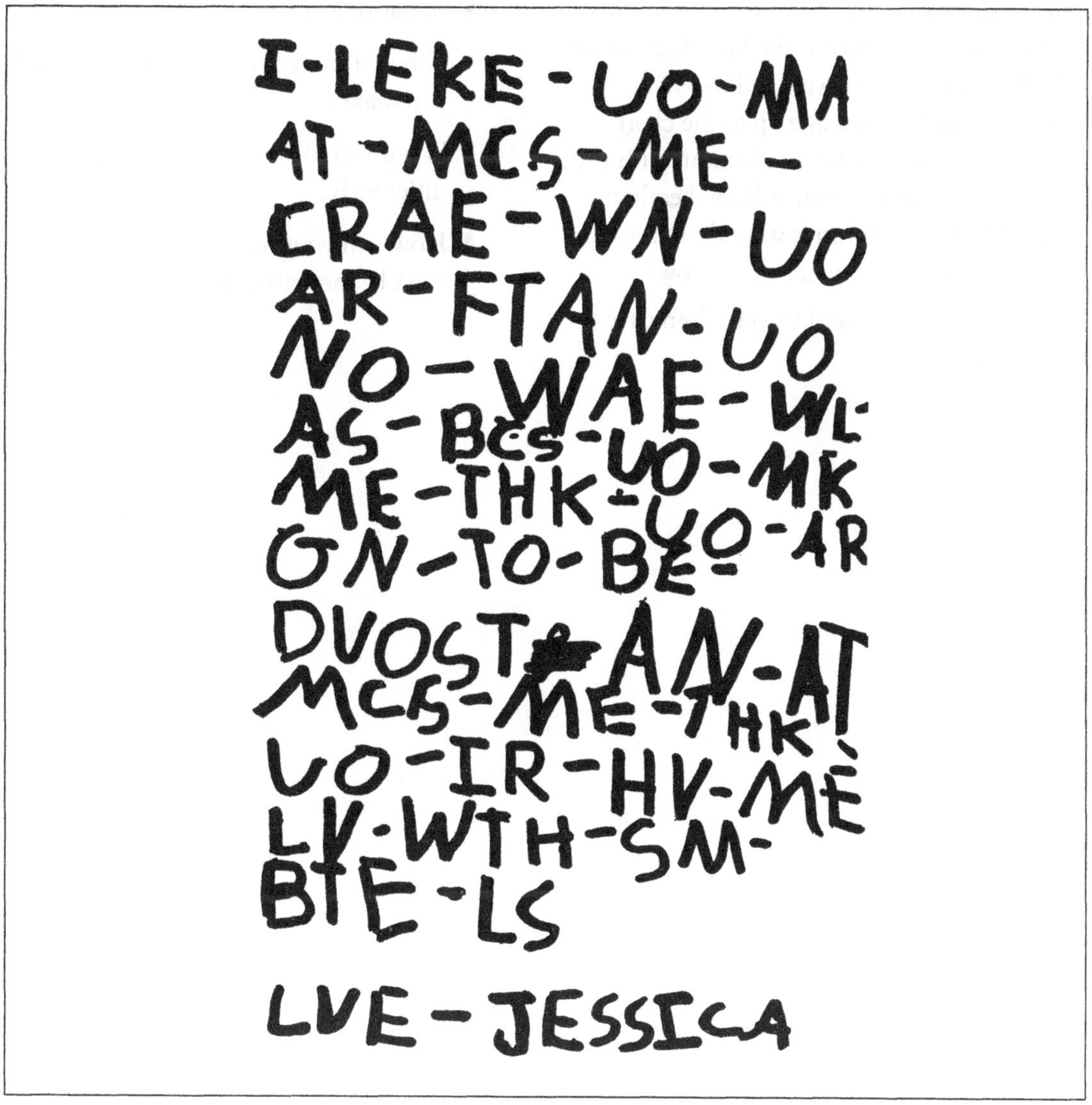

I-LEKE-UO-MA
AT-MCS-ME-
CRAE-WN-UO
AR-FTAN-UO
NO-WAE-UO
AS-BCS-WL-
ME-THK-UO-MK
ON-TO-BE-AR
DUOST-AN-AT
MCS-ME-THK-
UO-IR-HV-ME
LV-WTH-SM-
BIE-LS

LVE-JESSICA

FIGURE 15-12   Jessica's Writing

writing samples and/or the Letter Identification, Hearing and Recording Sounds in Words, and Writing Vocabulary Assessments from Clay's (1993a) *Observation Survey of Literacy Achievement* for each of the students.

2. Discuss with a group of colleagues what these children know and what they need to learn next about letters and words.

3. Think in advance how you could find opportunities to bring the principle to their attention during interactive writing.

4. Now, make a general plan for introducing interactive writing to the group. Use something simple—the retelling of a favorite story, a shopping list that you are really going to use, or something about the members of the group. You will need to explain the task to them and just get started as we described earlier in this chapter.

5. Afterwards, bring your finished piece of interactive writing to share with colleagues. Remember as much as you can about what individual children contributed. You will be

surprised at how easy it is to remember some individual contributions. We have found that children can almost always tell us which letters or words they came up to the chart and wrote. Compare your reflections with the data on children that you collected earlier:

■ What opportunities were there for children to use what they know?

■ What words could the children write easily?

■ What new learning took place?

■ What effective teaching decisions did you make?

■ What would you have done differently?

■ How will your reflections inform your next lesson with the group?

The Writing Workshop

Support for Word Learning

Guest Author: Mary Ellen Giacobbe

Within the community of a reading-writing classroom I have several goals. First, I am most interested in helping the writers I work with find and develop their own voices. Since voice is associated with what a person knows, thinks, and feels, I want to help find the language to communicate their voices both orally and in writing. Six-year-old Joey's voice comes through in his story "I Want A Dog," shown in Figure 16-1.

He tells why he wants a dog, how his mother is not agreeing, and what commitment he is willing to make. We discover a person who is passionate about his desire to be a dog owner. This is what we mean by voice; we get to know what Joey knows, thinks, and feels about his dogless situation. I would not want Joey to limit what he could write—to limit his voice—because he doesn't know how to spell correctly all the words he needs. Joey needs to have strategies to write the words he knows and uses, even though he may not know the conventional spellings.

My second goal is to help children acquire a way of thinking about writing: How do I choose a topic? How do I get started? Do I draw pictures? What will a reader want and

need to know in order to understand my story? Am I telling enough? Am I telling too much? How can I start this piece? How can I end this piece? I want writers to see that there are many ways of thinking about these issues. I want them to have ways to add, reorganize, and delete information from a text. I also want to help them acquire a way to think about the conventions of writing: spelling, punctuation, usage, and so on. How do I spell the word *required*? Where do I put periods in this writing? How do I proofread my writing?

My third goal is to help children revisit their work. I don't want children to finish their writing and immediately say, "I'm done!" Instead, I want them to return to their writing and read it with a critical eye. In order to do this, they need to have a way to think about text. They need to pose questions to themselves and to have classmates respond as readers, too. They also need to revisit the conventions of their writing. We don't just want more writing; we want to move children forward and help them extend and refine what they can do.

My fourth goal is to help children see purpose behind what they are doing and see why it's important for them to write every day. Our goal is to help them understand

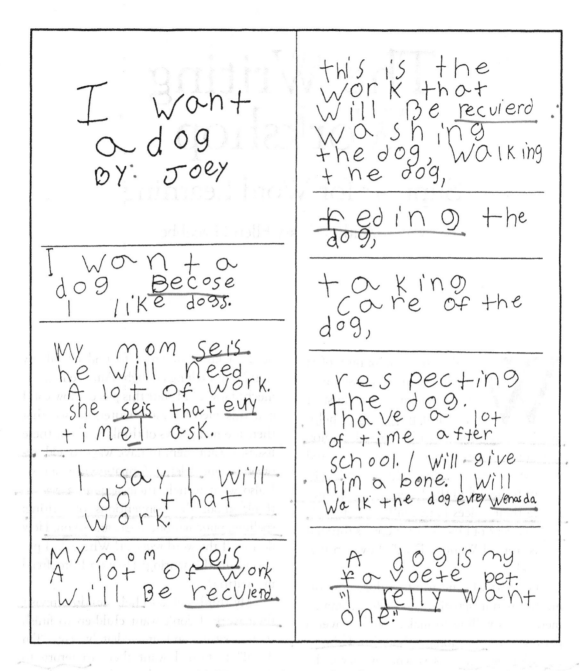

FIGURE 16-1 "I Want A Dog" by Joey

that writing is not just for when they're grown up. Writing can serve many purposes for them right now: to express themselves, to remember, to share the stories of their lives, to record information, and so on. Writing can also help us as readers.

One way of working toward these four goals is to engage children in a writers' workshop. A writers' workshop is a structured time for teaching and learning about writing. It includes time for a whole-group mini-lesson based on what most writers need to learn how to do. Children spend a good portion of the workshop time working on their own writing while the teacher confers with individuals or a small group. At the end of the workshop there is a short sharing time for writers to give feedback to each other.

In my current work, I do purposeful teaching of spelling based on my observations of what children are doing and what they need to know how to do to continue to grow as writers. This chapter is about that purposeful teaching, focusing on writers who have developed a way of representing words using alphabetic symbols, spacing, and punctuation marks.

The Writing Folder

In order to help students with their writing, it's essential to know them as spellers. What do they know about writing words? Spending time looking at their writing and trying to understand the thinking behind their spellings is a way to begin (Bissex 1980). I help each child keep an everyday working writing folder—a collection of their writing that shows what they know how to do as writers.

A writing folder is a way to keep a student's writing together and organized. In recent years I've been using a two-pocket folder with three fasteners in the center. I attach record-keeping pages and reference pages so they don't get lost and are always accessible. The first four pages of the folder are shown in reduced form in Figure 16-2 (full size reproducible forms are in Appendixes 45, 46, and 47).

The first page, titled "My Finished Writing," is a place for students to keep a record of the titles of their finished pieces. I like to keep this page at the beginning of the folder because it's the first thing that's noticeable, and it's a nice way of celebrating the writer's work. I ask students to place a number on their stories and then write the title by the corresponding number on the "My Finished Writing" page.

The second page is a place for students to keep a list of topics they can write about. One day while I was conferring with Chris, he described how he and his father had gone to a baseball game on Father's Day. As we talked I told him that it seemed like such a special time for the two of them. He smiled and said, "You've got that right. My sisters didn't get to come and spoil it." I learned that Chris had three sisters—and lots of sto-

ries to tell about them. He turned to the "Topics I Can Write About" page and began listing potential topics. ✓ * LOVE THIS IDEA *

Proofreading is an important part of what a writer does, so I begin a page called "My Proofreading List" with students as soon as I think they're ready for one. The list begins simply, reminding writers to put their names, titles, and dates on their writing; to number their finished stories; and to write the titles on their "Finished Writing Page." At first I am trying to help children get into the habit of checking over their work. I want them to be successful, so I give them only those items I know they can check. (In kindergarten I might start their proofreading lists with just the first two items.) The list then becomes an individualized list; as each writer acquires more skills, I add them onto the writer's list.

As writers fill in all the spaces on the first three pages, they'll need another sheet to continue their record keeping. The lined page with no heading is used for this purpose.

The next four pages of the folder are shown in Figure 16-3. Reproducible forms are provided in Appendixes 48, 49, and 50.

There are many lists available of "Frequently Used Words" (see Appendix 48). I've included such a list in the folders because "good spellers have a large number of remembered spellings and can therefore write a large number of words as whole units" (Bolton and Snowball 1993). I want to help writers develop fluency and speed in their writing and just know how a word is spelled. As children learn each word, it is highlighted. Many times these known words will act as springboards to solving unfamiliar words. For instance, a child who knows how to spell _when_ and _my_ could probably figure out _why_. Children need to learn not to depend on memorizing the spelling of all words. Clay (1991a) notes that "as the core of known words builds in writing, and the high-frequency words become known, these provide a series from which other words can

hahah

My Finished Writing	
1	Drawing Cartoos
2	Pictionary
3	The Disaster of the Christmas Tree
4	
5	
6	
7	
8	
9	
10	
11	
12	

Topics I Can Write About	
1	Voteing problems
2	The Election
3	The snow story
4	
5	
6	
7	
8	
9	
10	
11	
12	

My Proofreading List

1. I can write my name on my writing.

2. I can write a title on my writing.

3. I can write the date on my writing.

4. I can number my finished writing.

5. I can write the title of my writing on the page called My Finished Writing.

???

FIGURE 16-2   First Four Pages of a Writing Folder

Frequently Used Words			
✓ a	✓ for	little	she
✓ after	from	long	✓ so
all	✓ get	✓ look	✓ some
✓ am	✓ go	looked	✓ that
✓ an	going	✓ make	✓ the
✓ and	good	man	✓ then
✓ are	✓ had	mother	✓ there
as	✓ has	✓ me	✓ they
asked	✓ have	✓ my	✓ this
at	he	✓ no	three
away	her	not	✓ to
✓ back	here	✓ now	✓ too
be	him	✓ of	✓ two
✓ because	his	old	✓ up
before	house	✓ on	us
big	✓ how	✓ one	very
boy	✓ I	or	✓ was
✓ but	I'm	our	✓ we
✓ by	if	✓ out	✓ went
✓ came	✓ in	over	✓ were
can	into	✓ people	✓ what
come	✓ is	✓ play	✓ when
✓ could	✓ it	✓ put	where
✓ day	✓ just	ran	will
✓ did	keep	run	✓ with
do	kind	✓ said	✓ would
don't	know	saw	✓ you
down	✓ like	see	your

What I Know About Writing Words
1
2
3
4
5
6
7
8
9
10
11
12

Words I'm Learning

Aa	Bb	Cc	Dd
Ii	Jj	Kk	Ll
Qq	Rr	Ss	Tt
Yy	Zz	___ed	___ing

How to Write

Ee	Ff	Gg	Hh
Mm	Nn	Oo	Pp
Uu	Vv	Ww	Xx

FIGURE 16-3   Next Four Pages of a Writing Folder

be composed taking familiar bits from known words and getting to new words by analogy." The children can also use this list of frequently used words as a reference while proofreading their work.

"What I Know About Writing Words" is a place to record what writers can do as they attempt to write words. Later in this chapter, as I begin to analyze the spelling in some students' writing, I record what the child can do in spelling on this page.

The next two pages, "Words I'm Learning How to Write," are placed facing each other in the writing folder so they form a flat, continuous word wall when the folder is open. As a child masters many spellings of words, it is important to raise the level of expectations of what the child will do as a speller. These pages provide a place for you or the child to write words he knows or needs to know and for you to plan with him appropriate next words to work on. You can add these words to the "words to learn" list that's part of the word study system discussed in Chapter 14.

The "Writers' Workshop Guidelines" and "Alphabet Chart" are shown in Figure 16-4. The "Writers' Workshop Guidelines" are helpful routines for writers and provide me a glimpse of some of their problem solving. I ask them not to erase because I like to see their first thinking and any other thinking as they work toward the best expression of their ideas and their best spellings. If they want to try to write a word another way, I ask them to cross out the whole word and start it again next to their first attempt. This supports their ability to write a word in correct sequence from beginning to end. Most of all, I want to get them out of the habit of thinking that their work has to be perfect. If they change their mind while working, it doesn't mean they've made a mistake; it means they are reading and checking their work carefully. I ask them to save everything for the same reasons. In addition, sometimes they may want to refer back to earlier writing and, if they've thrown it away, it's gone. LIVE.

FIGURE 16-4   Writers' Workshop Guidelines & Alphabet Linking Chart

Writing on only one side of the paper allows the young writer who is using multiple pages, with a part of the story on each page, to insert new pages for additional writing and to rearrange pages if the parts are not in order.

Writing requires a degree of concentration, so it's important that children get into the habit of using a soft voice when they talk. This is a good guideline to consider throughout the day. So is working hard and trying one's best. Teachers will want to remind children that being right or wrong is not the focus; trying and taking risks is what learners must do.

The "Alphabet Linking Chart" (Appendix 3) provides a clear letter-sound link to key words. Children find this chart particularly useful because of the simple pictures. The alphabet on the chart is written as it would be phrased in the alphabet song. This chart can be included in the folder as a reference for those children who are *still learning letters and sounds*.

Analyzing the Spelling

Although I'm going to look at the total number of words used and the total number of words spelled correctly in the examples given here, it's certainly not necessary to do this with each piece of writing a child does. It's too time-consuming, and there are other things we need to focus our attention on if we are to help our students become better spellers. However, I do think it's amazing to see how well each writer is doing when we look at the total number of words used and the variety in the language they use to write their stories. These are not students who won't attempt to write because they are afraid of misspelling a word. Instead, they work hard and try their best.

I'll be looking at three other aspects of their writing. First, what do they know about writing words? Second, are the frequently used words becoming automatic? Third, what do they need to work on next?

An Analysis of Megan's Writing

Megan's first-grade class began their writers' workshop in mid-October. Her first story was "I Lik Going to Jmnasks" (I Like Going to Gymnastics). See Figure 16-5.

It's apparent from her circling (and perhaps the dots to separate her words) just how "hard" those cartwheels were! She spelled correctly fifty-three of the total eighty-seven words that she wrote, which means she spelled with 61 percent accuracy. As a speller, she knows how to do the following:

▌ She ~~attempts to~~ write all the words she needs to tell her story.

▌ She seems to know /ing/ sometimes and sometimes she doesn't. She uses /ing/ in *eitsiding-*(exciting), but she later writes *going* as *gowai*.

▌ She writes *wae* for *was*. Later she writes *was* in two places. Hmmm

▌ She writes *fan* for *fun*. Later she writes *fun*. (These inconsistencies in spellings are very typical of a writer who is experimenting with spellings.)

▌ In spelling difficult words, she almost always has a letter or letters for each consonant heard.

▌ She knows seventeen words from the "Frequently Used Words" list. My hunch is that she knows how to write others but she didn't need them in this particular piece of writing.

Megan is an accomplished beginning writer. However, there are two things I'd like to help her with. First, when you write about yourself and use the personal *I*, it is always spelled with a capital letter. Second, when you know a letter cluster such as /ar/ in *car* and *star*, you can use that information to help you get to other words such as *cartwheel* and *hard*. I am not necessarily interested in teaching her just how to spell those words correctly. Rather, I want her to understand

FIGURE 16-5 "I Lik Going to Jmnasks" by Megan

the process of using what she knows about one word to help her learn about other words.

An Analysis of John's Writing

Second grader John's story, "Blizzard '97" (Figure 16-6), is his seventh story. He uses a total of 121 words. He has spelled ninety-five words correctly for an accuracy rate of 78 percent. As a speller:

■ He attempts to write all the words he needs to tell his story.

■ He knows how to use a letter or letters for the sounds he hears.

■ He knows how to use the /ing/ ending.

■ He knows the correct spelling for forty-four of the frequently used words. Like Megan, he probably knows more, but this is what he reveals in this particular piece of writing.

John needs to work on /ed/ endings when that ending sounds like /t/. When he wrote *looked*, he wrote it as *lookd*. He wrote *asked, jumped, flopped, stepped,* and *slipped* as *asst, jimpit, flopt, saep,* and *sipt*. We need to talk about the action words and how we add /ed/ in the past tense. I also want him to understand that since he knows how to spell *then*, he can easily figure out *when* by analogy (sometimes he spells it *wen* and sometimes it's *wan*).

An Analysis of T. J.'s Writing

T. J.'s second-grade class started writing in December. By January he had written "Drawing Cartoons" and "Pictionary." Let's look at his third piece of writing, "The Disaster of the Christmas Tree," Figure 16-7, determine what he knows about how words work, and then consider the next appropriate instruction for him.

His story had a total of 194 words. He

FIGURE 16-6 "Bleserd '97" by John

misspelled twenty-three words. He is spelling with 88 percent accuracy. As a speller:

■ He uses a letter or letters to represent sounds in difficult words.

■ He knows how to add /s/ to make words plural.

■ He knows how to use /ing/.

■ He uses /ed/ to make a word past tense if the sound is /d/.

■ He knows how to write two contractions (*it's* and *we'll*).

■ He correctly spells sixty-two words from the list of frequently used words (this also includes words from two previous pieces of writing).

As I consider what is most important for him to study, I choose the /ed/ ending. He already knows how to spell *crushed*, *called*, *cracked*, *helped*, *picked*, and *started*. He also uses /ed/ in *exhausted* and *tried*, although he spells them *egsauted* and *tryed*. When you say three of those words ending in /ed/ you will hear a /t/, as in *cracked*, *helped*, and *picked*. He needs to know how to write *dressed* and *noticed* with /ed/ rather than *dresst* and *noetest*. Since he already knows something about the /ed/, it's a good skill to help him fine-tune. This would be a good minilesson to do with the class, because John needs some help with this, too.

T. J. knows the word *there*, so I would want to talk with him about the word *where*, which is very similar. I also would want to see if he knows that *didn't* is the contraction for *did not*.

FIGURE 16-7 "The Disaster of the Christmas Tree" by T. J.

Spelling Instruction Through Minilessons

Once we identify what students need to know, we then need to plan for instruction. Sometimes what we notice is only true for one student. In that situation, it's appropriate to take care of it individually with the writer. However, many times there are patterns that emerge from most of the class. Appendix 34 provides a list of some patterns teachers might observe; these are possible topics to address in minilessons.

What follows are some scripts of sample minilessons. Note that they tend to focus on one spelling topic, and children are encouraged to read their writing to see if they can find any words that fit the particular pattern discussed in the minilesson.

Sample Minilesson: Looking Carefully at a Word

The following is a minilesson designed to help students notice how particular words look (see Chapter 13).

Teacher: Today we're going to talk about two words that look almost the same but one letter is different. [Shows *were* on the magnetic board.] This word is *were*, as in "we were going to school" or "they were getting ready for recess."

Now watch this. When we put an *h* after the *w*, now it says *where*, as in "where are you going?" or "where is your book?" *Were* and *where* have lots of the same letters, but *where* has an *h* in it.

Mark: I have another way that I remember *where*. I know the word *there* and that helps me with *where* because the two words rhyme, *where* and *there*.

Teacher: Now we have two ways of thinking about the word *where*—we can add an *h* to *were* or we can think of *there* and how the two words rhyme. Today when you begin your writing and you are rereading your work from yesterday, listen for the word *where* and try to remember how to spell it correctly.

Sample Minilesson: Using What You Know About a Known Word to Help You Figure Out an Unknown Word

The following minilesson is designed to help children make connections (see Chapters 13 and 16).

We noted in Megan's writing that sometimes she uses *ar* and sometimes she just uses *r* to represent /ar/. Some of her classmates do the same.

Teacher: I noticed in Megan's writing that she is spelling *car* as *c-a-r*.

Several other children: That's the way I spell it, too.

Teacher: So, some of you know that when you hear the *ar* sound in a word, one way to write it is with the letters *a* and *r*. She also spells star as *s-t-a-r*. Once again the *ar* sound is written with an *a* and *r*. When Megan wrote the word *cartwheel*, she wrote *crtwl*. If you listen carefully, you will hear the word *car* in *cartwheel*. Megan, what do you need to add to your word *crtwl*? [Megan comes to the board and inserts an *a* before the *r*.]

Teacher: Now Megan has the first part of her word, *cartwheel*. I think she can also listen carefully to the word *hard*, which she spelled *hrd*, and figure out what other letter she needs to add to that word. [Megan comes to the board and inserts an *a* before the *r*.]

Teacher: Since Megan knows *car*, and *star*, she can figure out *cartwheel* and *hard*.

Billy: I'm writing about the treehouse in my backyard. I guess I spell *yard* *y-a-r-d*.

Susan: And *jar* would be *j-a-r*.

Teacher: And how would you write *are*, as in "We are going to . . ."

Juan: [interrupts] Oh, that's easy . . . *a r* . . . . same *ar* but with a silent *e*. [Teacher reminds children to use *ar* when they hear the *ar* sound in words.]

Sample Minilesson: What's Going to Help You Remember How to Spell _____?

This next minilesson is designed to help children use mnemonic devices to remember tricky words (see Chapter 13).

Teacher: There are some words that just don't seem to follow any pattern or patterns, and it's so easy to always have to question how we spell them. Sometimes it's helpful if we think of a little story that will serve as a memory aid to help us remember how to spell those words that trick us. For instance, when I was learning how to write words, I would get tricked on the word *piece*. Then one day my teacher mentioned that if you look carefully, you can see the word *pie* in *piece*. [Shows this on the easel.]

Another word that would fool me was *principal*. I would get confused trying to figure out whether the ending was *p-l-e* or *p-a-l*. A classmate mentioned that the principal is your *pal*, and so that's how I now remember how to spell *principal*.

Maria: Well, I was always writing *they* as *thay*. Then one day I thought that *they* means more than one. *A* is the first letter of the alphabet. In saying the alphabet you have to say lots of letters to get to *e*, and that's how I remember the *e* in *they*, because *they* means lots of people.

Jessica: I used to write *yousto*, like in "I used to play the piano." Then I realized it had nothing to do with *you*. Instead, I was using the piano. Now I know it's two words: *used to*.

Teacher: Another tricky word for me is *kindergarten*. I always want to spell it *kindergarden*, with a *d* instead of a *t*. Now I remember that it is a German word and they say it *garten*.

As you work on writing words, think about those words that trick you and see

what story or memory aid will help you remember how to spell them.

Spelling Minilesson: Past Tense Is *ed* Even Though You Might Hear /t/

The final sample minilesson illustrates how you might teach how words sound and mean (see Chapters 13 and 16).

Teacher: I've noticed in your writing that when you are using a word that means something you've done in the past, as in "I tried to hit the ball" or "I called my friend," you know to put *ed* for the ending. [Makes a list of other words from their writing: *crushed*, *started*, *excited*, etc.]

Sometimes there are words that mean something you did before (in the past), but when you say the words, they have a /t/ sound at the ending. Some words that have the /t/ sound at the end are *cracked*, *helped*, *picked*, and *noticed*. You need to know that even though you hear /t/ in these words, you would still use the *ed* when you write them.

Let's look at some words and think about the /ed/ ending.

Teaching about letters and words through the writing workshop requires a dynamic combination of explicit teaching and supporting children in making their own discoveries. Teaching decisions are guided by careful examination of children's written products as well as by watching and interacting with them during the workshop time. Observation is the key to designing powerful minilessons that bring children's attention to the new learning they need. In this way, teachers can accomplish more in a shorter time period. The ultimate goal is to assist students in becoming writers who:

■ Have developed personal voice. ✓

■ Know how to think about writing. ✓

■ Know how to revisit their work, asking ✓ themselves the questions they need to refine it, including the conventions of spelling, punctuation, and usage.

▮ See the purpose behind what they are doing in writing.

Many of the teaching points discussed in this chapter will be addressed in other writing contexts such as interactive writing. The important goal, however, is for each and every child to apply all that is known about writing, and in particular word solving in the writing process, in daily independent writing work. This will be the measure of our teaching success.

Suggestions for Professional Development

1. With colleagues, examine the writing of Megan, John, and T. J. In turn, discuss what each child knows about spelling and what each needs to learn.

2. Compare your own lists to Giacobbe's analysis and to her planned minilessons. How do you think the minilessons will help these young writers?

3. Then, examine writing samples from several children in one classroom (or several classrooms if you are working with a group of colleagues). Follow the same process, listing what these children know and what they need to know.

4. Plan a minilesson (or two) that recognizes the children's developmental level and then nudges them forward in their knowledge of spelling. Design the lesson so they learn strategies that they can use again and again (rather than just perfecting one piece of writing).

5. Try the minilesson or -lessons and bring back the results to share with colleagues a week later.

Reading Instruction
Systematic Observation and Teaching for Word Solving

We learn to do something by doing it; we get better with practice. So, it makes logical sense to say that children learn to read by reading. What does that mean? To understand, think of what a competent reader does. A competent reader:

❚ Maintains a focus on the meaning.

❚ Processes the print with fluency.

❚ Uses language cues to anticipate text and check on meaning.

❚ Recognizes most words instantly.

❚ Uses parts within wholes and larger chunks of written language.

❚ Solves words rapidly and easily.

❚ Uses several different kinds of information simultaneously.

❚ Demonstrates flexibility in the use of strategies, working in many different ways as needed for efficiency.

The competent reader described here and elsewhere in this book is demonstrating efficient word-solving skills. The reader has many ways of approaching unfamiliar words and is able to use these tools with ease, flu-ency, and flexibility. Poor readers are more specific in what they know and more rigid in what they can do with that knowledge (Clay 1991a).

Good readers simultaneously use many different kinds of cues—visual, phonological, meaning, and language structure—as they process print. The processing system involves using visual information as one critical aspect of reading. Information about letter-sound relationships becomes more available to readers because they are processing print and have seen and used many examples. The more they see a word, the more available are the phonological and orthographic elements of that word. That is also true about patterns. If readers see them frequently enough, it is easier to make connections between words.

In word study activities, teachers can be quite effective in helping students look at word patterns and learn about them. However, studying phonological and orthographic features of words in isolation will not guarantee that children will work these skills into an effective process for reading text. Instruction is needed to specifically support children's use of word-solving skills while they are actually reading continuous text.

Shared reading is a context in which the teacher and children read together from simple, enjoyable, enlarged texts, such as poems, songs, chants, rhymes, and stories. In shared reading, children who are just beginning to read can encounter words that are embedded in text. There are many opportunities as they read and reread to draw students' attention to letters, sounds, and words. Depending on the nature of the text, the teacher can emphasize different aspects of print, using masks, different-sized Post-its, or bright, translucent highlighter tape to help children attend to high-frequency words, letter patterns, and word parts. They may look for and find various categories of words—rhyming words, words that begin or end alike, homonyms, and so on—within a text they know well. Teacher and group support is important. Over time, teachers may increase the complexity of the task by choosing texts that offer children a greater range of opportunity to use more complex visual information.

Guided reading differs from shared reading in that children are reading unfamiliar texts for themselves rather than in unison with others. Guided reading is a group instructional setting designed to support individual readers in the development of the reading behaviors just described. In this chapter, we discuss the relationship between systematic observation and systematic teaching. Guided reading, shared reading, and word study are connected in a dynamic way:

■ Your observations of your students as readers determine the minilessons that you provide in planned word study. Knowing what children can do or are attempting to do contributes to the design of lessons on aspects of words. In this way, the word study curriculum is matched to children's emerging abilities.

■ You can analyze the appropriate level texts that you select for your students in shared and guided reading to determine the information in the text children need to solve words. Different texts make different demands on visual processing. This analysis also informs the word study curriculum.

■ The aspects of words explored during word study lessons and applications will be evident as children read texts because of the nature and complexity of the words at a particular reading level. In the shared and guided reading lessons, you can bring these aspects to children's attention briefly, almost as "echoes" of the word study minilesson, in ways that help children learn how they can use the information.

Shared and guided reading are intricately connected with learning about words. Shared reading offers a highly supported setting within which children can learn about how print works in a meaningful way. It is not about "memorizing" a text to say it with a group but about becoming familiar with some language patterns so that children can experience the whole act of reading for themselves even before they can decode many individual words. In the process, they learn much about words and how they work. Guided reading is not about *learning to read a specific book*; it is about *learning how to read*. Teachers select supportive texts and teach in powerful ways so children learn strategies they can use with a variety of books, not just with the ones encountered in lessons.

Systematic Observation During Guided Reading

Guided reading cannot be effective without information from close observation of students. Both informal and formal observation inform the teaching of word analysis in guided reading.

Informal Observation
During guided reading, teachers have numerous opportunities to observe how children use visual information as part of a reading process. The teacher can use a clipboard to take ongoing notes as children read familiar and new texts. Quick notes on reading be-

havior will provide valuable information over time. Several different options for recording observational notes can be found in Fountas and Pinnell (1996).

Formal Observation

Running Records and Analysis

Running records are a standardized tool for coding and scoring children's reading of text, and for analyzing children's reading behaviors. As we use running records, we are looking at children's solving of words as part of a process rather than simply counting the words read correctly. From children's attempts at word solving, we can get an idea about what they know about words and how they use their knowledge to solve them. Their attempts reveal understandings and strengths that we want to use as springboards for further learning. Children will make a few errors when they are reading a text that is "just right" in guided reading. That means the book is not so easy that the reader has no problems to solve (encounters unfamiliar words), but it is also not so hard that the whole process breaks down and the child can no longer read for meaning.

A young reader who is encountering a *just right* text is engaged in the kind of problem solving that keeps on building the reading process. That child, usually without realizing it, is practicing word solving in the most powerful situation for learning. The child is behaving like a reader—"reading for meaning with divided attention" (solving words while maintaining the meaning of a story or message). Readers need hundreds of experiences in solving words while reading text. That's how the self-extending system is built (see Clay 1991a). Readers who learn to work at their reading, try different strategies, and work for understanding are getting better at reading every time they read. In guided reading, they have two very important supports in the process:

▮ A text that is just right—with just a few new or unfamiliar words to solve.

▮ A teacher who is supporting the process before, during, and after the reading of the text.

Teaching for word solving requires noticing children's attempts at words and taking them further in their learning. As teachers develop their expertise in using running records, the following occur:

▮ The records become easier to use and seem almost automatic in nature.

▮ The records help teachers focus on the vital information they need to create their general plans for word study teaching.

▮ The records provide a great deal of specific information about individual readers.

▮ Colleagues can discuss the evidence of processing they see in the records.

Three sources for learning more about running records are:

1. *An Observation Survey of Early Literacy Achievement* (Clay 1993a). Marie Clay is the developer of the technique known as the "running record." In this comprehensive book, she provides the research base for running records, as well as thorough directions for coding, scoring, and analyzing records of reading behavior.

2. *Knowing Literacy: Constructive Literacy Assessment* (Johnston 1997). Peter Johnston provides valuable information about the running record, including many examples and directions.

3. *Guided Reading: Good First Teaching for All Children* (Fountas and Pinnell 1996). In this book we provide directions for taking running records and using them in guided reading.

Let's take a look at the kind of information teachers can glean from running records by focusing in on a few examples. Here our concern is to find out about each child's word-solving strategies, so we will discuss the records only from that perspective.

Tony Figure 17-1 shows Tony's reading of *Peaches the Pig* (Riley 1995), a level E book on our guided reading list (see Fountas and Pinnell 1996). *Peaches the Pig* has one or two lines of text on each page and an episodic structure that provides for some repeating patterns, although not on every page. To read *Peaches the Pig*, it would help a reader to know some high-frequency words, such as *to*, *with*, *you*, *I*, *can*, *she*. The reader might need to figure out some challenging words, such as *climb*, *called*, or *went*. There are words like *but* and *yes* at the beginning of sentences, a structure that will probably require attention to visual information as part of the word solving. Of course, the challenge in the book will vary for any given reader.

Tony's errors reveal many strengths in working at words. Notice that while he was doing a fair amount of word solving on this text, he was also reading fluently with smooth phrasing and lots of expression for longer stretches. In other words, he was solving words quickly and reading with high accuracy (97 percent). It is obvious that Tony recognized most of the words in this text without having to solve them. Several of his partially correct attempts included the following:

■ On page 1, the text says, "Peaches the Pig wanted to play." Tony read *waited* for *wanted* and continued to the end of the line. His attempt not only made sense but was close visually to the spelling pattern in *wanted*, but Tony was closely monitoring his reading. Perhaps *waited* didn't quite make sense to him. Tony went back to the word *wanted* and this time read it correctly, making his reading fit with the visual information and meaning.

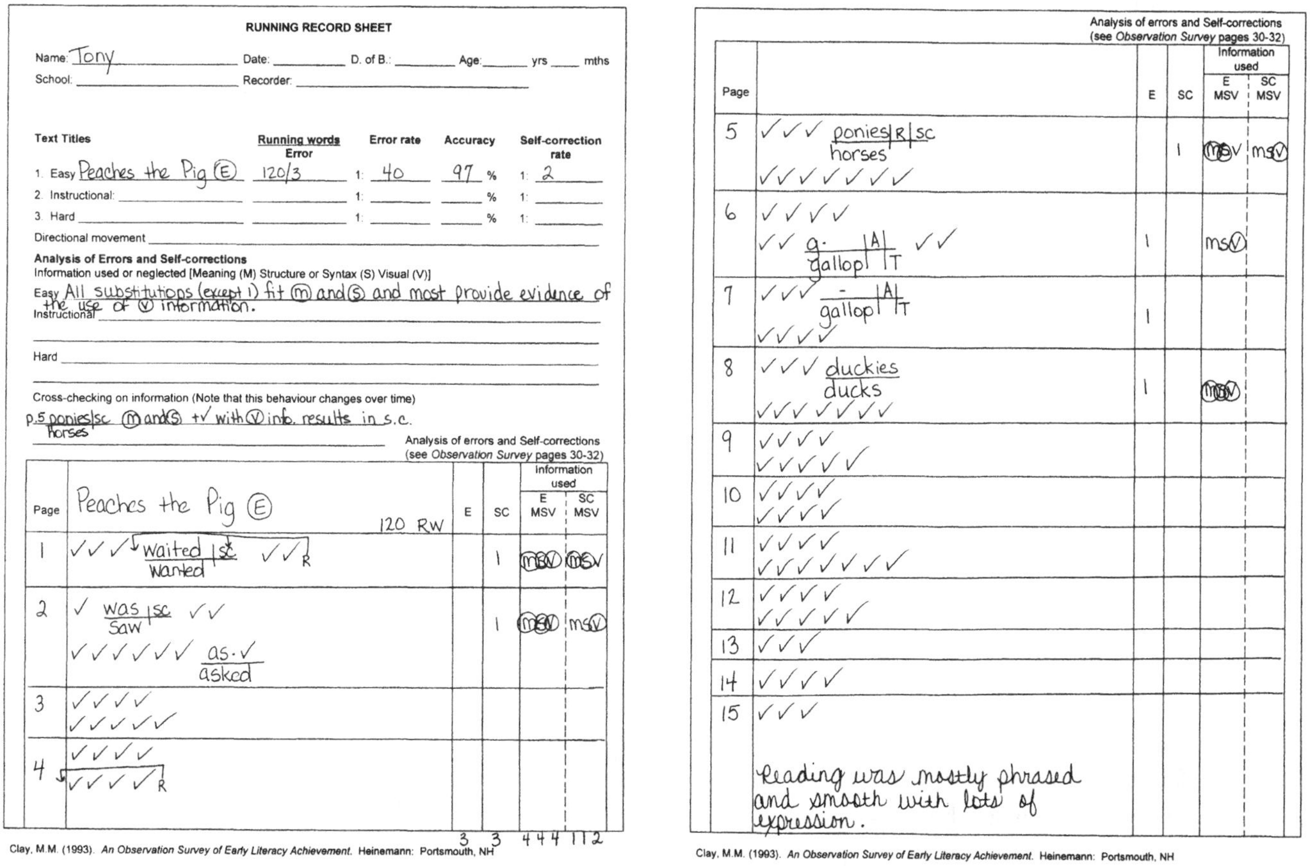

FIGURE 17-1   Running Record Sheet: Tony's Reading of *Peaches the Pig*

▮ On page 2, Tony read *was* for *saw* and then immediately corrected it before reading another word. His attempt was close to *saw* visually, but our hypothesis is that he immediately noticed the discrepancy in the order of letters. On the next line, Tony demonstrated some left-to-right word solving. He said the first part of the word (*as* in *asked*) and then solved the word quickly. This behavior indicates that Tony is able to use word components—the beginning part of the word.

▮ On page 5, Tony read *ponies* (which made sense) for *horses*, repeated the error, and then self-corrected, indicating that he was consistently making sure that his prediction "looked right."

▮ He appealed for help only twice during the reading of *Peaches the Pig*, on the same word, *gallop* on pages 6 and 7. The first time, Tony tried something: he made the sound of the first letter of the word and then asked. The second time, he probably was simply using the teacher as a resource on a word that was not at all familiar.

We would not make decisions about teaching Tony based on one or two particular errors. As we conduct our analysis of the running record, we are looking for broad patterns of behavior. We find that Tony can:

▮ Predict using meaning and language and can check with the visual information.

▮ Use his knowledge of many high-frequency words to read rapidly, with phrasing.

▮ Consistently monitor his reading to be sure that attempts fit with meaning and language as well as visual information.

▮ Use the first letter of the word he doesn't know to try a word that makes sense.

▮ Use the first part of the word (a letter cluster or consonant-vowel combination).

Based on these strengths, we might want to extend Tony's ability to use word parts in an analytic way so he can make stronger attempts at words like *gallop*, perhaps working out the first syllable or connecting it with another known word such as *gas* or *fall*. We also might want to check to be sure Tony simply understands the meaning of the word and have him look at some of the parts of the word later. Chances are, in the group reading of *Peaches the Pig*, there are other children who are consistently monitoring their reading, using first letters and some word parts in the initial position, who would profit from attending to different parts of the words in flexible ways.

Kassie   Now let's look at another reader, Kassie, who is reading *Ginger* (Fear 1995), a level I book on our list (Figure 17-2). *Ginger*, a story in which a cat seeks a new home, is quite a bit more difficult than *Peaches the Pig*, yet it is likely that we would find children reading at these two levels in the same classroom. In fact, Kassie and Tony are in the same first-grade classroom. The children in Kassie's group who are reading *Ginger* are encountering many more lines of text on each page.

In this book, there are many sentences that have two clauses joined by *and*, a more complex language structure. There are few repeating patterns, although there are several episodes to the story in which Ginger investigates a new house. There are many high-frequency words that are harder ones than the ones in *Peaches*, such as *saw, and, one, like, liked, then, all, this, for, in, out*. There are words in the text that children might not have seen before, such as *chased, place, nap, sunny*, and *either*. And, there are some more difficult words, such as *broccoli, building, sniffed, hungry, window*, and *perfect*, that will provide opportunities for word solving. Each of these words has some useful parts—either regular letter-sound association patterns or known endings such as *ing* or *y* that children will probably be able to use in the word-solving process.

RUNNING RECORD SHEET

Name: Kassie ___ Date: ___ D. of B.: ___ Age: ___ yrs ___ mths

School: ___ Recorder: ___

Text Titles	Running words / Error	Error rate	Accuracy	Self-correction rate
1. Easy Ginger (I)	232/10	1: 23	95 %	1: 2
2. Instructional		1:	%	1:
3. Hard		1:	%	1:

Directional movement ___

Analysis of Errors and Self-corrections
Information used or neglected [Meaning (M) Structure or Syntax (S) Visual (V)]

Easy / Instructional: Uses multiple sources of information to read. Her s.c. reflect flexible use of all sources of information.

Hard ___

Cross-checking on information (Note that this behaviour changes over time)

p.8 the|sc (M) and (S) +√ with (V) info results in s.c.
sniffed R|sc (S) and (V) info +√ with (M) results in s.c.
sniffed

Analysis of errors and Self-corrections (see *Observation Survey* pages 30-32)

Page	Ginger (I) 24 E / 232 RW	10 E	9 SC	Information used — E MSV	SC MSV
2	Uh|sc √ oh R|sc √ need|sc √√√√		3	M⊗V	msⓋ
	Oh no needed			M⊗V / M⊗V / MⓢV	m⊗V
	√√ around|sc √√ all		1	M⊗V	msⓋ
	√√√√ √ √√√ no painting				
4	√√ ⓐ the|sc building √√√ tall buildings		1	ⓜSV / MⓢV / MⓢV	msⓋ
	√√√√√ √√√√√		1		
	she liked the grass in front and		7		

Clay, M.M. (1993). *An Observation Survey of Early Literacy Achievement*. Heinemann: Portsmouth, NH

Kassie : Ginger

Analysis of errors and Self-corrections (see *Observation Survey* pages 30-32)

Page		E	SC	Information used — E MSV	SC MSV
6	√√√ / √√√√√ / √√√√				
	√√ around|sc √ all		1	M⊗V	msⓋ
	√√√√√√ / √√√√√ / √√√√√√				
8	√√√ −|⊗ √√ R the		1		msⓋ
	the|sc √√√ A		1	M⊗V	msⓋ
	√√√√ √ sniffed R|sc √√ sniffed		1	M⊗Ⓥ	mⓈV
	√√ b √ √√√ broccoli				
	√√√√ / √√√√√√				
10	√√√√√√				
	√√ − √√√√ √ wow		1		
	√√√ / √√√ / √√√√√√				

Clay, M.M. (1993). *An Observation Survey of Early Literacy Achievement*. Heinemann: Portsmouth, NH

Kassie : Ginger

Analysis of errors and Self-corrections (see *Observation Survey* pages 30-32)

Page		E	SC	Information used — E MSV	SC MSV
12	√√√√√√ / √√√√√√ / √√√√				
	√R √√ / √√√√ / √R √√				
14	√√√√ / √√√√ / √√√√√√				
15	√√ / √√√√√				
	√√ p-r|R √√ purr T		1	msⓋ	

snatches of phrased, expressive reading

Clay, M.M. (1993). *An Observation Survey of Early Literacy Achievement*. Heinemann: Portsmouth, NH

FIGURE 17-2 Running Record Sheet: Kassie's Reading of *Ginger*

Kassie read *Ginger* at 95 percent accuracy and her reading was fluent. Since the teacher was using assessment techniques to determine reading level, Kassie was given only a two-sentence introduction to this story. The teacher simply told her that the story was about a cat named Ginger who wanted to find a home. Kassie asked, "What was her name again?" Kassie knows that names are sometimes difficult and must be remembered while reading. Here are some of her errors on her first reading of the text:

❚ On page 2, Kassie did quite a bit of word solving. She began by saying *uh, oh,* but quickly self-corrected to *oh, no* as she noticed the words didn't look quite right. Approaching the word *needed,* she first said the base word *need* and then read *needed.* Kassie was either thinking about how the language didn't sound right, or was simply looking at the word in parts and then adding the inflectional ending.

❚ On page 4, the text says "Ginger saw tall buildings and short buildings." Kassie made two quick predictions for the word *all,* both of which would have made sense up to that point in the text, but instead of going on she slowed down to read *tall,* an indication that she was closely monitoring her reading using visual information. On that same page she read *building* for *buildings,* neglecting the *s,* but read both *building* and *buildings* accurately several more times on that page. If she had not left out the fourth line, her accuracy rate would have been much higher, and it's important to note that this error probably did not make any difference in her understanding of the text.

❚ Two more interesting errors appear on page 8. The text on lines 3 and 4 says, "Ginger looked all around and sniffed the air. She smelled broccoli. Ginger was hungry." Kassie read *snuffed* for *sniffed,* returned to the word before it, and self-corrected. Her attempt was very close to the

spelling pattern of *sniffed,* and might even sound like it made sense, but Kassie corrected her pronunciation. Our hypothesis is that she decoded the word, thought it wasn't quite right, and then conformed to the vowel pattern in the middle of the word. At the same time, she was probably thinking of a word she had heard in oral language and knew would make sense. On the next line, she said the *b* first for *broccoli* and then worked out the word in parts.

As a word solver in reading, Kassie can:

❚ Read many high-frequency words easily and quickly.

❚ Monitor her reading using her knowledge of letters, sounds, and words.

❚ Use single letters and word parts to figure out new words, even difficult words that she may not be familiar with.

❚ Solve words in flexible ways—with or without endings, in contracted form (*did* and *didn't*).

❚ Self-correct at the point of the error, indicating that she is able to hold meaning and language in her head while engaging in complicated word solving.

❚ Process words rapidly and fluently.

Mir Now let's look at Mir reading *Cam Jansen and the Mystery of the Stolen Diamonds* (Adler 1980), a level L book on our guided reading list (Figure 17-3). This Cam Jansen mystery requires the reader to process whole pages of small-print text in which the words are "wrapped around" (sentences stop and start in the middle of lines). There is a great deal of dialogue between the characters. The text has many difficult multisyllable words, such as *photographic memory, assignment, mental camera,* and *younger.*

The running record shown here covers only the first three pages of the book. Of the 228 words on which the record was taken, Mir read at 93 percent accuracy. This mys-

RUNNING RECORD SHEET

Name: Mir _____ Date: _____ D. of B.: _____ Age: ____ yrs ____ mths

School: _____ Recorder: _____

Text Titles	Running words / Error	Error rate	Accuracy	Self-correction rate
1. Easy _____		1: _____	____ %	1: _____
2. Instructional Cam... Stolen Diamonds ⓛ	228/23	1: 10	90 %	1: 7
3. Hard _____		1: _____	____ %	1: _____

Directional movement _____

Analysis of Errors and Self-corrections
Information used or neglected [Meaning (M) Structure or Syntax (S) Visual (V)]

Easy _____

Instructional *Errors generally sound right and look right and often make sense. A few uncorrected errors reflect an abandonment of meaning.*

Hard _____

Cross-checking on information (Note that this behaviour changes over time)

P.4 say/sc Ⓜ and Ⓢ +V with V info results in s.c.
in

		Analysis of errors and Self-corrections (see *Observation Survey* pages 30-32)			
				Information used	
Page	*Cam Jansen and the Mystery of the Stolen Diamonds* ⓛ	24 E 228 RW		E MSV	SC MSV
		23	4		
		E	SC		
3	✓✓✓✓✓✓				
	Clam ✓✓ his R/sc ✓✓ Stolen	2	1	ms⃝V	ms⃝V
	Cam ____ her ____ Shelton				
	✓✓✓ the beach ✓✓✓✓	2		m⃝s⃝V	
	____ a / bench			m⃝s⃝V	
	✓ shop mail ✓✓✓	2		m⃝s⃝V	
	shopping mall			m⃝s⃝V	
	✓✓✓✓✓				
	✓✓✓✓✓				
	✓✓✓				
	✓✓✓ ✓ Clam				
	✓✓✓✓✓ Cam				
	✓R ✓✓✓✓				

Clay, M.M. (1993). *An Observation Survey of Early Literacy Achievement.* Heinemann: Portsmouth, NH

Mir: Cam..... Stolen Diamonds

		Analysis of errors and Self-corrections (see *Observation Survey* pages 30-32)			
				Information used	
Page		E	SC	E MSV	SC MSV
4	✓✓✓✓✓✓✓				
	✓✓✓✓✓✓✓ finger in,				
	✓✓✓ then back out				
	✓R ✓✓✓✓				
	✓✓✓✓✓✓ Clam				
	✓✓✓✓✓✓ Cam				
	✓ of ✓✓✓✓	1		m⃝s⃝V	
	____ her				
	made/sc ✓R ✓		1	m⃝s⃝V	ms⃝V
	took				
	✓✓✓✓✓				
	✓ Clam had ✓ Then he asked	4		m⃝s⃝V	
	Cam hadn't				
	say/sc ✓✓✓		1	m⃝s⃝V	ms⃝V
	in				
	✓✓ Mother R ✓✓	1		m⃝s⃝V	
	Mother's				
	✓✓✓ and sure ✓	2		ms⃝V	
	____ she'll				
	✓				
	✓✓R ✓✓				
	✓✓✓✓ ✓✓ ✓				
	✓✓✓				
	✓ Clam/sc asked the ✓✓✓ potato	3	1	ms⃝V	ms⃝V
	Cam had what photo-			m⃝s⃝V	
	gearafic ✓✓✓✓✓			m⃝s⃝V	
	graphic			ms⃝V	

Clay, M.M. (1993). *An Observation Survey of Early Literacy Achievement.* Heinemann: Portsmouth, NH

Mir: Cam..... Stolen Diamonds

		Analysis of errors and Self-corrections (see *Observation Survey* pages 30-32)			
				Information used	
Page		E	SC	E MSV	SC MSV
5	___ ever ✓✓ but ✓✓✓✓	3		ms⃝V	
	of whatever ___				
	✓✓✓✓ didn't R ✓✓	1		m⃝s⃝V	
	did				
	✓✓✓✓✓✓				
	✓✓ the ✓ agreements ✓✓✓	2		m⃝s⃝V	
	assignment				

text was read rapidly
some punctuation was ignored
left some unmeaningful errors –
read right on

Clay, M.M. (1993). *An Observation Survey of Early Literacy Achievement.* Heinemann: Portsmouth, NH

FIGURE 17-3 Running Record Sheet: Mir's Reading of *Cam Jansen and the Mystery of the Stolen Diamonds*

tery is a novel with chapters. Possibly, the first part of the story was the most difficult for Mir, so we are seeing his work as he oriented himself to this longer text. He read fast, ignoring some punctuation. He also left a few meaningful errors after making an attempt at decoding. It is obvious that Mir reads most words quickly and automatically. Here are some of his errors:

■ On page 3, the text reads, "It was the first morning of spring vacation. Cam Jansen and her friend Eric Shelton were sitting on a bench in the middle of a busy shopping mall." Mir had some difficulty with the names of the characters. Names that are exotic or unfamiliar, which aren't possible to predict, give readers of all ages trouble with pronunciation. Mir read *clam* for *Cam* and did not correct this pronunciation until a later discussion with the teacher. He was probably relating the word to one he knows and neglecting to notice all of the details of the spelling pattern. He also substituted *Stolen* for *Shelton*, another name. Mir substituted *beach* for *bench* but self-corrected, indicating attention to the middle parts of the word. When he came to *shopping mall*, Mir said *shop mail*, and paused but went on. Our hunch is that he noticed the discrepancy but didn't quite understand what a shopping mall was, so he depended on his initial decoding without going farther.

■ Another place he had difficulty was with the words *photographic memory*, a concept that might be quite difficult to understand. He substituted *potato gearafic*.

■ Later in the text, for *assignment* he substituted *agreements*.

Mir was processing most of the text accurately, working out difficult words like *remember*, *younger*, *practicing*, and *mental* to read them correctly. Where he did not understand the word, Mir tried to simultaneously decode it by using the letter-sound associations and word parts, and he tried to connect it to a word he had heard before.

On his substitution *gearafic*, he was obviously trying to work out the word left to right. As a word solver in reading, Mir can:

■ Quickly and automatically read most words encountered in longer, complex chapter books.

■ Process a difficult text quickly, slowing down to problem solve when needed.

■ Use left-to-right word analysis either letter by letter or in chunks.

■ Use known words or word parts to figure out many unfamiliar words.

Assisting Mir to read books like the Cam Jansen series would involve helping him simultaneously think about the meanings of unfamiliar words while looking in more detail at their parts. A great deal of attention would center on understanding the story, so word solving can be supported. It might help, for example, to remind Mir to connect *photographic* with *photo*, and to engage in a discussion of the concept of *photographic memory* while looking at the word. Mir needs time to read and process texts and to talk about their meaning with others. This will enable him to consistently seek to ensure that the text makes sense without having to rely solely on his decoding abilities, which are considerable.

Even this brief examination shows us that readers are diverse not only in the *level* of text they can read or the *words* they can read, but also in the ways they process the whole text. All three readers were well underway in building a reading process. All three would read a bit differently on texts that were much easier or much harder. All three need instruction and practice.

Miscue Analysis and Informal Reading Inventories

With more proficient readers such as Mir, miscue analysis and informal reading inventories will provide additional information. Figure 17-4 is an example of a completed miscue analysis, including the coding form

MISCUE ANALYSIS PROCEDURE I CODING FORM

© 1987 Richard C. Owen Publishers, Inc.

READER Mir DATE 9/15/97

TEACHER ___ AGE/GRADE 6·6 SCHOOL ___

SELECTION Cam Jansen and the Mystery of the Stolen Diamonds (Chapter One)

LINE No./MISCUE No.	READER	TEXT	1 SYNTACTIC ACCEPTABILITY	2 SEMANTIC ACCEPTABILITY	3 MEANING CHANGE	4 CORRECTION	MEANING CONSTRUCTION (See 2,3,4) No Loss	Partial Loss	Loss	GRAMMATICAL RELATIONSHIPS (See 1,2,4) Strength	Partial Strength	Overcorrection	Weakness	5 GRAPHIC SIMILARITY H	S	N	6 SOUND SIMILARITY H	S	N
2/1	clam	Cam	Y	Y	N	N	✓			✓				✓			✓		
2/2	his	her	Y	Y	N	N	✓			✓				✓				✓	
2/3	stolen	shelton	Y	Y	N	N	✓			✓				✓			✓		
3/4	the	a	Y	Y	N	N	✓			✓					✓			✓	
3/5	beach	bench	P	P	Y	N		✓		✓				✓			✓		
4/6	shop	shopping	P	P	Y	N		✓				✓	✓				✓		
4/7	mall	mall	N	Y	N	N	✓					✓							
18/8	she	her	P	Y	N	N	✓			✓				✓			✓		
21/9	of	took	Y	Y	N	N	✓			✓									✓
22/10	mode	had	Y	Y	N	N	✓			✓				✓					✓
24/11	had	hadn't	Y	Y	N	N	✓			✓				✓			✓		
24/12	___	then	Y	Y	N	N	✓			✓									
24/13	___	he	Y	Y	N	N	✓			✓									
24/14	___	asked	Y	Y	N	N	✓			✓									
25/15	say	in	N	N	Y	N		✓				✓		✓					✓
27/16	mother	mother's	P	P	Y	N		✓				✓	✓				✓		
28/17	sure	and	P	P	Y	N		✓				✓	✓				✓		
33/18	clam	cam	Y	Y	N	N	✓			✓				✓			✓		
33/19	asked	had	P	P	Y	N		✓		✓				✓			✓		
33/20	the	what	P	P	Y	N		✓				✓		✓			✓		
33/21	potato	photo	N	N	Y	N		✓				✓	✓				✓		
34/22	gearafic	graphic	N	N	Y	N		✓				✓	✓				✓		
35/23	___	of	P	Y	N	N	✓			✓				✓			✓		
35/24	ever	whatever	N	N	Y	N		✓				✓	✓				✓		
35/25	but	___	N	N	N	N	✓			✓				✓					

a. TOTAL MISCUES 25

b. TOTAL WORDS 204

a ÷ b × 100 = MPHW 12

	No Loss	Partial	Loss	Str	Par	Over	Weak	H	S	N	H	S	N
COLUMN TOTAL	10	12	3	12	0	3	10	12	1	7	13	1	6
PATTERN TOTAL		25			25				20			20	
PERCENTAGE	40	48	12	48	0	12	40	60	5	35	65	5	30

(Goodman, Watson, Burke)

MISCUE ANALYSIS PROCEDURE I READER PROFILE

© 1987 Richard C. Owen Publishers, Inc.

READER Mir DATE 9/15/97

TEACHER ___ AGE/GRADE 6·6 SCHOOL ___

SELECTION Cam Jansen and the Mystery of the Stolen Diamonds (Chapter One)

	%	%
MEANING CONSTRUCTION		
No Loss	40	88
Partial Loss	48	
Loss	12	
GRAMMATICAL RELATIONS		
Strength	48	60
Partial Strength	0	
Overcorrection	12	
Weakness		
GRAPHIC/SOUND RELATIONS		
Graphic		
High	60	65
Some	5	
None	35	
Sound		
High	65	70
Some	5	
None	30	
RETELLING No retelling available		
Characters		
Events		
Total		
Holistic Score		

MPHW 12 TIME ___

REPEATED MISCUES ACROSS TEXT

LINE	READER	TEXT	COMMENTS (place in text, correction, etc.)
2	Clam	Cam	
6	Clam	cam	
18	Clam	Cam	
24	Clam	Cam	
33	Clam	Cam	self-corrected — on line 40 read it correctly (only other instance in the story)

COMMENTS

Self corrected 4 out of 25 miscues. Reliance on graphic and sound higher than on grammatical relationships. Meaning construction is only 40% no loss, but if taken together with partial loss becomes 88%. Needs increased reliance on grammatical relations and meaning construction.

(Goodman, Watson, Burke)

FIGURE 17-4 Mir's Miscue Analysis of *Cam Jansen and the Mystery of the Stolen Diamonds*

and reader profile. In these assessments the text is usually provided as a printed page and the teacher marks the child's miscues. It is followed by a retelling. The observer watches for various kinds of discrepancies between what the student reads and the words in the text. Miscues can then be analyzed in a way similar to the analysis presented for running records. For guidelines on miscue analysis, we refer you to Goodman, Watson, and Burke's (1987) Reading Miscue Inventory.

Moving from Systematic Observation to Systematic Instruction

Guided reading provides an ideal setting for systematic instruction in word solving while reading for meaning. In systematic instruction, we plan in *general terms*; the specifics of our teaching depend on the precise responses of the children at hand. Here are some examples of how teachers can plan in general but also take advantage of the moment's opportunity.

▮ Use the information from observation to think about introducing stories to children in guided reading. Whether you are using running records or miscue analysis, no lesson or interaction should be based on a single miscue but on the *kind of behaviors seen again and again*. The idea is to find out what a child's strengths are in word solving while reading and take that child further in learning. Examine the text. What words will the children need to hear so they can bring the knowledge to the processing of the print? What words might be good examples for the principles the class has been working on in word study? What words might be likely to give students opportunities to solve?

▮ Have in mind the kind of teaching during reading that will be important. Watch for opportunities to assist children at the word solving demanded by the text.

▮ Value partially correct responses. These responses give us important information to inform our teaching of word-solving strategies. One benefit of the *just right* text is that the child will be able to read for meaning and have only a few problems to solve while reading. If readers read only texts in which they know every word, they are not learning to use word-solving strategies.

▮ Using general knowledge of the children's reading behavior and specific observation of their reading on that day, explore principles more explicitly in one or two brief teaching points after they finish reading.

▮ Take one to two minutes, if appropriate, to work with letters using manipulatives such as magnetic letters following the reading of the text. For emergent readers, a minute or two of sorting letters is very helpful in teaching them how to look at and find letters embedded in print.

▮ If appropriate, following the text reading take one to two minutes with emergent readers to build some high-frequency words with magnetic letters.

▮ With early and transitional readers, following a text reading take two to three minutes for some quick work with magnetic letters or words written on an easel. Use prompts such as those provided in Chapter 16 for making connections to help your students develop ease and flexibility in working with word parts. Alternatively, as an oral or written activity quickly ask the children to find three or four words in the text that fit a particular category (e.g., a word that rhymes with *boy*, a compound word, a word with a prefix, a word that means *said*).

▮ Keep connecting word solving in guided reading to the word study curriculum. Use observation from guided reading to inform the minilessons in word study or to place examples on the word wall. Help children select examples of particular kinds of words that are important for them to know.

Isaac

Toni, working with her student, Isaac, provides us with a fine example of systematic observation that results in systematic teaching. Prior to the guided reading lesson, Toni had taken a running record of Isaac's reading. She had noticed that he was consistently using meaning in combination with attention to word parts. Isaac was reading *Rosie's Pool* (Riley 1995). His reading is shown in Figure 17-5.

In her interactions with Isaac, Toni was not simply using one or two partially correct responses. She wanted to encourage Isaac to continue using several different kinds of information to check on his reading and to solve words. Isaac's first analysis, resulting in *visit* (long *i* sound), was an excellent attempt. He attended to every part of the word. It was also significant that he stopped, indicating he knew that something wasn't quite right. Isaac had made a sound analysis but still wasn't satisfied. He was saying what was, to him, essentially a nonsense word, and it didn't make sense. Toni praised his partially correct response and encouraged him to search further. His second attempt, *invite*, was an interesting error. Toni could see that Isaac was thinking about the meaning of the whole story (in which some giants drop in on Rosie uninvited) and probably was also taking into account visual features such as letters in the words (the *v* and *i* are prominent in both *invited* and *visit*). The teacher wanted Isaac to think what the word could be in the story and still fit with the way he had noticed that it looks. Isaac reread the sentence up to the point of the original error, and then said, "Oh, *visit!*" He was able to make letter-sound analysis, meaning, and language structure come together. Even then, Toni did not simply say, "That's right" or "Good job!" She turned it back to the reader to check again with the meaning: "Try that and see if it would make sense and look right." Isaac was learning more than to sound out the word *visit*; he was learning how to solve words within a reading process.

This brief interaction took place while four children around Toni's table were also reading *Rosie's Pool* for themselves. During their reading, she had time for one or two brief but powerful interactions with each child. These interactions were not preplanned specifically, but they were systematic in that Toni was watching for opportunities to engage students in learning conversations around partially correct responses. The teaching moves were brief and unobtrusive. She

---

Isaac's Reading of *Rosie's Pool*

Text:	She looked up and saw three giants.
	They had come to visit her. (Page 2).
Isaac:	(Reading) She looked up and saw three giants. They had come to (pause) *visit*
	(pronounced with long *i* sound in first syllable). (He pauses and looks at teacher in appeal.)
Toni:	You're almost right. Try again and think what would make sense.
Isaac:	They had come to *invite* (pause).
Toni:	Can you think of something that looks like that and makes sense?
Isaac:	(Reading softly) They had come to . . . *Oh, visit!*
Toni:	Does that make sense and look right?
Isaac:	(Reading) The giants came to visit Rosie. (Comment) Yes.
Toni:	You really worked hard on that.

FIGURE 17-5   Isaac's Reading of *Rosie's Pool*

wanted each reader to keep going, processing the whole text. The assisted problem solving was based on each reader's strengths and needs.

We stress that the word-solving curriculum is not *carried* by these brief, powerful interactions. Remember that there are many other components—specific minilessons in word study followed by application and sharing, study of words in writing workshop and interactive writing, attention to words in introductions to stories, and teaching points following the guided reading lessons. We value, however, the power of supporting students while they read. In a sense, we are "coaching" these young students to put into action everything they have learned about words and how they work. In this way, they can see the value of using their knowledge as they read and enjoy text.

Suggestions for Professional Development

1. With colleagues, collect three books at each of the text levels that are most often used for guided reading with your children (see Fountas and Pinnell [1996] for more information on levels of text in a gradient).

2. Examine the books at each level, thinking about the demands for word solving.

3. Make lists of the kinds of words used in each text in several different categories. For example:
❚ Common high-frequency words.
❚ Words with regular spelling patterns (*cat, hat, sat; boy, toy*).

❚ Words with irregular spelling patterns (*eight, soap*).
❚ Words with affixes.
❚ Multisyllable words.
❚ Words that are spelled a particular way because of what they mean (*two, to; sail, sale*).
❚ Specialized vocabulary that children will use for a particular book but not analyze by sound or remember as a sight word.

4. Compare the books across the levels.
❚ How do the demands for word solving change?
❚ Remember that many of the words in books are accessible through broad support provided by the text and illustrations. At some levels children will not be expected to attend to all of the spelling patterns of words like *elephant* or *battery*. Discuss these words with colleagues.

5. Take some running records of children reading the books you have analyzed. In another meeting, compare your running records to the lists of words you have prepared, discussing the following:
❚ What word-solving behaviors do you notice?
❚ What were the relationships between the words in the text and the children's reading behavior?
❚ What aspects of words were children attending to successfully?
❚ What aspects of words were more challenging?
❚ What kinds of words were more challenging at each level?
❚ What did the children need to learn about how letters or words work?

Guided Reading
Powerful Teaching for Word Solving

There are two important aspects to becoming a competent word solver:

1. Knowing about words—the letters, the letter-sound relationships, the patterns, and the structures.

2. Being able to use one's knowledge while reading words that are embedded in phrases, sentences, paragraphs, and whole texts of different kinds.

Word study, as described in Section 3 of this volume, provides many active, interesting ways for children to develop knowledge of words. But guided reading makes the whole process come alive with purpose. There is a dynamic and ongoing relationship between the word study curriculum and the guided reading lessons that are taught every day.

In guided reading, instructional support helps children use what they know. We are not teaching for word solving using visual information alone. We recognize that readers are working on words embedded within continuous text. Word solving involves the orchestration of complex strategies that access many different kinds of information. It is not simply a process of looking at individual words, in a string,

and solving one at a time. The words are part of language systems involving meaning, world experience, grammar, or syntax, as well as visual patterns and their relation to sound and meaning. Our task as teachers is to help readers coordinate the understandings and behaviors while reading continuous text. In this chapter, we explore the teaching of word-solving skills within the guided reading lesson.

The Structure of Guided Reading Lessons

In general, lessons are organized into essential elements that may include introducing a new text and then having children read the text with support. After the reading, the teacher will make two or three important teaching points based on an ongoing observation of the readers' strengths and instructional needs. That same structure, in general, is used for all guided reading lessons, although as children begin reading silently and are engaging with longer texts, the structure may be modified.

There are opportunities to teach word solving in every part of the guided reading lesson structure:

❚ Before the children read the text, teachers provide an introduction that may include attention to words and word parts.

❚ While children are reading, teachers notice important behaviors to reinforce or prompt for word-solving action.

❚ After the children finish reading, teachers revisit part of the text to look at problem-solving examples, with the goal of helping children develop generative strategies that they can use again and again. Teachers may also provide opportunities through extensions for children to revisit the print or build a deeper understanding of word patterns.

The "before, during, and after" structure gives us a way to think about children's word solving throughout the lesson. Figure 18-1 gives an overall picture of this process.

Before the Reading

Before the children read the text, teachers must select it, plan for the introduction, and engage the children in conversation while introducing the story. Word solving is one element to consider while making these decisions.

Selecting Texts

The use of visual information and the nature of word-solving skills changes over time as readers learn more about how words work. The text a child reads acts as a medium for developing the kind of processing that will be required. To support children's word solving from the very early stages and to bring the children to a high level of competence with complex texts, teachers will need a book collection organized into a gradient of difficulty that moves from the easiest books to long, complex texts of a wide variety. The levels we refer to in this book are described in *Guided Reading* (Fountas and Pinnell 1996).

The easiest texts (levels A and B) have natural language arranged in predictable patterns, very few lines of print, and some easy high-frequency words (such as *the, a, I, is, an*). The pictures give a clear clue to the text so beginning readers, having learned from the teacher what the text is all about and maybe even having heard the language, can "read" it. They may actually be seeing "black blobs" and "white spaces" as they point and read. In this case, the emergent reader is not strictly decoding every letter of every word but is practicing important reading behaviors and, in the process, learning to notice a great deal more about print. High-frequency words and letter-sound relationships are learned through the reading and through the focused teaching that is provided.

There are many ways to analyze the characteristics of texts for guided reading (see Fountas and Pinnell 1996), but if we just think about words, we find that books increase in difficulty:

❚ From fewer lines of text, large print, and very clear spaces, to more lines with smaller print and smaller spaces (broken up by pictures), to whole pages of small print arranged in paragraphs.

❚ From a few easy, high-frequency words, to a more difficult and wider range of high-frequency words, to complex sentences with all categories of words in the language.

❚ From many phonetically regular words to irregular words with more difficult spelling patterns.

❚ From words with fewer syllables to texts with many more multisyllable words.

❚ From simple, everyday concepts to more specialized words, often used figuratively, with many meaning connotations, or connected to a kind of technology that requires specialized knowledge.

The kinds of texts that children are reading in third and fourth grades, for example, require different kinds of processing in word solving than those we give children

More advanced.

Teaching for Word Solving Within Guided Reading

	Before the reading	During the reading	After the reading
Teacher	• Selects book, considering words children know or can get to with strategies they control as well as format of text. • Introduces book—may have children find one or two familiar and new words. • Uses some of the new words in conversation so children can hear them. • Builds concepts for words that might be unfamiliar.	• Listens in to determine how readers are processing print. • Observes the readers' use of word-solving strategies. • Reinforces and comments on word solving—both successful and good tries. • Interacts with children to assist in word solving. • Prompts for word solving. • Tells the word when needed to help the reader move on through the text (when appropriate). • Makes observational notes to provide documentation.	• Returns to the text for one or two teaching opportunities such as problem solving on words. • Reinforces effective problem solving on the part of individual readers or the group. • Attends to specific words within the text. • May take words out of the text—using white board, easel and paper, or magnetic letters—for teaching demonstrations related to word analysis, moving back to the text at the end. • Discusses difficult vocabulary. • Engages readers in a few minutes of letter or word analysis work.
Students	• Notice particular words and find them. • Notice features of words that will help them when they encounter them while reading. • Think about the meaning of words in the text. • Say words as guided by the teacher. • Use words in conversation.	• Read the whole text or a unified part of the text. • Recognize most words without conscious attention. • Slow down to problem-solve new words when needed. • Apply strategies in flexible ways to solve words as needed. • Use print information in combination with meaning and language knowledge.	• Revisit the text at points of problem solving as guided by the teacher. • May become involved in some extended written work or work on word analysis or word solving.

FIGURE 18-1   Teaching for Word Solving Within Guided Reading

when they are just beginning to learn to read. The words are further away from the children's own experiences, so the text demands that the reader use visual information to gain access to the words. When encountering difficult and unfamiliar words, the reader will be called on to use a range of word-solving skills and also to search contextual information for the meaning. Good reading is based on the reader's understanding of the text and the reader's possession of a large reading vocabulary, which means far more than decoding the word. Readers must know what a word means or be able to figure out the meaning of a new word by connecting it to other known words.

Some early reading programs use what are called "decodable texts," texts that are written around and feature many regular letter-sound patterns. The purpose for using decodable texts is to require children to use phonetic elements of words to decode the text. By building the child's repertoire of knowledge of sound patterns over time, the goal is to enable the reader to eventually decode words using all possible letter-sound associations. For example, a "decodable" text might say something like this:

Pat had a hat.
Pat sat on her hat.
Pat's hat is flat.
Pat has a flat hat.

In this case, the children who are asked to read the text would have had explicit lessons on the *at*, *as*, and *ad* phonograms or "word families" (Chapter 9). These lessons would have followed a period of time learning the consonants, consonant clusters, and a few words such as *is*. When decodable texts are presented in a sequence, the first texts a child encounters are very simple and have only a few letter-sound combinations to decode. Usually the series of books builds so that children are using many different structures in the more complex texts that come later. The books are very carefully structured and are not considered "decodable" unless every structure in the book has been explicitly taught through a direct lesson. In the example given here, the writer would be thinking about whether the children had been taught the word *has* in an explicit lesson. If not, the the last line would have to read "Pat had a flat hat."

Obviously, decodable texts have limitations in terms of language, story, and interest. They may not enable all readers to use their knowledge of language and of the world as they learn about how to use the print information. A steady diet of such books, with few other literacy experiences, could convince the reader that reading doesn't make sense and decoding is the only way to "read," especially if these are the *first* books that children are asked to read for themselves. We have learned that when children have a very rich experience in interactive writing and shared reading, a large number of high-frequency words are built up. Children also learn *how to* attend to let-

ter-sound relationships and to common patterns in words. They learn how to use the parts to solve new words. For example, a child who has had many examples and understands the principle might be able to make quite a few connections (*had* is like *sad* and *hat*). Children are able to learn a great deal as they engage with pages of print. Sometimes, it is our job simply to "tidy up" knowledge by drawing children's attention to powerful elements of words, like phonograms, and other times make an explicit teaching point during a guided reading lesson. EXPLAIN↑

You might want to choose different books at different times for different purposes. Reading a variety of books that offer many different challenges will make readers more flexible. This means you might want to include some decodable texts in your guided reading collection. Here is a general sequence that we have found useful in selecting texts for emergent readers and early readers:

1. Begin with a shared reading of simple, natural language texts with specific attention to words.

2. Encourage children to "read" for themselves the small versions of books or poems they have encountered in shared reading.

3. Introduce simple caption books with a large font, clear space, many high-frequency words, and clear picture clues for children to read for themselves in their first guided reading lessons.

4. As children pay more attention to words, highlight teaching points that help them build a core of high-frequency words, notice the features of words, and connect words to each other.

5. Think about the words that children know and the ones they can figure out using their present word-solving skills. Then work to extend those skills gradually. Following

this principle—and as children read increasingly difficult texts—will ensure that texts contain good examples for directing children's attention to specific word elements such as phonograms, endings, prefixes, and other word parts that will help in solving words.

6. After children understand the processes involved in monitoring their reading and searching for information to solve words, you may decide to mix in some books that have many regular phonetic elements to challenge the reader and draw attention to words in different ways.

7. Continue to select books that have many high-frequency words, from easy to more difficult, and more lines of print so that children are reading more text that they can process easily. Sometimes books can be difficult but have only one or two lines of print, giving children a challenge but not much practice.

8. Continue to select books that have interesting content and build children's understanding of new words.

9. Move to the selection of a wide range of books of different genres at more difficult levels based on a complex combination of characteristics.

In summary, you will want to use many different kinds of books in your teaching of guided reading with the goal of efficient, flexible word solving. The effective teacher is always observing significant behaviors that indicate word solving is taking place within reading, and adjusting the book collection accordingly so that children will develop a good repertoire of strategies.

Introducing Texts

When you introduce a book, you provide a framework of meaning, language, and visual information that helps your students suc-cessfully process a new text. The book introduction usually includes some attention to the visual information in words. For beginning readers, this attention might be as simple as locating familiar or unfamiliar words; for more advanced readers, you might guide children in an exploration of how to analyze complex, multisyllable words for the parts and the meaning. The goal of attention to words during the introduction is *not* to preteach the words that the students will meet in the text. It is an opportunity to teach children something about the way words work as well as how to use word-solving strategies within reading. Here are three examples that illustrate teaching for word-solving during book introductions.

In our first example, Sue is introducing a very easy book, *Mom* (level A), to a group of emergent readers in one of their first guided reading lessons. She helps them understand that the character Mom is doing something interesting on every page. One goal is to help them match word by word while reading; another is to help them use visual information to check on their reading (Figure 18-2).

In this introduction, Sue shows this group of young readers how to use information in the pictures for meaning, but also how to check the word and discern how it looks. At this point they are using the salient feature, the first letter of the word. Our instructional goal is not for the children to learn the word *painting*, for example, but to learn the strategy of using the letter and related sound of the first part of the word to check on their reading.

In the sample introduction in Figure 18-3, Ron is introducing *I Can* to a group of emergent readers.[1] *I Can* is a level B book with a patterned text. In the book, a little sister tries to do everything a big sister does. In addition to linking this story to children's own experiences and supporting the meaning and

---

[1]The text of the complete book introduction is presented in Fountas and Pinnell (1996), p. 139.

Attention to Words During the Introduction of *Mom*

Teacher:	(*As children are looking at pictures in the book*) Let's see...Barry, what is Mom doing in this one? (*shows a page*) Take a close look.
Barry:	(*reading*) Mom is . . . fixing.
Teacher:	It could be fixing. It looks to me like she has a brush . . .
Ruth:	Painting.
Teacher:	. . . and a can here. So she might be . . . painting. Now, you know what? Barry has a way to figure out whether this word says *fixing*, because he thought it looked like she was fixing, or painting. He can think about how the word *fixing* would begin. *Fixing* . . .
Ruth:	F.
Teacher:	With an *f*, Ruth, and *painting* with a . . .
Children:	P
Teacher:	Let's look at the way it starts, so do you think, Barry, now it's going to say *fixing* or *painting*?
Barry:	*Painting.*
Teacher:	Good, that'll help you to do some good reading work, won't it?

FIGURE 18-2   Attention to Words During the Introduction of *Mom*

Attention to Words During the Introduction of *I Can*

Children:	*Point and read together the words, "I can swim, too"* (*Reflecting that the little sister wants to do what the big sister does.*)
Teacher:	Put your finger under the word *can*. Yes, that's *can*. Find *can* on this page.
Children:	*Locate* can *quickly*.
Later:	
Teacher:	They can both ride their bikes, can't they? Look, little sister's riding. Now, they're saying "Here we go!" *Here* starts with an uppercase *h*. Put your finger under *here* and say "here."
Children:	*Locate* here.
Teacher:	Here we go!

FIGURE 18-3   Attention to Words During the Introduction of *I Can*

---

language through conversation, Ron selects two important words, *can* and *here*, on which to focus the children's attention.

Amy is introducing her group of first graders to *The Three Billy Goats Gruff* (a level I book).[2] Because they are familiar with several versions of this story through hearing it read aloud, the introduction is brief. There is no need for Amy to concentrate on repeating the patterns of language in the book, but she does engage the children in a con-versation about what they know about those billy goats (Figure 18-4).

Amy has based her preparation of the introduction on the children's reading behavior and knowledge base. These children are able to hold the story in their heads while working on words; they also know many high-frequency words. Amy does not discuss every page of the story but focuses on the plot, the ideas, and the interesting language. She wants to demonstrate to children that

---

[2]The text of the complete book introduction is presented in Fountas and Pinnell (1996), p. 143.

Attention to Words During the Introduction of *The Three Billy Goats Gruff*

Teacher:	Do you think it was a good idea for the Billy Goats Gruff to cross the bridge? What would you expect to see at the beginning of the word *idea?*
Several children:	*I.*
Sara:	There's *idea.*
Teacher:	That's right. You're all pointing under *idea.* (*Says the word* idea *slowly as she writes it on a white board*). You can hear all of the sounds in that word, can't you?
Children:	(*Slowly*) Idea.
Teacher:	It was a good idea, wasn't it? They look like they're having a good time eating grass.

FIGURE 18-4   Attention to Words During the Introduction of *The Three Billy Goats Gruff*

they can take apart a word that is unfamiliar. She selects the word *idea* because it has regular letter-sound relationships, is easy to take apart, and also is a word that students are unlikely to have encountered before. She says the word, letting children hear her pronunciation, and then explicitly models, through writing, looking at all parts of the word.

In the next example, Claire introduces *Keep the Lights Burning, Abbie,* a level K chapter book, to a group of second graders (Figure 18-5).[3] This book is historical fiction, and Claire makes sure that her students understand the nature of this text and the island setting. They need to understand why it is important for the little girl Abbie to keep the lights burning. There are also some long and difficult words in the story that are completely unfamiliar to the students. An example is *Matinicus Island.* We have observed that students often balk at dealing with complicated names. Claire helps them sort it out by looking at the parts. Here, the idea is not for the children to learn the specific word but to know that it's possible to approach even a long and difficult word like this one.

The last example involves calling attention to word meanings. In *Amelia Bedelia and the Baby,* a Level K chapter book, word mean-

ings are very important.[4] In fact, Amelia consistently misinterprets words, which creates some very funny situations and provides an excellent setting for talking about alternative meanings. If students do not understand that the book is all about word meanings, they will miss the humor. In Claire's introduction, she reminds the children of a previously read Amelia Bedelia book and builds on the understanding they developed there (Figure 18-6).

All of these teaching techniques draw children's attention to the way words sound, look, and mean. Learning to use visual information also means attending to how the particular letter sequence communicates a particular meaning in text. For example, the meaning of a word in *Amelia Bedelia* is determined by the context in which the word is placed. When readers know a word very well, they can use it in many different contexts, interpreting the alternative meanings and even shades of meaning within those alternatives. Readers can increase their vocabulary through reading.

During the Reading

Children in guided reading lessons read the whole text or a unified part of the text. They read softly to themselves rather than in uni-

---

[3]The text of the complete book introduction is presented in Fountas and Pinnell (1996), p. 145.
[4]The text of the complete book introduction is presented in Fountas and Pinnell (1996), p. 147.

Attention to Words During the Introduction of *Keep the Lights Burning, Abbie*

Teacher: See if you can find *Matinicus* on this page. What do you notice about it?
Sheila: It has a capital letter. It's like a name.
Teacher: Uh, huh. Anything else?
Becky: It's really a long word.
Tiffany: It has "mat" and "in."
Sheila: And "us" too at the end! Cool! It's all parts.
Teacher: Those parts can help you if you have trouble with the name.

FIGURE 18-5   Attention to Words During the Introduction of *Keep the Lights Burning, Abbie*

Attention to Words During the Introduction of *Amelia Bedelia and the Baby*

Teacher: Do you remember the other Amelia Bedelia story we read in school?
Alice: The baseball one. It was *Amelia Bedelia Plays Ball*.
Teacher: Yes, it was about baseball: *Play Ball Amelia Bedelia*. What types of things did Amelia do in that story?
Sara: She did exactly whatever people told her to do, instead of what they meant for her to do. Like really stealing the base like a robber instead of just stealing the base like, uh, like in baseball.
Patrice: I loved when she tagged the boy with a tag instead of the ball!
Sara: And when they told her to run home, she ran all the way to her house.

FIGURE 18-6   Attention to Words During the Introduction of *Amelia Bedelia and the Baby*

---

son or in chorus, so each reader is processing the whole text. The readers know that their job is to keep going, reading as much as they can and solving any problems they have along the way. The teacher is there to assist if necessary, but a good text selection and a skillful story introduction make it possible for the children to read the text with only a few words to solve. A good rule of thumb is that each reader will be working at somewhere between 85 percent and 95 percent accuracy on the first reading of the new text. Later, with reading partners or independently, children will probably read the text again. On subsequent readings, the reader will process the text with increased accuracy, having solved most of the problem words on the first pass.

Observing and Supporting Reading

For the teacher, watching the children as they read the text provides a critical source of information. You can observe children's behavior, scan the group, and "listen in" to several readers for a few moments at a time. If older readers are reading silently most of the time, you can ask them to read aloud for a few minutes to provide information.

The emphasis is on helping individuals read text; each child's approach will be unique. Create a context within which you can teach individuals. While the stories have been selected for and introduced to a group of several children who are reading at similar levels, the reading is quite individual. Each young reader uses individual knowledge to approach the text. Of course, some of what each reader knows rests on the effectiveness of your introduction, so, inevitably, members of the group share some common understandings. But, each reader has unique ways of processing any particular text.

It is important not to break the momentum of the reading but to allow each reader to process the whole text with as little interruption as possible. At times it may be necessary to assist children in a bit of problem solving or to reinforce some behavior that indicates children are taking on new strategies. Powerful teaching can take place in the brief interactions you have with individual children or two or three children during a guided reading lesson. Here are two examples.

In the first example, Ruth was reading a page of the highly predictable book *Mom* (Figure 18-7). After the introduction, the children began to read. On each page the text says *Mom is* [action word]. When Ruth came to the page that said "Mom is digging," she read the familiar words *Mom is*, paused,

and then said "gardening," stopping again. Sue placed great value on Ruth's stopping to look closely at the text; it was evident that this emergent reader was checking on herself. Sue recognized Ruth's attempt but unobtrusively pointed her to an important piece of information, the first letter of the word. Ruth immediately came up with *digging*. This interchange took only a few seconds, and Ruth continued to read.

In the next example, Camilla was reading *Keep the Lights Burning, Abbie* (Figure 18-8). She substituted *picked* for *pecked* but was not satisfied with the way the sentence sounded, indicating that "it didn't make sense." Camilla's attempt was, in fact, very

---

Teaching for Word Solving During the Reading of *Mom*

Ruth:	(*Reading*) Mom is (*pause*) gardening. (*Pause*) "What's that word?"
Teacher:	It's looks like *gardening*, but look at (*points to the first letter of* digging)
Ruth:	Digging!
Teacher:	Digging!

FIGURE 18-7   Teaching for Word Solving During the Reading of *Mom*

Teaching for Word Solving During the Reading of *Keep the Lights Burning, Abbie*

Text:	Patience pecked Abbie's shoes.
Camilla:	(*Reading*) Patience picked Abbie's shoes. (*Says, "that doesn't make sense."*) Patience picked . . . (*pause*).
Teacher:	You've almost got that. Check the middle.
Camilla:	Patience pecked Abbie's shoes.

FIGURE 18-8   Teaching for Word Solving During the Reading of *Keep the Lights Burning, Abbie*

Teaching for Word Solving During the Reading of *Cam Jansen and the Mystery of the Monster Movie*

Text:	The lobby was crowded and warm.
Makala:	The lob-by (*with the last syllable rhyming with* my). Is that right?
Teacher:	It ends like *happy*.
Makala:	. . . lobby (*pronounced correctly*) was crowded and warm.

FIGURE 18-9   Teaching for Word Solving During the Reading of *Cam Jansen and the Mystery of the Monster Movie*

hard!

close visually to the actual word. However, *picked* was probably a more familiar word to her than *pecked*, especially if she had very little experience with chickens. She needed to look more closely at all the letters in the word. Her teacher's suggestion to "check the middle" pointed her to the right information.

In the last example, Makala was reading a Cam Jansen mystery (Figure 18-9). She read the word *lobby* by saying the first part and then the last part, rhyming it with *my*. Our hypothesis is that Makala did not understand what a lobby is and had not heard (or had seldom heard) the word said aloud. She was reading in syllables and doing a word analysis based on her understanding of some underlying rules. The teacher helped her by connecting *lobby* to a word that Makala knew. By doing so, the teacher was building implicit understanding of the principle that words that end in *y* have an *e* sound at the end. She did not stop to drive this point home but instead let Makala get back to reading the text. The principle could be explored further after the reading, and the teacher could also support Makala's understanding of the word.

Prompting During the Reading of the Text

Through the brief interactions in which teachers prompt for the use of strategies, they are supporting children's reading with divided attention—helping them learn to pay attention to multiple features of the text. The somewhat "spare" and specific language observed in the previous examples illustrates how unobtrusive these encounters are. These teachers were not talking much, but what they said was powerful, using specific language to help the child take specific action. At the same time, teachers need to be sure that the prompting is effective.

It is sometimes assumed that if we have provided systematic, direct teaching of a rule or principle, children have learned it. As teachers we know that is simply not always the case. Just because we have taught our

students a specific strategy to figure out a new word, there is no guarantee that they will use the strategy or concept and be able to apply it in the reading or writing process.

Systematicity requires thorough observation, teaching, observing for the effects of teaching, and, perhaps, teaching again. Prompting during reading can be effective only if the child knows what the teacher means and has the information to solve the problem. A prompt is not so much a question as a call to action. Figure 18-10 contains a list of prompts, generally organized by the kind of behavior they call for from the reader. Teachers have found lists such as this helpful to use for supporting children's word solving in guided reading. The advantage of using prompts like this is that by fine-tuning their language, teachers can get more teaching power out of a brief interaction.

After the Reading

Brief Teaching Points Related to the Text

After the children read the book or selection, it is typical for a teacher to make one or two teaching points. This teaching may be related to any aspect of reading—comprehension, fluency, self-monitoring, or self-correcting. If appropriate, teachers may choose to reinforce effective strategies used or to teach for word-solving strategies on new words, demonstrating how words work, showing examples, and inviting children to revisit the text and apply the word analysis strategy. The teaching for word solving will be directly related to the kinds of processing difficulties the children showed in the reading of the text in the lesson.

Going Back to the Text

The goal of the brief teaching following text reading is to prime children's strategies for solving words while reading text. It is always more meaningful, after working for a few minutes with word parts, to return to the text so that children can apply their knowledge as they read the words in text.

put into action

Prompts to Help Children Solve Words During Reading

To help the student notice errors:
You noticed what was wrong.
Find the part that's not quite right.
Check to see if that looks right.
Where's the tricky part? (after an error)
Get a good look.
There's a tricky word on this line.
What did you notice? (after hesitation or stop)
What's wrong?
Why did you stop?
Do you think it looks like _____?
Think about how that word looks.
Something wasn't quite right.
Were you right?

To help the student solve words:
Try that again and say the first sound.
What could you try?
It starts like _____.
It ends like _____.
Look at the parts.
What do you know that might help?
Do you see a part that can help?
Do you know a word like that?
Do you know a word that starts with those letters?
Do you know a word that ends with those letters?
What's that like?
Think of what the word means. Is it like another word you know?
What other word do you know like that?
What letter do you expect to see at the beginning (or end)?
Do you see a part that can help?
Look for a part you know.
Say the first part, the next part.

To help the student notice errors and fix them:
That sounds right, but does it look right?
That makes sense, but does it look right?
I like the way you worked that out.
It starts like that. Now check the last part.
Where's the tricky part? (after an error)
You made a mistake, can you find it?
You're nearly right.
You almost got that. See if you can find what is wrong.
Try it.
You've got the first part (last part) right.
Try that again.
Try it another way.

FIGURE 18-10   Prompts to Help Children Solve Words During Reading

For example, Toni returned to a problem-solving event that occurred while her first-grade children were reading *Rosie's Pool* (Figure 18-11). Several children had difficulty with the word *sitting*. Two of them had read *sweating* instead of *sitting*. With some prompting from the teacher, they self-corrected the error. After the reading, Toni chose to go back to that part of the text. She used the white board to illustrate a way to think about a tricky word. Writing the word *sitting* on the board, Toni illustrated how it's possible to cover up part of the word, then another part, and then say them all together. Not only did the children understand the concept, but one of them made a link to another word, noticing another principle—that the middle letter is sometimes doubled when you add *ing*. Toni asked the children to find the word in the text themselves, and then explored this new idea by writing *running* on the white board.

Guided reading provides a context before, during, and after the reading of a text that provides many opportunities to teach how words work, and perhaps even more important, to support children as they engage in word solving while reading. The understandings built in the guided reading lesson may be enriched through extending the text.

Extending the Text

Occasionally, the teacher may want to engage the children in follow-up activities that help them use the print in different ways. Writing or working with the words brings children back into the print and helps them attend to features of print in different ways. For example, when Sue's students finished reading *Mom*, Sue gave them a small, stapled blank book in which they wrote about things their moms were doing. They wrote the words *mom* and *is* on every page and finished the sentence to show a familiar activity. The words they added were, in most cases, approximated spellings, but the children had to say each word slowly, thinking about the sound.

Other examples of extended activities after guided reading include:

Teaching for Word Solving After Reading *Rosie's Pool*

Text:	Rosie was at her pool, sitting in the sun.
Teacher:	I'm going to help you think about a tricky part in the story. *She writes the word* sitting *on a white board for all children to see.* When you come to a tricky word, you can look at parts to help you. *She covers the* ting. What do you see in the first part?
Camilla:	It.
Edward:	Sit.
Teacher:	Yes, you're looking at a part that can help you. The first part says *sit. Uncovers the* ting. Do you see an ending you know?
Children:	ing.
Teacher:	Now say those parts together.
Children:	Sitting.
Maria:	That's like *running.*
Teacher:	*Writes* running *under the word* sitting *on the white board.* Yes. *Sitting* has two *t*'s and *running* has two *n*'s in the middle. You can notice the parts in the words. Now turn to page one and find *sitting*. Put your finger over the ending and read the first part.
Children:	Sit.
Teacher:	Now take your finger away. Now read the whole word, and then the whole sentence.
Children:	Sitting. Rosie was at her pool, sitting in the sun.

FIGURE 18-11   Teaching for Word Solving After Reading *Rosie's Pool*

❚ Children who read the little book *Food to Eat* (Peters 1995) cut pictures out of magazines and on each page wrote a sentence saying *This is a . . .*

❚ Children who read *Rosie's Tea Party* and *Rosie's Pool* wrote in their journals about how the giants behaved the same in the two stories.

❚ In interactive writing, children created a three-sentence summary of *Peaches the Pig*. The children contributed the initial and final consonants, some high-frequency words, and the word *pig*.

❚ A group of children who read *Amelia Bedelia* made a list of all the words that Amelia confused.

Letter and/or Word Work

We also recommend additional time (about a minute or two) with magnetic letters or written word work following the guided reading lesson for children who are not quickly processing the print information in the text. This is very helpful for particular groups of children. The word work might include letter sorting (see Chapter 12) or making or writing words as described in Chapter 13. The aim is to build children's strength in looking at print and thinking flexibly about words.

We find that using colorful magnetic letters on a large surface is ideal for teaching points. For emergent readers, you might want to demonstrate concepts about print and letters, such as:

❚ A group of letters make a word (*cat*).
❚ Words can be made from one or more letters (*I, to, can*).
❚ A word is the same in reading and writing.
❚ A word with a capital letter is the same as its lowercase form (*He, he*).
❚ Sounds in words are related to the letters in them (*m-a-n*).
❚ The letters in words represent sounds.
❚ Words can be short or long.
❚ Letters in words are read left to right.

If teachers engage children in working with letters and word parts and/or in writing letters and word parts, the children will develop flexible ways to word solve in reading and writing. Two to three minutes of word work on an easel with letters, on chart paper, or on a white board helps readers think in new ways. The following principles for manipulating letters and word parts may help you demonstrate to children how words work over time. Show the readers how to:

❚ Add letters to the beginning of a word to make a new word (*h + and = hand*).

❚ Add letters to the end of a word to make a new word (*sea + t = seat*).

❚ Change the first letter of a word to make a new word (*car, far*).

❚ Change the last letter of a word to make a new word (*had, has*).

❚ Add endings to make new words (*book, books; read, reading*).

❚ Use a word they know to solve a new word (*my, by*).

❚ Change the beginning and ending letters of a word to make new words (*his, hit, sit*).

❚ Change the beginning or ending clusters to solve new words (*spring, thing; wish, with*).

❚ Change the middle letter or letters to solve new words (*cat, cut; chair, cheer*).

❚ Add letters or letter clusters to solve new words (*it, pit, pitch, pitcher*).

❚ Use parts of words they know to figure out words they don't know (*tree + play = tray; she + make = shake*).

In addition, show children that:

❚ Some words sound the same and look different (*sail, sale*).
❚ Some words look the same and sound different (*read, read; present, present*).

Guided Reading—A Powerful Context for Word Solving

In the last two chapters we have explored guided reading as a context in which children learn how to be word solvers within the act of reading. We discussed systematic observation as the foundation for making decisions that will support the children's process of becoming word solvers while reading. Whatever the word study program implemented in a classroom, it will be necessary for us as teachers to intentionally work with children to help them solve words while reading continuous text. Many or even most cannot transfer these essential skills alone. We have stressed the importance of ensuring that children encounter challenging words within continuous print and apply word knowledge to what we call word solving. That is the skill that counts in reading.

Suggestions for Professional Development

1. On audio- or videotape, record yourself teaching a guided reading lesson.
2. Look at the lesson before the reading.
   - ❚ What did you do to help children attend to word solving?
3. Consider the section during the reading.
   - ❚ List the prompts that you used to help children in word solving.
   - ❚ Compare these prompts to our list.
   - ❚ Were they the most effective prompts?
   - ❚ Is there other language that might have been more effective?
4. Consider the section after the reading.
   - ❚ Reflect on any teaching points you made that were designed to help children learn more about how words work. Did your teaching points help children obtain learning skills that they can use in other texts (as opposed to simply reading the book)?
   - ❚ Look at children's attempts at words. What do they understand about words? What do their partially correct responses tell you?

Thinking Comprehensively About Word Matters

Every day our teaching focuses on the children in our own classrooms. We observe their individual growth and plan lessons to take them further in their learning. If we are to achieve our vision of helping every child become literate, including acquiring competence in word solving, we must consider our larger goals. It is not enough for a child to experience one good year of classroom instruction. As colleagues, we must work together to ensure year after year of excellent educational experience. Achieving that goal means working together toward a shared vision.

The last two chapters of this book are designed to support teachers in conceptualizing a continuum of learning, assessing the progress of a cohort of children, and connecting to children's homes. A continuum of learning helps us establish what children have previously learned, what they know, and where they need to go. In Chapter 19, we describe establishing benchmarks for progress, beginning with a broad continuum of learning that will be useful to you and your colleagues in your work across grade levels. In Chapter 20, we call for establishing common ground in reading instruction so that we can begin to design comprehensive, balanced programs. We present five steps to support the development of a comprehensive approach to word study with the understanding that no one action is sufficient to ensure that all children become literate. We must design excellent approaches, analyze classroom environments and the use of time, and reach out to parents and caregivers. With a step-by-step process, a team effort, and persistence over time, our goals are achievable.

Establishing Benchmarks for Progress

Learning words and learning about words is a lifelong process. In this chapter, we examine word learning as it changes over time. First we will look at a continuum of learning; then we will present a more formal view of broad categories of word learning that will help us shape and organize instruction.

Learning About Words— A Continuous Process

We start learning about words as soon as we are born. Everyone talks to babies; in fact, infants exist within a world of talk in which the sounds of the language quickly take on meaning. They interact with smiles, gurgles, and their first utterances, which receive almost the same response from adults as if they were part of a conversation. Soon, they use one- and two-word phrases in interactions with others. Indeed, the acquisition of oral language is an amazing accomplishment for young children. Children all over the world acquire the words and structures of oral language, with all its complexities, within the first four to five years of life. They seem to do so naturally, without any instruction except for the examples and the interactive support of those around them.

What about the representation of words in written form? Those understandings, too, begin very early, especially for children who are encouraged to explore print. They notice print in the environment, on the wrappings and containers of their favorite foods, on the covers of books and videotapes that they enjoy. All of these symbols begin to have meaning; they can interpret them and use them functionally. Even a very young child who is only two or three years old may be interested in seeing someone write her name. This process is accelerated when adults interact with children around written symbols.

Many children, if they have access to writing instruments, become interested in making their marks in writing. They use "scribble" writing, but eventually the figures they produce look more and more like letters. They may try to copy adults' writing to produce family names or make "shopping lists." Talking with children about letters almost always means using the names of the letters; it's a practical way that we can talk with them about these graphic symbols. Children begin learning the names of the letters that are most important to them. Distinguishing the first letter of one's name means paying closer attention to the details that make that letter different from others.

As they start to connect written and oral language in personal ways, we notice that children's approximated writing shows some awareness of sound-letter correspondence (for example, the child who writes *mother* as *MR*). Meanwhile, if children are hearing stories read aloud and are in a position to notice print, they are internalizing many important concepts about the way words are arranged in space on the page. They may even start to notice letters that are embedded in the print of the favorite stories they have heard many times.

Children who have many experiences with print are learning that reading and writing are related and that words and sentences are made up of component parts that go together in consistent ways. In fact, just learning that a word is written the same way every single time is an important concept children develop as they encounter a word in many different contexts through both reading and writing. And, as mentioned often in this book, that word might be one's name, as well as a ubiquitous word like *the*.

As they come to school, many children bring a solid understanding of the function of print; they know some letters as well as how to look at letters, and they may even be able to write some words. Children are then in a position to rapidly expand their knowledge of words and how words work.

Other children, while they may have interacted with written language and enjoyed stories, have not considered print directly or tried much writing themselves. They depend on school for first immersion in stories, attention to print, and chances to produce writing. For all children, those first years of school are critical. Here, they move from an approximate idea of written language and what it means to be a flexible, competent user of the written word. By providing a rich kindergarten and first-grade experience, it is possible to bring all children to this point.

Expanding and refining knowledge of words takes place within a curriculum that ensures that children will know the function of written language through hearing and sharing in stories. Children's vocabulary, for example, is constantly growing through the experiences they have that broaden their worlds and through the many books they hear read aloud. Reading, writing, and word study support encounters with words in many different ways.

In the first experiences, these young students will acquire some easy, high-frequency words and notice patterns in letter sequences. As their word knowledge grows, they begin to detect patterns in letter sequences. They learn that simple correspondence between one or two letters and the sounds is not sufficient to spell all the words they need. They begin to attend to larger visual patterns and match them up with words and parts of words. They also attend to the structural and semantic aspects of language as they utilize the variety of ways to solve words. Over time, their attention shifts to the importance of conventional spelling as they develop effective proofreading and reference skills.

In this "global" picture of change over time, we have referred to children from their earliest attention to print, which for some is at age two or three, to ten- or eleven-year-olds in the intermediate grades. Word learning is a continuous process. Even as adults we are always adding words to our vocabularies or learning new shades of meaning for the words we have used in our lives. Our learning is personal and individual. No two people have the exact same knowledge of word patterns and word meanings. Our knowledge is shaped by our experiences with life and language and the attention we give to the role of words.

Developmental Learning

Children's reading and writing behaviors are a guide to understanding the course of development. Sometimes we may view development as a process to watch and support; accordingly, we may approach teaching cautiously, not wanting to hurry or interfere with children's natural learning. Caution is appropriate; we do not want children to struggle but to enjoy reading. Developmental learning means more than waiting for the children to notice and explore aspects of print when they are "ready." To us and the teachers with whom we work, development is a natural process that takes into account assistance and skilled teaching.

It is our job to support children in their learning, and that includes showing them what they need to know and supporting them as they try it for themselves. If children have not noticed critical information on their own, it is our responsibility to bring it to their attention. They are not "on their own" to discover. We are right there to help. We create a context to help them attend to the details of print and connect those visual features to the sounds and meanings of language. In our society, many children depend on school to:

■ Provide their first experiences with print.

■ Make the experience meaningful and enjoyable.

■ Help them attend to the vital information they need to make sense of the written system.

■ Communicate the complex understandings they must learn in order to achieve control of literacy.

Waiting for the child to discover and develop is not the theme of this book. As we look at the continuum of development, we are always saying:

■ What does this child know and nearly know?

■ What instruction and support will help this child change—to move from here to there?

A Continuum of Learning

As we observe children's behavior in our efforts to determine where they are in their learning, we need to have in mind a broad continuum of learning. Clear, concrete terms describing learning on this continuum will help in thinking where children need to go next. The broad picture we just presented is interesting, but it is not specific enough to help in making decisions about a group of children we are expected to teach. We need to have some definitive characteristics and behaviors to look for as we accompany and guide children on their journey to becoming word solvers, realizing that each child will travel a different path to our goals.

Support children where they are but work for change.

No continuum can precisely represent the complexity and variability of individual learning. In other words, no child in a classroom will fit exactly any description on the continuum. But, you can use this tool to help think in general about the group of children you teach and how their learning is changing over time. The continuum presented here is not specific to any grade level because we must work with children from the knowledge base they have. Each level on the continuum has implications for our decisions as teachers. Learning is continuous; the goal is to see where children are, notice their strengths, and then teach for change.

Our evidence of children's understanding, on which we have built the continuum, comes from observation of behavior and samples of student work. Characteristics of student behavior, indicating understanding, are always interfaced with characteristics of the instructional program. Students attend to what teachers attend to, and they can learn effectively in a range of classroom programs. The specifics of what they know are related to the particular curriculum in which they have participated. One of the advantages of a continuum like this one is that you can examine the evidence of student learning, compare it to the behaviors placed in the categories on the continuum, and discover gaps in instruction that may need to be addressed.

Reading and writing are related in word learning.

In each of the following charts we have described both reading and writing behaviors. A strong connection exists between these two different but complementary areas of learning. We have created parallel categories, but the processes are not precisely parallel. There are relationships. Writing contributes to early reading progress. When children write, they must construct the features of the letters in sequence, making the motions necessary to construct the features of the letters. The movement helps children focus on the features and makes them memorable. Writing "slows down" the process so that it is easier to attend to the details of print. When children read, they perceive the features of the letters and letter sequences that represent words and match them up with language. Both reading and writing involve the same symbol system. Although the processes are different, the features of the words are the same. Children attend to them in different but complementary ways.

In this continuum we will broadly describe readers and writers from emergent to advanced categories. For each broad category we will touch on instructional implications. The chapters in the book have provided a rich repertoire of instructional approaches for helping children become word solvers through word study, reading, and writing. This continuum provides a road map for planning instruction.

Emergent Word Solvers   The chart in Figure 19-1 lists understandings and behaviors that are typical of emergent word solvers. This category parallels both "emergent readers" and "emergent writers," as development includes many understandings about reading and writing. Emergent *readers* rely on language and meaning to read simple texts. They are just beginning to control early behaviors such as left-to-right directionality, how print is arranged on the page, and word-by-word matching. Emergent *writers* are dis-

covering that they can present their messages in printed symbols that others can read. They are also discovering a relationship between the sounds of the language and the symbols that represent it. Emergent *word solvers* are puzzling out what a word really is, how letters go together, and how letters are different from each other.

What are our instructional goals for emergent word solvers? We want them to understand the functions of written language in conveying stories and messages—to look at print so they can distinguish letter features and word boundaries, hear the sounds in words, and connect sounds to letters. Phonological awareness, discussed in some detail in Chapter 8, is a critical understanding. The earliest learning involves attending to units of sound such as whole words, syllables, rimes, dominant consonants, and easier vowels.

In shared reading you focus on helping children notice letters and their features, attend to easy high-frequency words, recognize and use word boundaries, distinguish between letters and words, and develop an understanding that one spoken word matches one printed word. Emergent readers will experience, for the first time, guided and independent reading. They will make a transition from the shared reading that involves group support to reading very simple texts on their own. The emphasis is on matching word by word while reading and noticing important aspects of words that are embedded in one- or two-line texts.

In a writing workshop and interactive writing it is important for the teacher to help children notice many of the features of print listed for reading, and to help them learn the directional movements needed to form letters. Through early writing experiences, children learn to say words slowly and hear the sounds, eventually learning to hear them in sequence and connect them with letters and letter clusters.

Interactive writing provides a meaningful setting for you to demonstrate to children

Emergent Word Solvers	
Reading: Emergent word solvers . . .	Writing: Emergent word solvers . . .
Show interest in print and forms of writing.	Show interest in producing print for themselves.
Are moving from approximating reading to knowing that there is a consistent message.	Are moving from scribbling and letter-like forms to conventional letter forms.
Recognize some letter forms and some word forms; know some letter names.	Perform the motor action needed to form letters and words and know how to use the tools of writing.
Can hear sounds in words, make connections between words that sound alike, and recognize rhymes.	Can say words slowly, hear sounds in words and connect with some letters.
Know that print is read moving left to right and top to bottom.	Know how to write left to right on a line and return to the left for the next line. Know to write top to bottom on a page. Use both upper- and lowercase letters while writing; know the difference.
Are beginning to match voice and print while reading.	Are beginning to match voice and print to reread (either accurately or with approximation) some parts of message produced in writing.
Know that print represents meaning and language.	Know that writing can be used to communicate meaning to others.
Realize that letters grouped together form a word; words are defined by space on a page.	Know how to group letters together to form words and leave space between words.
Know that reading is something possible for them to do.	Know that writing is something that they can do.
Realize that ideas are represented in the written symbols rather than the pictures.	Realize that to produce a message that someone else can read, you must write letters and words.
Realize that letters and groups of letters are connected to sounds that we hear in words.	Know that letters represent sounds and how to represent individual sounds with letters or clusters of letters.
Recognize a few high-frequency words.	Know how to write a few high-frequency words.
Are making hypotheses about relationships between letters and sounds and how that information is used in reading.	Are making hypotheses about relationships between letters and sounds and how to use that information to write.
Have a core of ten to twenty simple words they can read.	Have a core of ten to twenty simple words they can write.

FIGURE 19-1   Emergent Word Solvers

the building-up process of writing. You will be doing much of the writing but inviting children to come up to the chart and participate. Explicitly model thinking of a message and involve children in the process. Then write the message or story word by word, saying each word slowly, writing the letters, and rereading it many times. You can write the harder words; children contribute the very easy high-frequency words that they know.

Encourage students to contribute letters they know and involve them in thinking about the directional movement to make the letter and the letter's visual features.

Word study experiences will include a range of hands-on experiences with letters of different colors, sizes, and media (sponge, magnetic, etc.). Children will profit from feeling letters, sorting letters, making words with letters, and painting letters. Also encourage children to work with simple words, particularly their names and some easy high-frequency words that they have encountered in writing and reading experiences. A small collection of "words we know" or "words we like" can be placed in a visible spot in the classroom, but the emphasis here is exploration and interest rather than memorization.

Children's names are a wonderful resource for emergent word solvers. Teachers should use name charts intensively, referring to them often during interactive writing, and encouraging children to find their names and their friends' names and to "read" the name chart. Name puzzles are also an appropriate and effective word-solving experience for emergent readers. We stress that word study must be active, personal, and fun. It is critical to notice interesting features of children's names (for example, whose names start or end alike) and to engage children in noticing letters and words. Children have a natural interest in the features of words and make many surprising connections.

Early Word Solvers Early word solvers have control of early strategies such as directionality and word-by-word matching (Figure 19-2). They are beginning to read without pointing. They can read books with several lines of print and have a small core of high-frequency words that they can write and read. Moreover, they have developed a system for learning words in reading and for constructing words in writing. They can hear and represent most of the sounds with letters or letter clusters. They use several sources of information to read and to check on themselves while reading. They can construct words by relating sounds to letters in a left-to-right sequence.

In guided reading, the sight vocabulary of early readers is expanding. They are using more of the letter-sound cues and reading longer stories with more text. Guided reading lessons focus on helping children read with fluency and phrasing while noticing vi-

sual information to solve words. The early reader is consistently cross-checking several sources of information—print or visual information, meaning, and language structure. Shared reading is a highly supportive context for helping early word solvers behave like readers, noticing aspects of words in a familiar text that they read over and over. Take the opportunity to point out features of words that are interesting; children will do the same, coming up with word discoveries in texts that they are reading together.

Writing workshops and interactive writing focus on continuing to build the core of high-frequency words with attention to common spelling patterns, representing all the sounds within a word, and noticing aspects of words such as double letters or inflectional endings. Interactive writing is a particularly powerful tool in helping early word solvers learn to construct words using many different techniques for connecting letters and sounds in words, as well as making connections among words that have similar features. Children contribute much more of the writing—the sounds within words in addition to dominant consonants. They use some vowels and make simple analogies such as *to* and *do*.

In word study, early word solvers continue to work with high-frequency words, adding to their personal spelling dictionaries or word banks. They make links among words to learn common spelling patterns. The word wall is an important tool, and so are interactive word charts. The word walls and charts represent children's first experiences in using references and resources, and they lead to independence. Children make words using letters and doing some simple word sorts, such as onsets and rimes, beginning and ending letters, and endings such as *s*, *ed*, and *ing*.

Transitional Word Solvers Transitional word solvers control the early behaviors. They can read texts with many lines of print, and they use multiple sources of information

Early Word Solvers	
Reading: Early word solvers . . .	Writing: Early word solvers . . .
Recognize almost all letters easily and know their names and associated sounds.	Produce the written forms of almost all upper- and lowercase letters quickly and easily.
Consistently notice gross mismatches while reading.	Produce approximations and attempts that closely represent the words intended; produce at least one letter for every sound they hear in a word.
Use most consonant sounds in words and many easy-to-hear vowels to check on their reading and solve simple words.	Hear and represent most of the sounds when they write words, especially consonant sounds and dominant, easy-to-hear vowels.
Have a core of high-frequency words that they can recognize both in isolation and when they meet them in text.	Have a core of high-frequency words that they can write quickly and easily.
Recognize many words that are not high frequency, particularly those with simple, regular patterns.	Can write many words that are not high frequency, particularly those with simple, easy-to-remember patterns.
Can use beginning and ending parts of words to figure out new words.	Can produce new words by using beginning and ending parts of words like "word families."
Use some visual features of words to check on their reading and to figure out unknown words.	Can write some words with visual patterns that are not consistent with simple phonetic patterns and can use one such word to figure out an unknown word.
Recognize and use inflectional endings of words in reading.	Produce written texts that have words with inflectional endings. Use words they know and add endings.
Make associations between simple words they know and use them to get to words they do not yet know.	Use simple words they know to derive new words by association or analogy.

FIGURE 19-2   Early Word Solvers

while reading for meaning. They are fluent and fast. They have a large core of frequently used words they can recognize quickly and easily. They notice pictures but do not rely on them for reading. In writing, transitional word solvers have a large vocabulary that they can produce quickly and efficiently. Transitional word solvers produce longer pieces of writing; their stories have more detail. They are spelling many words with standard spelling, and they are working out others with close approximations they can then check to learn more (Figure 19-3).

Even though transitional word solvers display many competencies, they are still working to develop self-extending systems. They are working on how to solve more complex words in reading, and they are just beginning to realize that letters and sounds

are not sufficient to achieve accurate spelling. They must recognize and use more complex orthographic patterns to spell words in writing.

In shared reading, help them focus on two- and three-syllable words and notice features of words such as prefixes, endings, and different cases and tenses. In guided reading, introduce longer, more complex texts that require students to recognize a large number of words and work out other words by analogy or word analysis. Teaching word solving in reading means helping students consistently use many different sources of information while reading, including visual information. They need to learn to use word-solving skills to take words apart without losing the sense of meaning and language structure.

Transitional Word Solvers	
Reading: Transitional word solvers . . .	Writing: Transitional word solvers . . .
Are building a large reading vocabulary, including but not limited to the harder high-frequency words and many words of high interest; can recognize this vocabulary easily and rapidly.	Have a large writing vocabulary, including many harder high-frequency words and many words of high interest that they can produce quickly and efficiently.
Have developed knowledge of many common spelling patterns and can use these patterns to figure out unknown words in reading.	Use many common spelling patterns quickly and automatically to form words while writing text.
Can use visual information quickly and efficiently while reading text.	Write most material quickly and efficiently, giving attention to the message being written.
Know that both letters and groups of letters can represent sounds	Use letters and groups of letters to represent sounds and know that the same sound can be represented in several different ways by different letters or groups of letters.
Know and use several different ways of analyzing a word—letter-sound relationships, analogy, and word parts.	Have a range of strategies for spelling words—remembering the spelling, working with a combination of letter-sound patterns and visual features, and using references.
Read longer texts with more varied vocabulary and more words.	Produce text that is less predictable, uses a wider variety of vocabulary, and has more words.
Can take words apart while reading for meaning; use component parts for analysis.	Can produce new words by analyzing them into component parts for easier writing.
Can take words apart by syllables and can analyze syllables using letters and sounds.	Hear most sounds, including harder-to-hear vowels, and understand that there is a vowel sound in each syllable.

FIGURE 19-3   Transitional Word Solvers

In interactive writing, share the pen with children on words that are powerful examples. Write easy high-frequency words yourself to move the writing along and invite children to participate on words that expand the learning of the group—such as multisyllable words or those that offer interesting connections to other words. Some teachers have found it productive to work with small groups in interactive writing, spending more time with students who are still at the beginning levels of learning to write. Grouping for interactive writing allows for work on basic concepts such as initial and final consonants for children who need them, and on more advanced concepts with other children.

In writing workshop and independent writing, students have a chance to write many words for themselves and use the sim-

ple references in the classroom such as word walls and charts. In minilessons teachers focus on all aspects of the writing process, including how to vary vocabulary, work out more complex words, and use classroom references and resources.

In word study, you may focus on categories of words such as contractions, compound words, and simple multisyllable words. Have students sort words into various categories and create word charts and word webs to help students explore patterns in words and connections among words. Depending on the students' behaviors, you may begin to engage transitional readers in using basic elements of the word study system (see Chapter 14), teaching them how to use simple resources such as the dictionaries available for children and encouraging them to continue using the word walls and word charts.

Self-Extending Word Solvers Self-extending readers use all sources of information flexibly while reading texts that are much longer and more complex. They have a large core of high-frequency words and many other words that they automatically recognize. Self-extending readers know what reading is "all about." They can learn from their reading and build high-level skills simply by encountering many different kinds of texts and figuring them out.

Self-extending writers have a large vocabulary of words that they can write quickly and easily (although it is much smaller than the reading vocabulary). They are fluent in thinking of the message or text, revising it in their heads as they go along, and writing it on the page. They are still developing the writing vocabulary as well as their ability to spell words in standard form. Their attempts show that they are connecting words and using rules and principles (Figure 19-4).

Students' reading and writing competencies do not always run parallel, of course. Students who have had a great deal of experience in reading but not much in writing

Self-Extending Word Solvers	
Reading: Self-extending word solvers . . .	Writing: Self-extending word solvers . . .
Use some or all of the print information along with meaning and language while reading longer, more difficult texts.	Understand that how words are written conveys and affects the meaning of the written piece.
Recognize most words quickly and easily; stop or pause in reading only occasionally when noticing difficult words or confused about meaning; reading sounds phrased and fluent.	Have a large and rapidly growing writing vocabulary that includes some complex, multisyllable words; can access writing vocabulary quickly, writing words fluently.
Can recognize parts of word that have meaning.	Can build words from word roots.
Notice when words they have read don't look right.	Have a growing level of awareness of alternative spelling patterns.
Recognize words in text that are similar in meaning but spelled differently or are spelled the same but have different meanings according to context and use this knowledge to help in comprehension.	Know many different ways to represent a sound and realize that meaning is different according to spelling.
Are able to analyze every part of a word when needed but use minimal information for efficiency in quick recognition of words.	Can represent all parts of multisyllable words in writing by using a combination of letter-sound patterns and visual features; analyze consonants and vowels in syllables.
Can use beginning level resources such as word charts or webs when differentiating similar words from one another or understanding the meaning of a word in reading.	Make effective use of beginning level resources such as dictionaries and word lists, are able to apply early dictionary skills such as alphabetizing, and can use beginning resources.
Try unfamiliar words using a range of strategies including relating known parts of words to new words.	Attempt to spell new words and recognize accurate parts of the attempt while checking with classroom resources.
Consistently notice discrepancies between their reading and the text, especially when meaning is lost; quickly self-correct at point of error.	Can locate more of their own errors because they have a greater sense of what words look like.
Can apply, when necessary, rules of pronunciation when reading aloud.	Are able to apply spelling generalizations and rules to many words they know.

FIGURE 19-4 Self-Extending Word Solvers

may be far ahead in reading skills but lack confidence in writing. Writing is a productive task that requires skills that are different from reading. We all recognize words in reading, for example, that we might have to think hard about if we were spelling them while writing. So, a student might roughly resemble characteristics of readers at one place on the continuum but resemble writers at another place.

Self-extending readers are still learning about reading. Shared reading becomes a community literacy experience in the classroom as students enjoy the rhythms of poetry, chants, and rhymes. It may also be a vehicle for using figurative or poetic language and attending to different ways words are put together for enjoyment and meaning.

As you work with self-extending word solvers in guided reading, select texts to offer challenge and variety. With instructional assistance, children encounter a wider variety of words. Also, texts will require more complex word solving related both to the structure of words and to their meaning. Texts will present content that may stretch students beyond their present worlds and understandings.

Word learning in reading means both vocabulary development as well as the structural analysis of more complex words. For example, we want students to be able to bring their own experiences to the interpretation of the words they meet in text, and to use context to acquire a strong understanding of the meaning. Moreover, we want them to go beyond the sentence or paragraph in which the word is embedded to think about the meaning of the whole text. Students must learn to monitor their reading for comprehension. For example, after they read a text, we would want to engage them in a discussion about the meaning of words. They can find morphological elements of words that help them make meaning connections among groups of words. As they use reading journals and personal notebooks, children can go beyond structural elements of individual words to explore complex meaning relationships among groups of words.

In writing, work with self-extending word solvers to create longer and more complex texts. Help students think about using in their own writing some of the interesting words they learn through reading. Word walls and interactive charts become constant references and resources for working out more complicated words. Most spelling of both easy and harder high-frequency words is standard. Students are using the word study system weekly to add to their repertoire of words. They are expanding their ability to proofread their own work.

Word study for self-extending word solvers continues to build on the understandings students have established earlier. By now, students fully understand that exploring and learning about words is part of their role in becoming literate. Continue to involve students in sorting words and making collections of words. It is still very important for word study to be active and to allow for discovery. Both closed and open sorts help students derive the categories that will enable them to generalize principles. Building words and making collections of words is also important. Students may have their own word notebooks in addition to the charts that everyone participates in creating. An important part of word study is teaching students to become more independent. It is also critical to help them continue to use the class references—word walls and charts—as well as beginning dictionaries.

Advanced Word Solvers Students who are advanced in reading, writing, and word solving have moved well beyond the early "learning to read and write" phases of literacy education. Of course, they are still learning and developing their skills. All along, they have been learning about reading and writing by using these skills for real purposes. Now, they vastly increase their capacity to use reading and writing as tools for learning.

The chart in Figure 19-5 provides general descriptions of their competencies.

Advanced word solvers continue to participate in guided reading lessons, although shared reading has become something more like choral reading, performance theater, or readers' theater. In guided reading, there is an emphasis on reading complex, longer texts of various genres. Your goal is not so much to move students "up" in difficulty (they actually can decode almost any word they meet) but to help them rapidly and fluently process and fully understand a wide variety of texts. For example, in guided reading, the introductions and conversations at points of reading a book with many chapters might help students learn how to read informational texts on a range of topics or to compare fantasy and realistic fiction. How would one read autobiography? How would it be different from biography? Help students sort out the subtle meanings of texts, analyze plots, and understand characters and how they change. And, of course, there is an emphasis on developing vocabulary while reading. Select the texts that provide challenges in the way the students use words:

Advanced Word Solvers	
Reading: Advanced word solvers . . .	Writing: Advanced word solvers . . .
Understand that words have meaning and that meaning varies within the texts in which they are embedded; search for subtle change in word meaning related to the texts they are reading.	Understand the linguistic and social functions of conventional spelling and produce products that are carefully edited.
Read almost all words in difficult texts quickly and automatically and read with high accuracy.	Understand that spelling is important and spell all words, except those that are technical and those that have the most difficult spelling patterns, conventionally.
Read novel texts with fluency and phrasing, slowing down briefly to solve difficult, unfamiliar words in the head.	Write most words quickly and easily with conventional spelling.
Solve technical words related to content areas of knowledge.	Write technical words related to content areas of knowledge; select words and put them together in a style suitable to the content area.
Use structural features or derive meanings of words.	Understand the structure of words, including affixes and word roots.
Analyze words using meaning units (roots and bases).	Combine meaning units to make words (roots and bases).
Use knowledge of complex letter patterns and word meanings to recognize words and derive their meanings.	Instead of trying to memorize each word, learn to spell words by analogy to other phonic patterns and by semantic or meaning relationship.
Learn many new words through reading.	Use new words to express meanings in writing.
Have a wide variety of word-solving strategies and can use context to develop new understandings.	Have a growing understanding of the wide variety of ways that words represent meaning (eponyms; acronyms).
Notice visual features of words that support quick word solving and automatic checking for accuracy while reading.	Use knowledge of visual patterns to notice when words don't look right; proofread and edit competently most of the time.
Use dictionaries or other references to explore pronunciation or word meanings.	Can use dictionary, thesaurus, computer spell check and other resources; understand organization plans for these resources (such as alphabetizing and guide words).

FIGURE 19-5   Advanced Word Solvers

❙ Words that students have already encountered but need to develop the complex understandings of alternative meanings.

❙ New words that students need to incorporate into their speaking, reading, and writing vocabularies.

In writing, students will be writing, editing, and publishing their own works for a variety of purposes. Engage them in research related to the content areas of the curriculum and at the same time showcase unique and functional words, helping students become independent writers who know how to use references and resources skillfully. As they grow in experience they realize that writing has a wide range of purposes, including:

❙ Notetaking to help learn in content areas.

❙ Lists to organize work and time.

❙ Outlines to organize ideas in writing.

❙ First, second, and later drafts in the composing and writing process.

❙ Communication with many different audiences from personal to distant.

❙ Writing that reflects one's thoughts in many different ways, including poetic language.

Word study for advanced word solvers recognizes the study of language as a viable content area of the curriculum. Students continue to work with word categories, engaging in complex word sorts to discover new principles and rules. They all use mnemonic devices to assist their learning. Work with the word study system continues, and there is an emphasis on students' taking over their own learning to a great extent. An important aspect of word study is making sure that students can independently and skillfully use complex references and resources. For example, we would want students to have good dictionary skills—using

guide words, pronunciation guides, and information on word origins. The study of words will include knowledge of historical relationships, word roots, and variations. All of this knowledge of words will help students not only in their performance on tests of vocabulary but also as they read for understanding and produce pieces of coherent, meaningful writing across a range of topics.

Using the Continuum

The charts we present in this chapter represent broad areas of learning. Again, no child will precisely fit the descriptions. As teachers we work with groups, but we always recognize that students learn as individuals. Depending on the grade level, the majority of the children in a classroom may fit over one or two of these categories.

We believe that thinking about the categories can prevent instructional decisions that really miss the mark by promoting word study activities that are much too simple or much too difficult for children. Of course, you will always find children who are inexperienced compared to the others in a class and need extra support; at the same time, other students will be quite advanced. Attention to multilevel activities or extra small-group support will help in meeting the challenges related to the range of experience that exists in every classroom.

After you consider which categories best fit your students' current levels of learning, think about the word study activities described in this book. You can make a "first match" by gathering some general ideas about the level and nature of the activities that might be appropriate. Then think more specifically about what you want children to know in terms of letters and words, using Chapter 9 as a resource and looking at the curriculum provided by your school district. Look carefully at the variety of word categories provided in the appendixes. Teaching for change involves designing instruction that will help individual students use what they know in active ways and introducing challenges and complexities that will help them move to the next level of learning.

Suggestions for Professional Development

1. Read and discuss with colleagues the continuum of learning described for word solving.

2. Gather the materials that describe your word study curriculum (basal readers, curriculum guides, etc.) and compare them to the continuum described here.

3. Using your own observations, running records, and writing samples from your classroom, try to place children in your class in one of the categories. Tolerate some ambiguity. Remember, no one child will perfectly fit a category.

4. After clustering students in tentative categories, draw some general implications for instruction:
   ∎ What kinds of word study activities might be appropriate?
   ∎ How can you introduce students to the activities? Be explicit in your plans for teaching the task when you embark on word study activities such as word sorting.

5. Design one or two word study activities that you think will be meaningful and will result in new learning for most of the children in your class. Try them out for a week or two.

6. Meet with colleagues to discuss your results.
   ∎ Were the activities too easy? Too hard?
   ∎ Did they result in learning that students could use in other ways? In other words, did the principles transfer from one learning context to another?
   ∎ Was there evidence that students used understandings developed in word study while they were reading or writing? Share examples.

7. Continue working on your word study curriculum using the continuum of progress. In time, your group of colleagues may want to adjust this continuum and add descriptions that particularly fit the children you teach and the way you are working in your school.

Thinking Comprehensively About Word Solving

Whatever the debate about the "best" way to teach reading and writing, teachers have the daily responsibility for designing learning experiences and supporting children in becoming competent readers, writers, and word solvers. If we examine experts' opinions and research, we find that there is common ground and that their theoretical differences are smaller than the rhetoric suggests. Rather than becoming involved in the debate, we need to focus energy on creating learning experiences that are supported by sound research and rooted in how children learn over time.

We need to think in a comprehensive way, working together and supporting each other to provide an excellent program for children. Word learning—phonics and spelling—is important, but these skills are only a part of the literacy program. They represent valuable tools that our students will use in learning and in communication. Some critical questions include:

■ How can we embed word learning in the curriculum so children become skillful, flexible word solvers in reading and writing?

■ How can we create in our students an interest in words so they learn more about

them as they read and write and, eventually, become lifelong learners of words?

■ How can we create clear expectations about word learning so all stakeholders in the education of children can work together to support our students?

■ How can we involve parents in supporting children's learning about words?

■ How can we develop our skills as teachers so we can provide a coherent, organized, quality program of word study?

In this chapter we present five steps that support the development of a comprehensive approach to word study. The previous chapters provide the support for taking each step.

1. Design a research-based word study program that is coherent, comprehensive, and rooted in how children learn over time.

In this book we have presented a dynamic combination of three strands that form a conceptual system for learning how letters and words work:

■ Focused word study activities that actively involve children in the exploration of how words work.

▮ Attention to words in reading that provide powerful examples to help children learn to take words apart while reading for meaning.

▮ Attention to words in writing to help children develop effective spelling strategies.

The approaches described in this book are based on current research on learning. These approaches have been thoroughly field-tested and implemented in classrooms where teachers experience all of today's challenges. But a word study program is not created simply by putting together a combination of activities. The challenge for us as teachers is to select teaching actions and create settings that enable children to *use* what they know, work at a level of success, and go to the next step. Implementing a good word study program involves thinking about an overall plan, organizing activities and materials, assessing children's strengths, and then finding a place to start. Research may support certain kinds of activities, but remember—it is not the activities *in and of themselves* that are of benefit to student learning—students progress as they participate in leveled activities that are "just right" for fostering new learning.

Teaching for Word Learning Throughout the Day

In this book we have described word learning through reading, writing, and word study. Our three-component model makes it clear that learning about letters, sounds, words, and how they work is not a simple matter of fifteen or twenty minutes of systematic instruction each day. To become fluent, flexible word solvers in reading and writing, children need many encounters with words. Thinking comprehensively means teaching about words throughout the day. For example, in a quality program, the teacher:

▮ Provides a focused minilesson on an aspect of word learning during the first hour of the day.

▮ Asks students to practice the principles presented through the minilesson in a word study center or other area.

▮ Follows the word study learning experience with a group share of discoveries about words and how they work.

▮ Encourages students in a writing workshop to check words using aspects they explored during the minilesson. In conferences, if appropriate, the teacher assesses how students are demonstrating their word knowledge and highlights the conceps or principles for them again.

▮ In reading, watches for opportunities to call students' attention to aspects of words—if appropriate, "echoes" the word study minilesson provided earlier.

▮ In content areas, such as health, social studies, or science, engages children in interactive writing, taking the opportunity to focus on how words work in the process of creating a meaningful message.

If teachers think about word solving—what children need to know matched with their current knowledge level—they can consciously call words to the children's attention. As students have numerous opportunities to encounter words in a variety of contexts, they use many words, become flexible as word solvers, and, in the process, build the vocabularies they need for quick, automatic reading and writing.

2. Create a shared vision for achievement in word learning.

In all of the chapters of this book we have emphasized finding out where children are in their learning and then teaching for change. Nothing else will work. No one can learn if, consistently, the learning task is too difficult. Yet there is always a tension between meeting children's instructional needs and having expectations for progress. All of us are familiar with the anxiety connected with reporting to parents about children's "below average," "average," or "above average" progress. At times, we find ourselves reluctantly reporting "below average" progress or even giving low letter grades when we know that students are working hard, using what they know, and learning. The dilemma is this: It is legitimate to require grade-level expectations; yet we want to motivate and help our individual students learn.

We believe that a shared vision for grade-level expectations can be a positive component of a comprehensive literacy education program. Word learning, in particular, is controversial because of the current debate about "phonics." In many school districts, teachers are handed grade-level expectations in terms of what they will *teach*. In this book, we stress that effective teaching begins with using the evidence of *learning* that our young students provide through their behavior. Here are some of the seemingly conflicting issues that teachers grapple with daily:

▌ We must meet students where they are and work from their strengths; nothing else will work effectively in the educational program.

▌ We must make it possible for students to work most of the time at a level of success so they see themselves as effective learners and build systems of understanding based on using what they know.

▌ We must teach for change; we have to help students make the fastest progress they can.

▌ If we do not have some kind of grade-level standard, our expectations of students may be too low and we may not work for the achievement they need.

A common vision for grade-level expectations will help us work together to create a rigorous and dynamic curriculum to help students learn about words.

Create and use grade-level benchmarks/expectations for understandings about letters and words.

Working with colleagues to establish benchmarks can be a remarkable professional ex-

perience, one that can contribute to building a vision for a school staff. We strongly encourage you to work with your colleagues rather than to simply adopt a set of benchmarks from an outside group or expert. You may, of course, want to consult many sources for samples and recommendations, but you should also trust your own observations of children who, over the years, have become very good word solvers. What could those children do and what did they know at the end of kindergarten? At the end of first and second grade? The goal is to set a standard that ensures that every child achieves these competencies. Following are some suggested steps in the process.

First, meet with colleagues interested in literacy education; ideally, this process should include teachers from all grade levels. As a group, think about some individual children and groups of children at each grade level who are good readers and spellers. What do they know about word solving and what can they do to word solve in reading and writing? Delving into the specific descriptions of these students' skills will make the process more productive. Observe children reading and writing, asking older children to read aloud. Use informal reading inventories or running records and talk about the evidence of strategies. Collect writing samples—early drafts and edited versions—to analyze word-solving and proofreading skills. Observe children in classroom work and also administer some of the assessments suggested in this book. Build a picture of the goals of the curriculum, realizing that individual variation will always be there.

Second, consult several lists of grade-level benchmarks or expectations for word learning to match the generated descriptions of student learning with those others have offered. Chances are, the generated characteristics will be consistent with published lists, but they will be in your own words, and the meaning will be clear because you and your colleagues will have grounded each statement with observation of students in your school. For example, we offer the suggested list of expectations in Figure 20-1.

Third, think about the level of achievement you want for your school. While comparing your own ideas about grade-level expectations to the ones you have read, it is possible that you will have set higher or lower expectations for a given grade level.

Our goals are always related to the experiences that we have had in our teaching. For example, if the school has a half-day kindergarten and the district program has not emphasized the integration of literacy in an active way, the kindergarten benchmarks listed in our chart may seem unrealistic. At the same time, the end-of-third-grade

---

Creating Benchmarks for Progress

Pre-kindergarten students will:
* Notice print in the environment.
* Distinguish print as different from pictures.
* Engage in role-play reading and writing.
* Show interest in hearing stories.
* Attend to picture books with an adult.
* Know or recognize some letters, especially in names.
* Recognize own name.
* Hold writing utensil and write using letter-like forms.
* Make some letter forms, though direction may not be consistently accurate.

By the end of kindergarten, students will:
* Understand most concepts about print, such as what letters and words are and how they are defined by space on a page.
* Understand words are made up of letters.
* Recognize and name most letters.
* Write most letters in the correct direction and in standard form.
* Say words slowly.
* Hear word boundaries (how space is used to define words).
* Hear and identify sounds in words, especially rhymes, syllables, and final or initial consonants or consonant clusters.
* Know most letter-sound associations for consonants and the easy-to-hear vowel sounds.
* Recognize own name and names of many classmates.
* Recognize some easy high-frequency words, such as *I*, *a*, *me*.
* Write some high-frequency words, such as *it*, *to*, *a*, *is*.
* Have a core of known words (ten to twenty) that they can write and read.

By the end of first grade, students will:
* Understand concepts about print—that words are made up of letters and defined by space, that letters are in a consistent order in words, that there are capital and small letters, that words are arranged from left to right and top to bottom in print.
* Know all letters names, forms, and related sounds.
* Hear syllables, rhyme, and sequences of sounds in words.
* Hear and write most sounds in words, including dominant and hard-to-hear consonants and the vowel sounds.
* Quickly and easily recognize a large number of words—both high-frequency words and other words—in reading texts.
* Write a large number of words (approximately seventy-five to one hundred) using conventional spelling.
* Write many more words representing all sounds heard, though spelling may not be conventional.
* Notice and use simple word patterns or clusters of letters that occur frequently together.
* Use known word parts to figure out unfamiliar words in reading or spell new words in writing.
* Understand that a letter can represent different sounds and that sounds can be represented by more than one letter or group of letters.
* Use common patterns to write words.
* Use a few simple resources, such as word walls, word lists, and simple dictionaries.

FIGURE 20-1 Creating Benchmarks for Progress: Sample Set of Expectations for Understandings About Letters and Words

By the end of second grade, students will:
- Understand that sounds are represented by a variety of letter sequences.
- Recognize automatically and rapidly a large reading vocabulary (hundreds of words).
- Write with ease and fluency a large number of words (hundreds) in conventional spelling.
- Write unfamiliar words by representing sounds with letters or letter patterns.
- Use word roots, prefixes, suffixes, and inflectional endings to read and write words.
- Recognize and write compound words, contractions, and easy plural forms.
- Use known word parts and patterns to figure out new words.
- Notice mismatches between words in reading and when words do not look right in writing.
- Know how to apply useful spelling principles to new words.
- Use a variety of strategies to spell words.
- Use a word wall, word lists, and dictionaries effectively in writing, proofreading, and editing.
- Know how to proofread to identify some words spelled incorrectly.

By the end of third grade, students will:
- Understand that spelling is important and use conventional spelling most of the time.
- Use sound, look, and meaning strategies to solve new words.
- Use common spelling patterns, word roots, prefixes, and suffixes to solve words in reading and spell words in writing.
- Use common plural rules to write words.
- Use spelling rules and exceptions to write words.
- Know many complex spelling patterns.
- Use effective proofreading skills to locate their own errors.
- Use resources such as dictionaries, thesauruses, and glossaries.
- Use mnemonic devices to help remember some words.

FIGURE 20-1   Creating Benchmarks for Progress, *continued*

benchmarks may be a good match. Participating in this exercise will inevitably lead to an examination of the curriculum at each grade level.

Establish goals for the upper grades and then work backwards, thinking of the foundational experiences that students need and working together for agreement on what is appropriate. In no way should establishing benchmark expectations restrict the curriculum to activities that are beyond students' understanding and that ruin their enjoyment of reading and writing. There are ways to integrate literacy that seem as natural to children as play, but it takes time and planning across grades to develop an effective program.

Fourth, create a tentative set of grade-level benchmarks to test over several years. If the school currently has low achievement, you will need to think simultaneously of what *is happening* and what you *want to happen* in the future. We want to set high standards, but the standards must be realistic ones that will serve students well. We must recognize that the standards for all children may take several years of program design and implementation to achieve.

Fifth, conduct assessment and observation to estimate how many students at each grade level currently meet the standard (or will by the end of the year). Making a graph or chart that includes each student who meets or exceeds the benchmark and each student who currently does not meet the benchmark will help you and your colleagues in two ways:

1. You will have a defined group of children who need extra help. For each of these children, you can work from the continuum of learning presented in the previous chapter and design daily instruction that will take them further. Some first-grade

students may need intensive extra help such as the one-to-one tutoring provided in Reading Recovery.

2. The data provide evidence of the success of the program over the years. We seldom examine historical data to assess our teaching; education is always a matter of trying this new program and that one and assessing the results, which may be no better or no worse than previous years. The purpose of assessment is to use the data to get better over the years. This first estimate provides a beginning. With the implementation of a quality program, the number of students who meet or exceed the benchmark will grow. Each year, using systematic assessment, chart the number of students who meet the benchmark. This simple statistic will help to fine-tune the program.

Sixth, try out the benchmarks over a period of time—perhaps two years. Meet periodically to share students' progress. It may be necessary to fine-tune statements and descriptions as you learn more about children and their learning. You may need to adjust some expectations. For example, kindergarten children may show much more knowledge and enthusiasm for word learning than you had previously expected.

3. Gather materials and organize classroom and school environments to support a high-quality word study program.

It is obvious that finding time for a word study program is a challenge. The classroom day is crowded. But word study, as we have presented it here, does not need to take much time if you are organized and have the appropriate materials. Throughout this book we have listed and described simple and inexpensive materials that will support word learning. You can acquire these materials over time. The next step is to be sure that the classroom environment is organized so that you and your students can use the mate-

rials efficiently. Wall space (or some kind of eye-level display space), for example, is absolutely necessary because the year's word learning is built day after day and displayed on charts, interactive writing, and other products produced by the teacher and the children. Make sure references are readily available. The final step is to teach children to use the environment so they can become independent.

4. Inform and involve parents and the community to support a high-quality word-learning program.

Parents and other caregivers are a resource for children's learning. In a handbook entitled *Help America Read: A Handbook for Volunteers*, we have described ways that volunteers and teaching assistants can be effective in helping children learn about words (see Fountas and Pinnell 1996). Many of the practical suggestions in this handbook will also be helpful for parents and caregivers.

One of the first tasks in implementing a word study program is to communicate with parents and help them understand their children's learning processes. Like many educators, parents may tend to look at the specifics of what is *taught* rather than *what is learned and how it is learned*. If we expect parents to value children's partially correct responses, we need to find ways to show them what children have learned and are learning. And, we need to reassure them that we have explicit goals for children's continuous achievement.

Through frequent communication with caregivers, we can help them understand the three-sided nature of the curriculum—that we will be teaching children about words but also making sure they use word knowledge in reading (phonics) and in writing (spelling) so they become highly skilled in each area. During conferences with caregivers, share student work with explicit examples; also, highlight student work in class newsletters or other communications.

Finally, parents and caregivers appreciate hearing about steps they can take to help their children. Over time, school staff can communicate many ways of supporting children that are part of the natural interactions in the home. For example, you can encourage parents to:

▮ Talk with children as much as possible to expand the use of words in spoken vocabulary.

▮ Enjoy reading books together. Parents can read favorites many times and encourage the children to join in, saying some of the words together, especially the ones that are inherently enjoyable and fascinating.

▮ Write for the children, talking out loud about the process.

▮ Encourage children to write for themselves. At first, parents should not expect correct forms but should praise children for first attempts. Over time, they can look for progress toward conventional spelling.

▮ Encourage children to find their own errors and correct them. Parents can gradually build in several different ways to see if a word looks right.

▮ Notice words in the environment—such as street names or store names—and draw the children's attention to them.

▮ Notice words on favorite foods, toys, or other items that interest the children.

▮ Play word games that draw children's attention to aspects of words such as beginning letters, sounds, and rhymes.

▮ Play family games that feature word learning as a component (Boggle, Pictionary, Scrabble, and Wheel of Fortune).

▮ Investigate technology supports such as computerized toys, computer games, and spell check programs that will assist in word learning.

Parents always appreciate any support the school can provide in the way of home materials. Kindergarten teachers can send home the child's name as a puzzle to be put together several times. Children may take home collections of words they know to play with and categorize. Some of the most interesting and effective home materials that we have used in recent years are Keep Books.[1] These simple books with black-and-white drawings are a way to greatly increase children's home reading. They range in level from the very easiest texts to second-grade level. Two sets of Keep Books explore math concepts; others present nursery rhymes, which are effective in developing phoneme awareness in young children. Two sets of titles are available in Spanish and a new set focuses on words and how they work.

Keep Books start at school, where the teacher may introduce them to the class or a small group of children, integrating them into a lesson. The children have their first successful experiences with the books and then bring them home to have more success. The important thing about these little books is that children take them home to keep. In our experience, they treasure these first books and share them with other young children in the family.

5. Become involved in ongoing professional development to increase skill in teaching about words and how they work.

The key to a quality word study program is in the teaching decisions that we make

---

[1]Keep Books are inexpensively published books designed for children to take home and keep. The cost of each book is $.25 when they are purchased in class-size quantities. Grants from the Charles Dana Foundation and the Martha Holden Jennings Foundation partially support the development and field testing of these little books. They are distributed on a not-for-profit basis by The Ohio State University. Keep Books may be obtained from The Ohio State University, Ramseyer Hall, 29 W. Woodruff, Columbus OH 43210 or call (614) 688-5770.

every day. It is unrealistic to expect new teachers or even those of us who have been teaching for a while to suddenly become expert in this area. We need to begin with a solid plan and approaches that work, but then we need to hone our skills so that powerful teaching interactions support learning. Again, the activities alone will not result in a large benefit for students. All instructional activities must be carefully planned and applied, and teachers need to become skilled in the moment-to-moment ways they help students focus their attention. Teachers apply sound practice when they:

❚ Have a personal interest in words, language, reading, and writing.

❚ Understand how children learn language and learn about the reading and writing processes, including word learning.

❚ Understand how letters and words work within languages.

❚ Understand the core goals of a word study curriculum.

❚ Use systematic observation and systematic teaching (the teaching-learning cycle) on a daily, weekly, and yearly basis.

❚ Know how to interact in ways that support students' learning of word-solving strategies in reading, writing, and word study.

❚ Attend to word learning throughout the day and across the curriculum.

❚ Engage in inquiry to learn more about how children become effective word solvers who are able to use their skills in reading and writing.

It is through seemingly casual interactions that you can make the powerful links among the three strands of the word study program. For example, teaching comments like the following create those "echoes" across the day as we have described:

❚ Oh, there's an interesting word. That's like the words we were talking about this morning!

❚ You found one of those words, didn't you? We were talking about homonyms just yesterday. *Knight* is a homonym. Would you like to add it to the chart?

❚ I notice that Jonathan wrote *enormous* in his story. That's like the words we were putting on the chart of words that mean *big*.

❚ Good for you! You were thinking about words with silent letters and found the word *know* on the word wall to help you.

Constantly drawing children's attention to words will not only have the beneficial effect of making links, but you will find that, after a while, children will bring aspects of words to each others' attention. Sometimes we have said that teachers are "born teachers" or "intuitive teachers" because they seem to spontaneously make these powerful links. Actually, it is a matter of attention, learning, and practice until learning conversations become almost automatic.

Professional development is essential to develop the necessary teaching skills. With colleague support, study groups can be quite effective, and we recommend that teachers study together rather than ask a consultant to provide an after-school session that may or may not relate to what the group is currently trying to achieve. A long-range plan for professional development may be established at the school or district level. A good plan will include time for you and your colleagues to work together, analyzing data from your own students as you learn more about word study.

Suggestions for Professional Development

1. Thinking comprehensively requires a long-range plan that takes into account systematic assessment, systematic instruction,

benchmarks or expectations for progress, and professional development. After reading this chapter, you may feel somewhat overwhelmed with the tasks ahead. You can break down the tasks by working with colleagues on a three- to four-year plan. At the end of this time, you will be surprised at how much has been accomplished. The most productive thing to do is to make a start.

2. Identify a group of colleagues to work with. Your group could be grade-level colleagues, but it is productive to communicate across grade levels.

3. Begin to plan. It can be helpful to write out the plan using chart paper so that every participant can see it. We like to leave the chart paper (or a typed version of it— perhaps enlarged slightly) in the staff room so we can discuss it or refer to it often. Another helpful action is to put specific time lines on your plan and schedule meetings to reflect on progress.

Here are some components that you may want to consider for your long-term plan:

- Begin work to establish expectations for progress at your school. Follow the process suggested in this chapter and plan to work on your benchmarks over the next three or four years.
- Create a plan for professional development so you will have colleague support over time in working on a quality word study program.
- Make a list of materials you will need and create a plan for acquiring them. Set a day for classroom organization. After trying a word study program for a while, set a day for reorganizing.
- Create a "phase in" plan for implementing systematic assessment at each grade level. Start with a few children but have a plan for expanding the system.
- Create a "phase in" plan for implementing a systematic word study program at each grade level.
- Be sure to make time in your plan for evaluation and reflection.

Finally, *Words Do Matter*

We wrote this book to help children become independent readers and writers who know how to use information about letter, sounds, and words to create meaning. But in the midst of teaching the practicalities of words, we do not forget their magic. The words of languages enable us to make meaning and to weave the texts that move and delight us. One such text is *The Perfectly Orderly H-O-U-S-E* by Ellen Kindt McKenzie (1994).

In this story a little old woman lived in a little old house that was terribly crowded with all of the things she would never throw away. She couldn't find anything that she wanted, so she decided to build a big new house where everything could be orderly. She said, "There is nothing more orderly than the alphabet. Everything I have begins with one letter or another. I'll just put it all in the order of the ABC's."

She did so but still couldn't find anything; so she decided that she needed a big house with a room for each letter of the alphabet. She asked her brother, Sam, to help her begin by building the Attic. There, the old woman put her aprons. As each room was constructed, she filled it with items starting with the appropriate letter: Basement, Closet, Dining room, and Entry (in which they put the eggs). Sam built a Family room, Garage, Hallway, Igloo, Junk room, Kitchen, Laundry room, Music room, Nautical Knickknack room, Observatory, and so on. Finally the old woman had a very long house with twenty-six rooms.

Now there were some problems in the process of moving in. For example, the car couldn't go into the Garage because it started with c, and it was too big for the Closet. Finally, she decided to park it in the Vestibule, along with a variety of other vehicles.

When the old woman's house was finished and all of her collected items were categorized, she started to get ready for a big party. She went to the Kitchen to bake a cake, but had to go to the Study for the sugar and to the Basement for the baking powder and butter. Then, she took the cake to the Observatory to put it in the oven and sat on the ottoman to rest. When the cake was ready, she went to the Igloo to write the invitations.

Finally, all the guests arrived. She sent them to the Closet for the cookies, the cakes, and the cold cuts. They went to the Igloo for ice cream and to the Attic for appetizers. The ladies had to eat in the Laundry room and the men in the Music room. Everyone had a wonderful time, but when the party was over, the old woman was very tired and wanted to rock in her rocking chair. Remembering that her rocking chair was still in her wee little old house, she walked back there and discovered Sam sitting in the rocking chair with just a few items of furniture. "Sam," she cried, "What a perfectly orderly house this is!" And that house stayed perfectly orderly forever.

This book is about language—specifically the words of our language and how we learn them and learn about them. The most important thing about words is how they are used to make meaning and create beauty. As teachers, we try to engage children in using words in interesting ways. In the process, we work to help them learn about words and their subtle and complex dimensions. Learning how words work is not a matter of acquiring a list of separate pieces of knowledge, such as letters and sounds, organized in a logical sequence. Learning how words work is a complex process in which children make the connections that catapult them to new learning.

For the final "word matters," we chose to share *The Perfectly Orderly H-O-U-S-E* because we find striking parallels between the author's message and our view of letter and word learning as part of a curriculum. The old woman's goal was to make her life completely orderly in a very simple way. By simplifying, she lost the meaningful connections that make living possible.

The old woman's rigid organization made her house too simple to make sense. We certainly don't want to make the same mistake with the learning process, forcing it into a rigid sequence that doesn't make sense to individual children. Learning for all children takes place sequentially, but it is not the same sequence for everyone. There are important milestones along the way and children generally progress from easier to more difficult ideas and concepts. Ideas build on each other, but they do so in complex ways as children bring all of their previous experiences to learning. Accordingly, we must adjust the curriculum to match individual strengths and needs, making sure each and every child achieves the desired outcomes.

McKenzie, in *The Perfectly Orderly H-O-U-S-E*, uses the alphabet as an organizational frame for an engaging story that makes children think about both the meaning of words and how they are spelled. Juxtaposing meaning and spelling in this ridiculous way creates delightful humor.

This book made us think about words and also about our own teaching. Our literacy curriculum must be designed to foster interest and joy in words and their use. Words matter because they provide us an entry into communication, humor, and pleasure. Teaching about words means recognizing—and reveling in—their meaning and their magic.

Appendixes

Alphabet Books

Ada, A. 1997. *Gathering the Sun*. New York: Lothrop, Lee & Shepard.

Amerikaner, S. 1989. *My Silly Book of ABCs*. New York: Silver Dollar Press.

———. 1994. *ABCs*. New York: Silver Dollar Press.

Angel, M. 1996. *An Animated Alphabet*. New York: David R. Godine.

Aylesworth, J. 1998a. *The Folks in the Valley*. New York: HarperCollins Juvenile.

———. 1998b. *Old Black Fly*. New York: Henry Holt.

Baker, A. 1994. *Black and White Rabbit's ABC*. New York: Kingfisher Press.

Balog, J. 1996. *James Balog's Animals A to Z*. New York: Chronicle Books.

Banks, K. 1988. *Alphabet Soup*. New York: Dragonfly Books.

Bannatyne-Cugnet, J. 1993. *A Prairie Alphabet*. Plattsburgh, NY: Tundra Books.

Baron, M. 1996. *Your Own ABC*. Toronto: Annick Press.

Bender, R. 1996. *The A to Z Beastly Jamboree*. New York: Lodestar Books.

Bond, M. 1991. *Paddington's ABC*. New York: Viking Press.

Bown, B. 1991. *Antler, Bear, Canoe: A Northwoods Alphabet Year*. Boston: Little, Brown.

Boynton, S. 1995. *A to Z*. New York: Little Simon.

Braybrooks, A. 1997. *Love Letters: A Book of ABCs*. New York: Golden Books.

Brown, M. 1994. *Sleepy ABC*. New York: HarperCollins Juvenile.

———. 1996. *A Child's Good Night Book*. New York: HarperCollins Juvenile.

Bruchac, J. 1997. *Many Nations: An Alphabet of Native America*. Mahwah, NJ: Bridgewater Books.

Bryan, A. 1997. *Ashley Bryan's ABC of African American Poetry*. New York: Atheneum.

Burningham, J. 1964. *John Burningham's ABC*. New York: Crown.

Bustard, A. 1989. *T Is for Texas*. Stillwater, MN: Voyageur Press.

Carter, D. 1994. *Alpha Bugs: A Pop-Up Alphabet*. New York: Little Simon.

Chin-Lee, C. 1997. *A Is for Asia*. New York: Orchard.

Cox, L. 1990. *Crazy Alphabet*. New York: Orchard.

Crowther, R. 1997. *The Most Amazing Hide and Seek Alphabet*. New York: Viking.

Darling, K. 1996. *Amazon ABC*. New York: Lothrop, Lee & Shepard.

Dillon, L., et al. 1997. *Ashanti to Zulu: African Traditions*. New York: Dial Books for Young Readers.

Doubilet, A. 1991. *Under the Sea from A to Z*. New York: Crown.

Edwards, M. 1992. *Alef-Bet: A Hebrew Alphabet Book*. New York: Lothrop, Lee & Shepard.

Ehlert, L. 1996. *Eating the Alphabet*. New York: Harcourt Brace.

Elting, M., & M. Folsom. 1980. *Q Is for Duck: An Alphabet Guessing Game*. New York: Clarion.

Feelings, M. 1974. *Jambo Means Hello: Swahili Alphabet Book*. New York: Dial Books For Young Readers.

Felix, M. 1995. *The Alphabet*. New York: Harcourt Brace.

Gardner, B. 1986. *Have you ever seen . . . ? An ABC Alphabet Book*. New York: Dodd, Mead.

Gaudrat, M. 1994. *My 1st ABC*. New York: Barrons Juveniles.

Geddes, A. 1995. *ABC (The Anne Geddes Collection)*. San Rafael, CA: Cedco Publishing.

———. 1997. *Down in the Garden Alphabet Book*. San Rafael, CA: Cedco Publishing.

Geisert, A. 1986. *Pigs from A to Z*. Boston: Houghton Mifflin.

George, P. 1995. *Gifts of Our People: An Alphabet of African History*. Valley Forge, PA: Judson Press.

Gibson, B. 1994. *ABC in the Woods*. Washington, DC: National Geographic Society.

Greenfield, E. 1994. *Aaron and Gayla's Alphabet Book*. New York: Writers & Readers.

Gretz, S. 1986. *Teddy Bear's ABC*. New York: Simon & Schuster.

Grover, M. 1996. *The Accidental Zucchini: An Unexpected Alphabet*. New York: Harcourt Brace.

Gustafson, S. 1994. *Alphabet Soup: A Feast of Letters*. Greenwich, CT: The Greenwich Workshop Press.

Hallinan, P. 1995. *When I Grow Up*. New York: Ideals Children's Books.

Harrison, T. 1989. *A Northern Alphabet*. Plattsburgh, NY: Tundra Books.

Hausman, G. 1994. *Turtle Island ABC*. New York: HarperCollins.

Hirashima, J. 1994. *ABC (A Chunky Shape Book)*. New York: Random House.

Hoban, T. 1987. *26 Letters and 99 Cents*. New York: Greenwillow.

———. 1990. *Exactly the Opposite*. New York: Greenwillow.

Horn, C. 1997. *Animals and Me ABC*. St. Louis, MO: Concordia.

Hudson, C. 1988. *Afro-Bets ABC Book*. East Orange, NJ: Just Us Books.

Johnson, S. 1995. *Alphabet City*. New York: Kingfisher.

Kaye, B. 1994. *A You're Adorable.* Cambridge, MA: Candlewick Press.

Kitamura, S. 1987. *What's Inside: The Alphabet Book.* New York: Farrar Straus & Giroux.

Kitchen, B. 1984. *Animal Alphabet.* New York: Dial Books for Young Readers.

Lear, E. 1997. *A Was Once an Apple Pie.* Cambridge, MA: Candlewick Press.

Lecourt, N. 1992. *Abracadabra to Zigzag: An Alphabet Book!* New York: Puffin.

Lessac, F. 1989. *Caribbean Alphabet.* New York: Tambourine Books.

Lobel, A. 1990. *Alison's Zinnia.* New York: Greenwillow Books.

MacDonald, S. 1986. *Alphabatics.* New York: Aladdin Books.

Maestro, B. 1989. *Taxi: A Book of City Words.* Boston: Houghton Mifflin.

Markle, S. et al. 1998. *Gone Forever: An Alphabet of Extinct Animals.* New York: Simon & Schuster.

Martin, B. 1989. *Chicka Chicka Boom Boom.* New York: Simon & Schuster.

Martin, M. 1996. *From Anne to Zach.* New York: Boyds Mills Press.

Mayers, F. 1994. *Baseball ABC.* New York: Harry N. Abrams.

McDonnell, F. 1997. *Flora McDonnell's ABC.* Cambridge, MA: Candlewick Press.

Merriam, E. 1992. *Goodnight to Annie: An Alphabet Lullaby.* New York: Hyperion.

Micklethwait, L. 1992. *I Spy: An Alphabet in Art.* New York: Greenwillow.

Miranda, A. 1996. *Pignic.* New York: Boyds Mills Press.

Mullins, P. 1997. *V for Vanishing: An Alphabet of Endangered Animals.* New York: HarperCollins Juvenile.

Onyefulu, I. 1993. *A Is for Africa.* New York: Cobblehill Books.

Pallotta, J. 1989a. *The Flower Alphabet Book.* Watertown, MA: Charlesbridge.

———. 1989b. *The Yucky Reptile Alphabet Book.* Watertown, MA: Charlesbridge.

———. 1990a. *The Bird Alphabet Book.* Watertown, MA: Charlesbridge.

———. 1990b. *The Dinosaur Alphabet Book.* Watertown, MA: Charlesbridge.

———. 1990c. *The Frog Alphabet Book.* Watertown, MA: Charlesbridge.

———. 1990d. *The Furry Alphabet Book.* Watertown, MA: Charlesbridge.

———. 1990e. *The Ocean Alphabet Book.* Watertown, MA: Charlesbridge.

———. 1991. *The Underwater Alphabet Book.* Watertown, MA: Charlesbridge.

———. 1992. *The Victory Garden Vegetable Alphabet Book.* Watertown, MA: Charlesbridge.

———. 1993a. *The Extinct Alphabet Book.* Watertown, MA: Charlesbridge.

———. 1993b. *Icky Bug Alphabet Book.* Watertown, MA: Charlesbridge.

———. 1994a. *The Desert Alphabet Book.* Watertown, MA: Charlesbridge.

———. 1994b. *The Spice Alphabet Book.* Watertown, MA: Charlesbridge.

———. 1995. *The Butterfly Alphabet Book.* Watertown, MA: Charlesbridge.

———. 1996. *The Freshwater Alphabet Book.* Watertown, MA: Charlesbridge.

———. 1997. *The Airplane Alphabet Book.* Watertown, MA: Charlesbridge.

———. 1998. *The Boat Alphabet Book.* Watertown, MA: Charlesbridge.

Paul, A. 1991. *Eight Hands Round: A Patchwork Alphabet.* New York: Dutton Books.

Pelham, D. 1991. *A Is for Animals: 26 Pop-Up Surprises.* New York: Simon & Schuster.

Pomeroy, D. 1997. *Wildflower ABC: An Alphabet of Potato Prints.* New York: Harcourt Brace.

Potter, B. 1995. *Peter Rabbit's ABC and 123.* London: F. Warne.

Pratt, K. 1992. *A Walk in the Rainforest.* Nevada City, CA: Dawn Publications.

———. 1996. *A Fly in the Sky.* Nevada City, CA: Dawn Publications.

Reasoner, C. 1989. *Alphabite! A Funny Feast from A to Z.* New York: Price Stern Sloan.

Reed, L. 1995. *Pedro, His Perro, and the Alphabet Sombrero.* New York: Hyperion.

Rey, H. A., & M. Rey. 1998. *Curious George's ABCs.* Boston: Houghton Mifflin.

Rice, J. 1991. *Cajun Alphabet Book.* Gretna, LA: Pelican Publishing.

Roberts, M. 1998. *The Jungle ABC.* New York: Disney Press.

Rotner, S. 1996. *Action Alphabet.* New York: Atheneum.

Ruurs, M. 1996. *A Mountain Alphabet.* Plattsburgh, NY: Tundra Books.

Sanders, E. 1995. *What's Your Name? From Ariel to Zoe.* New York: Holiday House.

Sandved, K. 1996. *The Butterfly Alphabet.* New York: Scholastic.

Sardegna, J. 1996. *K Is for Kiss Good Night: A Bedtime Alphabet.* New York: Picture Yearling.

Scarry, R. 1973. *Richard Scarry's Find Your ABCs.* New York: Random House.

Schories, P. 1996. *Over Under in the Garden: An Alphabet Book.* New York: Farrar Straus & Giroux.

Sendak, M. 1991. *Alligators All Around*. New York: HarperTrophy.

Seuss, Dr. 1996. *Dr. Seuss's ABC: An Amazing Book*. New York: Random House.

Shannon, G. 1996. *Tomorrow's Alphabet*. New York: Greenwillow.

Slate, J. 1996. *Miss Bindergarten Gets Ready for Kindergarten*. New York: Dutton Children's Books.

Smith, H. 1980. *ABCs of Maine*. Portland, ME: Down East Books.

Staake, B. 1998. *My Little ABC Book*. New York: Little Simon.

Stockham, P. 1990. *The Mother's Picture Alphabet*. New York: Dover Publications.

Stroud, V. 1996. *The Path of the Quiet Elk: A Native American Alphabet*. New York: Dial Books For Young Readers.

Stutson, C. 1996. *Prairie Primer: A to Z*. New York: Dutton Books.

———. 1997. *On the River ABC*. New York: Roberts Rinehart Publishers.

Tamer, E. 1996. *Alphabet City Ballet*. New York: HarperCollins Juvenile.

Tapahonso, L. 1995. *Navajo ABC: A Dine Alphabet Book*. New York: Simon & Schuster.

Thornhill, J. 1988. *The Wildlife ABC: A Nature Alphabet Book*. New York: Simon & Schuster.

Tryon, L. 1991. *Albert's Alphabet*. New York: Atheneum.

Van Allsberg, C. 1987. *The Z was Zapped*. Boston: Houghton Mifflin.

Versola, A., & M. Ajmera. 1997. *Children from Australia to Zimbabwe*. Watertown, MA: Charlesbridge.

Viorst, J. 1994. *The Alphabet from Z to A (With Much Confusion on the Way)*. New York: Atheneum.

Weaver, D. 1996. *New Mexico from A to Z*. Flagstaff, AZ: Rising Moon.

Wells, R. 1992. *A to Zen: A Book of Japanese Culture*. New York: Simon & Schuster.

Whitehead, P. 1989a. *Best Halloween Book (ABC Adventure)*. Mahwah, NJ: Troll Associates.

———. 1989b. *Dinosaur Alphabet Book*. Mahwah, NJ: Troll Associates.

Wildsmith, B. 1996. *Brian Wildsmith's ABC*. Austin, TX: Star Bright Books.

Wolf, J. 1987. *Adelaide to Zeke*. New York: Harper & Row.

Wood, J. 1993. *Animal Parade*. New York: Simon & Schuster.

Young, E. 1997. *Voices of the Heart*. New York: Scholastic

Zerner, A. 1993. *Zen ABC*. New York: Charles Tuttle.

Ziefert, H. 1997. *Night Knight*. Boston: Houghton Mifflin.

Books for Word Play

Ahlberg, J., & A. Ahlberg. 1978. *Each Peach Pear Plum.* New York: Puffin.

———. 1981. *Peek-a-Boo!* New York: Puffin.

Allington, R. 1990a. *Reading and Science—Words.* New York: Raintree/Steck Vaughn.

———. 1990b. *Talking.* New York: Raintree/Steck Vaughn.

Ancona, G. 1996. *Handtalk Zoo.* New York: Aladdin Paperbacks.

Anholt, C. 1992. *All About You.* New York: Viking Press.

Arnold, T. 1995. *Five Ugly Monsters.* New York: Scholastic.

Aylesworth, J. 1992. *The Cat and the Fiddle and More.* New York: Atheneum.

Baer, E. 1980. *Words Are Like Faces.* New York: Random House.

Baker, P. 1986. *My First Book of Sign.* New York: Kendall Green.

Base, G. 1986. *Animalia.* New York: Penguin.

Battles, E. 1979. *What Does the Rooster Say, Yoshio?* New York: Albert Whitman.

Benjamin, A. 1987. *Rat-a-Tat, Pitter-Pat.* New York: HarperCrest.

Berson, H. 1988. *A Moose Is Not a Mouse.* New York: Crown Publishers.

Bodecker, N. M. 1973. *It's Raining Said John Twaining.* New York: Atheneum.

Bond, M. 1985. *Paddington and the Knickerbocker Rainbow.* New York: Putnam.

Bossom, N. 1979. *A Scale Full of Fish and Other Turnabouts.* New York: Greenwillow.

Brown, M. W. 1947. *Goodnight Moon.* New York: HarperCollins Children's Books.

Carle, E. 1991. *My Very First Book of Words.* New York: HarperFestival.

Carlstrom, N. W. 1986. *Jesse Bear, What Will You Wear?* New York: Scholastic.

Chislett, G. 1991. *Melinda's No's Cold.* Toronto: Annick Press.

Chouinard, R., & M. Chouinard. 1988. *The Amazing Animal Alphabet Book.* New York: Doubleday.

Christelow, E. 1989. *Five Little Monkeys.* New York: Clarion.

Ciardi, J. 1961. *I Met a Man.* Boston: Houghton Mifflin.

Cohen, C. L. 1997. *Three Yellow Dogs.* New York: Mulberry Books.

Day, A. 1991. *Frank and Ernest.* New York: Scholastic.

De Regniers, B. S. 1972. *It Does Not Say Meow and Other Animal Riddles.* Boston: Houghton Mifflin.

Dodds, D. A. 1992. *Do Bunnies Talk?* New York: HarperCollins Juvenile.

Dragonwagon, C. 1987. *Alligator Arrived with Apples: A Potluck Alphabet.* New York: Macmillan.

Dunham, M. 1987a. *Colors: How Do You Say It?* New York: Lothrop, Lee & Shepard.

———. 1987b. *Numbers: How Do You Say It?* New York: Lothrop, Lee & Shepard.

———. 1987c. *Shapes: How Do You Say It?* New York: Lothrop, Lee & Shepard.

Edwards, P. D. 1995. *Four Famished Foxes and Fosdyke.* New York: HarperTrophy.

Ellentuck, S. n.d. *Did You See What I Said?* New York: Doubleday.

Elting, M., & M. Folsom. 1980. *Q Is For Duck: An Alphabet Guessing Game.* New York: Clarion.

Evans, L. 1997. *Snow Dance.* Boston: Houghton Mifflin.

Fallwell, C. 1991. *Clowning Around.* New York: Orchard.

Folsom, M. 1985. *Easy as Pie: A Guessing Game of Sayings.* Boston: Houghton Mifflin.

Fox, M. 1989. *Night Noises.* New York: Harcourt Brace.

Gibbons, G. 1992. *Weather Words and What They Mean.* New York: Holiday House.

Ginsburg, M. 1985. *Across the Stream.* New York: Puffin.

Goldstein, B. 1989. *Bear in Mind.* New York: Viking.

Gomi, T. 1991. *Seeing, Saying, Doing, Playing.* New York: Chronicle.

Gordon, J. R. 1993. *Six Sleepy Sheep.* Honesdale, PA: Boyds Mills Press.

Greenberg, J. E. 1985. *What Is the Sign for Friend?* New York: Franklin Watts.

Gwynne, F. 1970. *The King Who Rained.* New York: Windmill.

———. 1976. *A Chocolate Moose for Dinner.* New York: Windmill.

———. 1990. *A Little Pigeon Toad.* New York: Aladdin Paperbacks.

Hague, K. 1984. *Alphabears: An ABC Book.* New York: Scholastic.

Harter, D. 1997. *Walking Through the Jungle.* New York: Orchard.

Hartman, G. 1989. *For Strawberry Jam or Fireflies.* New York: Atheneum.

Hawkins, C. 1986. *Tog the Dog.* New York: Putnam.

———. 1988. *Zug the Bug: A Flip-the-Page Rhyming Book.* New York: Putnam.

Heller, R. 1988a. *A Cache of Jewels and Other Collective Nouns.* New York: Scholastic.

———. 1988b. *Kites Sail High.* New York: Grosset and Dunlap.

———. 1989. *Many Luscious Lollipops: A Book About Adjectives.* New York: Grosset and Dunlap.

Hepworth, C. 1992. *Antics.* New York: Putnam.

Hill, E. 1986. *Spot's First Words: El Libro Grande de las.* New York: Putnam

———. 1989. *Spot's Big Book of Words.* New York: Putnam.

Hirschi, R. 1992. *Seya's Song.* Seattle, WA: Sasquatch Books.

Hoban, T. 1981. *More Than One.* New York: William Morrow.

———. 1991. *All About Where.* New York: Greenwillow.

Hopkins, L. B. 1995. *Good Rhymes, Good Times.* New York: HarperCollins.

Hunt, B. K. 1976. *Your Ant Is a Witch.* New York: Harcourt Brace.

Hutchins, P. 1976. *Don't Forget the Bacon.* New York: Puffin.

Johnston, J. 1974. *Speak Up, Eddie!* New York: Putnam.

Kalish, M., & L. Kalish. 1993. *Bears on the Stairs: A Beginners Book.* New York: Scholastic.

Keats, E. J. 1971. *Over in the Meadow.* New York: Scholastic.

Kellogg, S. 1987. *Aster Aardvark's Alphabet Adventures.* New York: William Morrow/Mulberry.

Koch, M. 1989. *Just One More.* New York: Greenwillow.

Krauss, R. 1989. *A Hole Is to Dig.* New York: HarperTrophy.

Krupp, R. R. 1988. *Get Set to Wreck!* New York: Atheneum.

Kuskin, K. 1956. *Roar and More.* New York: Harper & Row.

Luton, M. 1983. *Little Chick's Mother and All the Others.* New York: Puffin.

Maestro, B. 1979. *On the Go: A Book of Adjectives.* New York: Random House.

Maestro, G. 1984. *What's Frank Frank? Tasty Homophone Riddles.* New York: Clarion.

———. 1986. *What's Mite Might? Homophone Riddles.* New York: Clarion.

Martin, B. 1967. *Brown Bear, Brown Bear, What Do You See?* New York: Henry Holt.

———. 1970. *Fire! Fire! Said Mrs. McGuire.* New York: Holt, Rinehart and Winston.

Moncure, J. B. 1989. *Play with "a" and "t."* Elgin, IL: The Child's World.

Most, B. 1991. *Pets in Trumpets: And Other Word Riddles.* New York: Harcourt Brace.

Nash, O. 1992. *The Adventures of Isabel.* Boston: Little, Brown.

O'Neill, M. 1961. *Hailstones and Halibut Bones.* New York: Doubleday.

Parish, P. 1993. *Thank You, Amelia Bedelia.* New York: HarperTrophy.

———. 1994a. *Amelia Bedelia.* New York: HarperCollins Juvenile.

———. 1994b. *Amelia Bedelia and the Surprise Shower.* New York: HarperCollins Juvenile.

———. 1995a. *Come Back, Amelia Bedelia.* New York: HarperCollins Juvenile.

———. 1995b. *Teach Us, Amelia Bedelia.* New York: Demco Media.

———. 1996a. *Amelia Bedelia and the Baby.* New York: Camelot.

———. 1996b. *Good Driving, Amelia Bedelia.* New York: Camelot.

———. 1996c. *Good Work, Amelia Bedelia.* New York: Camelot.

———. 1996d. *Merry Christmas, Amelia Bedelia.* New York: Camelot.

———. 1996e. *Play Ball, Amelia Bedelia.* New York: HarperCollins Juvenile.

———. 1997a. *Amelia Bedelia Goes Camping.* New York: Camelot.

———. 1997b. *Amelia Bedelia Helps Out.* New York: Camelot.

———. 1997c. *Amelia Bedelia's Family Album.* New York: Camelot.

———. 1997d. *Bravo, Amelia Bedelia.* New York: William Morrow.

Preiss, B. 1982. *The First Crazy Word Book: Verbs.* New York: Franklin Watts.

Prelutsky, J. 1984. *The New Kid on the Block.* New York: Scholastic.

———. 1983. *The Random House Book of Poetry for Children.* New York: Random House.

Presson, L. 1996. *What in the World Is a Homophone?* Hauppauge, NY: Barron's.

Rand, A. 1991. *Sparkle and Spin: A Book About Words.* New York: Harry N. Abrams.

Rankin, L. 1991. *The Handmade Alphabet.* New York: Dial Books.

Scarry, R. 1985. *Richard Scarry's Best Word Book Ever!* New York: Random.

Schwartz, A. 1982. *Busy Buzzing Bumble Bees and Other Tongue Twisters.* New York: Harper & Row.

Sendak, M. 1962. *Chicken Soup with Rice.* New York: Scholastic.

Sesame Street. 1980. *Sesame Street Sign Language Fun.* New York: Random House.

———. 1983. *Sesame Street Word Book.* New York: Golden Press.

Sherman, I. 1983. *Walking, Talking Words.* New York: Harcourt Brace.

Steig, W. 1980. *The Bad Speller.* New York: Windmill.

Steinmetz, L., & S. Steinmetz. 1994. *The Dangerous Journey of Doctor McPain to . . .* Littleton, MA: Sundance.

Terban, M. 1982. *Eight Ate: A Feast of Homonym Riddles*. New York: Clarion.

———. 1983. *In a Pickle and Other Funny Idioms*. New York: Clarion.

———. 1984. *I Think I Thought*. Boston: Houghton Mifflin.

———. 1985. *Too Hot to Hoot: Funny Palindrome Riddles*. New York: Clarion.

———. 1987. *Mad as a Wet Hen! And Other Funny Idioms*. Boston: Houghton Mifflin.

———. 1988. *The Dove Dove. Funny Homograph Riddles*. New York: Clarion.

Tester, S. R. 1977. *What Did You Say?* New York: Children's Press.

Verboven, A. 1996. *Ducks Like to Swim*. New York: Orchard.

Whatley, B., & S. Whatley. 1994. *Whatley's Quest: An Alphabet Adventure*. Sydney, Australia: HarperCollins.

Wildsmith, B. 1978. *What the Moon Saw*. New York: Oxford University Press.

Williams, S. 1990. *I Went Walking*. New York: Harcourt Brace.

Woods, A. 1982. *Quick as a Cricket*. Auburn, ME: Child's Play.

Ziefert, H. 1997. *Baby Buggy, Buggy Baby*. Boston: Houghton Mifflin.

Alphabet

abcd efg hijk lmnop

qrs tuv wx yz

A a	B b
apple	bear

C c	D d	E e	F f
cat	dog	elephant	fish

G g	H h	I i	J j
gate	hat	igloo	jack-in-the-box

K k	L l	M m	N n
kite	leaf	moon	nest

O o	P p	Q q	R r
octopus	pig	queen	ring

S s	T t	U u	V v
sun	turtle	umbrella	vacuum

W w	X x	Y y	Z z
window	x-ray	yo-yo	zipper

Appendix 3   Alphabet Linking Chart

One Hundred High-Frequency Words

a	I	they
after	I'm	this
all	if	to
am	in	too
an	into	two
and	is	up
are	it	us
as	just	very
asked	like	was
at	little	we
away	look	went
back	make	were
be	man	what
because	me	when
before	mother	where
big	my	who
but	no	will
by	not	with
came	now	you
can	of	your
come	on	
could	one	
day	or	
did	our	
do	out	
don't	over	
for	play	
from	put	
get	said	
go	saw	
going	see	
had	she	
has	so	
have	than	
he	that	
her	the	
here	their	
him	them	
his	then	
how	there	

Appendix 4   One Hundred High-Frequency Words

Five Hundred High-Frequency Words

a	became	care
able	because	carry
about	become	cat
above	bed	catch
across	been	caught
add	before	certain
after	began	change
again	begin	children
against	behind	city
air	being	class
all	believe	clean
almost	below	close
along	best	clothes
already	better	cold
also	between	come
although	big	coming
always	bike	complete
am	black	could
among	boat	couldn't
an	body	country
and	books	cut
animal	boot	dad
another	both	dark
answer	box	day
any	boy	deep
anything	bring	did
are	broke	didn't
around	brother	died
as	brought	different
ask	build	dinner
asked	bus	do
at	but	does
ate	buy	dog
away	by	doing
baby	call	done
back	called	don't
bad	came	door
ball	can	down
be	can't	draw
beautiful	car	dream

dry	full	house
during	fun	how
each	funny	however
early	game	hurt
earth	gave	I
easy	get	I'd
eat	getting	idea
either	girl	if
else	give	I'm
end	go	important
enough	goes	in
even	going	inside
ever	gone	instead
every	good	into
everyone	got	is
everything	grade	it
fact	great	it's
family	green	job
fare	group	jump
fast	grow	just
father	had	keep
favorite	half	kept
feel	hand	kids
feet	happy	killed
fell	hard	kind
few	has	knew
field	have	know
fight	having	lady
finally	he	land
find	head	large
fine	hear	last
fire	heard	later
first	heart	learn
fish	heavy	leave
five	help	left
fix	her	less
follow	here	let
food	high	life
for	hill	light
form	him	like
found	his	line
four	hit	list
free	hold	little
friend	home	live
from	hope	lived
front	hour	lives

long	now	ride
look	number	right
looking	of	river
lost	off	room
lot	often	round
lots	old	run
love	on	running
lunch	once	said
mad	one	same
made	only	sat
main	or	saw
make	order	say
making	other	scared
man	our	school
many	out	sea
may	outside	second
maybe	over	see
me	own	seen
mean	page	set
men	paper	several
might	park	shall
mind	part	she
miss	party	ship
mom	past	short
money	people	shot
moon	perhaps	should
more	person	show
morning	pick	shown
most	picture	sick
mother	place	side
move	plants	simple
much	play	since
must	possible	sister
my	pretty	sit
myself	probably	size
name	problem	sky
near	put	sleep
need	rain	small
never	ran	snow
new	read	so
next	ready	some
nice	real	someone
night	really	something
no	reason	soon
not	red	sound
nothing	rest	space

special	to	with
stand	today	without
start	together	woke
started	told	work
state	too	world
stay	took	would
still	top	wouldn't
stood	tree	yard
stop	tried	year
store	trouble	yes
story	try	you
street	trying	your
stuff	turned	
such	two	
summer	under	
sun	until	
sure	up	
take	upon	
talk	us	
teach	use	
teacher	used	
tell	very	
ten	walk	
than	want	
that	wanted	
that's	was	
the	wasn't	
their	watch	
them	water	
themselves	way	
then	we	
there	week	
these	well	
they	went	
they're	what	
things	when	
think	where	
third	which	
this	while	
those	who	
though	whole	
thought	why	
three	will	
through	win	
throw	winter	
time	wish	

Words with Consonants (initial and final)

Words with b

b-	-b
bake	bathtub
basket	bulb
beetle	crab
black	drab
book	cub
boss	jab
butter	scrub

Words with c

c-	-c
candy	attic
clean	elastic
climb	frantic
clothes	gigantic
come	hectic
cream	plastic
cuddle	rustic

Words with d

d-	-d
damp	food
dear	read
drop	road
dry	send
duck	told
dull	tried
dye	wired

Words with f

f-	-f
fast	cuff
father	half
find	if
flavor	leaf
five	off
friend	puff
funny	shelf

Words with g

g-	-g
gas	big
go	bug
grab	fog
grasp	mug
great	peg
gum	rug
gym	tag

Words with h

h-	-h
had	ash
hand	brush
help	crash
hill	flash
hit	push
hot	rush
hunt	smash

Words with j

j-

jelly
jest
jiggle
jolly
joy
jump
jungle

Words with k

k-

kangaroo
keen
keep
kennel
kernel
kick
king

Words with l

l-	**-l**
land	doll
latch	pail
leg	pill
like	shell
little	wall
low	well
lung	yell

Words with m

m-	-m
many	clam
meat	drum
miles	ham
miss	scream
mom	stem
music	storm
my	warm

Words with n

n-	-n
near	begin
nest	fun
net	green
new	men
nice	seen
no	ten
none	win

Words with p

p-	-p
person	cheap
pig	deep
play	drip
pocket	help
pony	nap
pretty	shrimp
puppy	trip

Words with q

qu-

quack
queen
quick
quiet
quilt
quit
quiz

Words with r

r-	**-r**
rain	air
read	bear
really	car
ride	dear
rise	door
rope	roar
rug	wear

Words with s

s-	**-s**
second	bus
seven	class
sister	dress
smooth	lakes
stop	seasons
sudden	ties
summer	wires

Words with t

t-	-t
talk	cannot
tell	cut
tie	dirt
tired	jacket
today	quit
train	right
trouble	want

Words with v

v-	
vacation	
vacuum	
van	
velvet	
violet	
violin	
vote	

Words with w

w-	-w
wagon	arrow
was	bow
water	cow
we	how
went	now
wind	row
word	willow

Words with x

x-	-x
xylophone	box
	fox
	mix
	ox
	sax
	six
	wax

Words with y

y-	-y
yard	bay
yarn	boy
year	day
yell	key
yellow	say
yes	toy
yet	tray

Words with z

z-	-z
zap	buzz
zebra	fuzz
zero	jazz
zoo	quiz
zipper	
zip	
zone	

Words with Consonant Clusters (initial)

A consonant cluster is a group or two or three consonants that are often clustered together in words. A sampling of words is provided. It is useful to look at the clusters in families.

"r" family clusters

br-	tr-	gr-
branch	trace	grain
brand	track	grand
brake	trash	grape
brass	treat	grass
brick	trick	grease
bronze	trip	greet
broth	truck	grip
brush	try	ground

fr-	cr-	wr-
freckle	crack	wrap
fresh	crayon	wreck
fright	cream	wrench
frog	crib	wriggle
from	crop	wrinkle
frost	crowd	wrist
froze	crumble	write
fry	crush	wrong

dr-	pr-
drain	pray
dream	press
dress	prince
drink	print
drip	prize
drizzle	problem
drum	program
dry	proved

"l" family clusters

bl-	cl-	fl-
black	clap	flag
bland	class	flame
blank	clay	flat
blend	clean	flavor
bliss	clever	flea
blister	closet	flew
blot	cloud	flip
blue	club	fly

gl-	pl-	sl-
glad	place	sleeve
glass	plan	slept
glide	planet	slice
glimpse	plaster	slid
globe	plate	slide
glove	play	slim
glow	plum	slip
glue	plus	slot

"s" family clusters

sc-
scale
scan
scar
scarf
scat
scatter
school
scout

sk-
skeleton
sketch
skid
skim
skin
skip
skirt
sky

sm-
smack
smart
smash
smell
smile
smog
smoke
smooth

sn-
snack
snail
snake
snap
sneak
sneeze
sniff
snow

sp-
space
speak
spell
spend
spider
spill
spoil
spot

st-
stand
star
station
stem
stick
still
stop
storm

sw-
swam
sweat
sweet
swell
swept
swift
swim
switch

"3 letter" family clusters

scr-

scramble
scrape
scratch
scream
screw
script
scrub
scruff

squ-

squad
square
squash
squeak
squeal
squeeze
squint
squirrel

str-

straw
stream
street
stress
stretch
string
strong
struck

thr-

thread
threat
three
thrift
thrill
throat
throb
throw

spr-

sprain
spray
spread
sprig
spring
sprint
sprout
sprung

spl-

splash
splat
splatter
splendid
splice
splinter
split
splotch

shr-

shrank
shred
shrill
shrimp
shrine
shrink
shrub
shrug

sch-

schedule
scheme
scholar
scholastic
school
schooner

other

tw-

twelve
twice
twig
twill
twin
twine
twirl
twist

Words with Consonant Clusters (final)

-ct	-dge	-nd
act	bridge	and
duct	edge	band
fact	fudge	bend
pact	fridge	hand
strict	judge	send
tact	ledge	pond
tract	lodge	sand
	pledge	send

-lt		
belt	-mp	-ft
felt	bump	craft
knelt	camp	gift
melt	damp	left
quilt	chomp	lift
tilt	jump	raft
welt	shrimp	shift
wilt	slump	soft
	stomp	swift

-nch		
bench		-nce
branch		chance
bunch		dance
crunch		fence
inch		glance
lunch		prance
pinch		prince
punch		since

Appendix 8   Words with Consonant Clusters (final)

©1998 by G. S. Pinnell and I. C. Fountas from *Word Matters: Teaching Phonics and Spelling in the Reading/Writing Classroom*. Portsmouth, NH: Heinemann

-nge	-st	-nt
binge	cost	ant
cringe	dust	bent
fringe	fast	dent
hinge	lost	front
lunge	nest	plant
twinge	past	sent
	rest	tent
-nk	test	went
bank		
blink		
chunk	-nse	-sp
drank	dense	clasp
honk	rinse	crisp
sunk	sense	gasp
think	tense	grasp
trunk		lisp
	-sk	rasp
	ask	wisp
-pt	brisk	
crept	disk	
kept	desk	
script	dusk	
slept	mask	
swept	risk	
wept	task	

Words with Consonant Digraphs (initial)

A consonant digraph is two consonants that together make one unique sound.

ch-

challenge

chance

check

cheese

chill

choose

chop

church

sh-

shack

shade

she

shell

shine

ship

shop

shut

wh-

whale

wheat

wheel

when

which

while

white

why

th-

than

that

then

these

thin

think

third

thorn

Words with Consonant Digraphs (final)

-ch	-ng	-th
beach	bring	bath
coach	fang	cloth
grouch	king	death
peach	long	math
pouch	sing	mouth
slouch	sting	smooth
speech	strong	teeth
teach	ring	tooth

-tch	-nk	-sh
catch	blink	blush
ditch	drink	cash
fetch	ink	crush
itch	link	dash
patch	sank	dish
scratch	sink	fish
stretch	think	smash
witch	trunk	trash

-ck

back
beck
check
cluck
deck
duck
flick
slick

Words with Double Consonants

apple	funny	mitten
attic	furry	muddle
banner	fussy	passage
batter	giggle	pepper
belly	glitter	penny
better	haddock	pillow
bidding	hammer	puddle
bitten	happen	puppy
bitter	happy	rabbit
buffet	hello	raccoon
buggy	hidden	riddle
butter	holler	session
carrot	hollow	shallow
carry	hotter	silly
cellar	hurry	simmer
chatter	juggle	smaller
coffee	kitten	smelly
collect	lesson	smitten
connect	letter	sorry
cottage	little	squiggle
dollar	manner	sudden
dresser	marry	suggest
fiddle	matter	summer
flutter	message	sunny
follow	messy	surround

Appendix 11   Words with Double Consonants

©1998 by G. S. Pinnell and I. C. Fountas from *Word Matters: Teaching Phonics and Spelling in the Reading/Writing Classroom*. Portsmouth, NH: Heinemann

taller	twitter	willow
tattered	valley	worry
tennis	village	yellow

Words with Short Vowel Sounds

Words with *a* as in *apple*

ban	pan	grand
bat	ran	hand
can	sad	land
cap	sag	lamb
cat	sat	last
fan	back	rack
fat	band	rash
ham	candy	sand
mad	fast	tack
map	flag	

Words with *e* as in *elephant*

bed	net	head
beg	peg	help
bet	pet	kept
egg	set	nest
end	wet	ready
fed	bend	send
led	best	sled
leg	bread	step
let	dent	tend
met	fetch	went

Words with *i* as in *igloo*

bib	mitt	gills
bit	mix	hitch
dig	pig	pill
fig	rig	quill
fit	sit	ring
hit	brim	still
if	bring	swim
is	dish	twitch
jig	ditch	will
kit	fill	witch

Words with *o* as in *octopus*

box	clock
dot	crop
fox	flop
got	long
hop	plop
hot	pond
jot	shock
not	soft
pop	song
top	stop

Words with *u* as in *umbrella*

bun	bunk
bus	duck
cup	just
cut	must
fun	pluck
hut	puppet
run	skunk
rut	truck
sun	trunk
up	trust

Words with a Vowel and "r"

ar	er	ir
arm	fender	birth
bar	her	dirt
barn	longer	fir
card	mother	girl
car	player	hair
far	reader	shirt
farm	sender	sir
hard	shower	stir
tar	tender	twirl
yarn	were	whirl

or	ur
born	burn
corn	fur
form	hurt
horn	purr
more	spurt
morning	turn
storm	urn
torn	furnish
worm	furniture
worn	

Appendix 13   Words with a Vowel and "r"

©1998 by G. S. Pinnell and I. C. Fountas from *Word Matters: Teaching Phonics and Spelling in the Reading/Writing Classroom.* Portsmouth, NH: Heinemann

Words with Silent "e"

a with silent *e*

ate
base
came
face
game
gave
late
made
make
name
place
plane
same
space
state
table
tale
wave

i with silent *e*

bite
drive
fire
five
life
like
live
mile
mine
ride
side
size
time
white
wide
wife
wire
write

u with silent *e*

blue
clue
cube
cute
flute
glue
hue
huge
mule
tube

e with silent *e*

Pete

o with silent *e*

bone
globe
home
hope
joke
nose
note
phone
rode
rose
smoke
those
vote

Phonograms

A phonogram, or *rime*, is a cluster of letters, a word part, or a spelling pattern. It is usually a vowel sound plus a consonant sound. The phonograms or word families can also be parts of multisyllable words (e.g., *cab·in*). When a child wants to write a word, he may think of one other word or word part that is like it. Note the rime at the beginning of the line and words that share the pattern following it. The thirty-seven most frequently used patterns (Wylie and Durrell 1970) are marked with an asterisk.

-ab	cab, dab, jab, lab, nab, tab, blab, crab, drab, grab, scab, slab
-ace	face, lace, mace, pace, race, brace, grace, place, space, trace
-ack*	back, hack, lack, pack, quack, rack, sack, tack, black, clack, crack, knack, shack, slack, smack, snack, stack, track, whack
-act	act, fact, pact, tact, tract
-ad	bad, dad, fad, had, lad, mad, pad, sad, tad, clad, glad
-ade	bade, fade, jade, made, wade, blade, glade, grade, shade, spade, trade
-aff	gaff, chaff, staff
-aft	draft, raft, waft, craft, graft, shaft
-ag	bag, gag, hag, jag, lag, nag, rag, sag, tag, wag, brag, crag, drag, flag, slag, snag, stag, swag
-age	age, cage, gage, page, rage, sage, wage, stage
-aid	aid, laid, maid, paid, raid, braid, staid
-ail*	ail, bail, fail, hail, jail, mail, nail, pail, quail, rail, sail, tail, wail, flail, frail, snail, trail
-ain*	lain, main, pain, rain, vain, wain, brain, chain, drain, gain, grain, plain, slain, Spain, sprain, stain, strain, train
-aint	faint, paint, saint, taint, quaint
-air	fair, hair, lair, pair, chair, flair, stair, air
-aise	raise, braise, chaise, praise

-ait	bait, gait, wait, strait, trait
-ake*	bake, cake, fake, lake, make, quake, rake, take, wake, brake, drake, flake, shake, snake, stake, sake
-ale*	bale, dale, gale, hale, male, pale, sale, tale, scale, shale, stale, whale
-alk	balk, calk, talk, walk, chalk, stalk
-all	all, ball, call, fall, gall, hall, mall, pall, tall, wall, small, squall, stall
-alt	halt, malt, salt
-am	am, cam, dam, ham, jam, ram, tam, yam, clam, cram, dram, gram, scam, scram, sham, slam, swam, tram
-ame*	came, dame, fame, game, lame, name, same, tame, blame, flame, frame, shame
-amp	camp, damp, lamp, ramp, tamp, vamp, champ, clamp, cramp, scamp, stamp, tramp
-an*	an, ban, can, fan, man, pan, ran, tan, van, bran, clan, flan, plan, scan, span, than
-ance	dance, lance, chance, France, glance, prance, stance, trance
-anch	ranch, blanch, branch, stanch
-and	and, band, hand, land, sand, bland, brand, gland, stand, strand, grand
-ane	bane, cane, lane, mane, pane, sane, vane, wane, crane, plane
-ang	bang, fang, gang, hang, pang, rang, sang, tang, clang, slang, sprang, twang
-ank*	bank, dank, hank, lank, rank, sank, tank, yank, blank, clank, crank, drank, flank, plank, prank, shrank, spank, thank
-ant	ant, can't, pant, rant, chant, grant, plant, scant, slant
-ap*	cap, gap, lap, map, nap, rap, sap, tap, yap, chap, clap, flap, scrap, slap, snap, strap, trap, wrap

-ape	cape, gape, nape, tape, drape, grape, scrape, shape
-ar	bar, car, far, jar, mar, par, tar, char, scar, spar, star
-ard	bard, card, guard, hard, lard, yard, shard
-are	bare, care, dare, fare, hare, mare, pare, rare, ware, blare, flare, glare, scare, share, snare, spare, square, stare
-arge	barge, large, charge
-ark	bark, dark, hark, lark, mark, park, shark, spark, stark
-arm	arm, farm, harm, charm
-arn	barn, darn, yarn,
-arp	carp, harp, tarp, sharp
-art	cart, dart, mart, part, tart, chart, smart, start
-ase	base, case, vase, chase
-ash*	ash, bash, cash, crash, dash, gash, hash, lash, mash, rash, sash, brash, clash, flash, slash, smash, stash, thrash, trash
-ask	ask, cask, mask, task, flask
-asm	chasm, plasm, spasm
-asp	gasp, hasp, rasp, clasp, grasp
-ass	bass, lass, mass, pass, brass, class, glass, grass
-ast	cast, fast, last, mast, past, vast, blast
-aste	baste, haste, paste, taste, waste, chaste
-at*	at, bat, cat, fat, gnat, hat, mat, pat, rat, sat, tat, vat, brat, chat, flat, that
-atch	batch, catch, hatch, latch, match, patch, scratch, thatch
-ate*	ate, date, fate, gate, hate, late, mate, rate, crate, grate, plate, skate, state
-ath	bath, lath, math, path, wrath

-aught	caught, naught, taught, fraught
-aunch	haunch, launch, paunch
-aunt	daunt, gaunt, haunt, jaunt, taunt, flaunt
-ave	cave, gave, pave, rave, save, wave, brave, crave, grave, shave, slave, stave
-aw*	caw, gnaw, jaw, law, paw, raw, saw, claw, draw, flaw, slaw, squaw, straw
-awl	bawl, brawl, crawl, drawl, shawl, scrawl, trawl
-awn	dawn, fawn, lawn, pawn, yawn, brawn, drawn, prawn, spawn
-ax	ax, lax, tax, wax, flax
-ay*	bay, day, gay, hay, jay, lay, may, nay, pay, quay, ray, say, way, bray, clay, cray, ray, gray, play, pray, slay, spray, stay, stray, sway, tray
-aze	daze, faze, gaze, haze, maze, raze, blaze, craze, glaze, graze
-ea	pea, sea, tea, flea, plea
-each	beach, each, leach, peach, reach, teach, bleach, breach, preach
-ead	dead, head, lead, read, bread, dread, spread, thread, tread
-ead	bead, lead, read, knead, plead
-eak	beak, leak, peak, teak, weak, bleak, creak, freak, sneak, speak, squeak, streak, tweak
-eal	deal, heal, meal, peal, real, seal, teal, veal, zeal, squeal, steal
-ealth	health, wealth, stealth
-eam	beam, ream, seam, cream, dream, gleam, scream, steam, stream, team
-ean	bean, dean, lean, mean, wean, clean, glean
-eap	heap, leap, reap, cheap
-ear	dear, ear, fear, gear, hear, near, rear, sear, tear, year, clear, shear, smear, spear
-ear	bear, pear, wear, swear

-east	beast, east, feast, least, yeast
-eat*	beat, feat, heat, meat, neat, peat, seat, bleat, cheat, cleat, pleat, treat, wheat
-eath	breath, death, feather, heather
-eave	heave, leave, weave, cleave, sheave
-eck	deck, heck, neck, peck, check, fleck, speck, wreck
-ed	bed, fed, led, red, wed, bled, bred, fled, shed, shred, sled, sped
-edge	hedge, ledge, wedge, dredge, pledge, sledge
-ee	bee, fee, knee, lee, see, tee, wee, flee, free, glee, tree
-eech	beech, leech, breech, screech, speech
-eed	deed, feed, heed, kneed, need, reed, seed, weed, bleed, breed, creed, freed, greed, speed, steed, tweed
-eek	leek, meek, peek, reek, seek, week, cheek, creek, Greek, sleek
-eel	feel, heel, keel, kneel, peel, reel, creel, steel, wheel
-eem	deem, seem, teem
-een	keen, queen, seen, teen, green, preen, screen, sheen
-eep	beep, deep, jeep, keep, peep, seep, weep, cheep, creep, sheep, sleep, steep, sweep
-eer	beer, deer, jeer, leer, peer, queer, seer, sneer, steer
-eet	beet, feet, meet, fleet, greet, sheet, skeet, sleet, street, sweet, tweet
-eeze	breeze, freeze, sneeze, squeeze, tweeze, wheeze
-eft	deft, heft, left, cleft, theft
-eg	beg, keg, leg, Meg, peg
-eigh	neigh, weigh, sleigh
-eld	held, meld, weld

-ell*	bell, cell, dell, dwell, fell, jell, knell, sell, tell, well, yell, quell, shell, smell, spell, swell
-elp	help, kelp, yelp
-elt	belt, felt, knelt, melt, pelt, welt, dwelt, smelt
-em	gem, hem, stem, them
-en	den, hen, men, pen, ten, yen, glen, then, when, wren
-ence	fence, hence, whence
-ench	bench, wench, clench, drench, French, quench, stench, trench, wrench
-end	bend, end, fend, lend, mend, rend, send, tend, vend, wend, blend, spend, trend
-ense	dense, sense, tense
-ent	bent, cent, dent, gent, Kent, lent, rent, sent, tent, vent, went, scent, spent
-ep	pep, prep, step
-ept	kept, wept, crept, slept, swept
-erge	merge, serge, verge
-erk	jerk, clerk
-erm	berm, germ, term
-ern	fern, tern, stern
-erve	nerve, serve, verve, swerve
-esh	mesh, flesh, fresh
-ess	less, mess, bless, chess, dress, press, stress, tress
-est*	best, guest, jest, lest, nest, pest, rest, test, vest, west, zest, blest, chest, crest, quest, wrest
-et	bet, get, jet, let, met, net, pet, set, wet, yet, fret, whet

-etch	etch, fetch, retch, sketch, wretch
-ew	dew, few, hew, knew, new, pew, blew, brew, chew, crew, drew, flew, screw, stew, threw
-ex	hex, vex, flex
-ey	hey, grey, prey, they, whey
-ib	bib, fib, jib, rib, crib, glib
-ibe	jibe, bribe, scribe, tribe
-ice*	dice, ice, lice, mice, nice, rice, vice, price, slice, spice, splice, twice, thrice
-ick*	kick, lick, pick, quick, sick, tick, wick, brick, chick, click, flick, slick, stick, thick, trick
-id	bid, did, hid, kid, lid, mid, quid, rid, grid, skid, slid, squid
-ide*	bide, hide, ride, side, tide, wide, bride, chide, glide, pride, slide, snide, stride
-ie	die, fie, lie, pie, tie, vie
-ied	died, lied, dried, fried, tried
-ief	brief, chief, grief, thief
-ield	field, yield, shield
-ier	brier, crier, drier, flier
-ies	dies, lies, pies, ties, cries, dries, flies, fries, skies, tries
-ife	fife, knife, life, rife, wife, strife
-iff	miff, tiff, cliff, skiff, sniff, whiff
-ift	gift, lift, rift, sift, drift, shift, swift, thrift
-ig	big, dig, fig, gig, jig, pig, rig, wig, sprig, swig, twig
-igh	high, nigh, sigh, thigh

-ight*	knight, light, might, night, right, sight, tight, blight, bright, flight, fright, plight, slight
-ike	bike, dike, hike, like, pike, spike, strike
-ild	mild, wild, child
-ile	bile, file, mile, pile, tile, vile, smile, stile, while
-ilk	bilk, milk, silk
-ill*	bill, dill, fill, gill, hill, ill, Jill, kill, mill, pill, quill, rill, sill, till, will, chill, drill, frill, grill, skill, spill, still, swill, thrill, trill, twill
-ilt	gilt, jilt, hilt, kilt, tilt, wilt, quilt, stilt
-im	dim, him, rim, vim, brim, grim, prim, slim, swim, trim, whim
-ime	dime, lime, mime, time, chime, clime, crime, grime, prime, slime
-imp	limp, chimp, crimp, primp, skimp, blimp
-in*	bin, din, fin, gin, kin, pin, sin, tin, win, chin, grin, shin, skin, spin, thin, twin
-ince	mince, since, wince, prince
-inch	cinch, inch, finch, pinch, winch, clinch, flinch
-ind	bind, find, hind, kind, mind, rind, wind, blind, grind
-ine*	dine, fine, line, mine, nine, pine, tine, vine, wine, brine, shine, shrine, spine, swine, whine
-ing*	bing, ding, king, ping, ring, sing, wing, zing, bring, cling, fling, sling, spring, sting, string, swing, thing, wring
-inge	binge, hinge, singe, tinge, cringe, fringe, twinge
-ink*	kink, link, mink, pink, rink, sink, wink, blink, brink, chink, clink, drink, shrink, slink, stink, think
-int	hint, lint, mint, tint, glint, print, splint, sprint, squint, stint

-ip*	dip, hip, lip, nip, quip, rip, sip, tip, zip, blip, chip, clip, drip, flip, grip, ship, skip, slip, snip, strip, trip, whip
-ipe	pipe, ripe, wipe, gripe, snipe, stripe, swipe, tripe
-ir	fir, sir, stir, whir
-ird	bird, gird, third
-ire	fire, hire, tire, wire, spire
-irk	quirk, shirk, smirk
-irt	dirt, flirt, shirt, skirt, squirt
-irth	birth, firth, girth, mirth
-ise	rise, wise
-ish	dish, fish, wish, swish
-isk	disk, risk, brisk, frisk, whisk
-isp	lisp, wisp, crisp
-iss	hiss, kiss, miss, bliss
-ist	fist, list, mist, wrist, grist, twist
-it*	bit, fit, hit, kit, knit, lit, pit, quit, sit, wit, flit, grit, skit, slit, spit, split, twit
-itch	ditch, hitch, pitch, witch, switch
-ite	bite, kite, mite, quite, rite, site, white, write, sprite
-ive	dive, five, hive, jive, live, chive, drive, strive, thrive
-ix	fix, mix, six
-o	do, to, who
-o	go, no, so, pro
-oach	coach, poach, roach, broach
-oad	goad, load, road, toad
-oak	soak, cloak, croak

-oal	coal, foal, goal, shoal
-oam	foam, loam, roam
-oan	loan, moan, groan
-oar	boar, roar, soar
-oast	boast, coast, roast, toast
-oat	boat, coat, goat, moat, oat, bloat, gloat, float, throat
-ob	cob, fob, gob, job, knob, lob, mob, rob, sob, blob, glob, slob, snob
-obe	lobe, robe, globe, probe
-ock*	dock, hock, knock, lock, mock, rock, sock, tock, block, clock, crock, flock, frock, shock, smock, stock
-od	cod, mod, nod, pod, rod, sod, clod, plod, prod, shod, trod
-ode	code, mode, node, rode, strode
-oe	doe, foe, hoe, toe, woe
-og	bog, cog, dog, fog, hog, jog, log, tog, clog, flog, frog, grog, slog, smog
-ogue	brogue, rogue, vogue
-oil	boil, coil, foil, oil, soil, toil, spoil, broil
-oin	coin, join, loin, groin
-oint	joint, ointment, point
-oist	foist, hoist, joist, moist
-oke*	joke, poke, woke, yoke, broke, choke, smoke, spoke, stoke, stroke
-old	bold, cold, fold, gold, hold, mold, old, sold, told, scold
-ole	dole, hole, mole, pole, role, stole, whole
-oll	poll, roll, toll, droll, knoll, scroll, stroll, troll
-oll	doll, loll
-olt	bolt, colt, jolt, molt, volt
-ome	dome, home, Rome, tome, gnome, chrome

-ome	come, some
-omp	pomp, romp, chomp, stomp
-on	son, ton, won
-ond	bond, fond, pond, blond, frond
-one	bone, cone, hone, lone, tone, zone, clone, crone, drone, phone, prone, shone, stone
-ong	bong, dong, gong, long, song, tong, prong, strong, thong, wrong
-oo	boo, coo, goo, moo, too, woo, zoo, shoo
-ood	good, hood, wood, stood
-ood	food, mood, brood
-oof	goof, roof, proof, spoof
-ook	book, cook, hook, look, nook, took, brook, crook, shook
-ool	cool, fool, pool, tool, drool, school, spool, stool
-oom	boom, doom, loom, room, zoom, bloom, broom, gloom, groom
-oon	loon, moon, noon, soon, croon, spoon, swoon
-oop	coop, hoop, loop, droop, scoop, sloop, snoop, stoop, swoop, troop
-oor	poor, boor, moor, spoor
-oose	goose, loose, moose, noose
-oot	boot, hoot, loot, moot, root, toot, scoot, shoot
-ooth	booth, smooth, tooth
-op*	bop, cop, hop, mop, pop, sop, top, chop, crop, drop, flop, plop, prop, shop, slop, stop
-ope	cope, hope, lope, mope, nope, pope, rope, grope, scope, slope
-orch	porch, torch, scorch
-ord	cord, ford, lord, chord, sword

-ore*	bore, core, fore, gore, more, pore, sore, tore, wore, chore, score, shore, snore, spore, store, swore
-ork	cork, fork, pork, stork
-orm	dorm, form, norm, storm
-orn	born, corn, horn, morn, torn, worn, scorn, shorn, sworn, thorn
-ort	fort, port, sort, short, snort, sport
-ose	hose, nose, pose, rose, chose, close, prose, those
-oss	boss, loss, moss, toss, cross, floss, gloss
-ost	cost, lost, frost
-ost	host, most, post, ghost
-ot*	cot, dot, got, hot, jot, knot, lot, not, pot, rot, tot, blot, clot, plot, shot, slot, spot, trot
-otch	botch, notch, blotch, crotch
-ote	note, quote, rote, vote, wrote
-oth	moth, broth, cloth, froth, sloth
-ouch	couch, ouch, pouch, vouch, crouch, grouch, slouch
-oud	loud, cloud, proud
-ough	rough, tough, slough
-ought	bought, fought, ought, sought, brought, thought
-ould	could, would, should
-ounce	bounce, pounce, flounce, trounce
-ound	bound, found, hound, mound, pound, round, sound, wound, ground
-oup	soup, group
-our	hour, sour, flour, scour
-ouse	douse, house, mouse, rouse, souse, blouse, grouse, spouse

-out	bout, gout, lout, pout, tout, clout, flout, grout, scout, shout, snout, spout, sprout, stout, trout
-outh	mouth, south
-ove	cove, wove, clove, drove, grove, stove, trove
-ove	dove, love, glove, shove
-ow	bow, know, low, mow, row, sow, tow, blow, crow, flow, glow, grow, show, slow, snow, stow
-ow	bow, cow, how, now, row, sow, vow, brow, chow, plow, prow, scow
-owl	fowl, howl, jowl, growl, prowl, scowl
-own	down, gown, town, brown, clown, crown, drown, drown
-own	known, mown, sown, blown, flown, grown, shown, thrown
-owse	dowse, browse, drowse
-ox	box, fox, lox, pox
-oy	boy, coy, joy, Roy, soy, toy, ploy
-ub	cub, dub, hub, nub, pub, rub, sub, tub, club, drub, flub, grub, scrub, shrub, snub, stub
-ube	cube, rube, tube
-uch	much, such, touch
-uck*	buck, duck, luck, muck, puck, suck, tuck, cluck, pluck, shuck, stuck, struck, truck
-ud	bud, cud, dud, mud, spud, stud, thud
-ude	dude, nude, rude, crude, prude
-udge	budge, fudge, judge, nudge, drudge, grudge, sludge, smudge, trudge
-ue	cue, due, hue, blue, clue, flue, glue, true
-uff	buff, cuff, huff, puff, ruff, bluff, fluff, gruff, scuff, sluff, snuff, stuff

-ug*	bug, dug, hug, jug, lug, mug, pug, rug, tug, chug, drug, plug, shrug, slug, smug, snug, thug
-uke	duke, nuke, fluke
-ule	mule, rule, yule
-ulk	bulk, hulk, sulk
-ull	cull, dull, gull, hull, lull, mull, skull
-ull	bull, full, pull
-um	bum, gum, hum, mum, rum, sum, chum, drum, glum, plum, scum, slum, strum, swum
-umb	dumb, numb, plumb, thumb
-ume	fume, flume, plume, spume
-ump*	bump, dump, hump, jump, lump, pump, chump, clump, frump, grump, plump, slump, stump, thump, trump
-un	bun, fun, gun, nun, pun, run, sun, shun, spun, stun
-unch	bunch, hunch, lunch, munch, punch, brunch, crunch
-une	June, tune, prune
-ung	hung, lung, rung, sung, clung, slung, sprung, stung, strung, swung, wrung
-unk*	bunk, dunk, funk, hunk, junk, punk, sunk, chunk, flunk, plunk, shrunk, skunk, slunk, spunk, stunk, trunk
-unt	bunt, hunt, punt, runt, blunt, grunt, shunt, stunt
-up	cup, pup, sup
-ur	cur, fur, blur, slur, spur
-ure	cure, lure, pure, sure
-url	burl, curl, furl, hurl, purl, churl, knurl
-urn	burn, turn, churn, spurn

-urse	curse, nurse, purse
-urt	curt, hurt, blurt, spurt
-us	bus, pus, plus, thus
-use	fuse, muse
-ush	gush, hush, lush, mush, rush, blush, brush, crush, flush, plush, slush, thrush
-uss	buss, cuss, fuss, muss, truss
-ust	bust, dust, gust, just, must, rust, crust, thrust, trust
-ut	but, cut, gut, hut, jut, nut, rut, glut, shut, smut, strut
-utch	hutch, clutch, crutch
-ute	cute, jute, lute, mute, brute, chute, flute
-utt	butt, mutt, putt
-y	by, my, cry, dry, fly, fry, ply, pry, shy, sky, sly, spy, spry, try, why
-ye	aye, dye, eye, lye, rye

Two-Syllable Words

absent	flavor	pencil
action	hammer	planet
applaud	helpful	plastic
balloon	insect	pocket
because	insist	pumpkin
before	inspect	pretzel
center	jolly	sandbox
contest	joyous	special
cricket	kicking	stubborn
dinner	laughing	subtract
dessert	louder	surprise
exclaim	monster	unlock
excuse	notebook	water
fastest	paper	

Three-Syllable Words

activate	factory	magical
adventure	fantastic	mosquito
banana	forever	multiply
bicycle	gigantic	normally
butterfly	habitat	poisonous
cantaloupe	honestly	popular
caravan	however	terrible
carousel	icicle	tornado
crocodile	invention	underneath
curious	kangaroo	vacation
different	listening	watery
difficult	magnify	whichever
elephant	marshmallow	wonderful
fabulous	marvelous	

©1998 by G. S. Pinnell and I. C. Fountas from *Word Matters: Teaching Phonics and Spelling in the Reading/Writing Classroom.* Portsmouth, NH: Heinemann

Four-Syllable Words

absolutely

activity

adorable

affectionate

alligator

calculator

caterpillar

considerate

conversation

dedicated

dependable

demonstration

differences

energetic

enjoyable

entertainment

escalator

especially

exaggerate

fortunately

hysterical

independent

information

interested

interrupted

kindergarten

magnificent

material

motorcycle

mysterious

necessary

operation

pepperoni

populated

refrigerate

regularly

spectacular

stationery

tarantula

unusual

watermelon

Words with Silent Letters

b

comb

climb

lamb

doubt

thumb

g

bought

gnat

though

through

h

ghost

ghastly

ghoul

k

knew

knife

knit

knock

know

l

chalk

talk

walk

would

t

castle

listen

often

thistle

whistle

w

wrap

wren

wrist

write

wrong

Contractions

A contraction is one word made from two longer words, with some letters omitted and replaced with an apostrophe.

am	**have**	**not**	**us**
I'm	could've	aren't	let's
	I've	can't	
are	might've	couldn't	**will**
they're	should've	didn't	I'll
we're	they've	doesn't	it'll
you're	we've	don't	he'll
	would've	hadn't	she'll
had, would	you've	hasn't	that'll
I'd		haven't	they'll
it'd		isn't	we'll
she'd	**is, has**	mustn't	you'll
there'd	here's	needn't	
they'd	he's	shouldn't	
we'd	it's	wouldn't	
you'd	she's		
	that's		
	there's		
	what's		
	where's		
	who's		

Compound Words

Compound words are two whole words that are combined to make a new word.

airplane	cookbook	grapefruit
airport	crosswalk	grasshopper
another	daylight	haircut
anybody	daytime	hairdresser
anyone	doorbell	hamburger
anyplace	downstairs	handsome
anything	dugout	headache
anywhere	earring	headquarters
applesauce	earthquake	headset
audiotape	earthworm	herself
background	everybody	highway
barefoot	everyone	hilltop
baseball	everything	himself
basketball	everywhere	homemade
bedroom	fingernail	homesick
birdhouse	fireproof	housework
birthday	flashlight	however
boyfriend	football	indoor
breakfast	forever	infield
campfire	girlfriend	inside
cannot	grandchildren	into
chalkboard	grandfather	itself
classmate	grandmother	jellyfish
cockpit	grandparent	keyboard

maybe	sandpaper	teammate
meanwhile	seashell	themselves
motorcycle	seesaw	today
myself	skateboard	toenail
network	skyscraper	toothbrush
newscast	snowball	toothpick
nobody	snowflake	touchdown
noontime	snowman	tryout
oatmeal	somebody	tugboat
ourselves	someday	turnpike
outline	somehow	underground
outside	someone	understand
playground	something	upset
pushcart	sometimes	videotape
railroad	somewhere	watermelon
rainbow	starfish	wheelchair
rainfall	strawberry	whenever
rattlesnake	sunlight	windshield
rollerblade	sunrise	without
rosebud	sunshine	woodland
sailboat	suntan	woodpecker
salesperson	sweetheart	yourself

Suffixes

Suffixes are groups of letters added after a base word or root. The following is a sample of the wide variety.

Suffix	Meaning	Example
-ant	one who	assistant
-ar	one who	liar
-arium	place for	aquarium
-ble	inclined to	gullible
-ent	one who	resident
-er	one who	teacher
-er	more	brighter
-ery, ry	products	pottery
-ess	one who (female)	actress
-est	most	most
-ful	full of	mouthful
-ing	material	roofing
-ing	(present tense)	smiling
-less	without	motherless
-ling	small	fledgling
-ly	every	weekly
-ly	(adverb)	happily
-ness	state of being	happiness
-ology	study of	biology
-or	one who	doctor
-ous	full of	wondrous
-s, es	more than one	boxes
-y	state of	sunny

Prefixes

Prefixes are letter groups added before a base word or root. Prefixes generally add to or change the meaning of the word.

Prefix	Meaning	Examples
ab-	away from	absent, abnormal
ad-	to, toward	advance, addition
after-	later, behind	aftermath, afterward
anti-	against, opposed	antibiotic, antigravity
auto-	self	automobile, autobiography
be-	make	believe, belittle
bi-	two	bicycle, biceps
com, con, co-	with, together	commune, concrete
contra-	against	contradict, contrary
de-	downward, undo	deflate, defect
deci-	ten	decibels, decimal
dis-	not	dislike, distrust
e, ex-	out of, prior to	explain, expense
en, em-	in, into, cover	engage, employ
extra-	outside	extravagant, extraterrestrial
im-	not	impose, imply
in-	into, not	include, incurable
inter-	among	interact, internal
macro-	large	macroeconomics, macrobiotic
magni-	great	magnify, magnificent
mega-	huge	megaphone, megabucks
micro-	small	microscope, microbe
mis-	wrongly	mistake, mislead

non-	not	nonsense, nonviolent
over-	above, beyond	overflow, overdue
post-	after	postdate, postmark
pre-	before, prior to	preheat, prehistoric
pro-	in favor of	protest, protect
re-	again	repeat, revise
re-	back	return, rebel
sub-	under, beneath	submarine, subject
super-	above, beyond	superior, supernatural
tele-	far	telescope, telephone
trans-	across	transfer, transit
tri-	three	tricycle, triangle
un-	not	unknown, unjust
ultra-	beyond	ultraviolet, ultrasuede
under-	beneath, below	underneath, underline
uni-	one, single	unicorn, uniform

Adding Endings

Adding "ed"

"d" sound	"ed" sound	"t" sound	"y" to "i"
grilled	added	dressed	buried
grabbed	branded	fished	carried
piled	landed	kissed	cried
played	melted	liked	dried
screamed	needed	walked	fried
yelled	quilted	wished	tried

Adding "er" and "est"

base	er	est
big	bigger	biggest
bright	brighter	brightest
cold	colder	coldest
dark	darker	darkest
early	earlier	earliest
fast	faster	fastest
friendly	friendlier	friendliest
nice	nicer	nicest
pretty	prettier	prettiest
quick	quicker	quickest
rich	richer	richest
scary	scarier	scariest
small	smaller	smallest
soft	softer	softest
tall	taller	tallest
white	whiter	whitest

Synonyms

Synonyms are words that have similar meanings.

add/total	demonstrate/show
after/following	different/diverse
all/every	dislike/detest
anger/rage	divide/split
appear/look	during/while
appreciative/thankful	earth/world
arrive/reach	eat/consume
ask/question	end/finish
baby/infant	enough/sufficient
back/rear	error/mistake
before/prior	fat/chubby
begin/start	fetch/get
below/under	find/locate
bitter/tart	fix/mend
brave/courageous	forgive/excuse
call/yell	fortune/wealth
car/vehicle	fragile/delicate
change/swap	freedom/liberty
city/town	frequent/often
close/shut	giant/huge
continue/persist	gift/present
dangerous/hazardous	give/donate
decrease/lesson	grab/take
delay/postpone	grow/develop

guide/lead	mean/cruel
happy/glad	messy/sloppy
hasten/hurry	mend/repair
heal/cure	mistake/error
high/tall	model/example
hold/grasp	move/transport
hop/skip	naughty/bad
huge/vast	near/close
idea/concept	neat/tidy
illegal/wrong	need/require
income/earnings	new/fresh
injure/hurt	obey/follow
insult/offend	odor/smell
job/occupation	often/frequently
jump/leap	omit/delete
just/fair	operate/use
keep/save	overdue/late
kind/considerate	own/have
large/big	pack/fill
last/persist	pain/ache
late/tardy	pair/couple
leave/depart	part/piece
like/enjoy	peak/summit
listen/hear	perform/act
little/small	pick/choose
make/build	praise/applaud
mark/label	quaint/odd

quake/shake	tiny/small
quick/fast	touch/feel
quiet/silent	trail/path
quit/stop	try/attempt
quiz/test	tug/pull
rage/fury	understand/know
rain/shower	undo/untie
raise/increase	unstable/wobbly
record/write	untamed/wild
relax/rest	untidy/messy
repeat/echo	uproar/noise
revise/change	use/apply
rule/law	usual/common
safe/secure	utter/talk
say/tell	vacant/empty
scrape/scratch	vacation/break
scream/shout	value/worth
sharp/pointed	vanish/disappear
shove/push	vary/change
slam/bang	violent/rough
splash/spray	vital/necessary
spring/bounce	wag/wave
sour/tart	wail/cry
take/steal	walk/stroll
tear/rip	warn/alert
terrify/scare	wash/clean
thin/slender	well/healthy

whack/hit

whole/entire

yank/pull

yell/shout

yummy/tasty

zilch/nothing

zoom/rush

Antonyms

Antonyms are words that mean the opposite or nearly opposite of each other.

above/below	come/go	give/take
absent/present	cry/laugh	go/stop
achieve/fail	defend/attack	good/bad
add/subtract	dirty/clean	half/whole
admire/dislike	dry/wet	hard/soft
admit/reject	dull/bright	harm/help
adult/child	eager/lazy	happy/sad
afraid/confident	early/late	hate/love
alive/dead	earn/spend	heal/hurt
all/none	east/west	hear/ignore
allow/forbid	easy/difficult	heavy/light
appear/vanish	empty/full	hot/cold
arrive/depart	ending/beginning	improve/damage
asked/told	enemy/friend	icy/warm
asleep/awake	enjoy/hate	ill/healthy
beginning/end	enter/exit	illegal/legal
big/little	fact/fiction	in/out
blame/forgive	fail/pass	joy/grief
blunt/sharp	fancy/plain	laugh/cry
bottom/top	fat/thin	lead/follow
break/fix	flexible/rigid	left/right
buy/sell	friend/stranger	little/big
cause/effect	front/back	long/short
cheap/expensive	girl/boy	loose/tight

lose/find	over/under	short/long
lose/gain	pass/fail	simple/complex
lose/win	plain/fancy	slow/fast
loud/soft	pleasure/pain	small/large
love/hate	private/public	smooth/rough
low/high	push/pull	start/finish
morning/evening	question/answer	stop/start
multiply/divide	quick/slow	sweet/sour
night/day	raise/lower	to/from
noisy/quiet	remain/change	top/bottom
north/south	repair/break	true/false
nothing/everything	rich/poor	ugly/pretty
obey/command	right/wrong	up/down
often/seldom	sad/funny	white/black
old/young	sad/glad	whole/part
on/off	same/different	with/without
open/close	shallow/deep	work/play

Homographs

Homographs are words that are spelled the same but differ in meaning and origin. When they are pronounced differently they are called heteronyms.

bass	My father enjoys fishing for *bass*.
	Since his voice is so low, my brother sings the *bass* in the school musical.
conduct	I would like to learn to *conduct* an orchestra.
	Chewing gum is not appropriate *conduct* for school.
content	I would be *content* with a piece of chocolate cake for dinner.
	It is a good idea to read the *contents* of some foods before eating them.
contest	My sister always wins the frog-jumping *contest* at the State Fair.
	I am expected in court this week to *contest* my speeding ticket.
contract	I signed a *contract* to mow the school lawn for one year.
	The lungs expand and *contract* to enable you to breathe.
converse	Love is the *converse* of hate.
	I was able to *converse* with the school principal during his recent visit.
desert	All of his friends seemed to *desert* him after his candy was gone.
	The *desert* is hot and dry.
does	He always *does* his homework on time.
	On the way home, we saw two *does* and their fawns crossing the road.
excuse	My brother had no *excuse* for the broken vase.
	My mother could not *excuse* his inappropriate behavior.

©1998 by G. S. Pinnell and I. C. Fountas from *Word Matters: Teaching Phonics and Spelling in the Reading/Writing Classroom.* Portsmouth, NH: Heinemann

lead	It was my turn to *lead* the class in the Pledge of Allegiance today.
	Our teacher insisted we all use *lead* pencils.
minute	The chances of finding a needle in a haystack are quite *minute*.
	I could see more clearly the *minute* I put my glasses on.
object	My brother could not identify the wrapped *object* under the Christmas tree.
	I did not think my parents would *object* to a new puppy.
present	I was given a new bike as a birthday *present*.
	I was very nervous when I was asked to *present* the winner with the trophy.
primer	Before we painted the walls, we had to coat them with a *primer*.
	We were all given *primers* in our reading classes.
read	I was asked to *read* two books for my English class.
	I only *read* one book.
record	My brother is trying to set a new world *record* for pie eating.
	As part of my science project, I had to *record* the phases of the moon for one week.
refuse	I cannot *refuse* a chocolate chip cookie.
	On Monday mornings, we put all of our *refuse* out to be collected.
sow	The *sow* at my uncle's farm just had a litter of piglets.
	October seems to be the best time to *sow* our crop.
subject	The new teacher is the *subject* of much discussion.
	I would not want to *subject* anyone to my little brother's singing.
tear	After I fell, I noticed a *tear* in my jeans.
	Even though the scratch hurt, I did not shed a single *tear*.

wind   It is not a good idea to *wind* a clock too tightly.

I could hear the strong *wind* during the storm this morning.

use   A bucket with a hole in the bottom is of no *use* to me.

As a special favor, my dad let me *use* the car on Friday.

Homophones

Homophones are words that sound the same, or almost the same, but look different and have different meanings.

accept/except	cent/sent/scent	feat/feet
ad/add	cents/scents/sense	find/fined
affect/effect	cereal/serial	fir/fur
aisle/I'll/isle	chalk/chock	flair/flare
aloud/allowed	cheap/cheep	flea/flee
altar/alter	chews/choose	flew/flu/flue
ant/aunt	choral/coral	flour/flower
arc/ark	close/clothes	for/fore/four
ate/eight	creak/creek	forth/fourth
be/bee	days/daze	foul/fowl
bear/bare	dear/deer	gate/gait
beat/beet	forth/fourth	great/grate
been/Ben	dense/dents	groan/grown
blue/blew	desert/dessert	guessed/guest
board/bored	dew/do/due	hail/hale
break/brake	die/dye	hair/hare
brews/bruise	doe/dough	hall/haul
capital/capitol	dual/duel	hay/hey
carat/caret/carrot	earn/urn	heal/heel/he'll
caught/cot	ewe/yew/you	hear/here
ceiling/sealing	eye/I	heard/herd
cell/sell	fair/fare	hi/high
cellar/seller	fairy/ferry	higher/hire

him/hymn	moose/mousse	rain/reign/rein
hoarse/horse	none/nun	raise/rays/raze
hoes/hose	oar/or/ore	rap/wrap
hole/whole	oh/owe	real/reel
hour/our	one/won	red/read
in/inn	our/hour	right/rite/write
its/it's	overdo/overdue	ring/wring
Jim/gym	paced/paste	road/rode/rowed
knead/need	pail/pale	role/roll
knew/new	pain/pane	root/route
knight/night	pair/pare/pear	rose/rows
knot/not	past/passed	rote/wrote
know/no	patience/patients	rough/ruff
knows/nose	pause/paws	rung/wrung
lead/led	peace/piece	sail/sale
leak/leek	peak/peek	scene/seen
lessen/lesson	peal/peel	sea/see
lie/lye	pear/pare/pair	seam/seem
loan/lone	pedal/peddle	seas/sees/seize
made/maid	plain/plane	sew/so/sow
mail/male	pole/poll	shear/sheer
main/Maine/mane	poor/pour/pore	shoe/shoo
Mary/marry/merry	praise/prays/preys	shone/shown
meat/meet	presence/presents	side/sighed
might/mite	prince/prints	sight/cite
mind/mined	principal/principle	some/sum
missed/mist	quarts/quartz	son/sun

stair/stare	theirs/there's	ware/wear/where
stairs/stares	threw/through	wave/waive
stake/steak	throne/thrown	way/weigh
stationary/stationery	thyme/time	we'd/weed
steal/steel	tide/tied	we/wee
straight/strait	to/too/two	weak/week
suite/sweet	toad/towed	weather/whether
sundae/Sunday	told/tolled	weave/we've
tacks/tax	tow/toe	which/witch
tail/tale	vain/vane/vein	who's/whose
tea/tee	vary/very	wood/would
team/teem	wade/weighed	you'll/yule
teas/tease/tees	waist/waste	you/ewe
their/there/they're	wait/weight	your/you're

Plurals

There are a variety of useful categories for forming most plurals. Some samples follow.

Add *s*
(*to most*)

apple	apples
bag	bags
crab	crabs
can	cans
desk	desks
dog	dogs
face	faces
mop	mops
tree	trees
radio	radios

Add *es*
(*end in s, sh, ch, x, z*)

arch	arches
buzz	buzzes
bus	buses
box	boxes
dish	dishes
fox	foxes
kiss	kisses
patch	patches
peach	peaches
quiz	quizzes

Add *s*
(*end in vowel + y*)

boy	boys
day	days
key	keys
play	plays
say	says
valley	valleys

Change the *f* to *v*
(*some words that end in f*)

calf	calves
half	halves
hoof	hooves
knife	knives
life	lives
scarf	scarves
self	selves
shelf	shelves
wife	wives
wolf	wolves

Rare plurals

child	children
foot	feet
goose	geese
man	men
mouse	mice
ox	oxen
woman	women

Stay the same

deer
lamb
moose
sheep

Add *ies*
(*end in consonant + y*)

baby	babies
candy	candies
city	cities
country	countries
fly	flies
family	families
lady	ladies
pony	ponies
sky	skies
story	stories

Spelling Demons

A spelling demon is a tricky word to spell. The following is a list of words that are often misspelled.

a lot	close	forty	many
a while	clothes	friend	might
about	come	getting	myself
again	coming	guess	new
all right	could	happily	no (yes)
almost	didn't	have	none
also	different	having	off
always	does	heard	often
another	doesn't	here	once
answer	don't	he's	one (number)
any	eighth	hole	our
anyone	enough	I'd	people
are	especially	I'm	piece
beautiful	every	into	probably
because	everybody	it's (it is)	ready
been	everyone	its	really
before	except	knew	receive
beginning	excited	know	right
believe	favorite	laugh	said
buy	February	let's	says
by	field	loose	school
can't (cannot)	finally	lose	separate
cannot	first	making	shoes

since	threw	was	who
something	through	wear (shirt)	whole
sometimes	tired	weather (rain)	with
sure	to	Wednesday	won
tear	tonight	week	won't
terrible	too	we're (we are)	women
that's	trouble	went	would
their (belongs to)	Tuesday	were	wouldn't
then	two	what	write
there	until	when	writing
they	upon	where	wrote
they're (they are)	usually	whether	your
though	very	which	you're (you are)
thought	want		

Shortened Words (Clipped Words)

Clipped words exist in the language as people shorten forms for greater efficiency.

ad	advertisement	**lunch**	luncheon
auto	automobile	**mart**	market
bike	bicycle	**math**	mathematics
burger	hamburger	**memo**	memorandum
cab	cabriolet	**mum**	chrysanthemum
champ	champion	**phone**	telephone
clerk	cleric	**photo**	photograph
cuke	cucumber	**plane**	airplane
doc	doctor	**ref**	referee
dorm	dormitory	**specs**	spectacles
exam	examination	**stereo**	stereophonic
fan	fanatic	**taxi**	taxicab
flu	influenza	**teen**	teenager
gas	gasoline	**tux**	tuxedo
grad	graduation	**typo**	typographical error
gym	gymnasium	**vet**	veterinarian
lab	laboratory	**zoo**	zoological gardens
limo	limousine		

Onomatopoeic Words

Onomatopoeic words are words that, when spoken, sound like their meaning.

bark	plop
boom	quack
buzz	rip
chirp	roar
clang	rustle
click	screech
crackle	smash
fizz	snap
groan	splash
hiss	sputter
kerchoo	squeak
oink	zoom

Greek Roots

Root	Meaning	Example
aero	air	aerobics
bio	life	biology
chron	time	chronological
cycl	circle	cycle
gen	race	gender
geo	earth	geography
graph	write	autograph
homo	same	homophone
hydr	water	hydroplane
log	word	logo
mech	machine	mechanic
meter	measuring	centimeter
nym	name	antonym
path	feeling	pathetic
phobea	fear	claustrophobia
phone	sound	telephone
photo	light	photograph
poli	city	metropolis
phys	nature	physical
psych	mind	psychiatrist
soph	wise	sophisticated
therm	heat	thermostat

Latin Roots

Root	Meaning	Example
aud	hear	audible
agri	field	agriculture
aqua	water	aquarium
cap	head	capital
dent	tooth	dentist
dict	speak	dictate
form	shape	formula
grat	please	grateful
liber	free	liberate
loc	place	location
lum	light	illuminate
man	hand	manual
mar	ocean	marina
min	small	minimal
miss	send	amiss
mob	move	mobile
mort	death	mortician
multi	many	multitude
nat	born	natural
nov	new	novel
opt	best	option
ped	foot	pedal
port	carry	transport
sci	know	science
sect	cut	section

sens	feel	sense
sign	mark	signature
spec	see	spectacles
temp	time	temporary
terr	land	territory
tract	pull	tractor
urb	city	urban
vac	empty	vacate
vid/vis	see	video/vision
volv	roll	evolve

Portmanteau Words

Portmanteau words are words that are made of two words that are blended into one.

autobus	automobile & bus
brunch	breakfast & lunch
clash	clap & crash
hi-fi	high fidelity
o'clock	of the clock
skylab	sky & laboratory
smash	smack & mash
smog	smoke & fog
splatter	splash & splatter
squiggle	squirm & wiggle

©1998 by G. S. Pinnell and I. C. Fountas from *Word Matters: Teaching Phonics and Spelling in the Reading/Writing Classroom*. Portsmouth, NH: Heinemann

Word-Solving Strategies

- Using the strategies that good spellers use.

- Listening for syllables in words.

- Saying words slowly.

- Saying words slowly, listening for sounds, recording letters, rereading/touching, listening for next sound, and so on.

- If you've crossed out part of a word while you are figuring out the whole word, go back and write the whole word so you can get a good look at the new spelling.

- Writing high-frequency words correctly and quickly.

- Noticing and using particular letters or letter clusters (*sh, ch, wh, th, ar, oa*).

- Knowing what the vowels and consonants are.

- Writing words that begin the same (letter, or cluster of letters).

- Writing words that end the same (letter, cluster of letters, or same pattern).

- Writing words that sound the same but look different (homophones).

- Writing words in a category (contractions, question words, compound words).

- Writing words with different middles (*ball, bell*).

- Writing words with the same sounds but different spellings (*play, wait, eight*).

- Writing words that have the same letter that makes two different sounds (*car, circus; go, ginger*).

- Writing plurals for words by adding *s*.

- Writing plurals for words by adding *es* (*boxes, churches*).

- Writing plurals for words by changing their spelling (*man, men*).

- Writing plurals for words that end in *y* by adding *es*.

- Writing plurals for words that end in an *f* by changing to a *v* and adding *es*.

- Writing possessives by adding apostrophe *s*.

- Writing words with prefixes.

- Writing words with silent letters (*gh, kn, wr*).

- Writing contractions and observing the role of the apostrophe.

- Doubling consonants when adding *ing* or *ed* (if preceded by a short vowel).

- When adding *er* or *est* to a word ending in *y*, change the *y* to *i* then add *er* or *est*.

- Writing words where the /c/ and /k/ and /ck/ all represent the same sound; never use /ck/ at the beginning of a word.

- Including at least one vowel in every syllable.

- Usually forming the past tense with *ed* (even though you might hear *t*).

- Usually representing or following a long *a*, *e*, or *i*, sound at the end of a word with a *y* (*may*, *monkey*, *sky*).
- Writing words with common patterns (*ake*, *ack*, *tion*, *ite*).
- Positioning of letters *f* and *ph* (beginning); *ff*, *ph*, *gh* (ending).
- Exploring base words (*jump*, *jumped*, *jumping*, *jumps*, *jump rope*).
- Talking about what will help you remember how to spell words.
- Using what you know about words to write new words.
- Breaking words into syllables.
- Writing base words and adding endings.

Using References and Resources

- Using word references and resources in classroom.
- Using a dictionary for finding words.
- Using the spelling checker or thesaurus on the computer.

Procedures for Buddy Study System

- Writing words on a spelling card.
- Adding words to your Words to Learn list.
- Choosing appropriate words for your weekly word study list.
- Marking a buddy's spelling test or buddy check.
- Giving a buddy test.
- Proofreading written work for spelling errors.

- Using the Look, Say, Cover, Write, Check sheet.

- Mixing and fixing words with magnetic or other types of letters.

- Caring for and using word study system materials.

- Highlighting tricky parts of words.

- Writing strings of words that connect.

Process Interiew: Reading

Name: _____

Date: _____

What do you do when you come to a word you don't know how to read? What else do you do?

What were some tricky words for you in reading today? What made them hard to figure out?

If you were teaching a kindergartner how to read words, what would you do? Anything else?

How can you get better at reading new words?

Process Interview: Writing

Name: _____

Date: _____

What do you do when you come to a word you don't know how to write? What else do you do?

What are some words that are tricky for you? Why do you think they are hard?

How do you learn to write new words? What else do you do?

If you were teaching a kindergartner how to write words, what would you do? Anything else?

How can you get better at writing new words?

Why is correct spelling important?

Have a Try

Try 3

Try 2

Try 1

a	be	call	day	each
about	because	came	did	else
after	been	can	do	end
all	before	come	does	every
am	but	could	don't	
an	by		down	
and				
are				
as				
at				

fall	get	had	I	just
for	go	has	I'm	
from	going	have	if	
	got	he	in	
		her	into	
		here	is	
		him	it	
		his	its	
		house	it's (it is)	
		how		

keep key kind	last late left let like little live long look love	make man many may me met mine mom more most mother much my	name near need nice no not now	of off on one or other our out over own
page play please put	quick quiet quite	ran read red ride run	said same saw see she so some	take than that the them then their there they this time to too took two

under until up upon us	very visit	was we went were what when where which who why will with would
excited	yes you your	zoo

Word Search

Crossword Puzzle

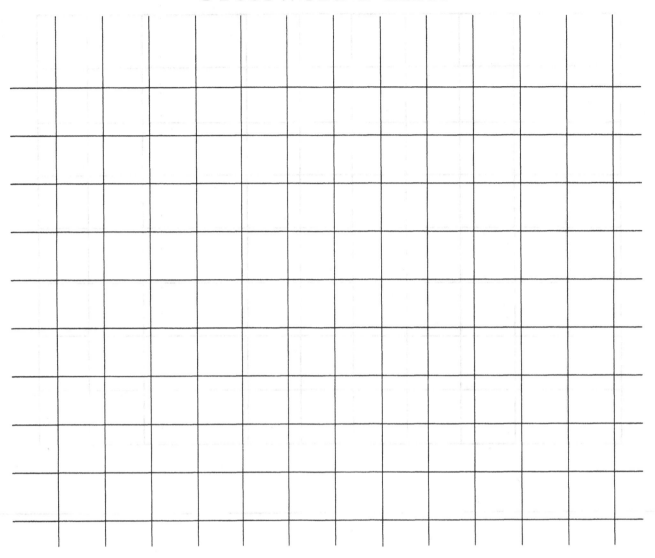

Across   Down

Appendix 40   Crossword Puzzle

©1998 by G. S. Pinnell and I. C. Fountas from *Word Matters: Teaching Phonics and Spelling in the Reading/Writing Classroom.* Portsmouth, NH: Heinemann

Words to Learn

Words to Learn

Words to Learn

Look, Say, Cover, Write, Check

Look, Say, Cover, Write, Check

Buddy Check

Name: _____   Date: _____

1. Buddy reads your words to you and then checks them.

2. Try again if they were not right.

3. Use your list to write it correctly in last column, if it wasn't right.

4. Highlight or circle parts you want to remember and make the word with magnetic letters.

Word	**Try Again**	**Correct Spelling** [Highlight parts to remember and make the word with magnetic letters.]
_____	_____	_____
_____	_____	_____
_____	_____	_____
_____	_____	_____
_____	_____	_____
_____	_____	_____
_____	_____	_____
_____	_____	_____
_____	_____	_____
_____	_____	_____
_____	_____	_____

Score: /   Score: /

Appendix 43   Buddy Check Sheets (three versions)

©1998 by G. S. Pinnell and I. C. Fountas from *Word Matters: Teaching Phonics and Spelling in the Reading/Writing Classroom*. Portsmouth, NH: Heinemann

Buddy Check

Name: _____   Date: _____

Word	**Try Again**	**Correct Spelling** [Highlight parts to remember and make the word with magnetic letters.]
_____	_____	_____
_____	_____	_____
_____	_____	_____
_____	_____	_____
_____	_____	_____
_____	_____	_____
_____	_____	_____
_____	_____	_____
_____	_____	_____
_____	_____	_____
_____	_____	_____
_____	_____	_____
_____	_____	_____
_____	_____	_____
_____	_____	_____

Score: /   **Score:**   /   Over ⟶

Write the words misspelled correctly; highlight parts to remember.	Tell why they were misspelled and what you will need to remember.

Buddy Check

Name: _____   Date: _____

	Words	Try Again	Correct Spelling
1.	_____	_____	_____
2.	_____	_____	_____
3.	_____	_____	_____
4.	_____	_____	_____
5.	_____	_____	_____
6.	_____	_____	_____
7.	_____	_____	_____
8.	_____	_____	_____

Score: /   Score: /

For words not right in the second column, what do you need to remember?
(Use a highlighter to mark parts you want to remember.)

Make Connections

Name: _____   Date: _____

Write your words:

_____   _____   _____

_____   _____   _____

_____   _____   _____

Make Connections . . .

_____

- -

_____

Over ⟶

Appendix 44   Make Connections (two versions)

©1998 by G. S. Pinnell and I. C. Fountas from *Word Matters: Teaching Phonics and Spelling in the Reading/Writing Classroom.* Portsmouth, NH: Heinemann

Make Connections

Name: _____   Date: _____

Write Your Words

Sounds Like [have some of the same sounds]		Looks Like [other words are spelled the same way]

My Finished Writing

1

2

3

4

5

6

7

8

9

10

11

12

Appendix 45   My Finished Writing

©1998 by M. E. Giacobbe. In *Word Matters* by G. S. Pinnell and I. C. Fountas. Portsmouth. NH: Heinemann, © 1998.

Topics I Can Write About

1

2

3

4

5

6

7

8

9

10

11

12

Appendix 46   Topics I Can Write About

©1998 by M. E. Giacobbe. In *Word Matters* by G. S. Pinnell and I. C. Fountas. Portsmouth. NH: Heinemann, © 1998.

My Proofreading List

1. I can write my **name** on my writing.

2. I can write a **title** on my writing.

3. I can write the **date** on my writing.

4. I can number my finished writing.

5. I can write the **title** of my writing on the page called **My Finished Writing**.

Frequently Used Words

a	for	little	she
after	from	long	so
all	get	look	some
am	go	looked	that
an	going	make	the
and	good	man	then
are	had	mother	there
as	has	me	they
asked	have	my	this
at	he	no	three
away	her	not	to
back	here	now	too
be	him	of	two
because	his	old	up
before	house	on	us
big	how	one	very
boy	I	or	was
but	I'm	our	we
by	if	out	went
came	in	over	were
can	into	people	what
come	is	play	when
could	it	put	where
day	just	ran	will
did	keep	run	with
do	kind	said	would
don't	know	saw	you
down	like	see	your

Appendix 48   Frequently Used Words

©1998 by G. S. Pinnell and I. C. Fountas from *Word Matters: Teaching Phonics and Spelling in the Reading/Writing Classroom*. Portsmouth, NH: Heinemann

What I Know About Writing Words

1

2

3

4

5

6

7

8

9

10

11

12

Appendix 49   What I Know About Writing Words

©1998 by M. E. Giacobbe. In *Word Matters* by G. S. Pinnell and I. C. Fountas. Portsmouth. NH: Heinemann, © 1998.

Words I'm Learning

Aa	Bb	Cc	Dd
Ii	Jj	Kk	Ll
Qq	Rr	Ss	Tt
Yy	Zz	___ed	___ing

How to Write

Ee	Ff	Gg	Hh
Mm	Nn	Oo	Pp
Uu	Vv	Ww	Xx

Writers' Workshop Guidelines

Cross out, don't erase.

Save everything, don't throw anything away.

Write on one side of the paper.

When you talk, use a soft voice.

Work hard and try your best.

Appendix 51   Writers' Workshop Guidelines

©1998 by M. E. Giacobbe, illus. by JoAnn C. Smith. In *Word Matters* by G. S. Pinnell and I. C. Fountas. Portsmouth. NH: Heinemann, © 1998.

Error Analysis

Date	Word	High-Frequency Words	Consonants: Initial, Final, Cluster, Digraph	Vowels: Long, Short Vowel Patterns *y* as a Vowel	Contractions, Compounds, Plurals	Base Words and Affixes: Prefixes, Suffixes, Inflectional Endings	Homophones Homographs	Other: e.g. Letter Form, Letter Order, Silent Letters

Appendix 52   Error Analysis Chart

Choose, Write, Build
Mix, Fix, Mix

Look, Say, Cover,
Write, Check

Buddy Check

Make Connections

Buddy Test

Buddy Test

Word Study Notebook

Make Your Own

Bibliography

Adams, M. J. 1990. *Beginning to Read: Thinking and Learning About Print.* Cambridge, MA: MIT Press.

Adler, D. A. 1980. *Cam Jansen and the Mystery of the Stolen Diamonds.* New York: Scholastic.

———. 1992. *Cam Jansen and the Mystery of the Monster Movie.* New York: Scholastic.

Bear, D. R., M. Invernizzi, S. Templeton, and F. Johnston. 1996. *Words Their Way.* Saddle River, NJ: Prentice Hall.

Bissex, G. 1980. *GNYS AT WORK: A Child Learns to Write and Read.* Cambridge, MA: Harvard University Press.

Bolton, F., and D. Snowball. 1993. *Teaching Spelling: A Practical Resource.* Portsmouth, NH: Heinemann.

Brown, M. W. 1947. *Goodnight Moon.* New York: HarperCollins Children's Books.

Clay, M. M. 1975. *What Did I Write?* Portsmouth, NH: Heinemann.

———. 1991a. *Becoming Literate: The Construction of Inner Control.* Portsmouth, NH: Heinemann.

———. 1991b. "Introducing a New Storybook to Young Readers." *The Reading Teacher* 45: 264–273.

———. 1993a. *An Observation Survey of Early Literacy Achievement.* Portsmouth, NH: Heinemann.

———. 1993b. *Reading Recovery: A Guidebook for Teachers in Training.* Portsmouth, NH: Heinemann.

Clymer, T. 1963. "The Utility of Phonics Generalizations in the Primary Grades." *The Reading Teacher* 16: 252–258.

Cowley, J. 1990a. *Farm Concert.* Bothell, WA: The Wright Group.

———. 1990b. *The Hungry Giant.* Bothell, WA: The Wright Group.

Cunningham, P. M. 1995. *Phonics They Use: Words for Reading and Writing.* 2d ed. New York: HarperCollins.

Ehri, L. C. 1998. "Grapheme-phoneme Knowledge is Necessary for Learning to Read Words in English." In *Word Recognition in Beginning Literacy,* edited by J. Metsala and L. C. Ehri. Hillsdale, NJ: Lawrence Erlbaum.

Elkonin, D. B. 1973. "U.S.S.R." In *Comparative Reading,* edited by J. Downing. New York: Macmillan.

Fear, S. 1995. *Ginger.* Boston: Houghton Mifflin.

Fitzgerald, J.A. 1951. *A Basic Life Spelling Vocabulary.* Bruce.

Fountas, I. C., and G. S Pinnell. 1996. *Guided Reading: Good First Teaching for All Children.* Portsmouth, NH: Heinemann.

Gentry, J. R. 1987. *Spel . . . Is a Four-Letter Word.* Portsmouth, NH: Heinemann.

Gentry, J. R., & J. W. Gillet. 1993. *Teaching Kids to Spell.* Portsmouth, NH: Heinemann.

Goodman, K. 1996. *Reading Strategies: Focus on Comprehension.* New York: Routledge & Kegan Paul.

Goodman, Y. M., D. J. Watson, and C. L. Burke. 1987. *Reading Miscue Inventory: Alternative Procedures.* Katonah, NY: Richard C. Owen.

Goswami, U., and P. Bryant. 1990. *Phonological Skills and Learning to Read.* Hillsdale, NJ: Lawrence Erlbaum.

Harris, T. L., and R. E. Hodges. 1995. *Literacy Dictionary.* Newark, DE: International Reading Association.

Henderson, E. H. 1990. *Teaching Spelling.* 2d ed. Boston: Houghton Mifflin.

Holdaway, D. 1979. *The Foundations of Literacy.* Sydney: Ashton Scholastic.

Horn, E. 1954. *Teaching Spelling.* Washington, D.C.: National Education Association.

Johnston, P. H. 1997. *Knowing Literacy.* York, ME: Stenhouse.

McKenzie, E. K. 1994. *The Perfectly Orderly H-O-U-S-E.* New York: Henry Holt.

Moats, L. C. 1995. *Spelling: Development, Disability, and Instruction.* Baltimore, MD: York Press.

Moustafa, M. 1997. *Beyond Traditional Phonics: Research Discoveries and Reading Instruction.* Portsmouth, NH: Heinemann.

Peters, C. 1995a. *At the Zoo.* Boston: Houghton Mifflin.

———. 1995b. *Foods to Eat.* Lexington, MA: D.C. Heath.

Pinnell, G. S., and I. C. Fountas. 1997. *Help America Read: A Handbook for Volunteers.* Portsmouth, NH: Heinemann.

Read, C. 1971. "Pre-school Children's Knowledge of English Phonology." *Harvard Educational Review* 41: 1–34.

———. 1986. *Children's Creative Spellings.* New York: Routledge & Kegan Paul.

Riley, K. 1995a. *Peaches the Pig.* Boston: Houghton Mifflin.

———. 1995b. *Rosie's Pool.* Boston: Houghton Mifflin.

Sitton, R. 1995. *Spelling Source Book.* Spokane, WA: Northwest Textbook.

Stanovich, K. 1994. "Romance and Reality." *The Reading Teacher* 47: 280–291.

Templeton, S., and D. R. Bear, eds. 1992. *Development of Orthographic Knowledge and the Foundation of Literacy: A Memorial Festschrift for Edmund H. Henderson.* Hillsdale, NJ: Lawrence Erlbaum.

Treiman, R. 1985. "Onsets and Rimes as Units of Spoken Syllables: Evidence from Children." *Journal of Experimental Child Psychology* 39: 161–181.

Wilde, S. 1992. *You Kan Red This! Spelling and Punctuation for Whole Language Classrooms, K–6.* Portsmouth, NH: Heinemann.

———. 1997. *What's a Schwa Sound Anyway? A Holistic Guide to Phonetics, Phonics, and Spelling.* Portsmouth, NH: Heinemann.

Wylie, R. E., and D. D. Durell. 1970. "Teaching Vowels Through Phonograms." *Elementary English* 47: 787–791.

Zutell, J. 1996. "The Directed Spelling Thinking Activity (DSTA): Providing an Effective Balance in Word Study Instruction." *The Reading Teacher* 50 (2): 98–108.

Index

Voices on Word Matters
Learning About Phonics and Spelling in the Literacy Classroom

Edited by **Irene C. Fountas** and **Gay Su Pinnell**

Are you interested in learning more about implementing an effective word study program? To this end, you'll find our new book, *Voices on Word Matters: Learning About Phonics and Spelling in the Literacy Classroom,* an excellent resource. This companion volume to *Word Matters* is an edited collection of chapters by noted scholars and practitioners. It provides a rich extension of our instructional system for spelling and phonics with chapters on interactive and independent writing, word sorting and word walls, letter learning, word-solving strategies, shared reading, language and word play, assessment, and much more.

Special guest authors include:
- Billie J. Askew
- David Booth
- Diane E. DeFord
- Dorothy P. Hall and Patricia M. Cunningham
- Justina Henry
- Susan Hundley and Diane Powell
- Carol B. Jenkins
- Carol A. Lyons
- Andrea McCarrier and Ida Patacca
- William Stokes
- Sandra Wilde
- Barbara Joan Wiley
- Jerome Zutell

This comprehensive volume will extend your learning as it takes you into rich literacy classrooms, provides you with concrete learning activities, and expands your understanding of our conceptual framework. Once again, we provide many reproducible sheets and lists for classroom application as well as professional development activities at the end of each chapter.